# 1

## CHITOSE KAIDO

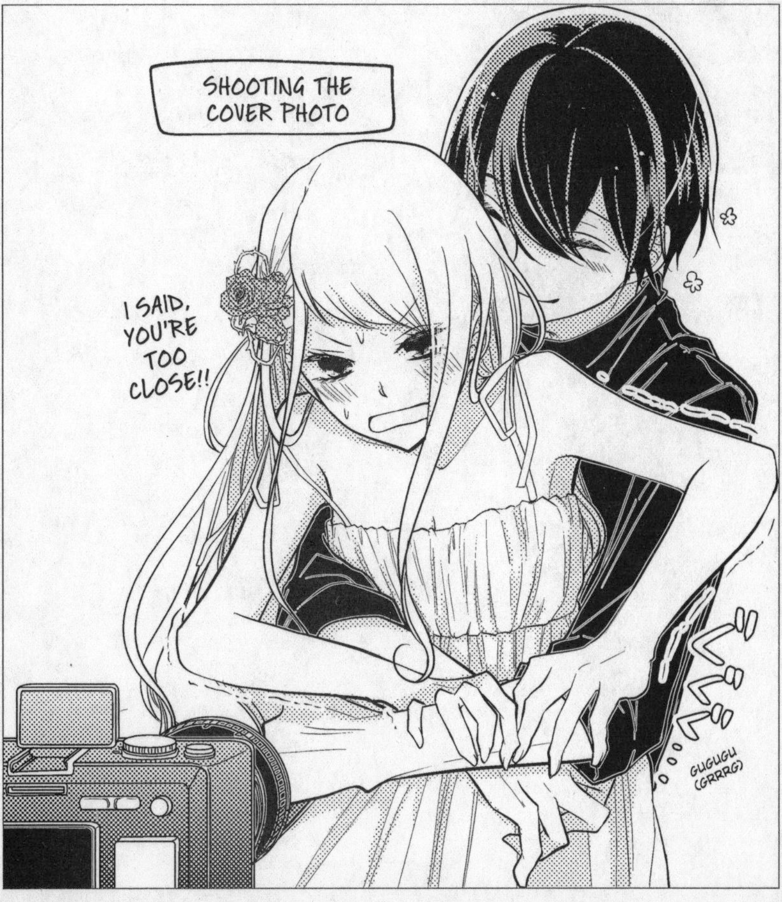
SHOOTING THE COVER PHOTO
I SAID, YOU'RE TOO CLOSE!!
GUGUGU (GRRRG)

# CONTENTS

LOVE AND HEART

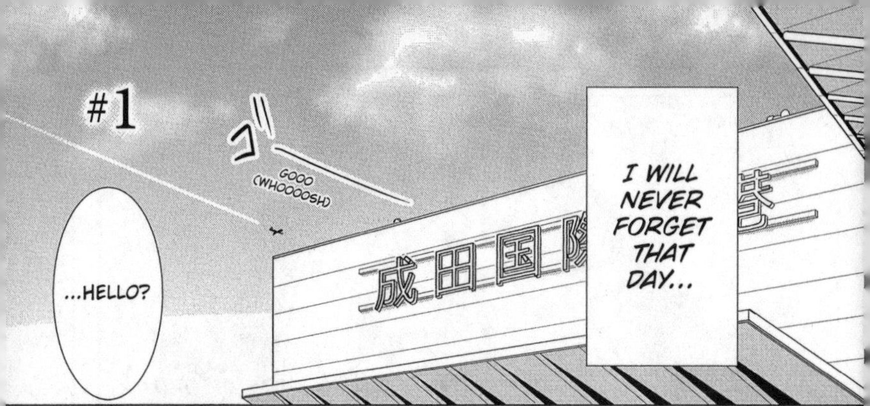
I WILL NEVER FORGET THAT DAY...
ゴー
GOOO (WHOOOOSH)
...HELLO?
#1

SIGN: NARITA INTERNATIONAL AIRPORT

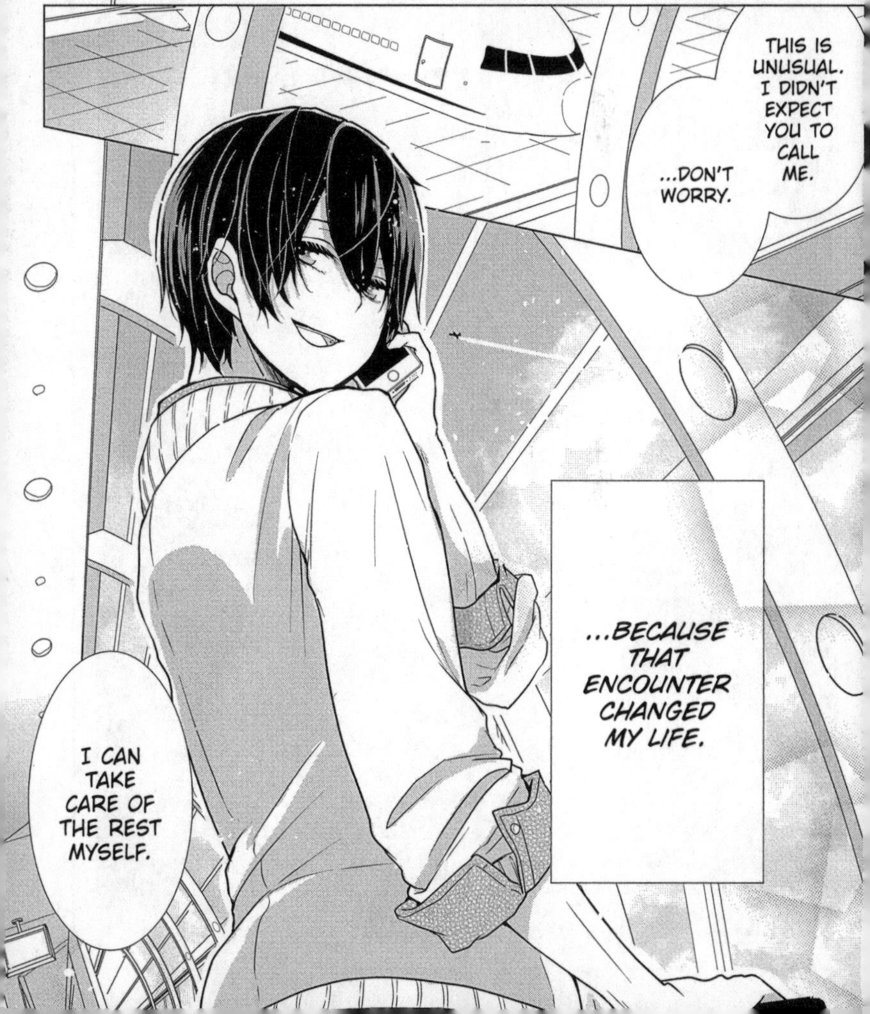
THIS IS UNUSUAL. I DIDN'T EXPECT YOU TO CALL ME.
...DON'T WORRY.
...BECAUSE THAT ENCOUNTER CHANGED MY LIFE.
I CAN TAKE CARE OF THE REST MYSELF.

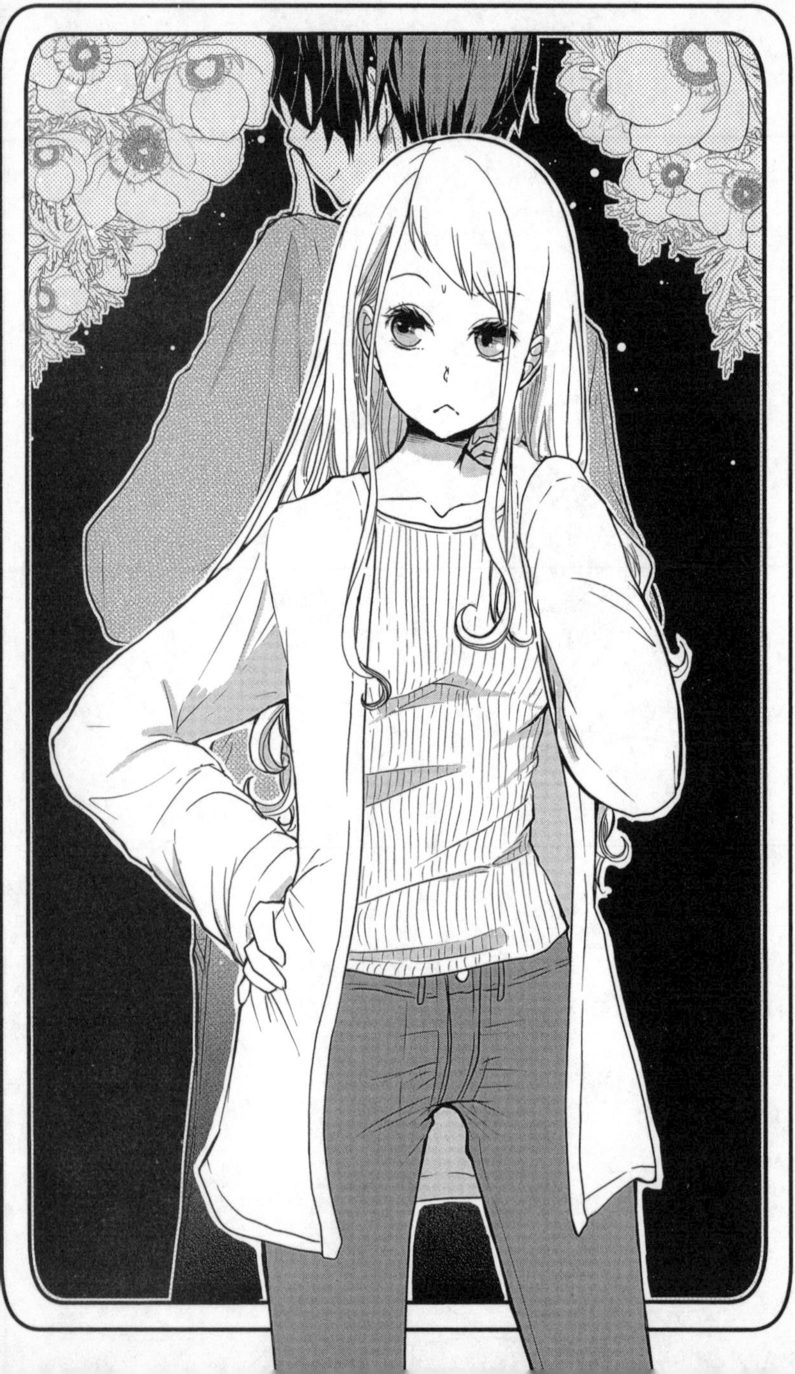

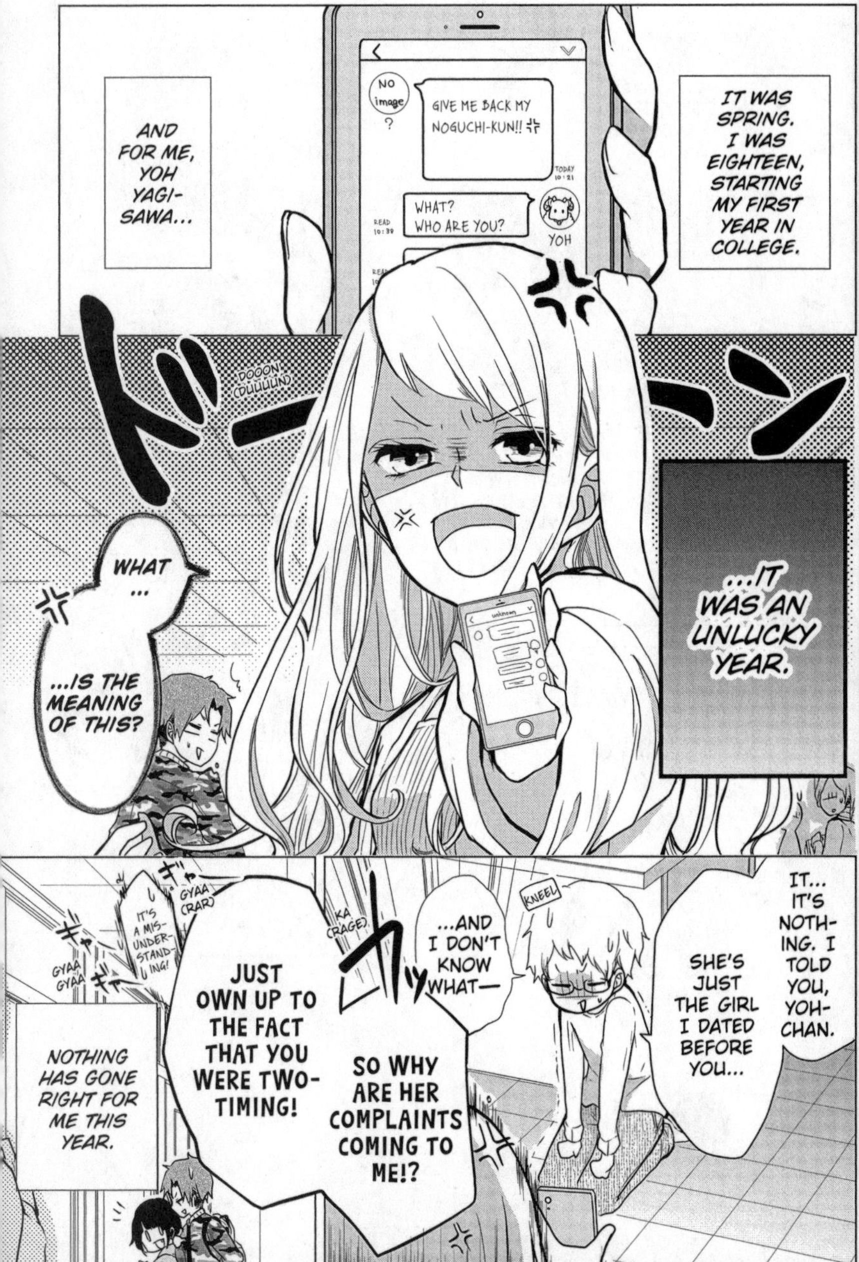
IT WAS SPRING. I WAS EIGHTEEN, STARTING MY FIRST YEAR IN COLLEGE.
No image ?
GIVE ME BACK MY NOGUCHI-KUN!!
TODAY 10:21
WHAT? WHO ARE YOU?
YOH
READ 10:38
AND FOR ME, YOH YAGI-SAWA...
DOOON (DUUUUUN)
...IT WAS AN UNLUCKY YEAR.
WHAT... ...IS THE MEANING OF THIS?
IT... IT'S NOTH-ING. I TOLD YOU, YOH-CHAN.
SHE'S JUST THE GIRL I DATED BEFORE YOU...
KNEEL
...AND I DON'T KNOW WHAT—
KA (RAGE)
SO WHY ARE HER COMPLAINTS COMING TO ME!?
JUST OWN UP TO THE FACT THAT YOU WERE TWO-TIMING!
GYAA (RAR)
IT'S A MIS-UNDER-STAND-ING!
GYAA GYAA
NOTHING HAS GONE RIGHT FOR ME THIS YEAR.

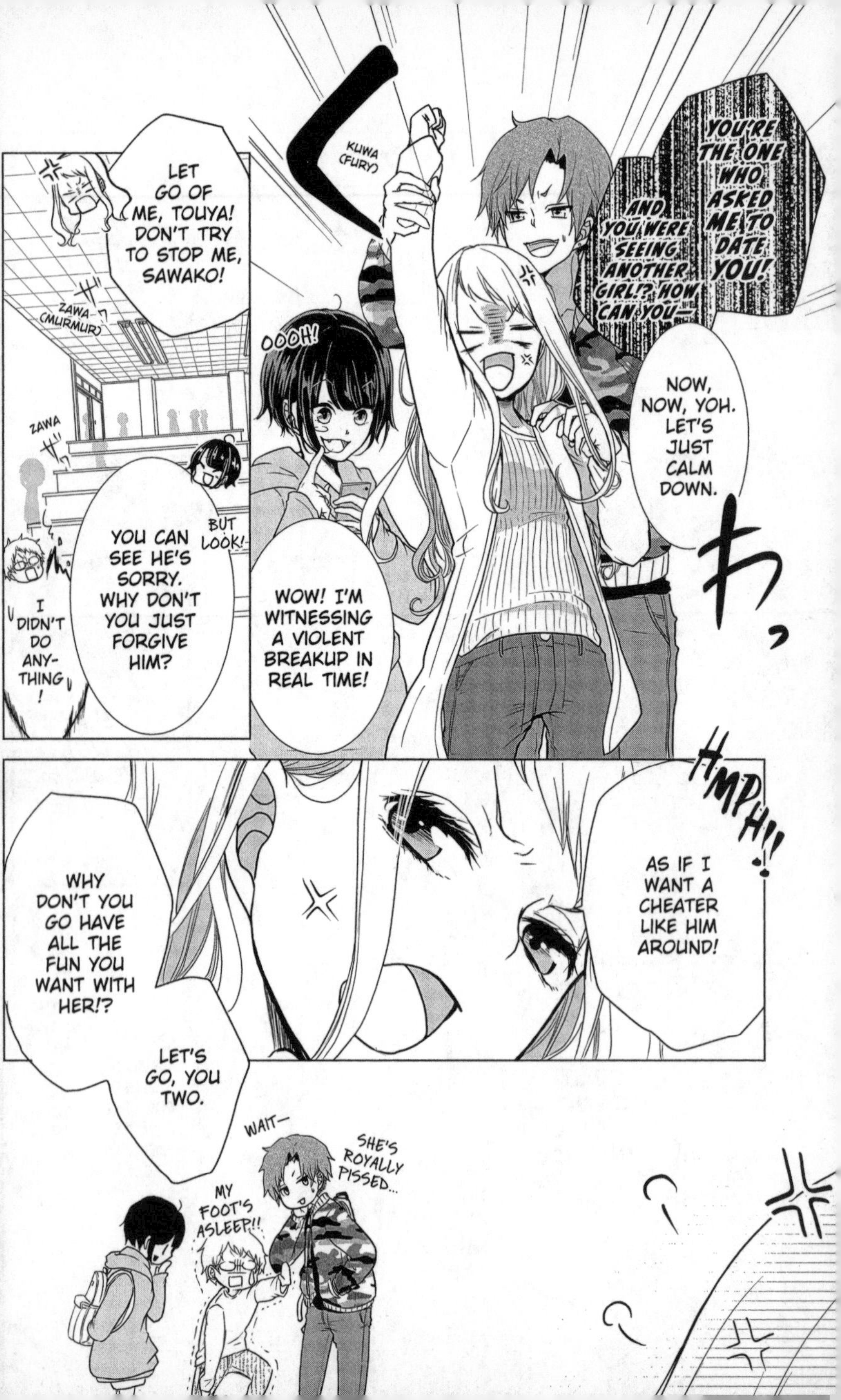
YOU'RE THE ONE WHO ASKED ME TO DATE YOU!
AND YOU WERE SEEING ANOTHER GIRL!? HOW CAN YOU—
KUWA (FURY)
NOW, NOW, YOH. LET'S JUST CALM DOWN.
OOOH!
WOW! I'M WITNESSING A VIOLENT BREAKUP IN REAL TIME!
LET GO OF ME, TOUYA! DON'T TRY TO STOP ME, SAWAKO!
ZAWA (MURMUR)
ZAWA
BUT LOOK!
YOU CAN SEE HE'S SORRY. WHY DON'T YOU JUST FORGIVE HIM?
I DIDN'T DO ANYTHING!
HMPH!!
AS IF I WANT A CHEATER LIKE HIM AROUND!
WHY DON'T YOU GO HAVE ALL THE FUN YOU WANT WITH HER!?
LET'S GO, YOU TWO.
WAIT—
SHE'S ROYALLY PISSED...
MY FOOT'S ASLEEP!!

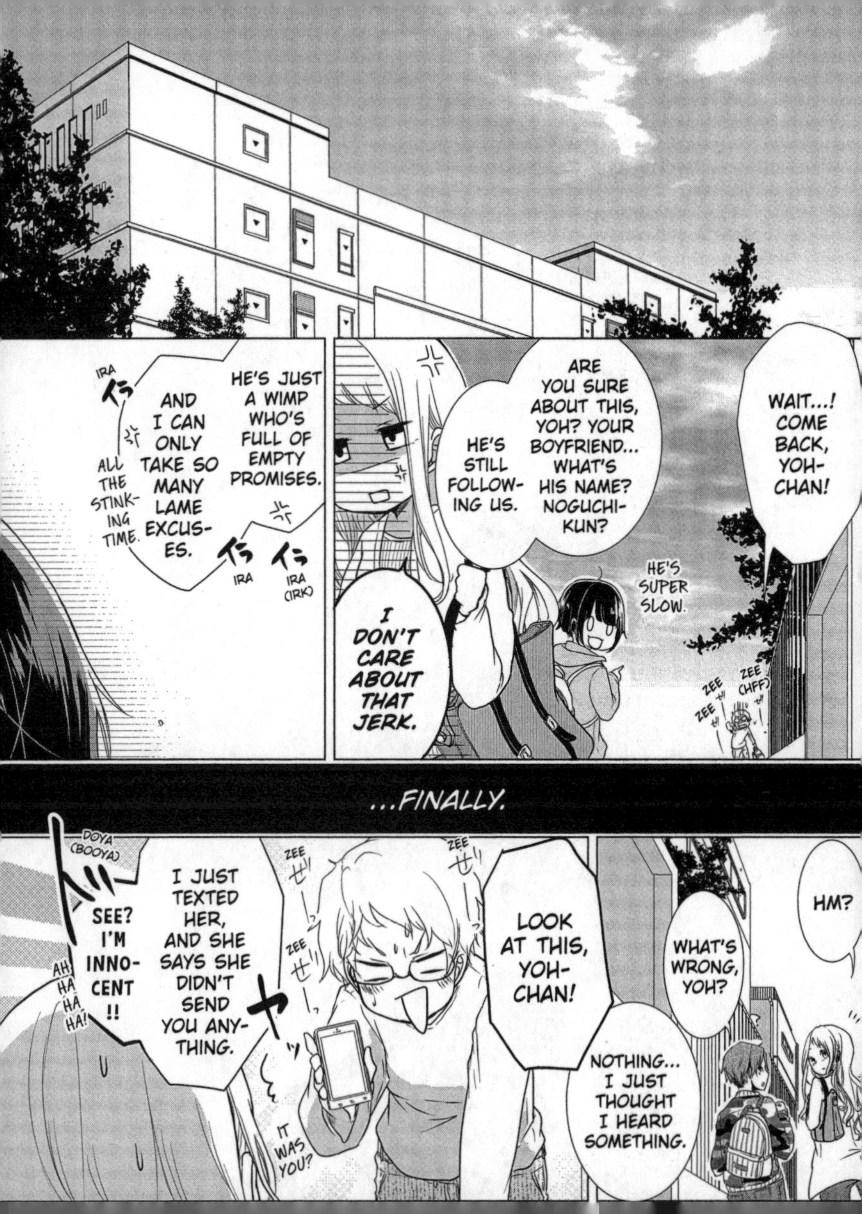
WAIT...! COME BACK, YOH-CHAN!
ARE YOU SURE ABOUT THIS, YOH? YOUR BOYFRIEND... WHAT'S HIS NAME? NOGUCHI-KUN?
HE'S STILL FOLLOWING US.
HE'S SUPER SLOW.
ZEE (CHFF)
ZEE ZEE
I DON'T CARE ABOUT THAT JERK.
HE'S JUST A WIMP WHO'S FULL OF EMPTY PROMISES.
AND I CAN ONLY TAKE SO MANY LAME EXCUSES.
ALL THE STINKING TIME.
IRA
IRA
IRA (IRK)
...FINALLY.
HM?
WHAT'S WRONG, YOH?
NOTHING... I JUST THOUGHT I HEARD SOMETHING.
LOOK AT THIS, YOH-CHAN!
ZEE
ZEE
ZEE
I JUST TEXTED HER, AND SHE SAYS SHE DIDN'T SEND YOU ANYTHING.
SEE? I'M INNOCENT!!
DOYA (BOOYA)
AH HA HA HA!
IT WAS YOU?

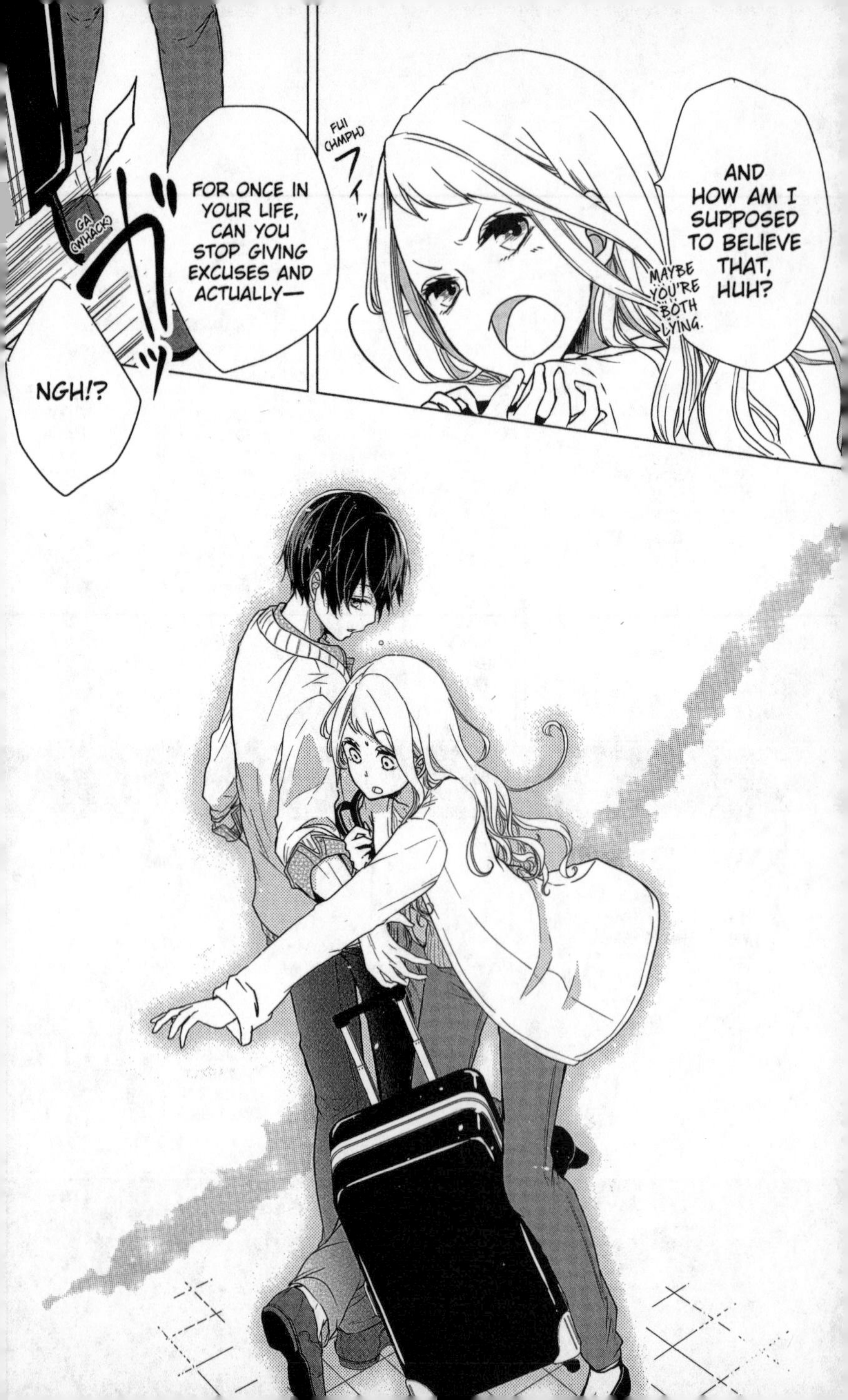
AND HOW AM I SUPPOSED TO BELIEVE THAT, HUH?
MAYBE YOU'RE BOTH LYING.
FUI (HMPH)
FOR ONCE IN YOUR LIFE, CAN YOU STOP GIVING EXCUSES AND ACTUALLY—
GA (WHACK)
NGH!?

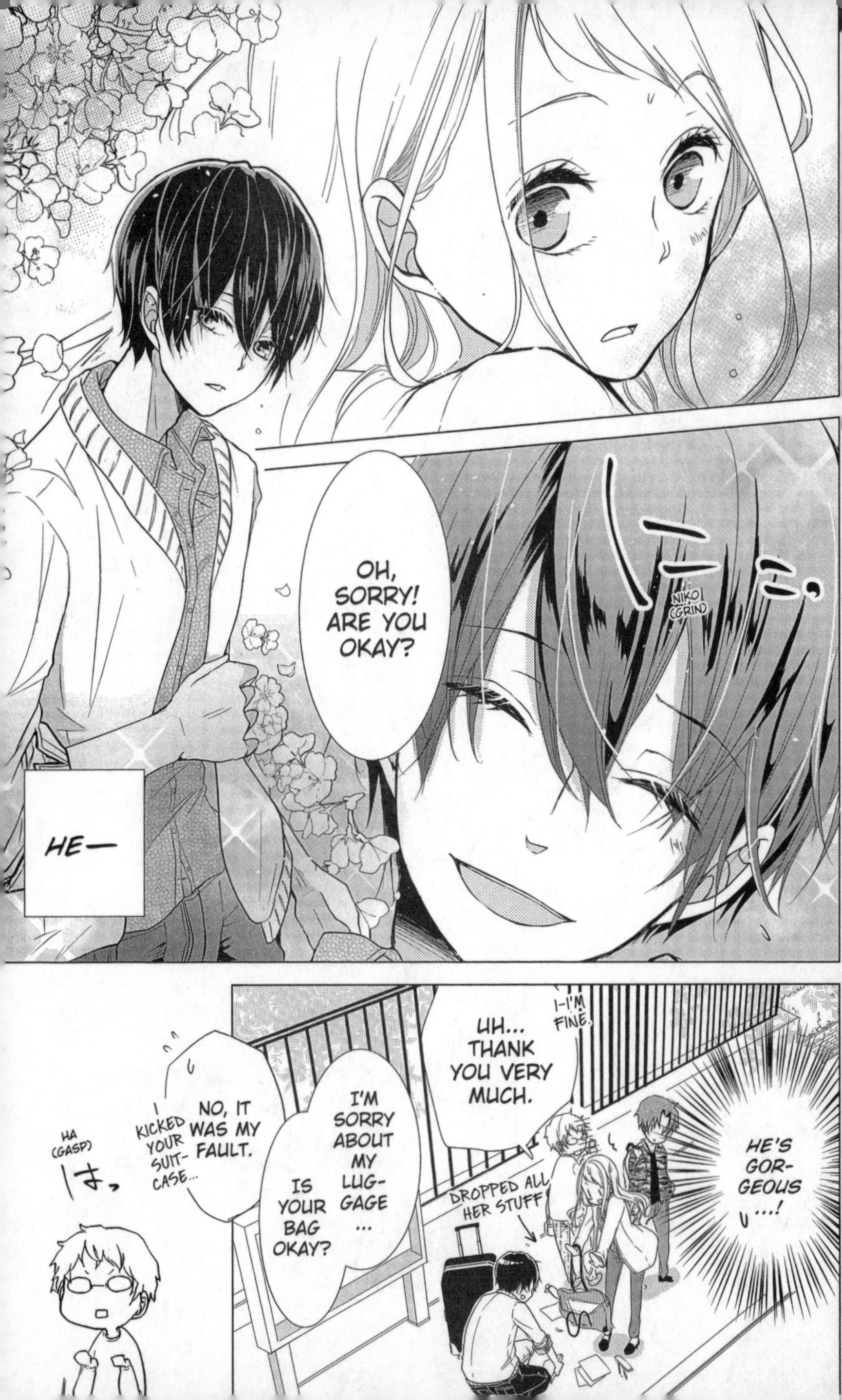
OH, SORRY! ARE YOU OKAY?
NIKO (GRIN)
HE—
HE'S GORGEOUS...!
UH... THANK YOU VERY MUCH.
I-I'M FINE.
DROPPED ALL HER STUFF
I'M SORRY ABOUT MY LUGGAGE...
IS YOUR BAG OKAY?
NO, IT WAS MY FAULT.
I KICKED YOUR SUITCASE...
HA (GASP)
はっ

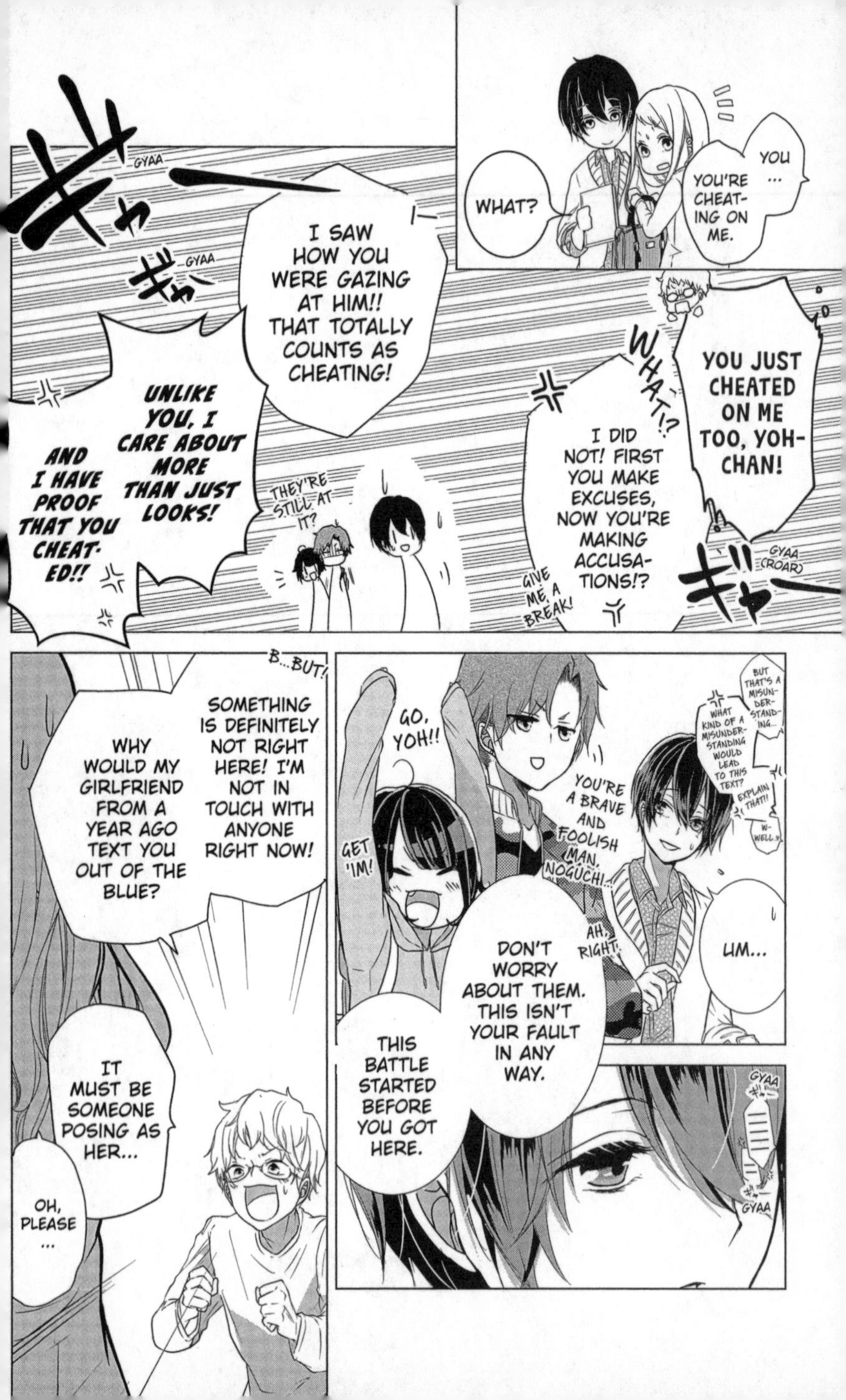
YOU ... YOU'RE CHEATING ON ME.
WHAT?
YOU JUST CHEATED ON ME TOO, YOH-CHAN!
WHAT!?
I DID NOT! FIRST YOU MAKE EXCUSES, NOW YOU'RE MAKING ACCUSATIONS!?
GIVE ME A BREAK!
GYAA (ROAR)
I SAW HOW YOU WERE GAZING AT HIM!! THAT TOTALLY COUNTS AS CHEATING!
GYAA
GYAA
THEY'RE STILL AT IT?
UNLIKE YOU, I CARE ABOUT MORE THAN JUST LOOKS!
AND I HAVE PROOF THAT YOU CHEATED!!
BUT THAT'S A MISUNDERSTANDING...
WHAT KIND OF A MISUNDERSTANDING WOULD LEAD TO THIS TEXT? EXPLAIN THAT!!
W-WELL...
GO, YOH!!
GET 'IM!
YOU'RE A BRAVE AND FOOLISH MAN, NOGUCHI...
AH, RIGHT.
UM...
DON'T WORRY ABOUT THEM. THIS ISN'T YOUR FAULT IN ANY WAY.
THIS BATTLE STARTED BEFORE YOU GOT HERE.
GYAA
GYAA
B...BUT!
SOMETHING IS DEFINITELY NOT RIGHT HERE! I'M NOT IN TOUCH WITH ANYONE RIGHT NOW!
WHY WOULD MY GIRLFRIEND FROM A YEAR AGO TEXT YOU OUT OF THE BLUE?
IT MUST BE SOMEONE POSING AS HER...
OH, PLEASE ...

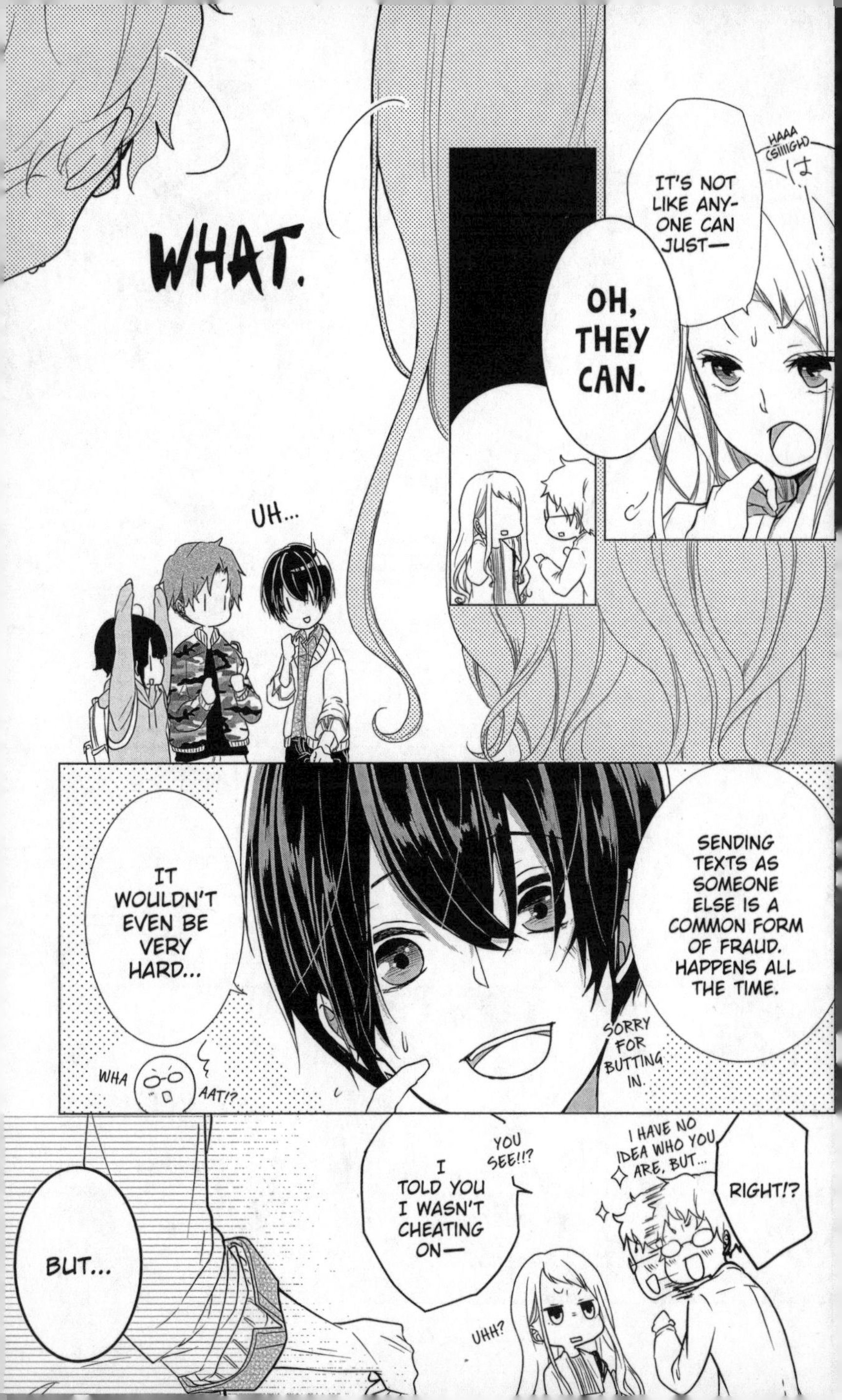

HAAA (SIIIGH) は
IT'S NOT LIKE ANY-ONE CAN JUST—
OH, THEY CAN.
WHAT.
UH...
SENDING TEXTS AS SOMEONE ELSE IS A COMMON FORM OF FRAUD. HAPPENS ALL THE TIME.
SORRY FOR BUTTING IN.
IT WOULDN'T EVEN BE VERY HARD...
WHA AAT!?
RIGHT!?
I HAVE NO IDEA WHO YOU ARE, BUT...
YOU SEE!!?
I TOLD YOU I WASN'T CHEATING ON—
UHH?
BUT...

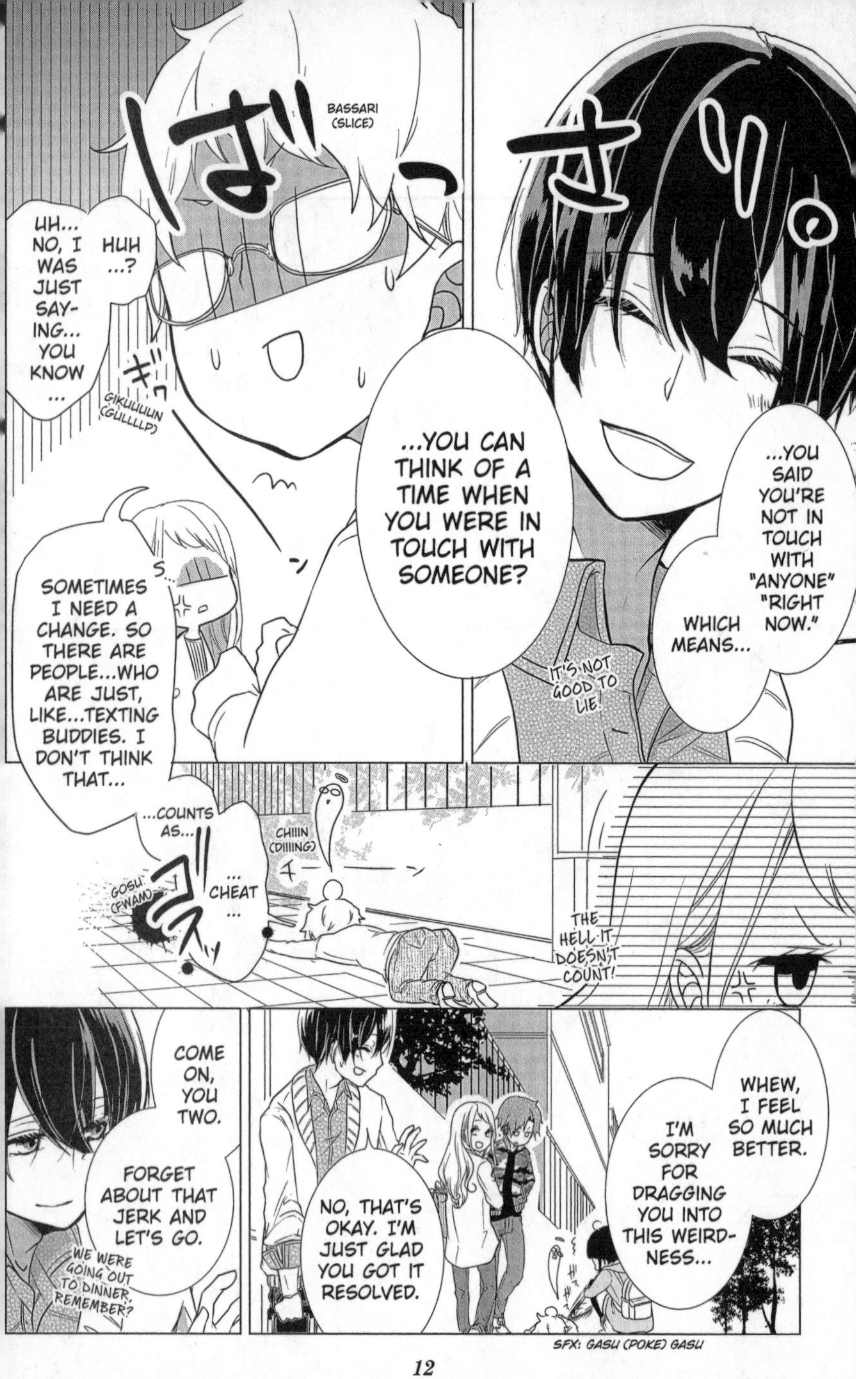
BASSARI (SLICE)
...YOU SAID YOU'RE NOT IN TOUCH WITH "ANYONE" "RIGHT NOW."
WHICH MEANS...
...YOU CAN THINK OF A TIME WHEN YOU WERE IN TOUCH WITH SOMEONE?
IT'S NOT GOOD TO LIE!
HUH ...?
UH... NO, I WAS JUST SAY-ING... YOU KNOW ...
GIKUUUUN (GULLLLP)
S...
SOMETIMES I NEED A CHANGE. SO THERE ARE PEOPLE...WHO ARE JUST, LIKE...TEXTING BUDDIES. I DON'T THINK THAT...
THE HELL IT DOESN'T COUNT!
...COUNTS AS...
... CHEAT ...
GOSU (FWAM)
CHIIN (DIIIING)
WHEW, I FEEL SO MUCH BETTER.
I'M SORRY FOR DRAGGING YOU INTO THIS WEIRD-NESS...
NO, THAT'S OKAY. I'M JUST GLAD YOU GOT IT RESOLVED.
COME ON, YOU TWO.
FORGET ABOUT THAT JERK AND LET'S GO.
WE WERE GOING OUT TO DINNER, REMEMBER?

SFX: GASU (POKE) GASU

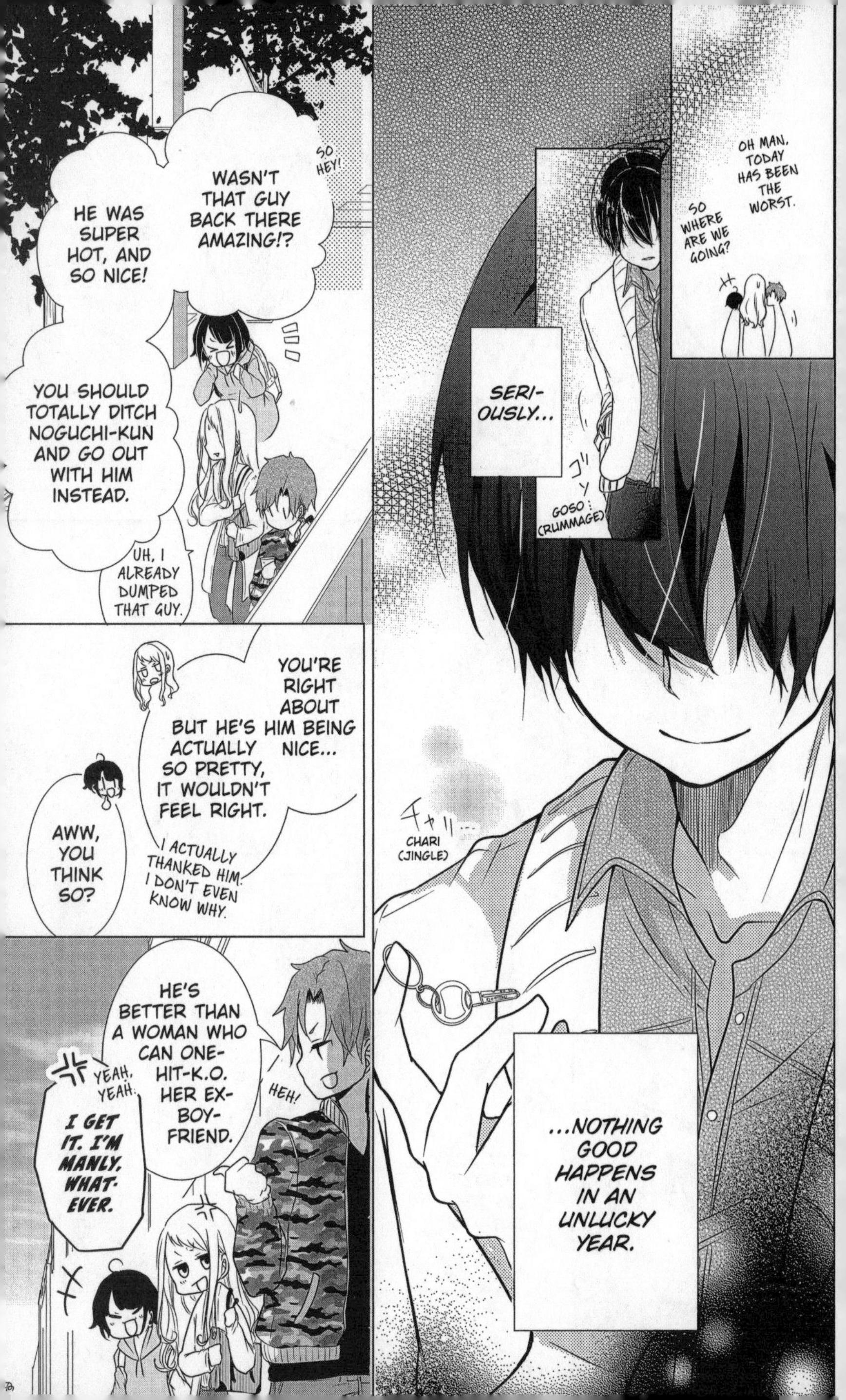
OH MAN, TODAY HAS BEEN THE WORST.
SO WHERE ARE WE GOING?
SERI-OUSLY...
GOSO (RUMMAGE)
CHARI (JINGLE)
...NOTHING GOOD HAPPENS IN AN UNLUCKY YEAR.
SO HEY!
WASN'T THAT GUY BACK THERE AMAZING!?
HE WAS SUPER HOT, AND SO NICE!
YOU SHOULD TOTALLY DITCH NOGUCHI-KUN AND GO OUT WITH HIM INSTEAD.
UH, I ALREADY DUMPED THAT GUY.
YOU'RE RIGHT ABOUT HIM BEING NICE...
BUT HE'S ACTUALLY SO PRETTY, IT WOULDN'T FEEL RIGHT.
I ACTUALLY THANKED HIM. I DON'T EVEN KNOW WHY.
AWW, YOU THINK SO?
HE'S BETTER THAN A WOMAN WHO CAN ONE-HIT-K.O. HER EX-BOYFRIEND.
HEH!
YEAH, YEAH.
I GET IT. I'M MANLY. WHAT-EVER.

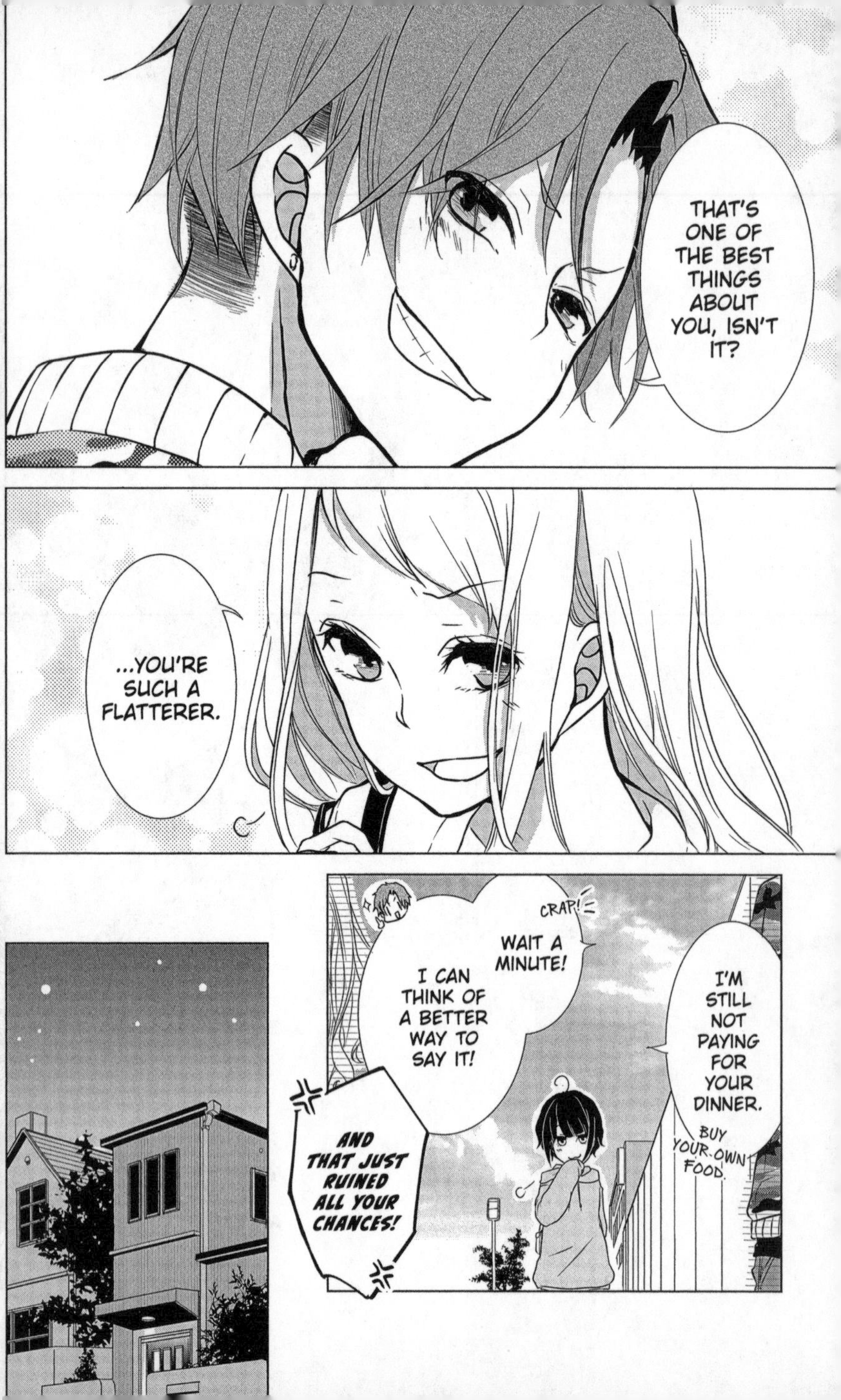
THAT'S ONE OF THE BEST THINGS ABOUT YOU, ISN'T IT?
...YOU'RE SUCH A FLATTERER.
I'M STILL NOT PAYING FOR YOUR DINNER.
BUY YOUR OWN FOOD.
CRAP!
WAIT A MINUTE!
I CAN THINK OF A BETTER WAY TO SAY IT!
AND THAT JUST RUINED ALL YOUR CHANCES!

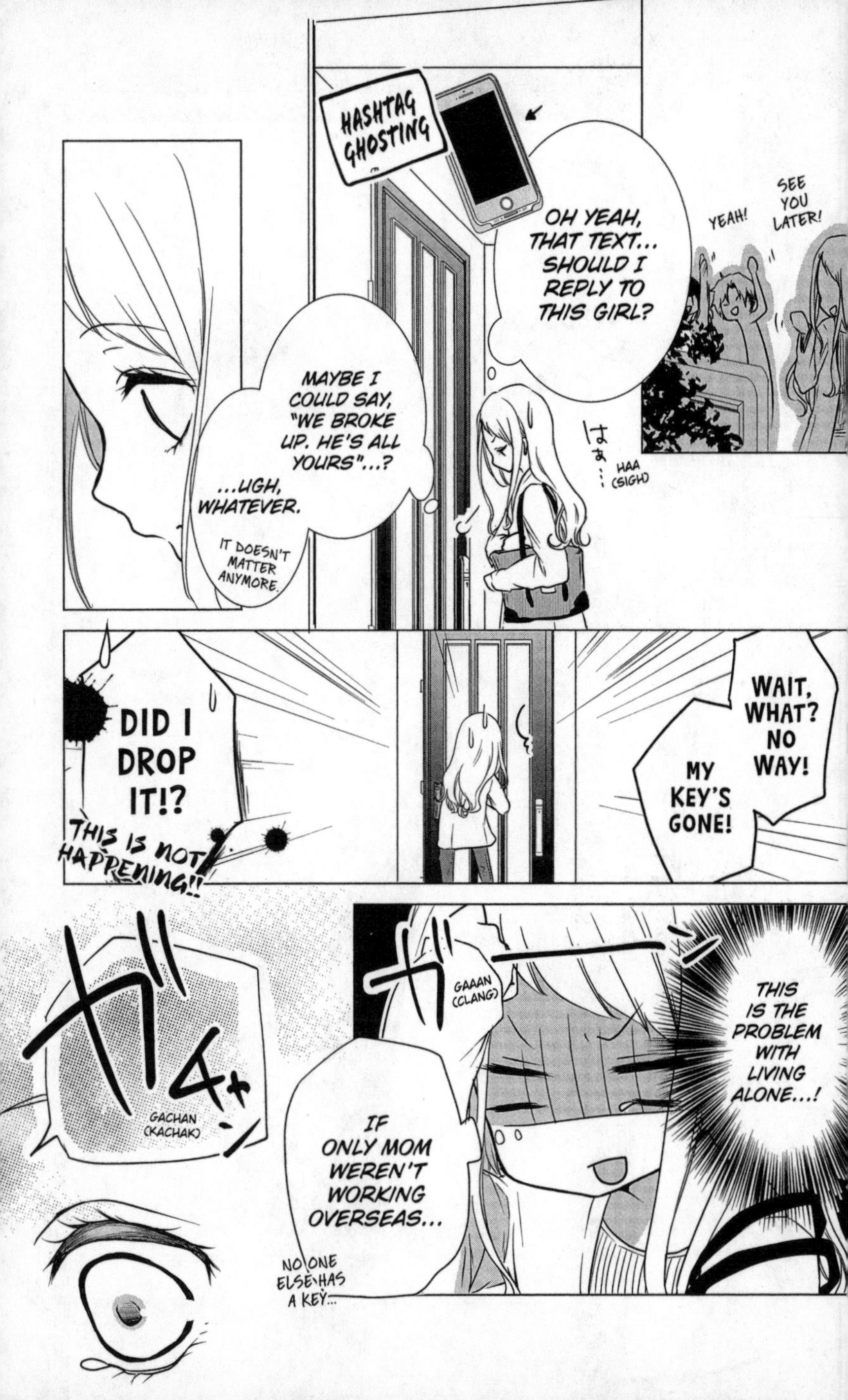
SEE YOU LATER!
YEAH!
HASHTAG GHOSTING
OH YEAH, THAT TEXT... SHOULD I REPLY TO THIS GIRL?
はぁ…
HAA (SIGH)
MAYBE I COULD SAY, "WE BROKE UP. HE'S ALL YOURS"...?
...UGH, WHATEVER.
IT DOESN'T MATTER ANYMORE.
WAIT, WHAT? NO WAY!
MY KEY'S GONE!
DID I DROP IT!?
THIS IS NOT HAPPENING!!
THIS IS THE PROBLEM WITH LIVING ALONE...!
ガーン
GAAAN (CLANG)
IF ONLY MOM WEREN'T WORKING OVERSEAS...
NO ONE ELSE HAS A KEY...
ガチャ
GACHAN (KACHAK)

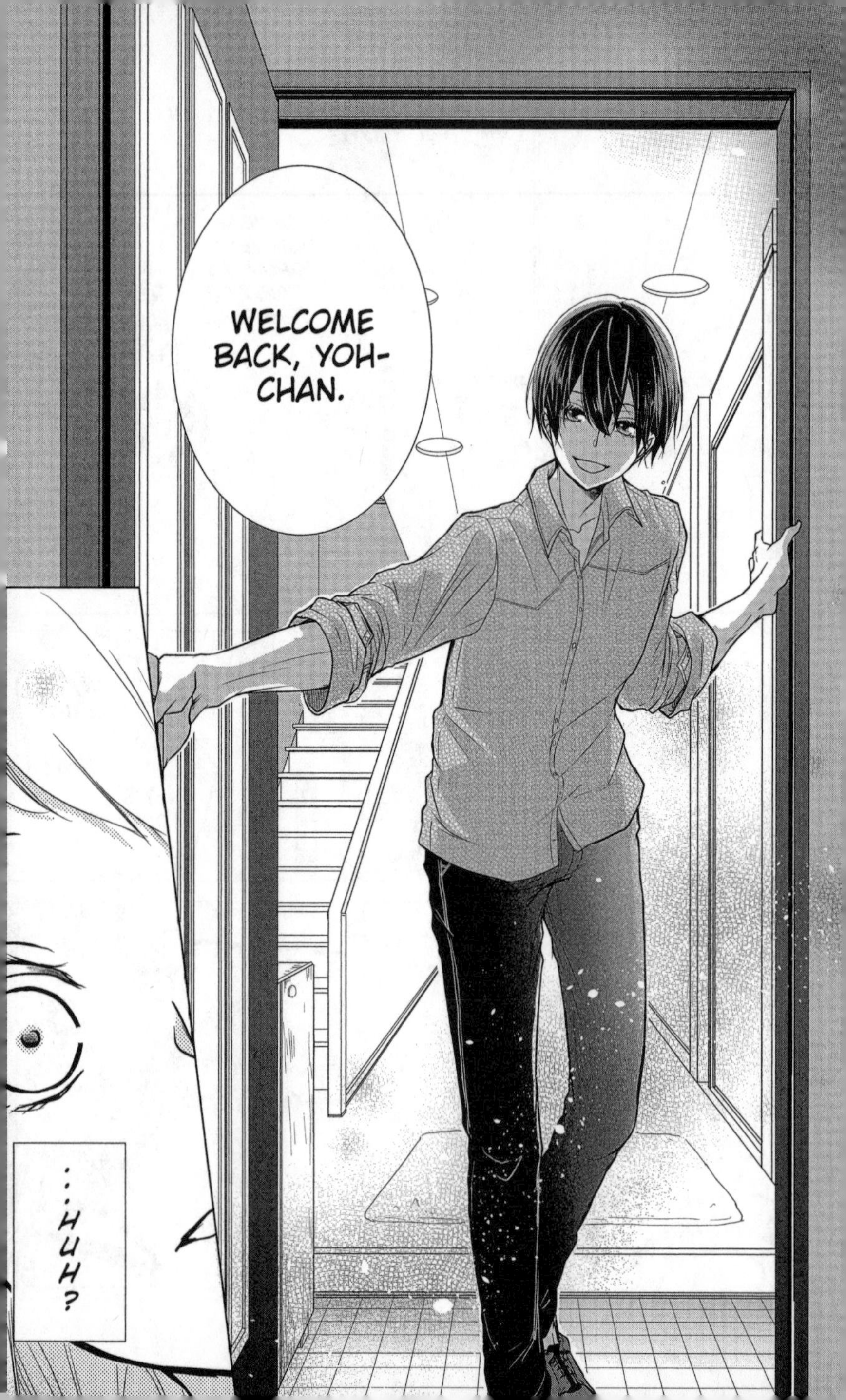
WELCOME BACK, YOH-CHAN.
...HUH?

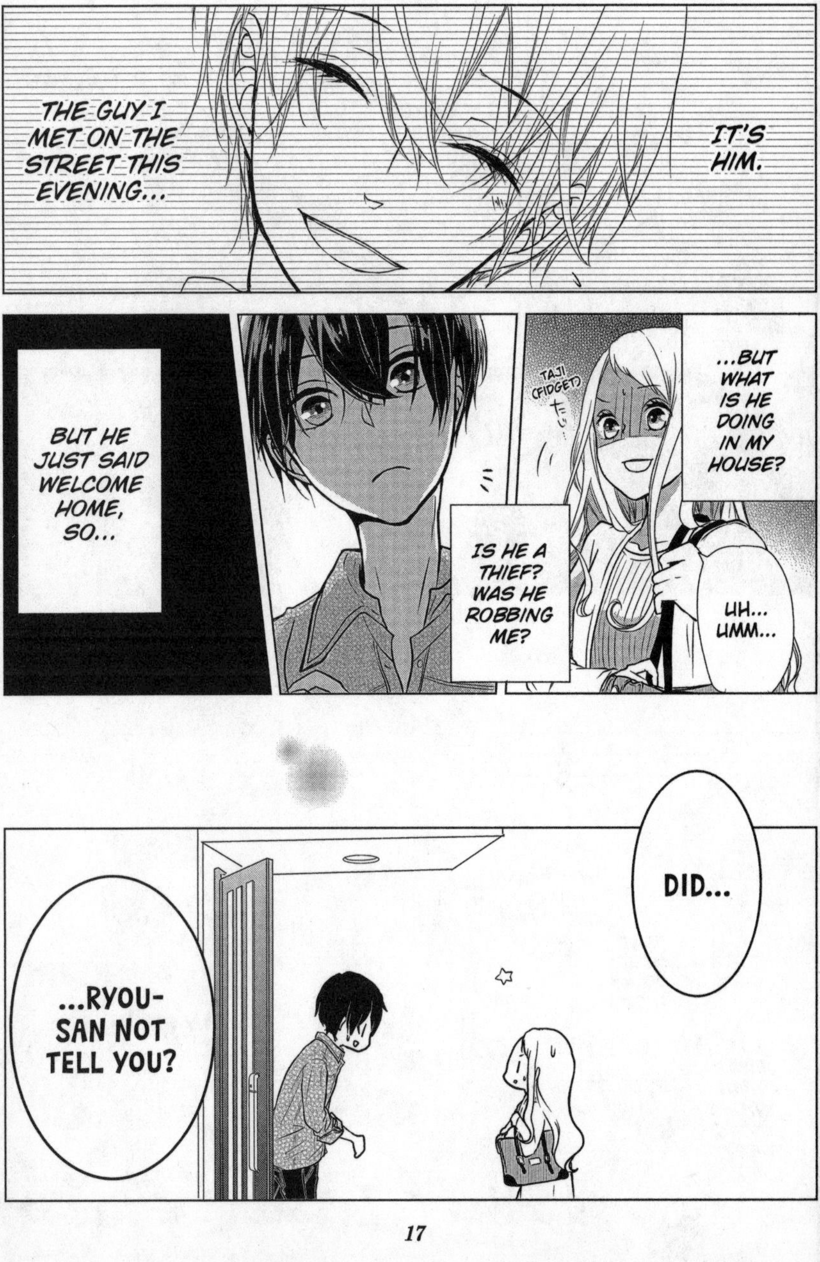
THE GUY I MET ON THE STREET THIS EVENING...
IT'S HIM.
...BUT WHAT IS HE DOING IN MY HOUSE?
TAJI (FIDGET)
UH... UMM...
IS HE A THIEF? WAS HE ROBBING ME?
BUT HE JUST SAID WELCOME HOME, SO...
DID...
...RYOU-SAN NOT TELL YOU?

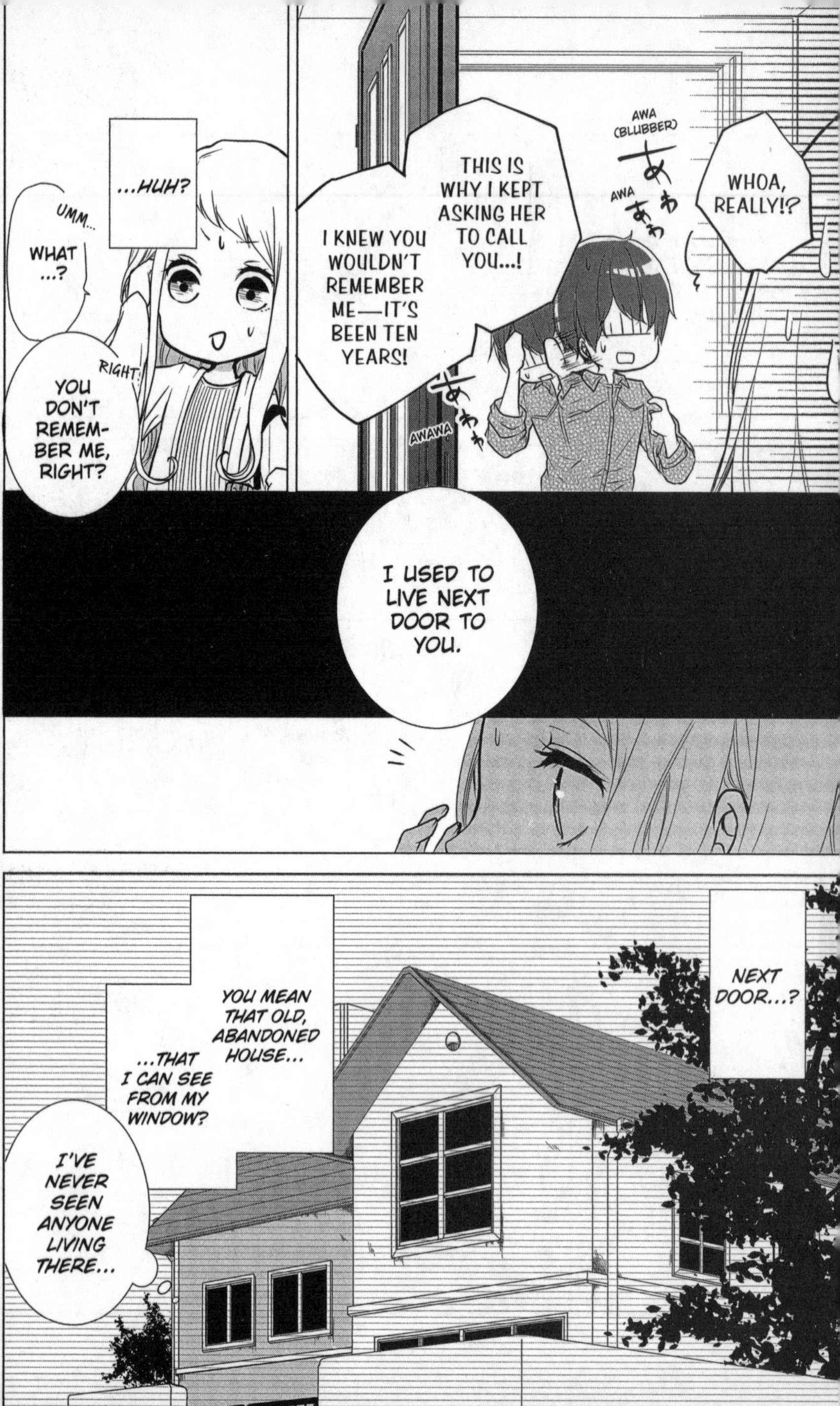
WHOA, REALLY!?
AWA (BLUBBER)
あ
AWA
あわ
THIS IS WHY I KEPT ASKING HER TO CALL YOU...!
I KNEW YOU WOULDN'T REMEMBER ME—IT'S BEEN TEN YEARS!
あわわ
AWAWA
...HUH?
UMM...
WHAT ...?
RIGHT
YOU DON'T REMEM-BER ME, RIGHT?
I USED TO LIVE NEXT DOOR TO YOU.
NEXT DOOR...?
YOU MEAN THAT OLD, ABANDONED HOUSE...
...THAT I CAN SEE FROM MY WINDOW?
I'VE NEVER SEEN ANYONE LIVING THERE...

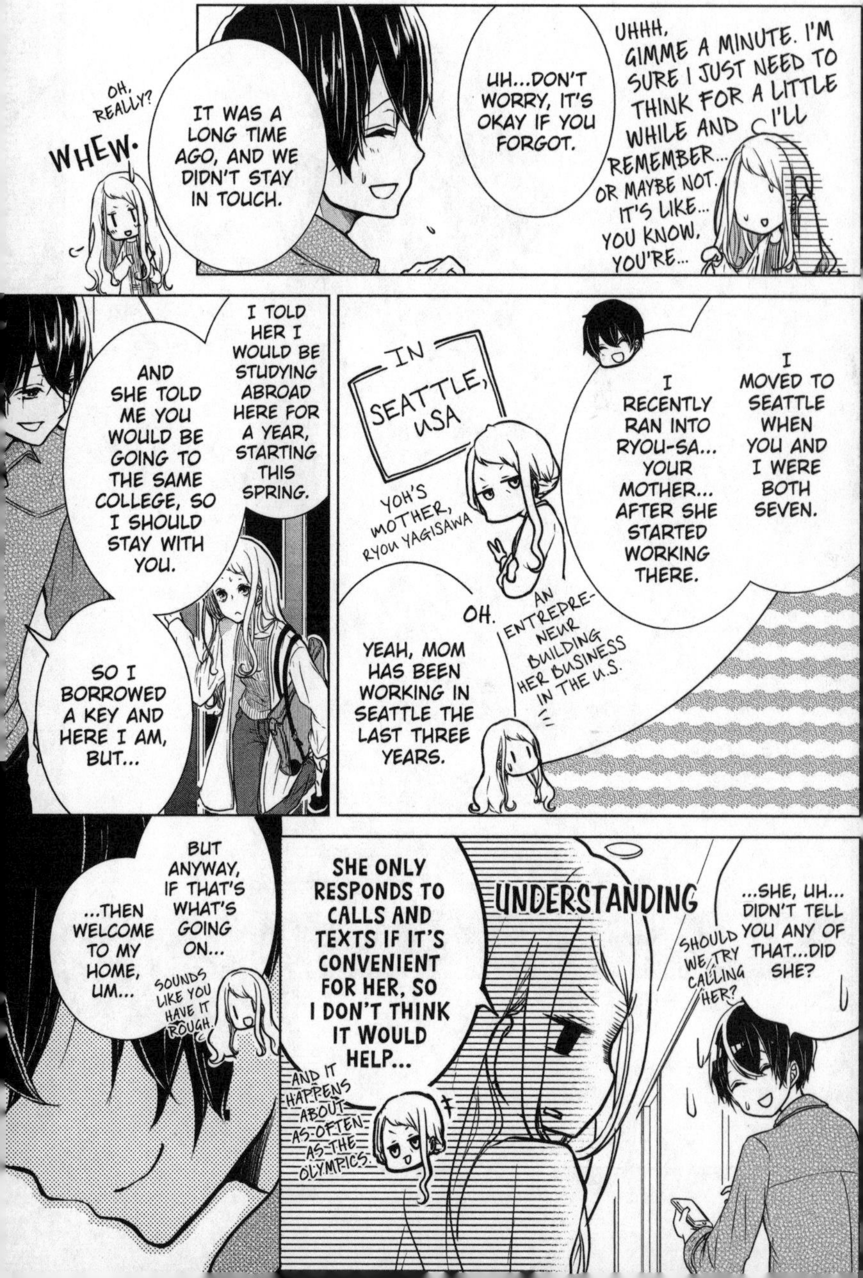
UHHH, GIMME A MINUTE. I'M SURE I JUST NEED TO THINK FOR A LITTLE WHILE AND I'LL REMEMBER... OR MAYBE NOT. IT'S LIKE... YOU KNOW, YOU'RE...
UH...DON'T WORRY, IT'S OKAY IF YOU FORGOT.
IT WAS A LONG TIME AGO, AND WE DIDN'T STAY IN TOUCH.
OH, REALLY?
WHEW.
I MOVED TO SEATTLE WHEN YOU AND I WERE BOTH SEVEN.
I RECENTLY RAN INTO RYOU-SA... YOUR MOTHER... AFTER SHE STARTED WORKING THERE.
IN SEATTLE, USA
YOH'S MOTHER, RYOU YAGISAWA
OH.
AN ENTREPRE-NEUR BUILDING HER BUSINESS IN THE U.S.
YEAH, MOM HAS BEEN WORKING IN SEATTLE THE LAST THREE YEARS.
I TOLD HER I WOULD BE STUDYING ABROAD HERE FOR A YEAR, STARTING THIS SPRING.
AND SHE TOLD ME YOU WOULD BE GOING TO THE SAME COLLEGE, SO I SHOULD STAY WITH YOU.
SO I BORROWED A KEY AND HERE I AM, BUT...
...SHE, UH... DIDN'T TELL YOU ANY OF THAT...DID SHE?
SHOULD WE TRY CALLING HER?
UNDERSTANDING
SHE ONLY RESPONDS TO CALLS AND TEXTS IF IT'S CONVENIENT FOR HER, SO I DON'T THINK IT WOULD HELP...
AND IT HAPPENS ABOUT AS OFTEN AS THE OLYMPICS.
BUT ANYWAY, IF THAT'S WHAT'S GOING ON...
...THEN WELCOME TO MY HOME, UM...
SOUNDS LIKE YOU HAVE IT ROUGH.

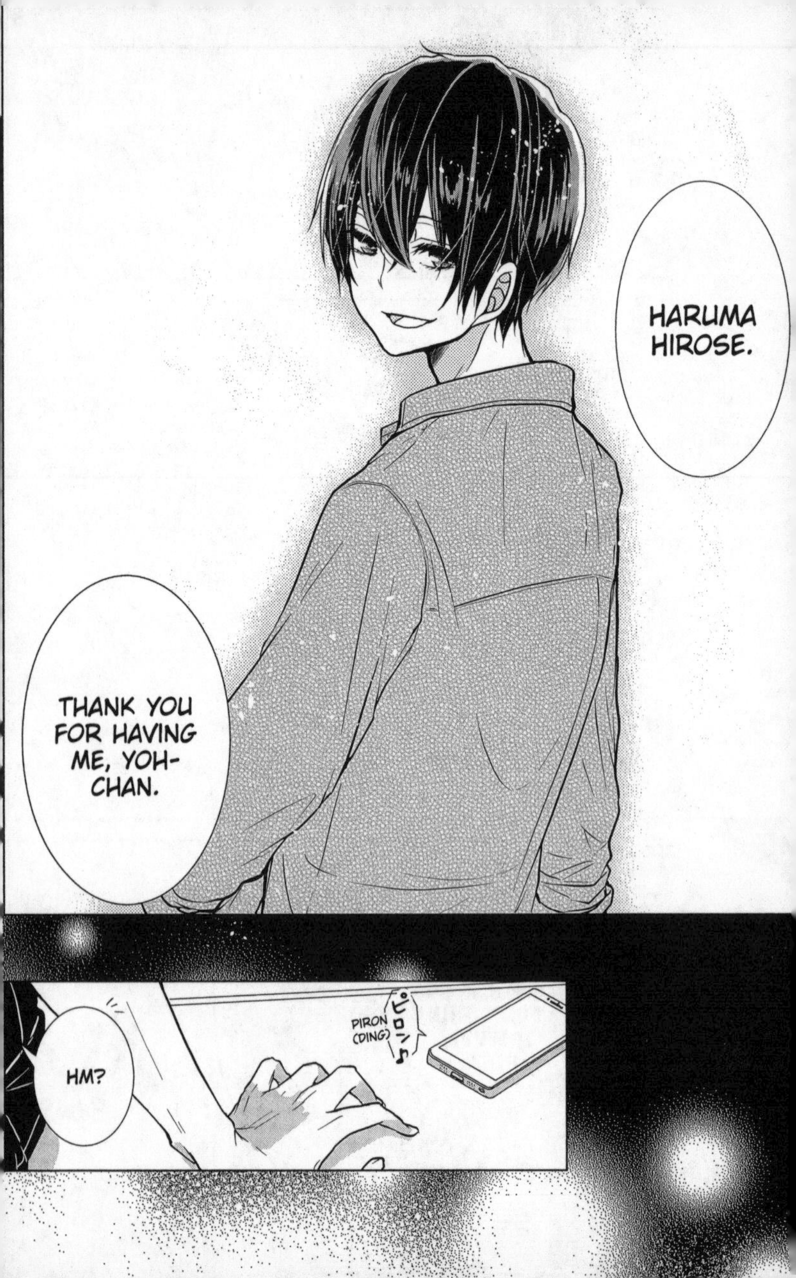
HARUMA HIROSE.
THANK YOU FOR HAVING ME, YOH-CHAN.
ピロン♪
PIRON (DING)
HM?

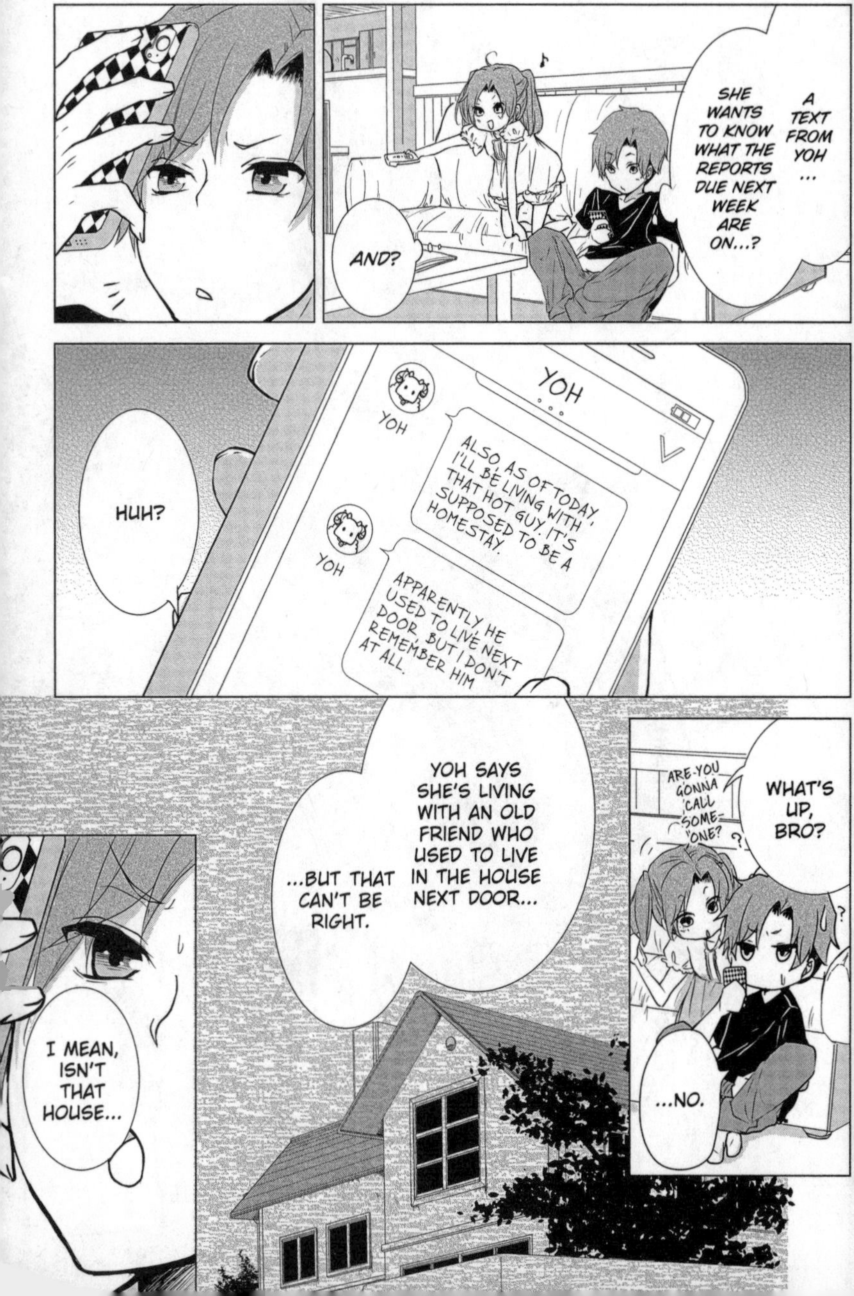
A TEXT FROM YOH...
SHE WANTS TO KNOW WHAT THE REPORTS DUE NEXT WEEK ARE ON...?
AND?
YOH
YOH
ALSO, AS OF TODAY, I'LL BE LIVING WITH THAT HOT GUY. IT'S SUPPOSED TO BE A HOMESTAY.
YOH
APPARENTLY, HE USED TO LIVE NEXT DOOR, BUT I DON'T REMEMBER HIM AT ALL.
HUH?
WHAT'S UP, BRO?
ARE YOU GONNA CALL SOMEONE?
...NO.
YOH SAYS SHE'S LIVING WITH AN OLD FRIEND WHO USED TO LIVE IN THE HOUSE NEXT DOOR...
...BUT THAT CAN'T BE RIGHT.
I MEAN, ISN'T THAT HOUSE...

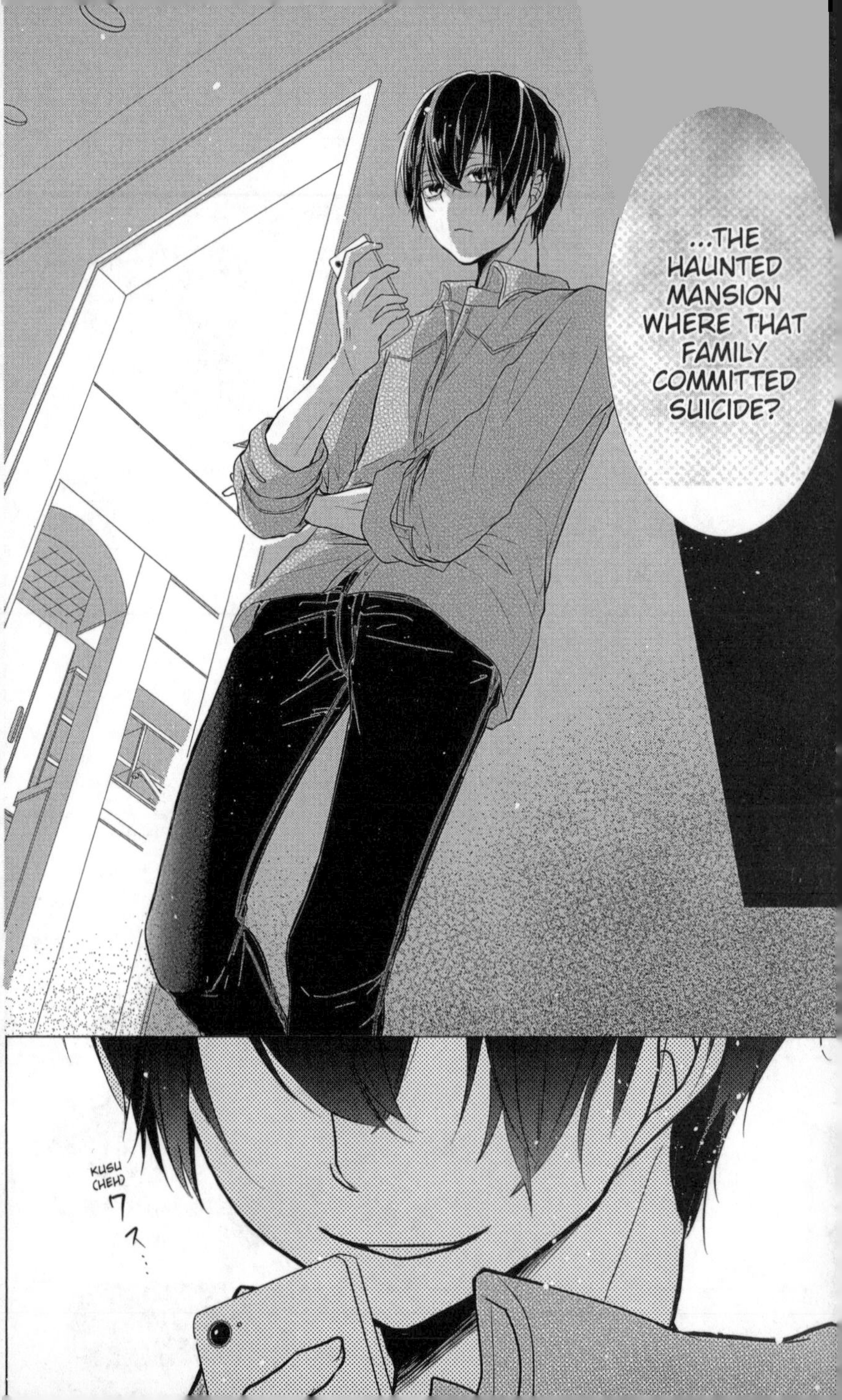
...THE HAUNTED MANSION WHERE THAT FAMILY COMMITTED SUICIDE?
KUSU CHEH

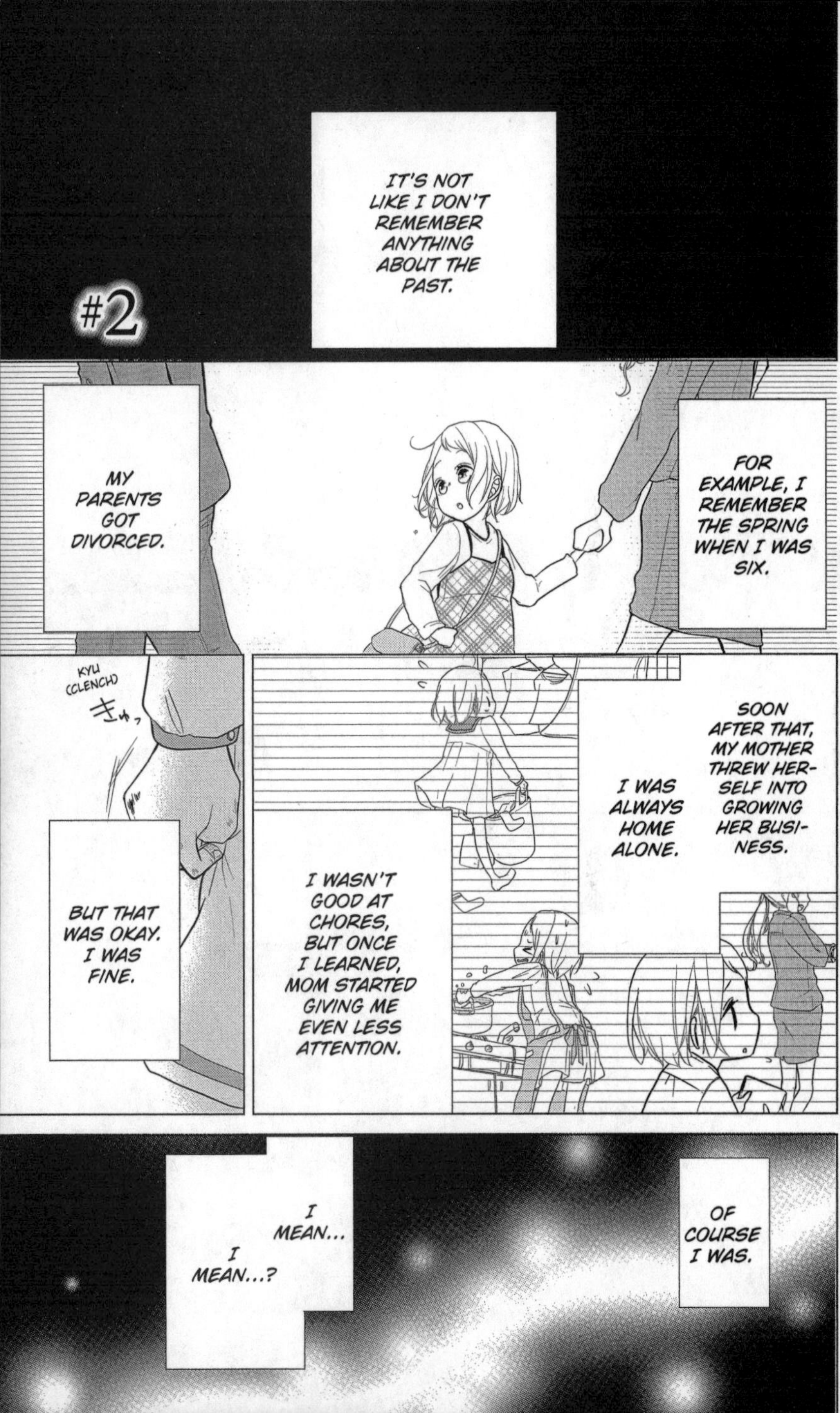
IT'S NOT LIKE I DON'T REMEMBER ANYTHING ABOUT THE PAST.
#2
FOR EXAMPLE, I REMEMBER THE SPRING WHEN I WAS SIX.
MY PARENTS GOT DIVORCED.
SOON AFTER THAT, MY MOTHER THREW HER-SELF INTO GROWING HER BUSI-NESS.
I WAS ALWAYS HOME ALONE.
I WASN'T GOOD AT CHORES, BUT ONCE I LEARNED, MOM STARTED GIVING ME EVEN LESS ATTENTION.
KYU (CLENCH)
きゅっ
BUT THAT WAS OKAY. I WAS FINE.
OF COURSE I WAS.
I MEAN...
I MEAN...?

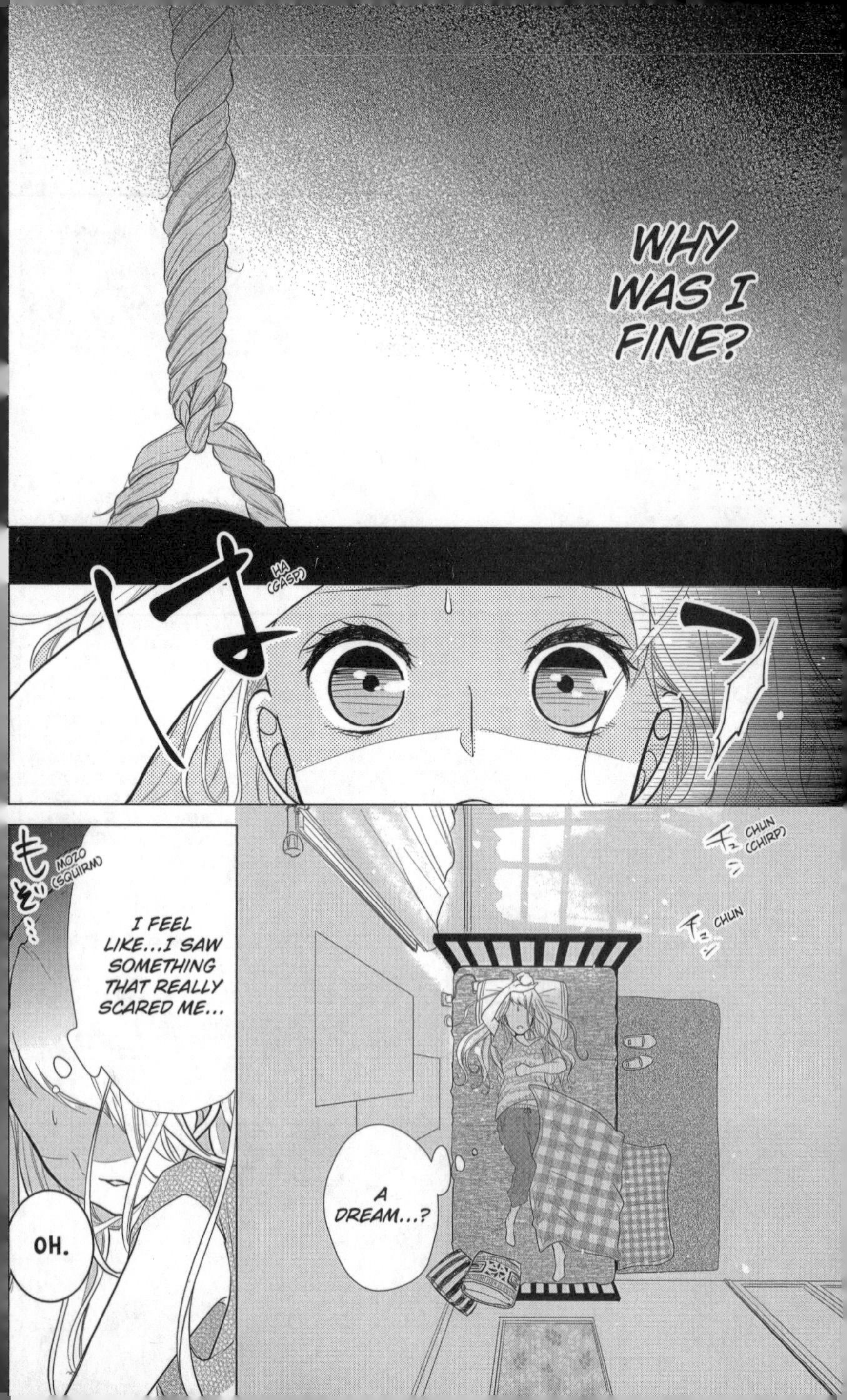
WHY WAS I FINE?
HA (GASP)
CHUN (CHIRP)
CHUN
A DREAM...?
MOZO (SQUIRM)
I FEEL LIKE...I SAW SOMETHING THAT REALLY SCARED ME...
OH.

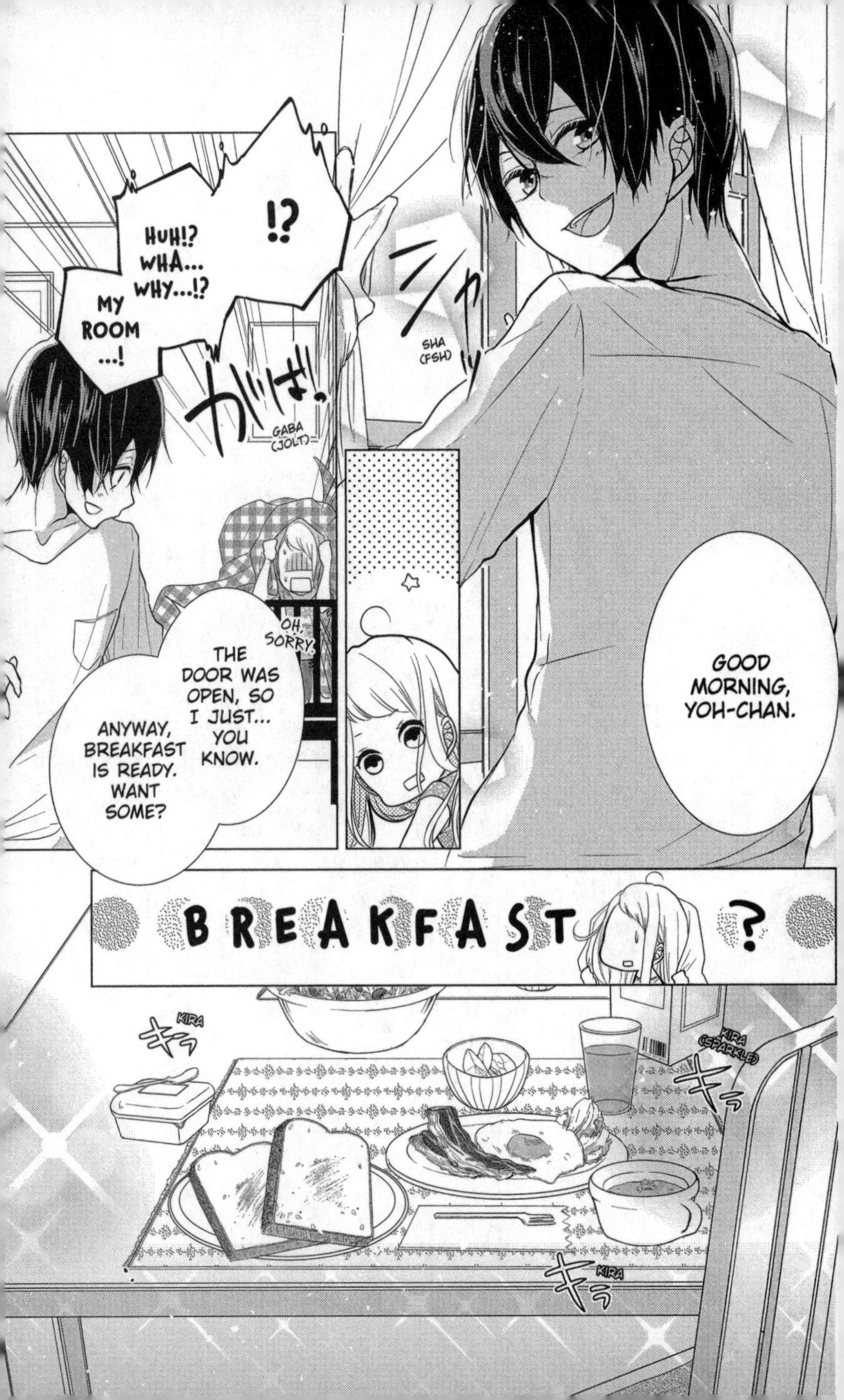

SHA (FSH)
!?
HUH!? WHA... WHY...!?
MY ROOM ...!
GABA (JOLT)
GOOD MORNING, YOH-CHAN.
OH, SORRY.
THE DOOR WAS OPEN, SO I JUST... YOU KNOW.
ANYWAY, BREAKFAST IS READY. WANT SOME?
BREAKFAST ?
KIRA (SPARKLE)
KIRA
KIRA

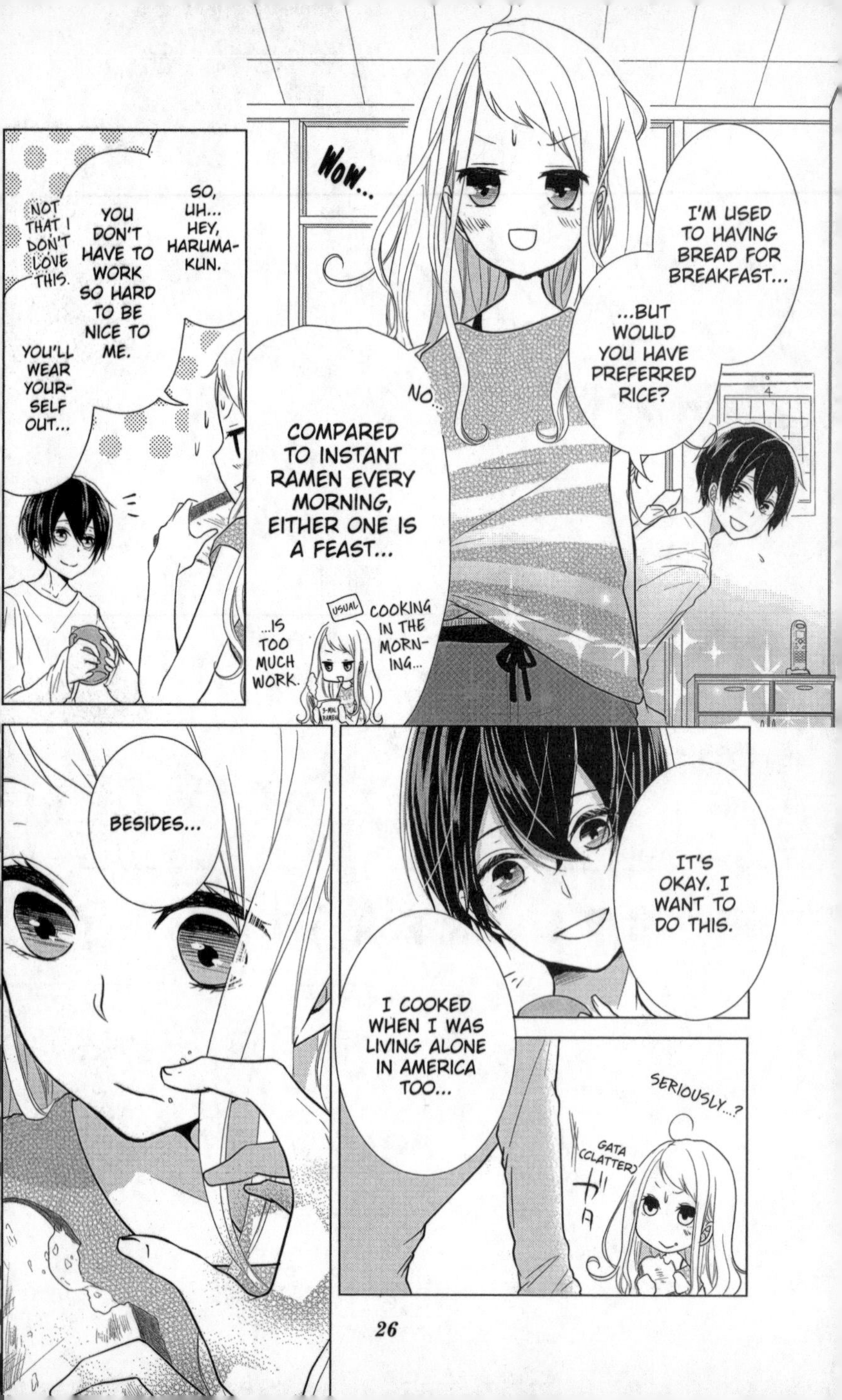
I'M USED TO HAVING BREAD FOR BREAKFAST...
...BUT WOULD YOU HAVE PREFERRED RICE?
WOW...
NO...
COMPARED TO INSTANT RAMEN EVERY MORNING, EITHER ONE IS A FEAST...
USUAL
COOKING IN THE MORNING...
...IS TOO MUCH WORK.
SO, UH... HEY, HARUMA-KUN.
YOU DON'T HAVE TO WORK SO HARD TO BE NICE TO ME.
NOT THAT I DON'T LOVE THIS.
YOU'LL WEAR YOURSELF OUT...
IT'S OKAY. I WANT TO DO THIS.
I COOKED WHEN I WAS LIVING ALONE IN AMERICA TOO...
SERIOUSLY...?
GATA (CLATTER)
BESIDES...

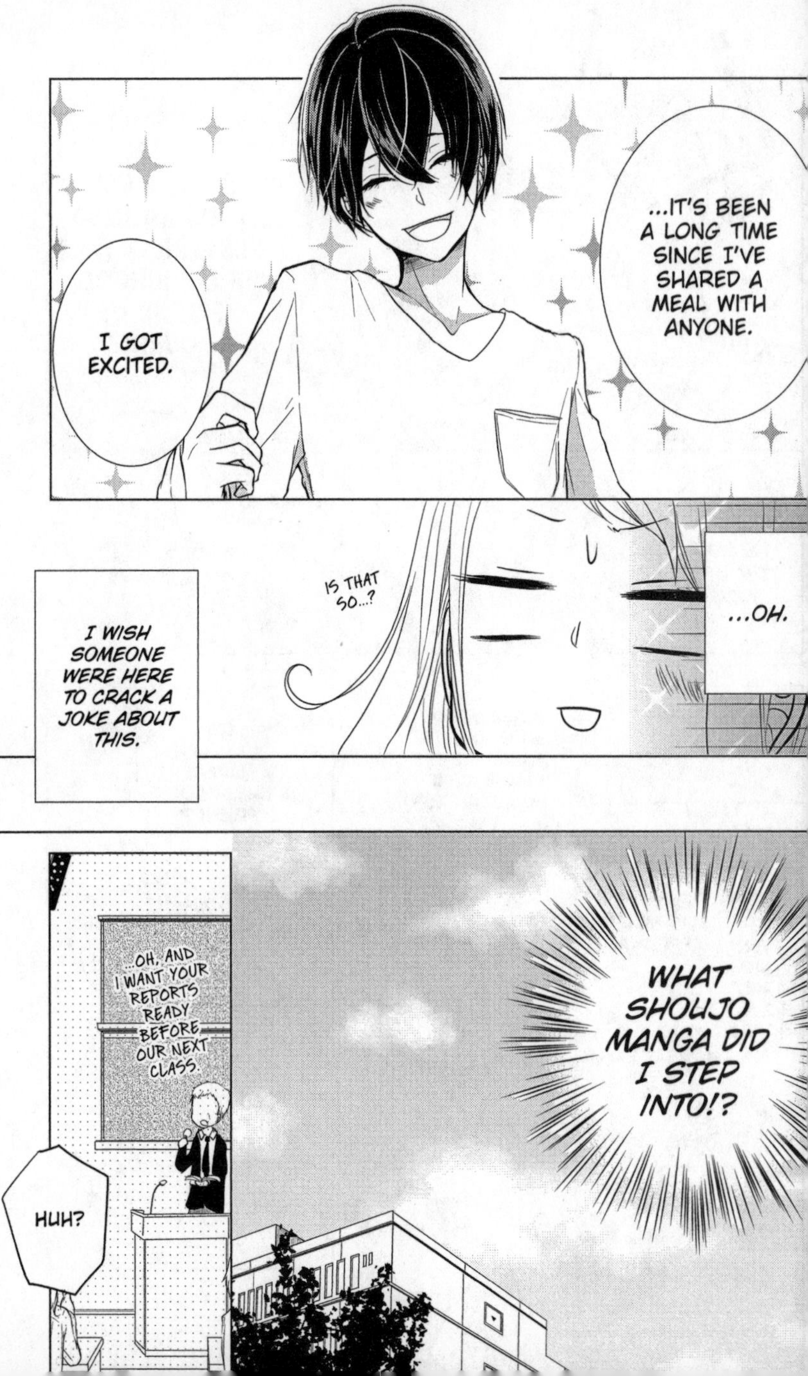
...IT'S BEEN A LONG TIME SINCE I'VE SHARED A MEAL WITH ANYONE.
I GOT EXCITED.
...OH.
IS THAT SO...?
I WISH SOMEONE WERE HERE TO CRACK A JOKE ABOUT THIS.
WHAT SHOUJO MANGA DID I STEP INTO!?
...OH, AND I WANT YOUR REPORTS READY BEFORE OUR NEXT CLASS.
HUH?

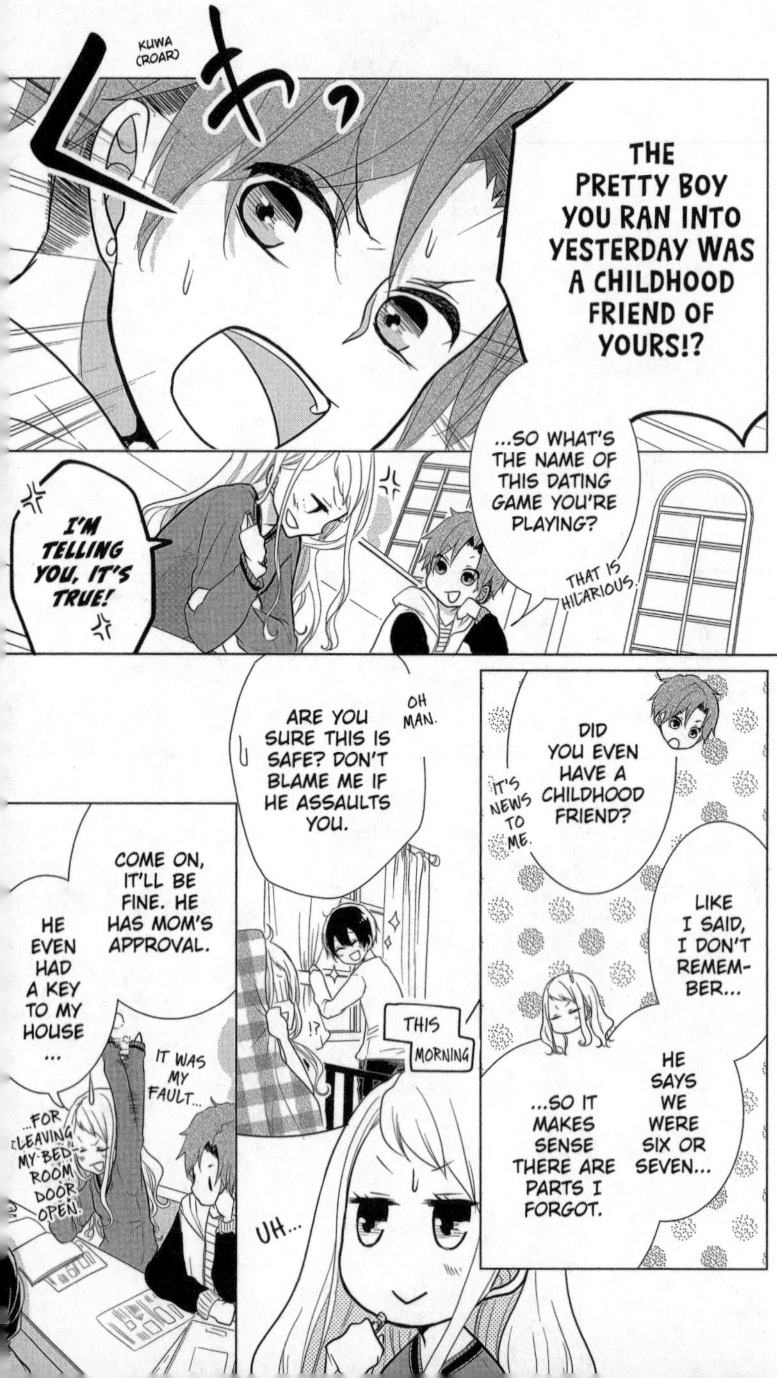
KUWA (ROAR)
THE PRETTY BOY YOU RAN INTO YESTERDAY WAS A CHILDHOOD FRIEND OF YOURS!?
...SO WHAT'S THE NAME OF THIS DATING GAME YOU'RE PLAYING?
THAT IS HILARIOUS.
I'M TELLING YOU, IT'S TRUE!
DID YOU EVEN HAVE A CHILDHOOD FRIEND?
IT'S NEWS TO ME.
LIKE I SAID, I DON'T REMEMBER...
HE SAYS WE WERE SIX OR SEVEN...
...SO IT MAKES SENSE THERE ARE PARTS I FORGOT.
ARE YOU SURE THIS IS SAFE? DON'T BLAME ME IF HE ASSAULTS YOU.
OH MAN.
THIS MORNING
!?
UH...
COME ON, IT'LL BE FINE. HE HAS MOM'S APPROVAL.
HE EVEN HAD A KEY TO MY HOUSE...
IT WAS MY FAULT...
...FOR LEAVING MY BEDROOM DOOR OPEN.

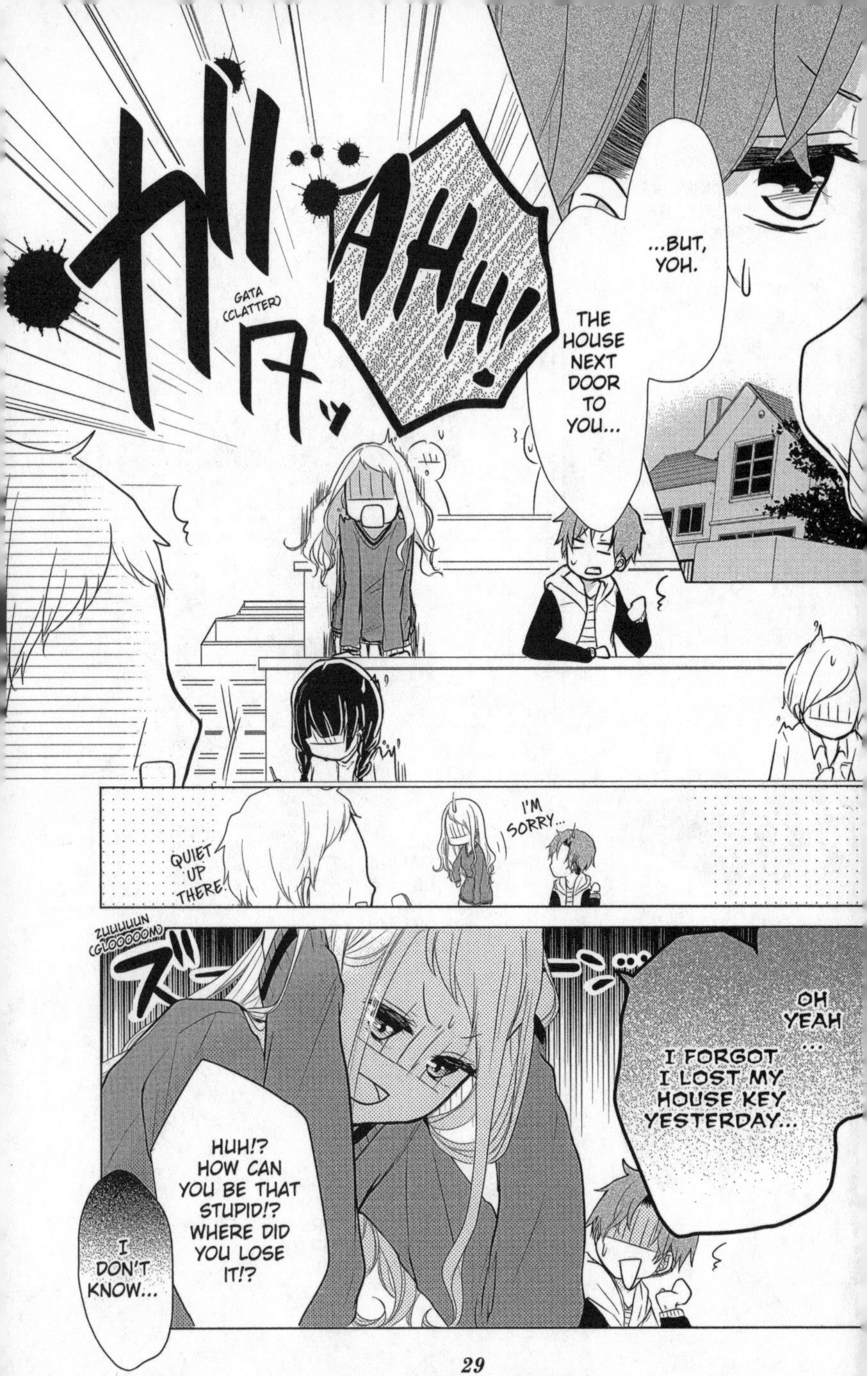
...BUT, YOH.
THE HOUSE NEXT DOOR TO YOU...
AAHH!
GATA (CLATTER)
I'M SORRY...
QUIET UP THERE.
ZUUUUUN (GLOOOOOM)
OH YEAH...
I FORGOT I LOST MY HOUSE KEY YESTERDAY...
HUH!? HOW CAN YOU BE THAT STUPID!? WHERE DID YOU LOSE IT!?
I DON'T KNOW...

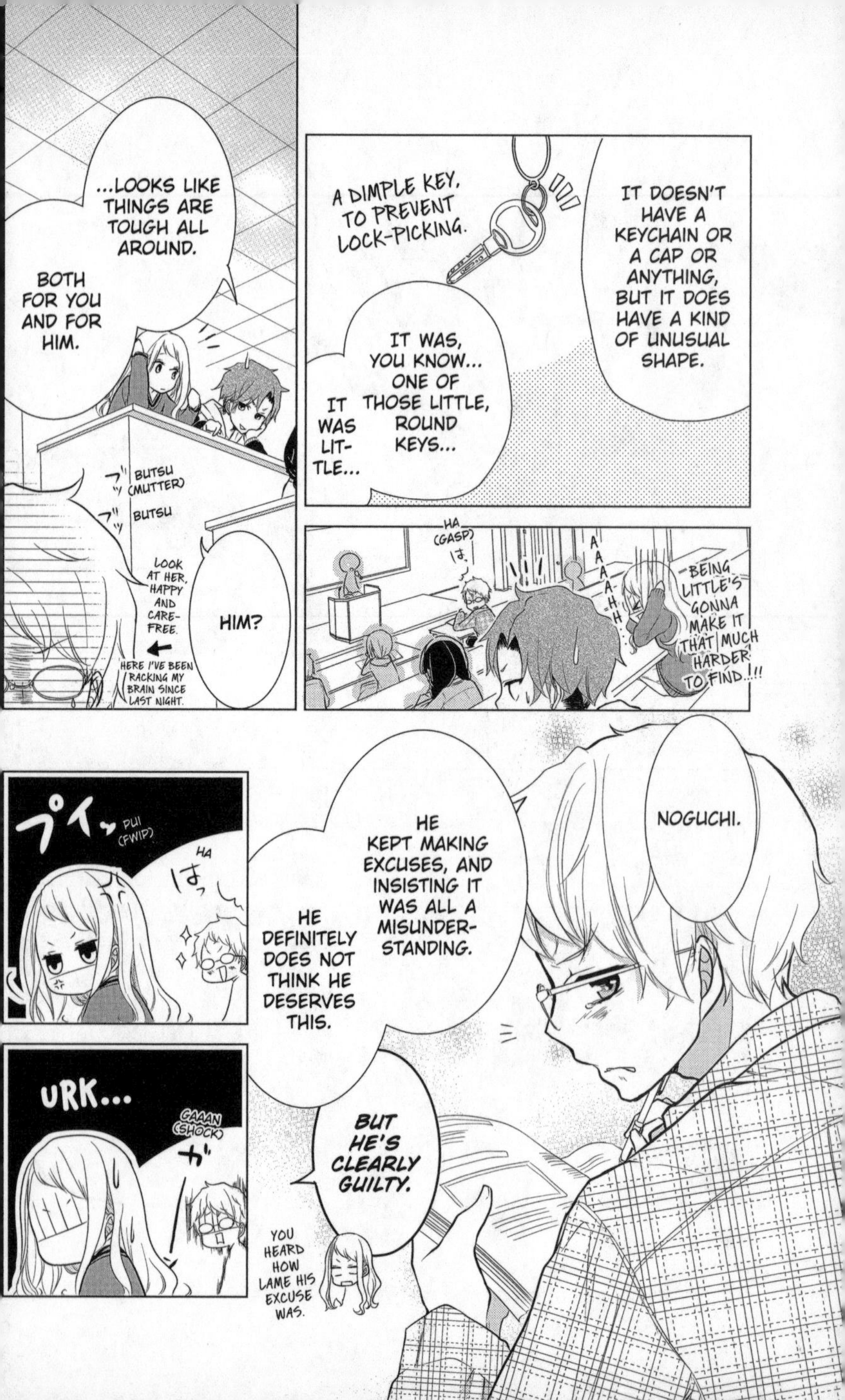
IT DOESN'T HAVE A KEYCHAIN OR A CAP OR ANYTHING, BUT IT DOES HAVE A KIND OF UNUSUAL SHAPE.
A DIMPLE KEY, TO PREVENT LOCK-PICKING.
IT WAS, YOU KNOW... ONE OF THOSE LITTLE, ROUND KEYS...
IT WAS LIT-TLE...
BEING LITTLE'S GONNA MAKE IT THAT MUCH HARDER TO FIND!!!
AAAAHH
は HA (GASP)
...LOOKS LIKE THINGS ARE TOUGH ALL AROUND.
BOTH FOR YOU AND FOR HIM.
HIM?
ブツ BUTSU (MUTTER)
ブツ BUTSU
LOOK AT HER, HAPPY AND CARE-FREE.
HERE I'VE BEEN RACKING MY BRAIN SINCE LAST NIGHT.
NOGUCHI.
HE KEPT MAKING EXCUSES, AND INSISTING IT WAS ALL A MISUNDER-STANDING.
HE DEFINITELY DOES NOT THINK HE DESERVES THIS.
BUT HE'S CLEARLY GUILTY.
YOU HEARD HOW LAME HIS EXCUSE WAS.
プイッ PUI (FWIP)
はっ HA
URK...
ガ GAAAN (SHOCK)

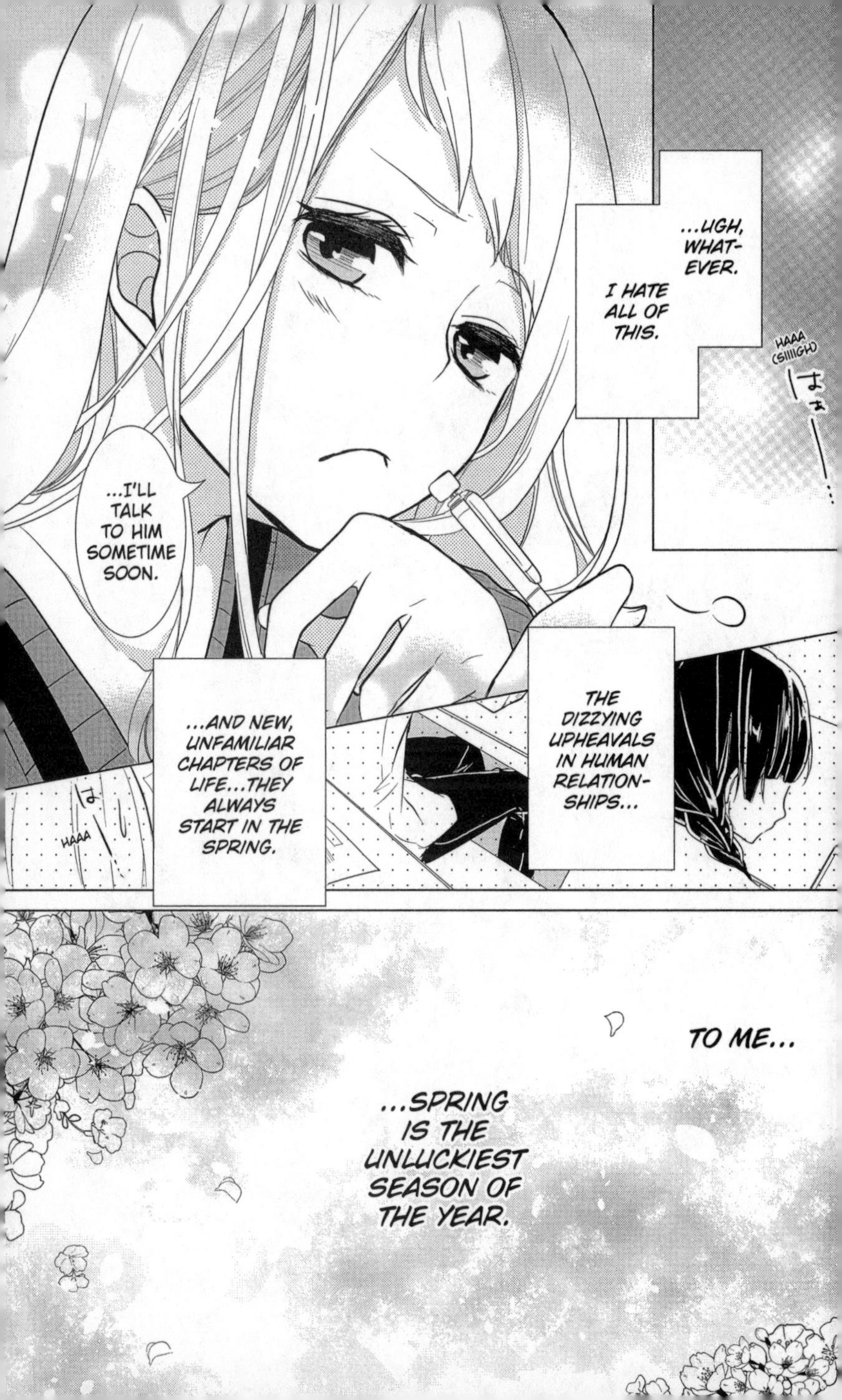
...UGH, WHATEVER.
I HATE ALL OF THIS.
HAAA (SIIIIGH)
はぁー…
...I'LL TALK TO HIM SOMETIME SOON.
THE DIZZYING UPHEAVALS IN HUMAN RELATIONSHIPS...
...AND NEW, UNFAMILIAR CHAPTERS OF LIFE...THEY ALWAYS START IN THE SPRING.
HAAA
は
TO ME...
...SPRING IS THE UNLUCKIEST SEASON OF THE YEAR.

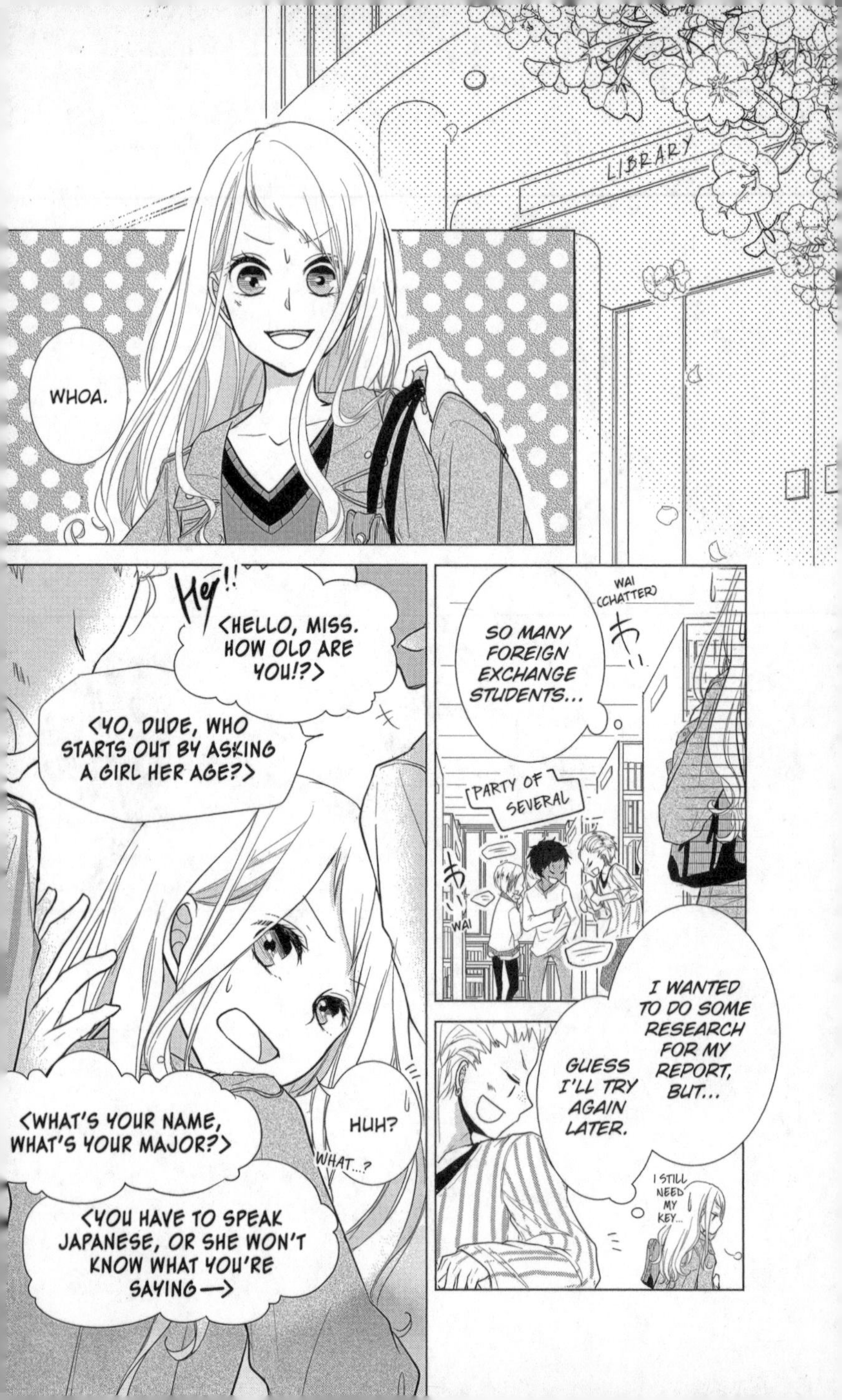
LIBRARY
WHOA.
WAI (CHATTER)
SO MANY FOREIGN EXCHANGE STUDENTS...
PARTY OF SEVERAL
WAI
I WANTED TO DO SOME RESEARCH FOR MY REPORT, BUT...
GUESS I'LL TRY AGAIN LATER.
I STILL NEED MY KEY...
Hey!!
<HELLO, MISS. HOW OLD ARE YOU!?>
<YO, DUDE, WHO STARTS OUT BY ASKING A GIRL HER AGE?>
HUH?
WHAT...?
<WHAT'S YOUR NAME, WHAT'S YOUR MAJOR?>
<YOU HAVE TO SPEAK JAPANESE, OR SHE WON'T KNOW WHAT YOU'RE SAYING—>

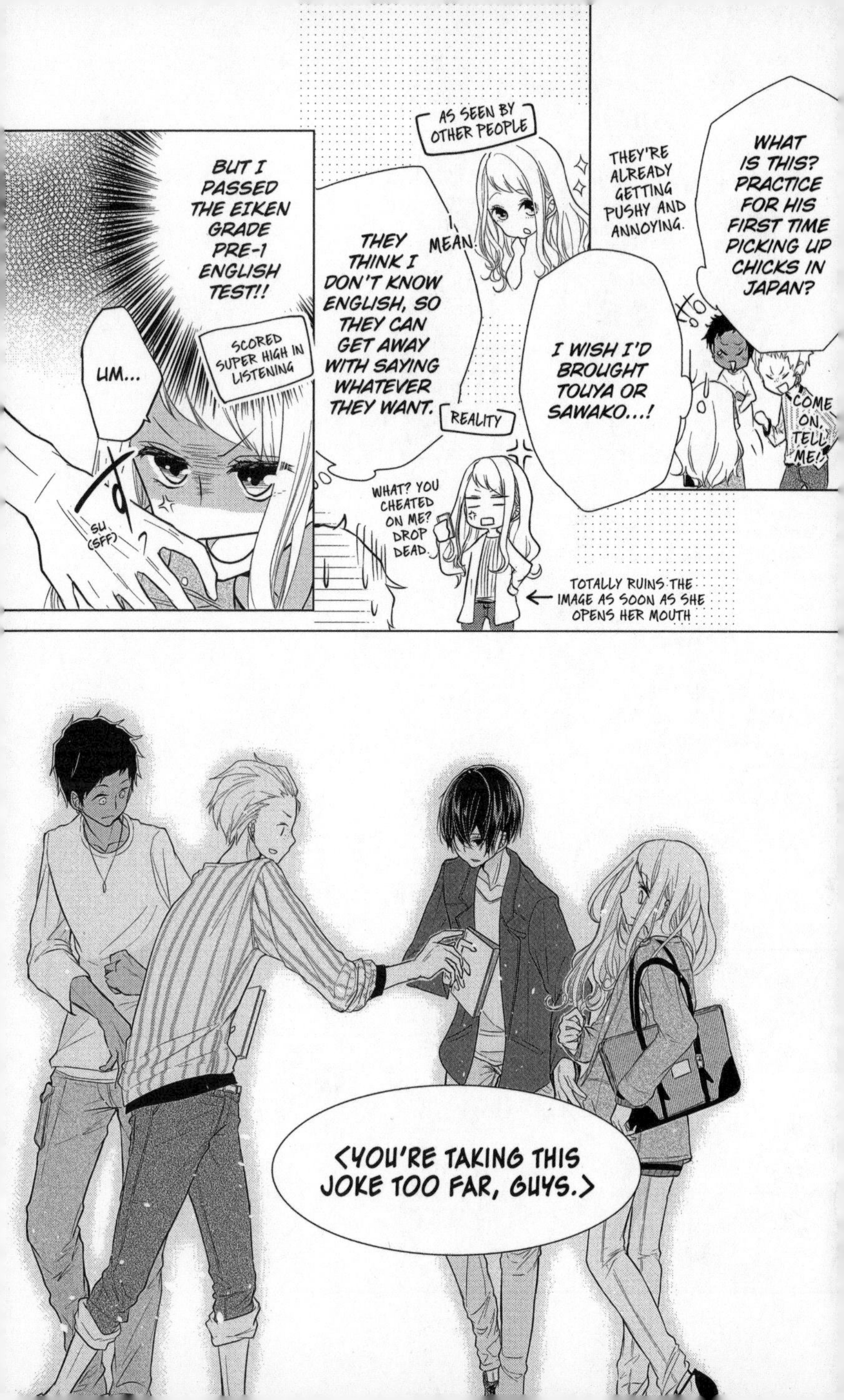
WHAT IS THIS? PRACTICE FOR HIS FIRST TIME PICKING UP CHICKS IN JAPAN?
THEY'RE ALREADY GETTING PUSHY AND ANNOYING.
COME ON, TELL ME!
I WISH I'D BROUGHT TOUYA OR SAWAKO...!
AS SEEN BY OTHER PEOPLE
I MEAN.
THEY THINK I DON'T KNOW ENGLISH, SO THEY CAN GET AWAY WITH SAYING WHATEVER THEY WANT.
REALITY
WHAT? YOU CHEATED ON ME? DROP DEAD.
TOTALLY RUINS THE IMAGE AS SOON AS SHE OPENS HER MOUTH
BUT I PASSED THE EIKEN GRADE PRE-1 ENGLISH TEST!!
SCORED SUPER HIGH IN LISTENING
UM...
SU (SFF)
<YOU'RE TAKING THIS JOKE TOO FAR, GUYS.>

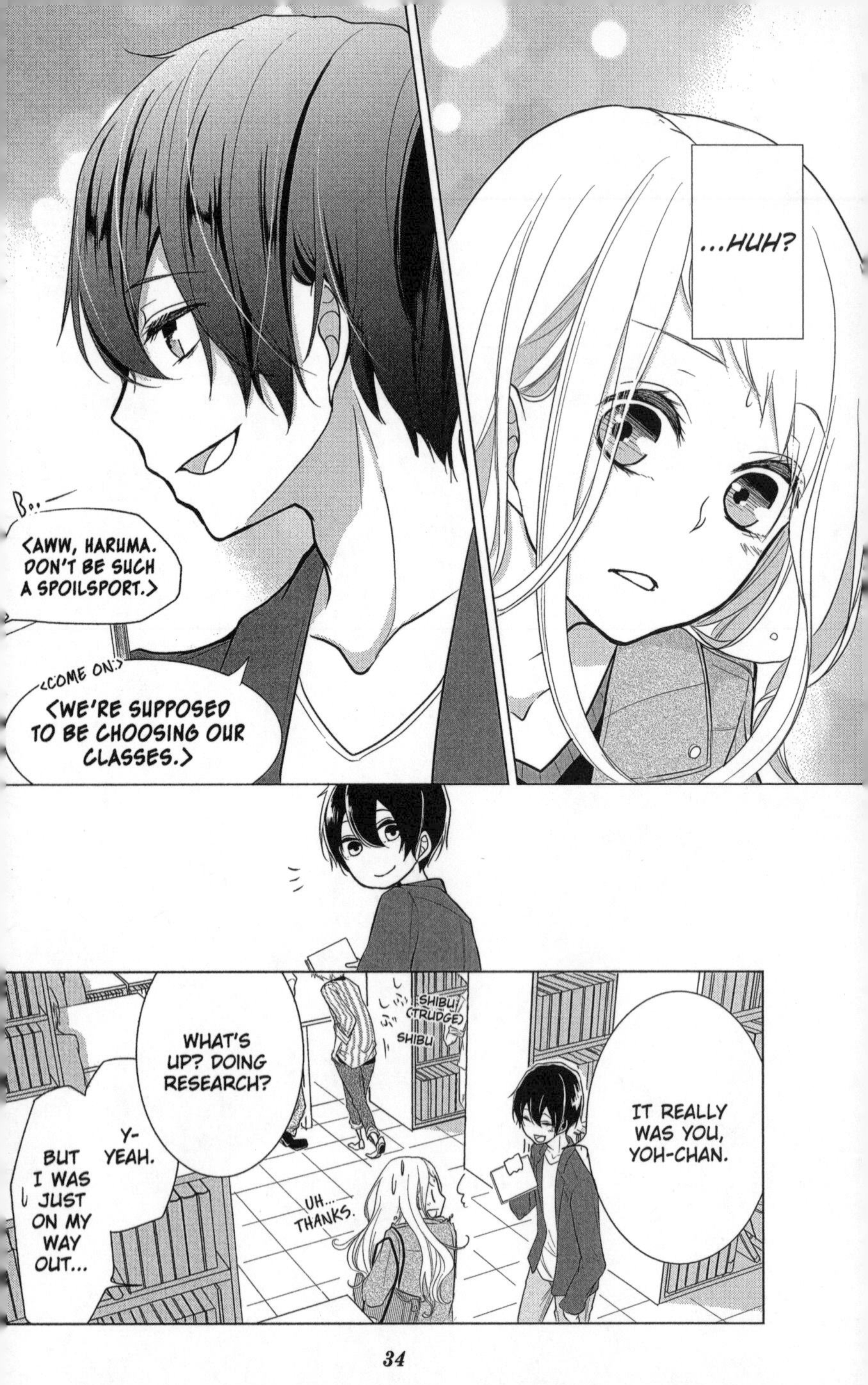
...HUH?
B..
<AWW, HARUMA. DON'T BE SUCH A SPOILSPORT.>
<COME ON.>
<WE'RE SUPPOSED TO BE CHOOSING OUR CLASSES.>
IT REALLY WAS YOU, YOH-CHAN.
SHIBU
(TRUDGE)
SHIBU
UH... THANKS.
WHAT'S UP? DOING RESEARCH?
Y- YEAH.
BUT I WAS JUST ON MY WAY OUT...

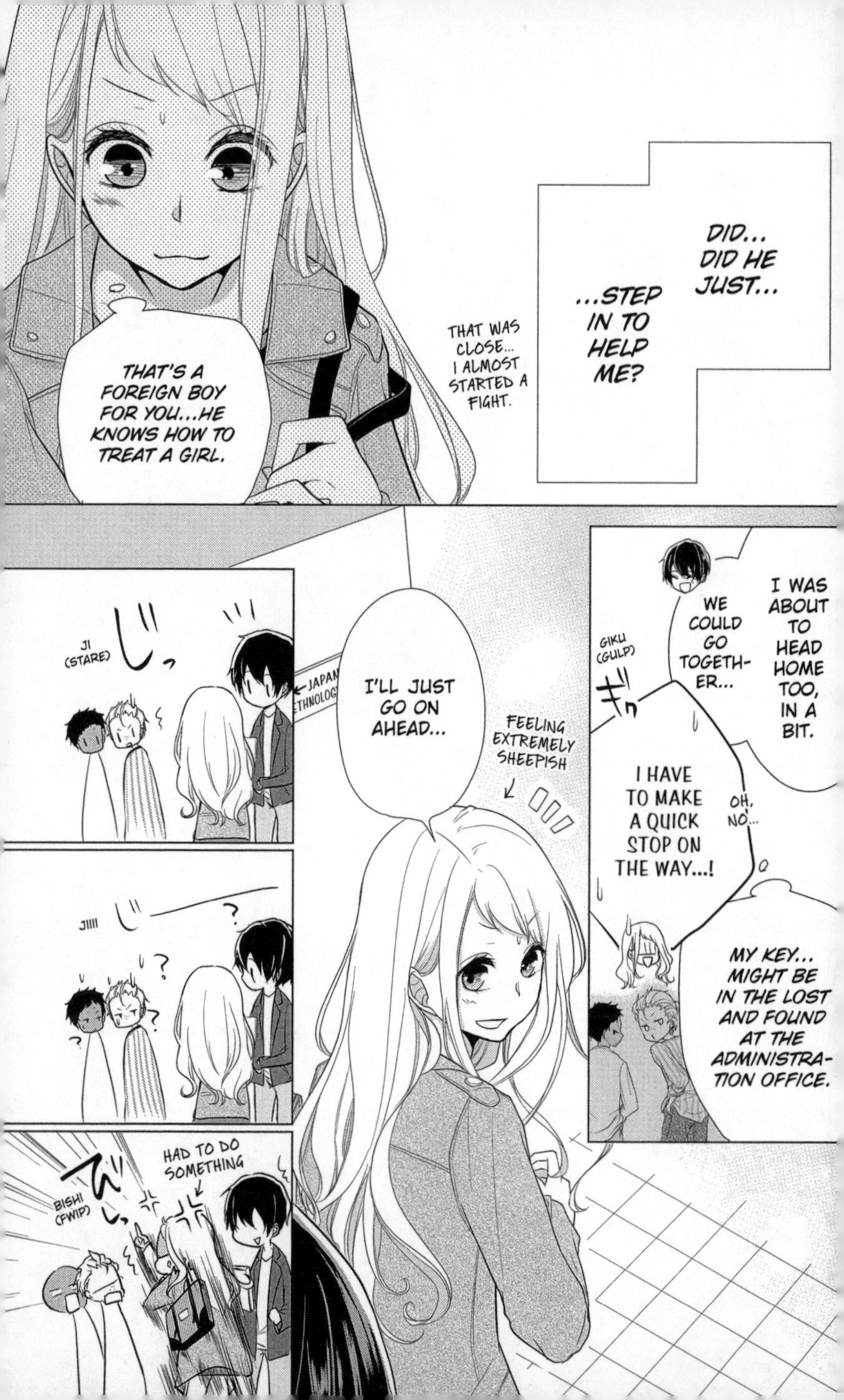
DID... DID HE JUST...
...STEP IN TO HELP ME?
THAT WAS CLOSE... I ALMOST STARTED A FIGHT.
THAT'S A FOREIGN BOY FOR YOU...HE KNOWS HOW TO TREAT A GIRL.
I WAS ABOUT TO HEAD HOME TOO, IN A BIT.
WE COULD GO TOGETHER...
GIKU (GULP)
I HAVE TO MAKE A QUICK STOP ON THE WAY...!
OH, NO...
MY KEY... MIGHT BE IN THE LOST AND FOUND AT THE ADMINISTRATION OFFICE.
I'LL JUST GO ON AHEAD...
FEELING EXTREMELY SHEEPISH
JI (STARE)
JIIII
HAD TO DO SOMETHING
BISHI (FWIP)

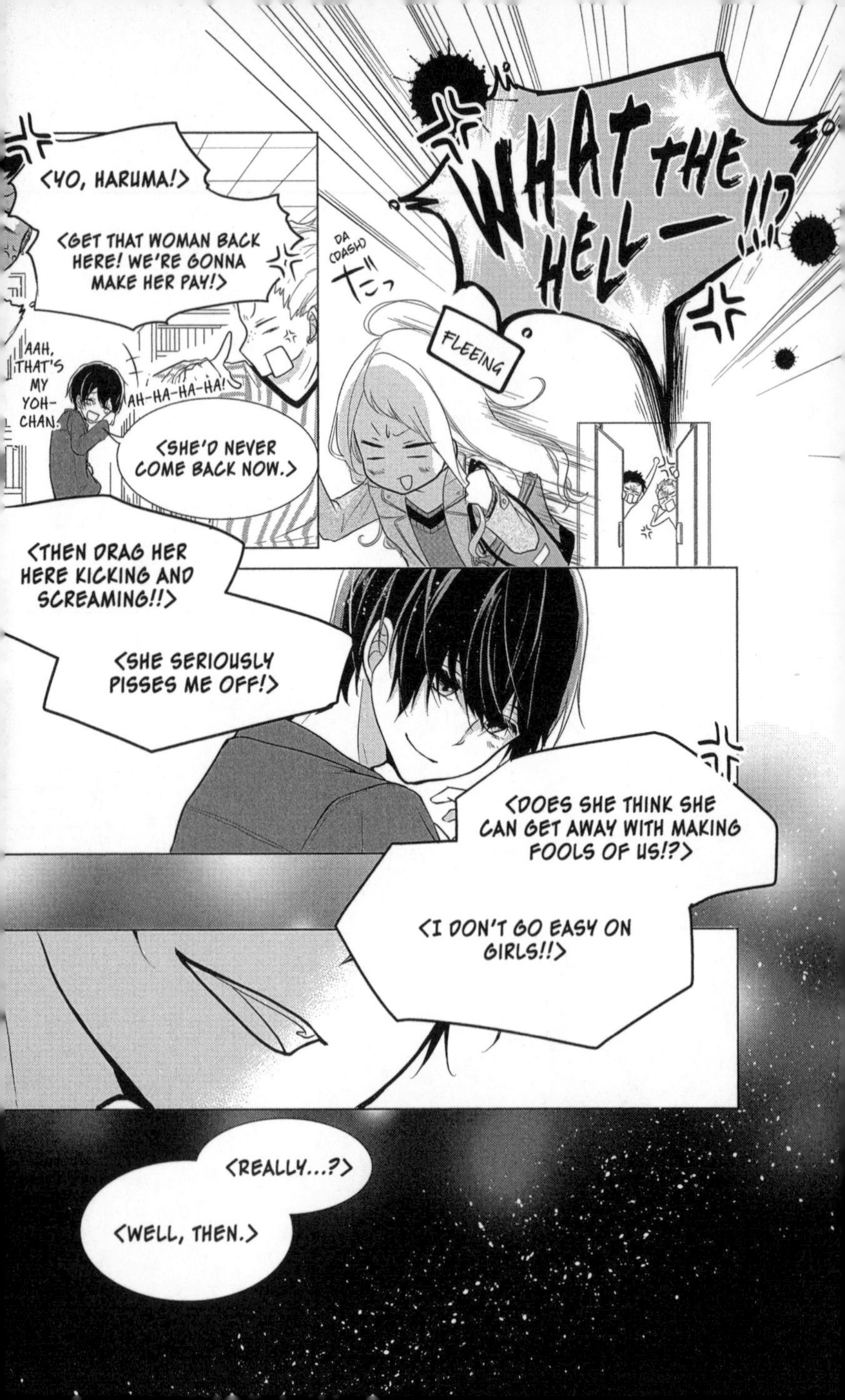
WHAT THE HELL—!!?
DA (DASH)
だっ
FLEEING
<YO, HARUMA!>
<GET THAT WOMAN BACK HERE! WE'RE GONNA MAKE HER PAY!>
AAH, THAT'S MY YOH-CHAN.
AH-HA-HA-HA!
<SHE'D NEVER COME BACK NOW.>
<THEN DRAG HER HERE KICKING AND SCREAMING!!>
<SHE SERIOUSLY PISSES ME OFF!>
<DOES SHE THINK SHE CAN GET AWAY WITH MAKING FOOLS OF US!?>
<I DON'T GO EASY ON GIRLS!!>
<REALLY...?>
<WELL, THEN.>

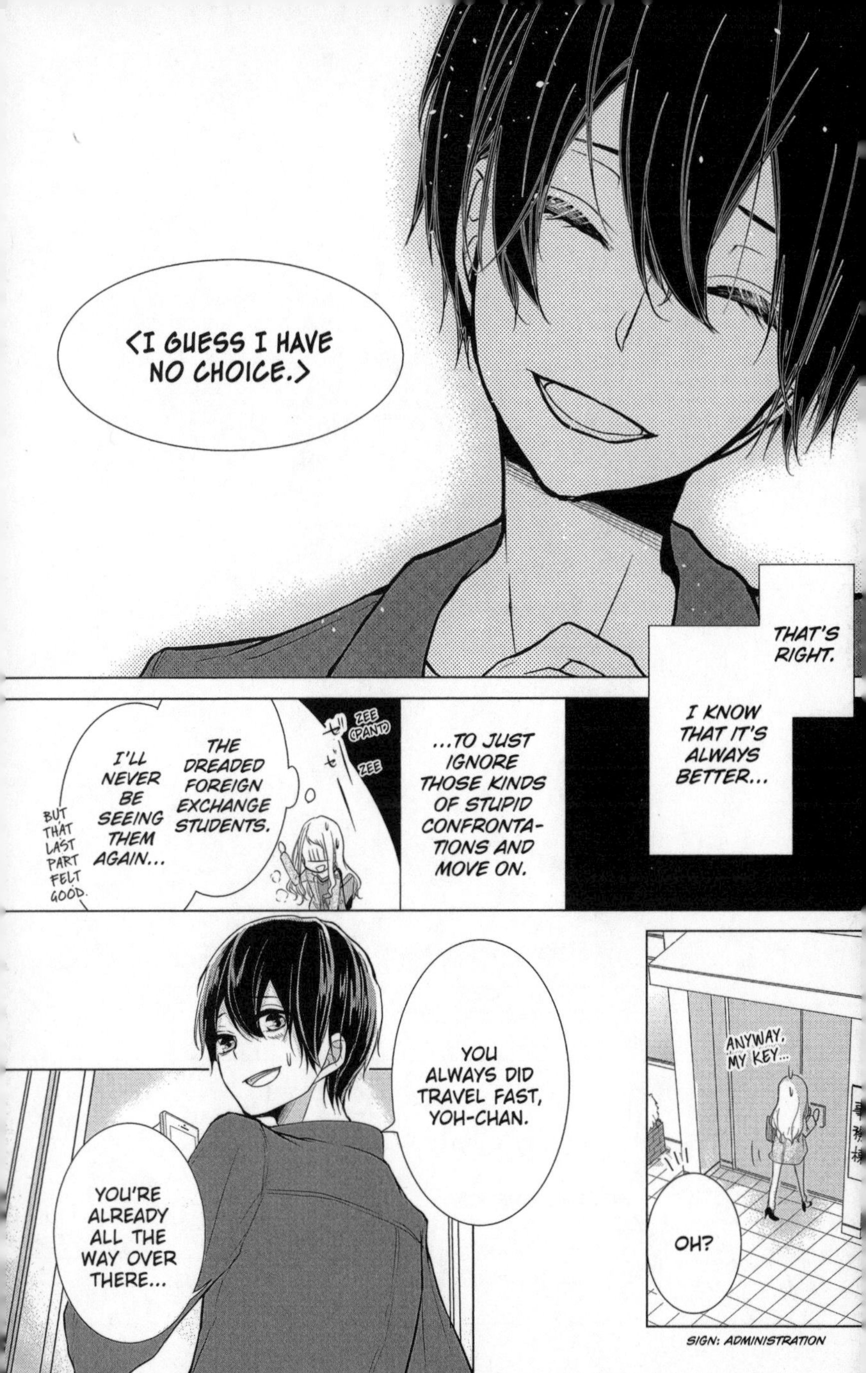
<I GUESS I HAVE NO CHOICE.>
THAT'S RIGHT.
I KNOW THAT IT'S ALWAYS BETTER...
...TO JUST IGNORE THOSE KINDS OF STUPID CONFRONTATIONS AND MOVE ON.
ZEE (PANT)
ZEE
THE DREADED FOREIGN EXCHANGE STUDENTS.
I'LL NEVER BE SEEING THEM AGAIN...
BUT THAT LAST PART FELT GOOD.
ANYWAY, MY KEY...
OH?
YOU ALWAYS DID TRAVEL FAST, YOH-CHAN.
YOU'RE ALREADY ALL THE WAY OVER THERE...

SIGN: ADMINISTRATION

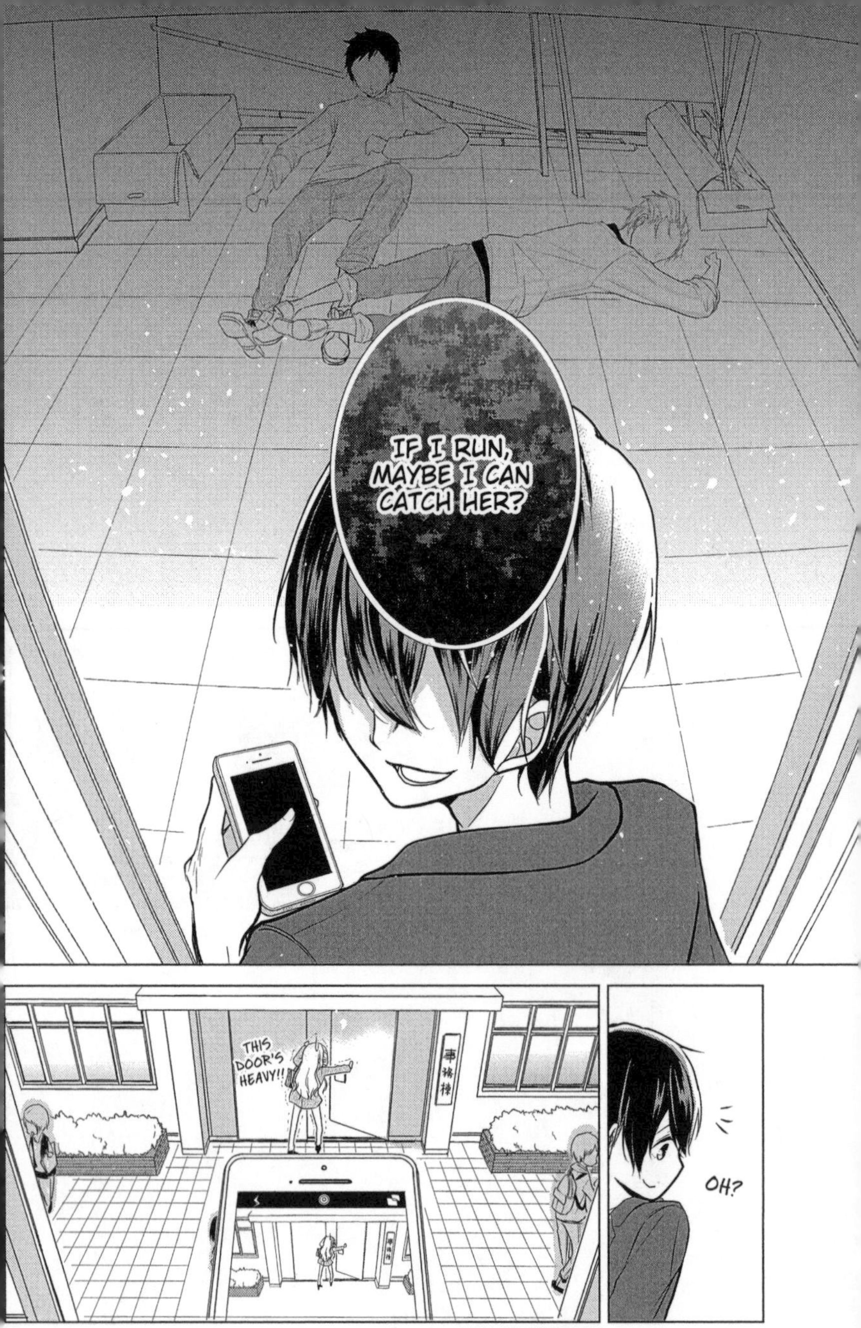
IF I RUN, MAYBE I CAN CATCH HER?
OH?
THIS DOOR'S HEAVY!!

SIGN: ADMINISTRATION

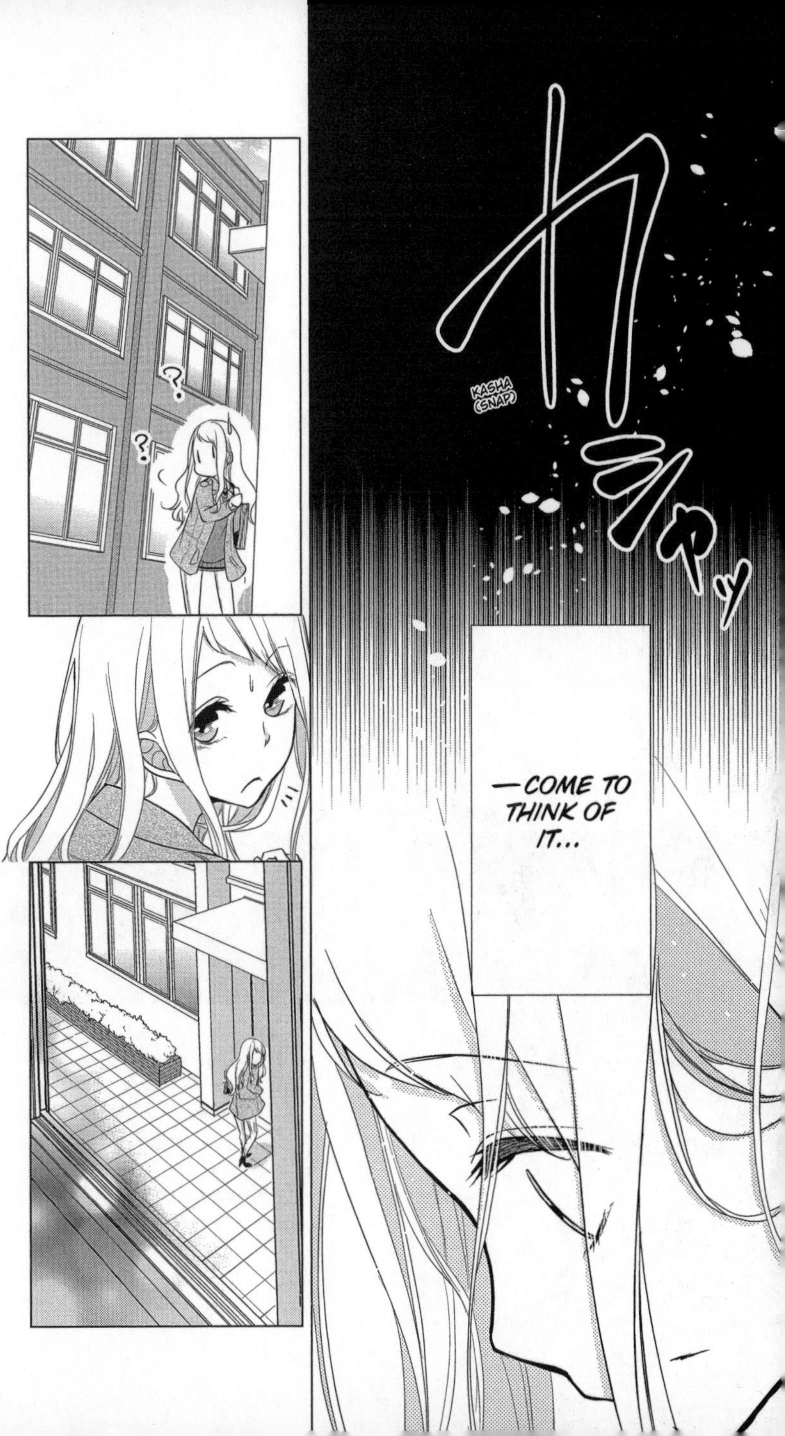
カシャッ
KASHA (SNAP)
—COME TO THINK OF IT...
?
?

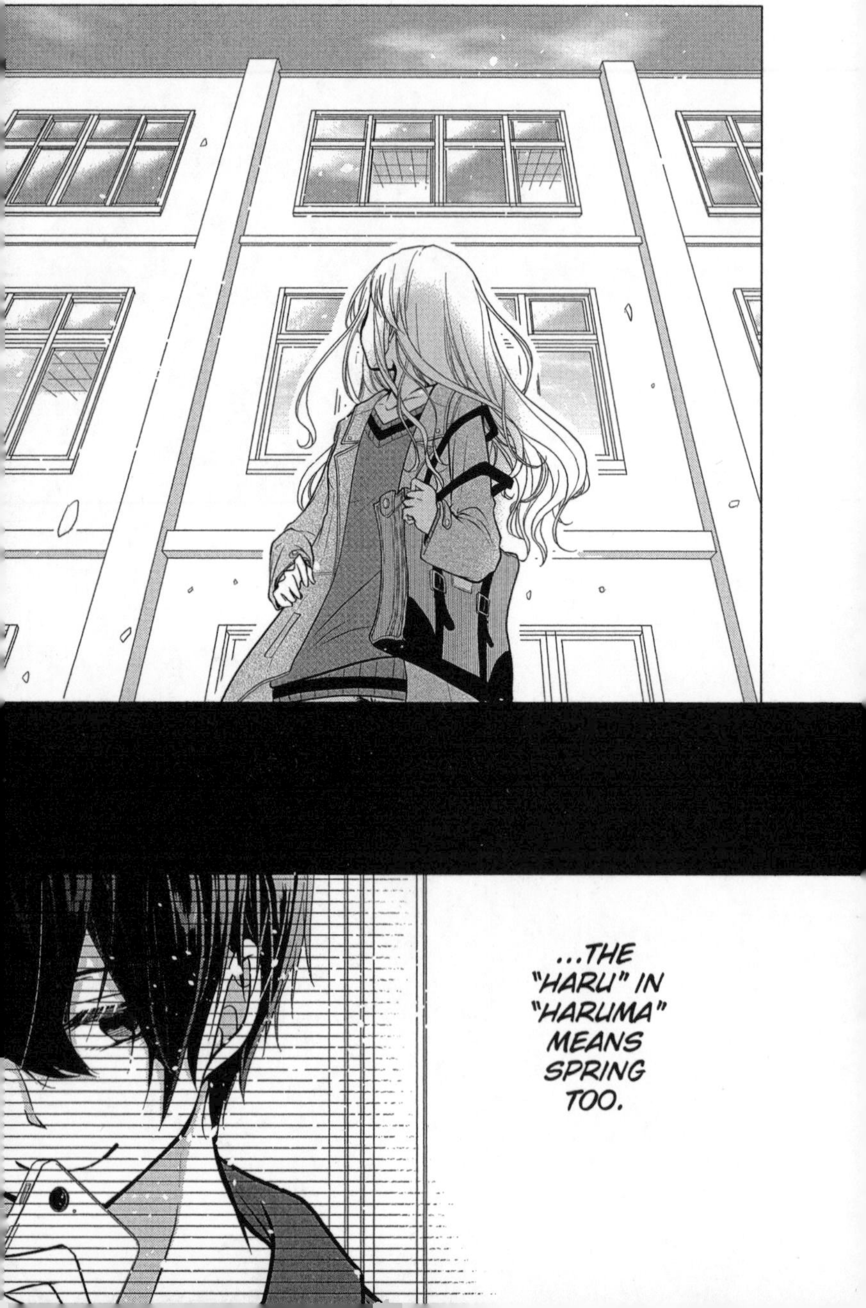
...THE "HARU" IN "HARUMA" MEANS SPRING TOO.

# #3

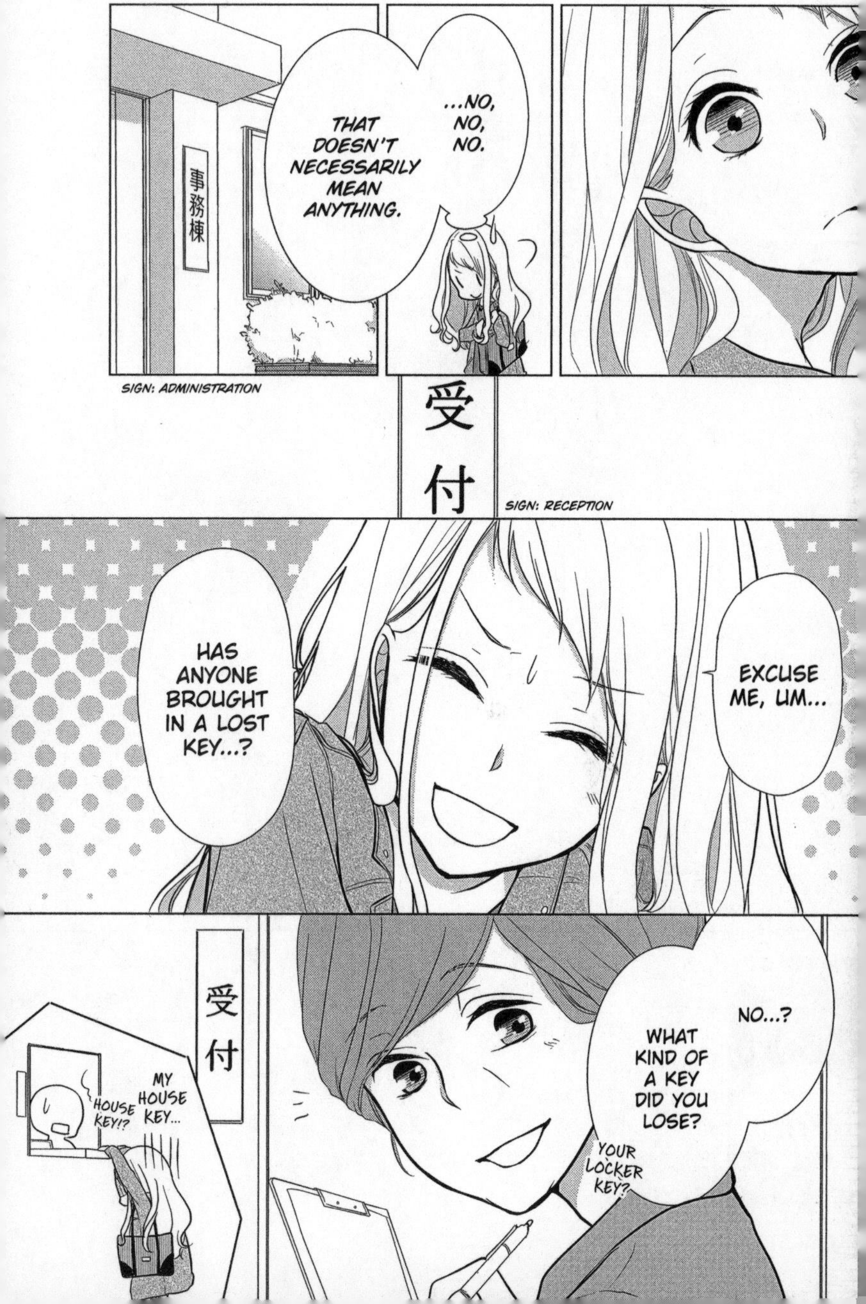
...NO, NO, NO.
THAT DOESN'T NECESSARILY MEAN ANYTHING.
事務棟
SIGN: ADMINISTRATION
受付
SIGN: RECEPTION
EXCUSE ME, UM...
HAS ANYONE BROUGHT IN A LOST KEY...?
NO...?
WHAT KIND OF A KEY DID YOU LOSE?
YOUR LOCKER KEY?
受付
MY HOUSE KEY...
HOUSE KEY!?

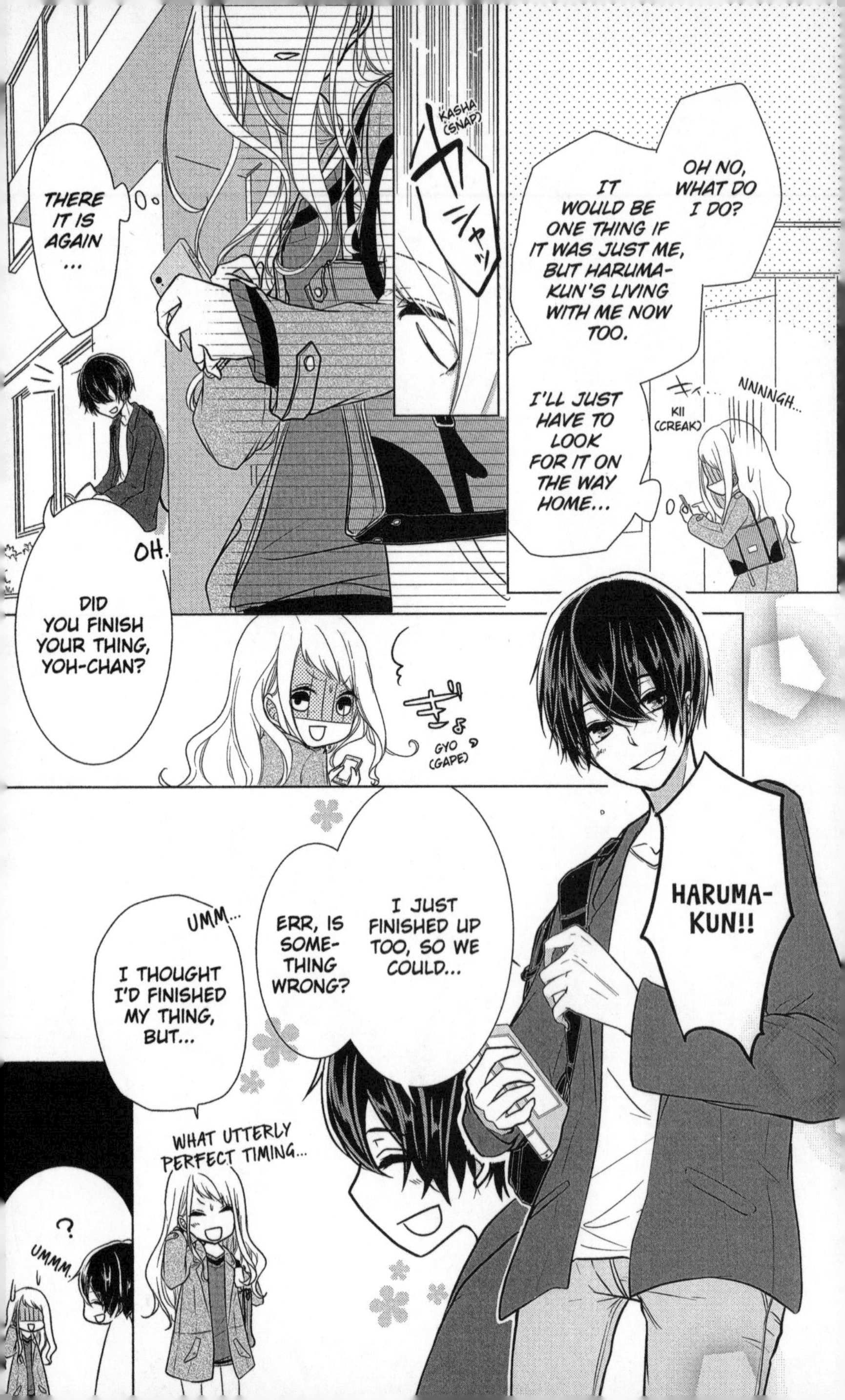
OH NO, WHAT DO I DO?
IT WOULD BE ONE THING IF IT WAS JUST ME, BUT HARUMA-KUN'S LIVING WITH ME NOW TOO.
I'LL JUST HAVE TO LOOK FOR IT ON THE WAY HOME...
NNNNGH...
KII (CREAK)
KASHA (SNAP)
THERE IT IS AGAIN...
OH.
DID YOU FINISH YOUR THING, YOH-CHAN?
GYO (GAPE)
HARUMA-KUN!!
I JUST FINISHED UP TOO, SO WE COULD...
ERR, IS SOME-THING WRONG?
UMM...
I THOUGHT I'D FINISHED MY THING, BUT...
WHAT UTTERLY PERFECT TIMING...
?
UMM.

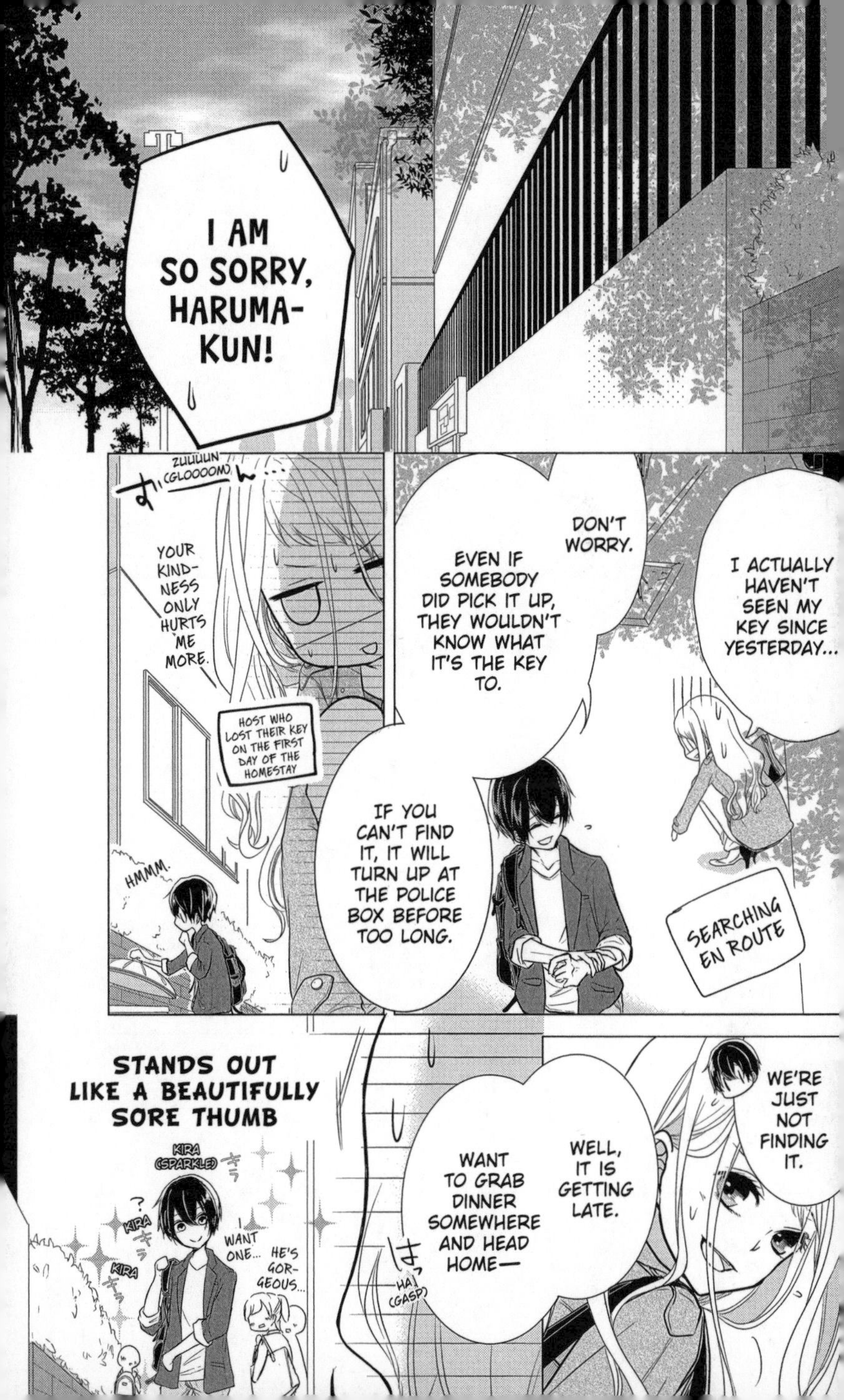
I AM SO SORRY, HARUMA-KUN!
I ACTUALLY HAVEN'T SEEN MY KEY SINCE YESTERDAY...
SEARCHING EN ROUTE
DON'T WORRY.
EVEN IF SOMEBODY DID PICK IT UP, THEY WOULDN'T KNOW WHAT IT'S THE KEY TO.
IF YOU CAN'T FIND IT, IT WILL TURN UP AT THE POLICE BOX BEFORE TOO LONG.
ZUUUUN (GLOOOOM)
YOUR KINDNESS ONLY HURTS ME MORE.
HOST WHO LOST THEIR KEY ON THE FIRST DAY OF THE HOMESTAY
HMMM.
WE'RE JUST NOT FINDING IT.
WELL, IT IS GETTING LATE.
WANT TO GRAB DINNER SOMEWHERE AND HEAD HOME—
HA! (GASP)
STANDS OUT LIKE A BEAUTIFULLY SORE THUMB
KIRA (SPARKLE)
?
KIRA
KIRA
I WANT ONE...
HE'S GORGEOUS...

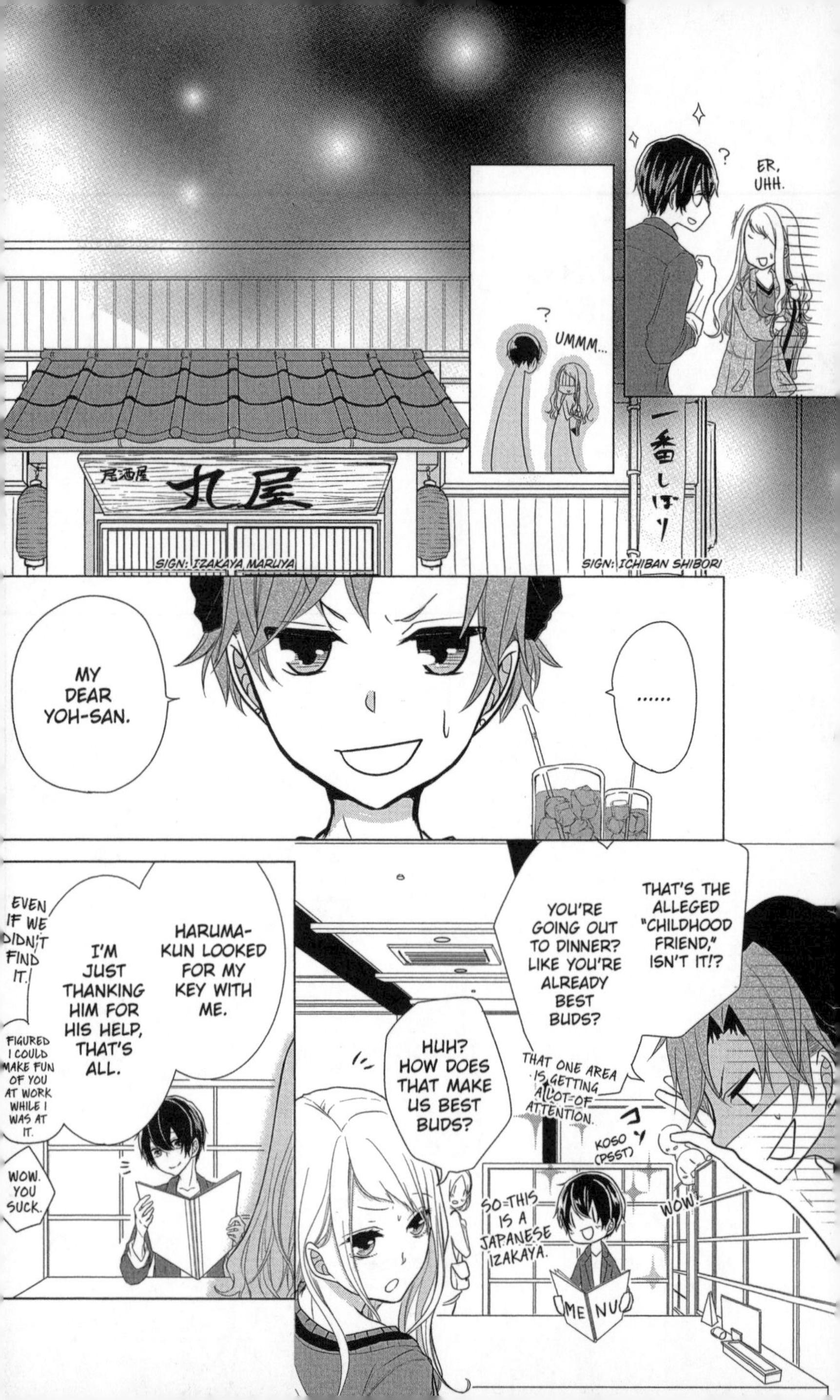

ER, UHH.
UMMM...
一番しぼり
SIGN: ICHIBAN SHIBORI
居酒屋 丸屋
SIGN: IZAKAYA MARUYA
......
MY DEAR YOH-SAN.
THAT'S THE ALLEGED "CHILDHOOD FRIEND," ISN'T IT!?
YOU'RE GOING OUT TO DINNER? LIKE YOU'RE ALREADY BEST BUDS?
THAT ONE AREA IS GETTING A LOT OF ATTENTION.
KOSO (PSST)
WOW!
SO THIS IS A JAPANESE IZAKAYA.
MENU
HUH? HOW DOES THAT MAKE US BEST BUDS?
HARUMA-KUN LOOKED FOR MY KEY WITH ME.
I'M JUST THANKING HIM FOR HIS HELP, THAT'S ALL.
EVEN IF WE DIDN'T FIND IT.
FIGURED I COULD MAKE FUN OF YOU AT WORK WHILE I WAS AT IT.
WOW. YOU SUCK.

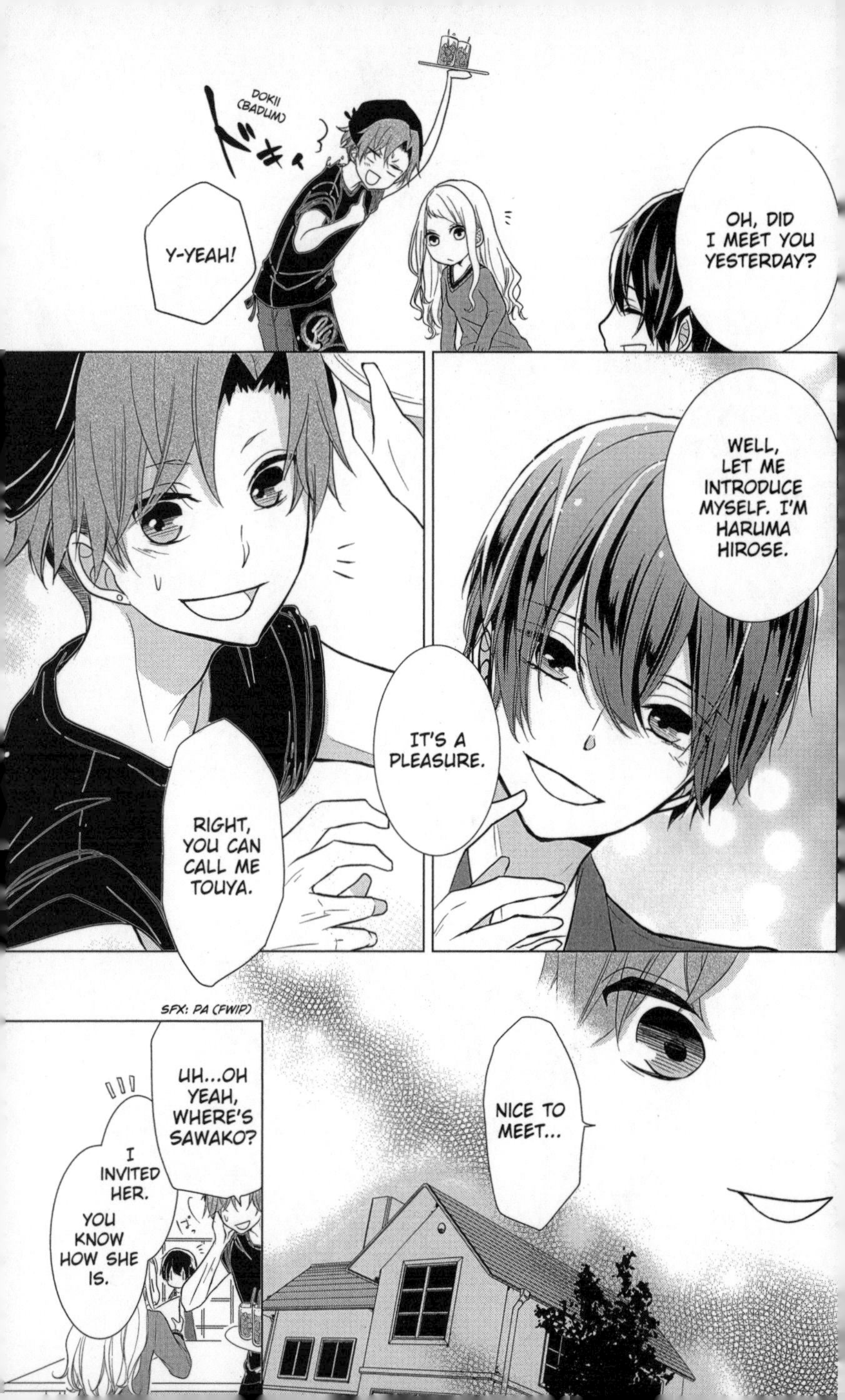
OH, DID I MEET YOU YESTERDAY?
DOKII (BADUM)
Y-YEAH!
WELL, LET ME INTRODUCE MYSELF. I'M HARUMA HIROSE.
IT'S A PLEASURE.
RIGHT, YOU CAN CALL ME TOUYA.
NICE TO MEET...
SFX: PA (FWIP)
UH...OH YEAH, WHERE'S SAWAKO?
I INVITED HER. YOU KNOW HOW SHE IS.

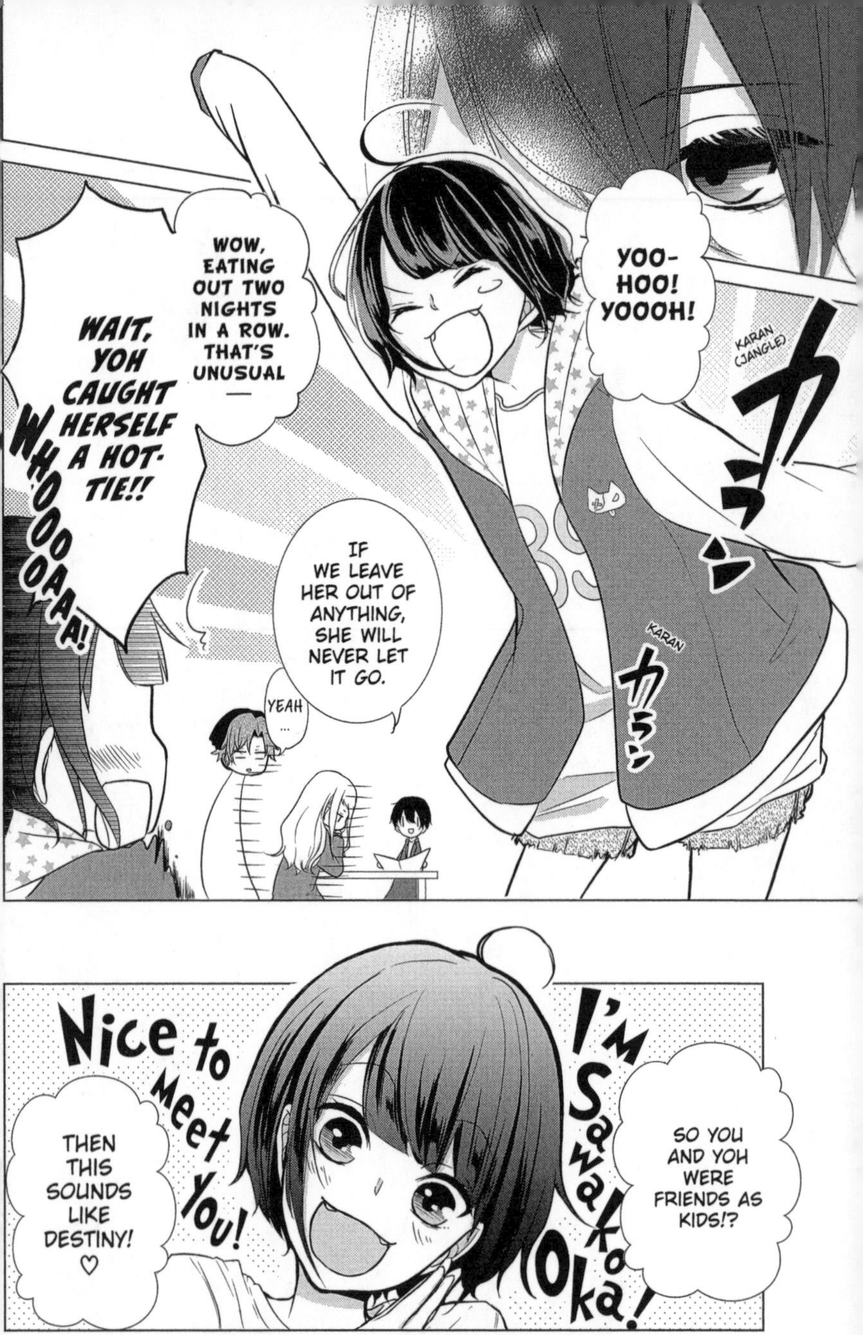
YOO-HOO! YOOOH!
KARAN (JANGLE)
KARAN
WOW, EATING OUT TWO NIGHTS IN A ROW. THAT'S UNUSUAL —
WAIT, YOH CAUGHT HERSELF A HOT-TIE!!
WHOOOOOAAA!
IF WE LEAVE HER OUT OF ANYTHING, SHE WILL NEVER LET IT GO.
YEAH ...
I'M Sawako Oka!
SO YOU AND YOH WERE FRIENDS AS KIDS!?
Nice to Meet You!
THEN THIS SOUNDS LIKE DESTINY! ♡

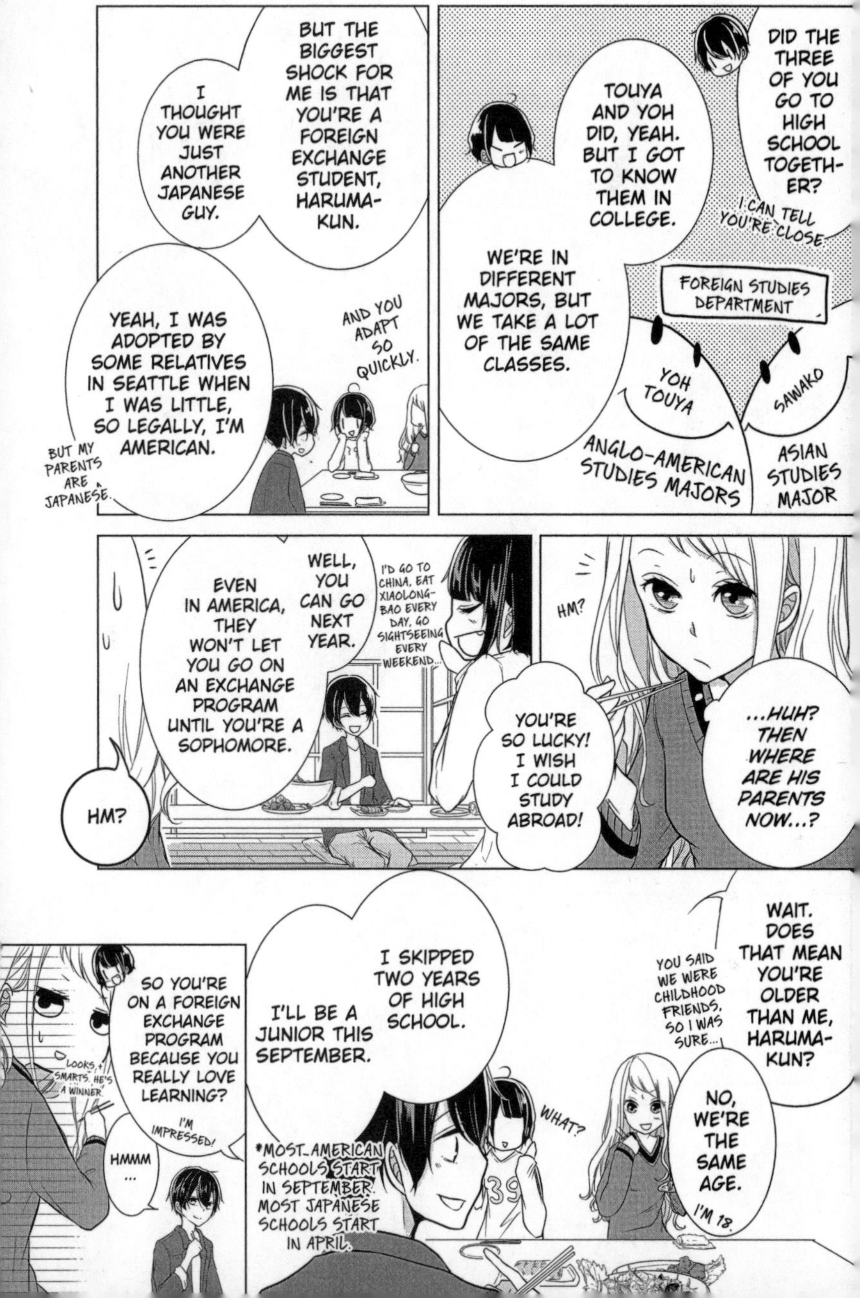
DID THE THREE OF YOU GO TO HIGH SCHOOL TOGETH-ER?
I CAN TELL YOU'RE CLOSE.
TOUYA AND YOH DID, YEAH. BUT I GOT TO KNOW THEM IN COLLEGE.
FOREIGN STUDIES DEPARTMENT
YOH TOUYA
SAWAKO
ASIAN STUDIES MAJOR
ANGLO-AMERICAN STUDIES MAJORS
WE'RE IN DIFFERENT MAJORS, BUT WE TAKE A LOT OF THE SAME CLASSES.
BUT THE BIGGEST SHOCK FOR ME IS THAT YOU'RE A FOREIGN EXCHANGE STUDENT, HARUMA-KUN.
I THOUGHT YOU WERE JUST ANOTHER JAPANESE GUY.
AND YOU ADAPT SO QUICKLY.
YEAH, I WAS ADOPTED BY SOME RELATIVES IN SEATTLE WHEN I WAS LITTLE, SO LEGALLY, I'M AMERICAN.
BUT MY PARENTS ARE JAPANESE.
HM?
...HUH? THEN WHERE ARE HIS PARENTS NOW...?
YOU'RE SO LUCKY! I WISH I COULD STUDY ABROAD!
I'D GO TO CHINA, EAT XIAOLONG-BAO EVERY DAY, GO SIGHTSEEING EVERY WEEKEND...
WELL, YOU CAN GO NEXT YEAR.
EVEN IN AMERICA, THEY WON'T LET YOU GO ON AN EXCHANGE PROGRAM UNTIL YOU'RE A SOPHOMORE.
HM?
WAIT. DOES THAT MEAN YOU'RE OLDER THAN ME, HARUMA-KUN?
YOU SAID WE WERE CHILDHOOD FRIENDS, SO I WAS SURE...
NO, WE'RE THE SAME AGE.
I'M 18.
WHAT?
I SKIPPED TWO YEARS OF HIGH SCHOOL.
I'LL BE A JUNIOR THIS SEPTEMBER.
*MOST AMERICAN SCHOOLS START IN SEPTEMBER. MOST JAPANESE SCHOOLS START IN APRIL.
SO YOU'RE ON A FOREIGN EXCHANGE PROGRAM BECAUSE YOU REALLY LOVE LEARNING?
LOOKS, SMARTS. HE'S A WINNER.
I'M IMPRESSED!
HMMM...

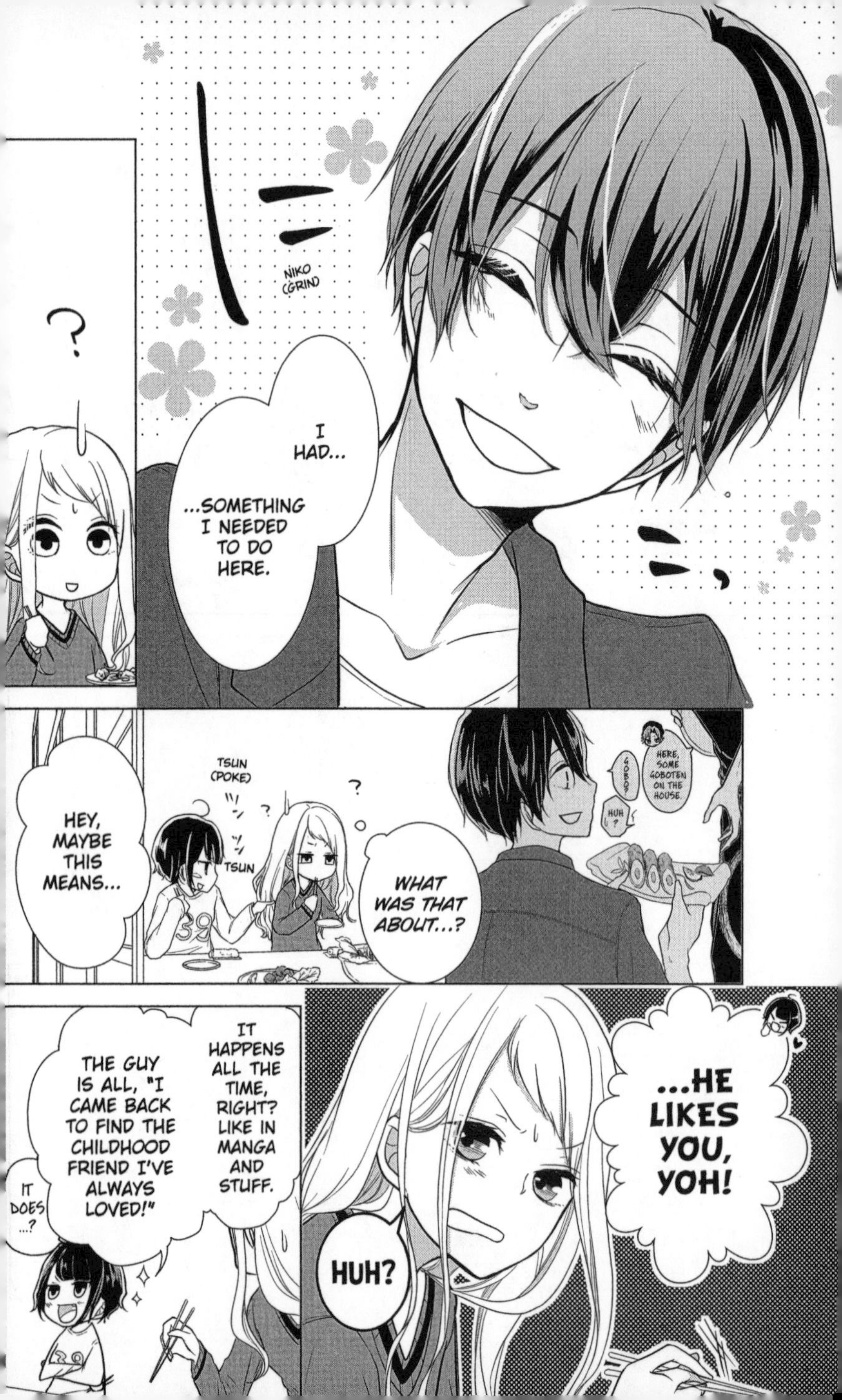
NIKO (GRIN)
I HAD...
...SOMETHING I NEEDED TO DO HERE.
?
HERE, SOME GOBOTEN ON THE HOUSE.
GOBO?
HUH?
WHAT WAS THAT ABOUT...?
?
TSUN (POKE)
TSUN
HEY, MAYBE THIS MEANS...
...HE LIKES YOU, YOH!
HUH?
IT HAPPENS ALL THE TIME, RIGHT? LIKE IN MANGA AND STUFF.
THE GUY IS ALL, "I CAME BACK TO FIND THE CHILDHOOD FRIEND I'VE ALWAYS LOVED!"
IT DOES ...?

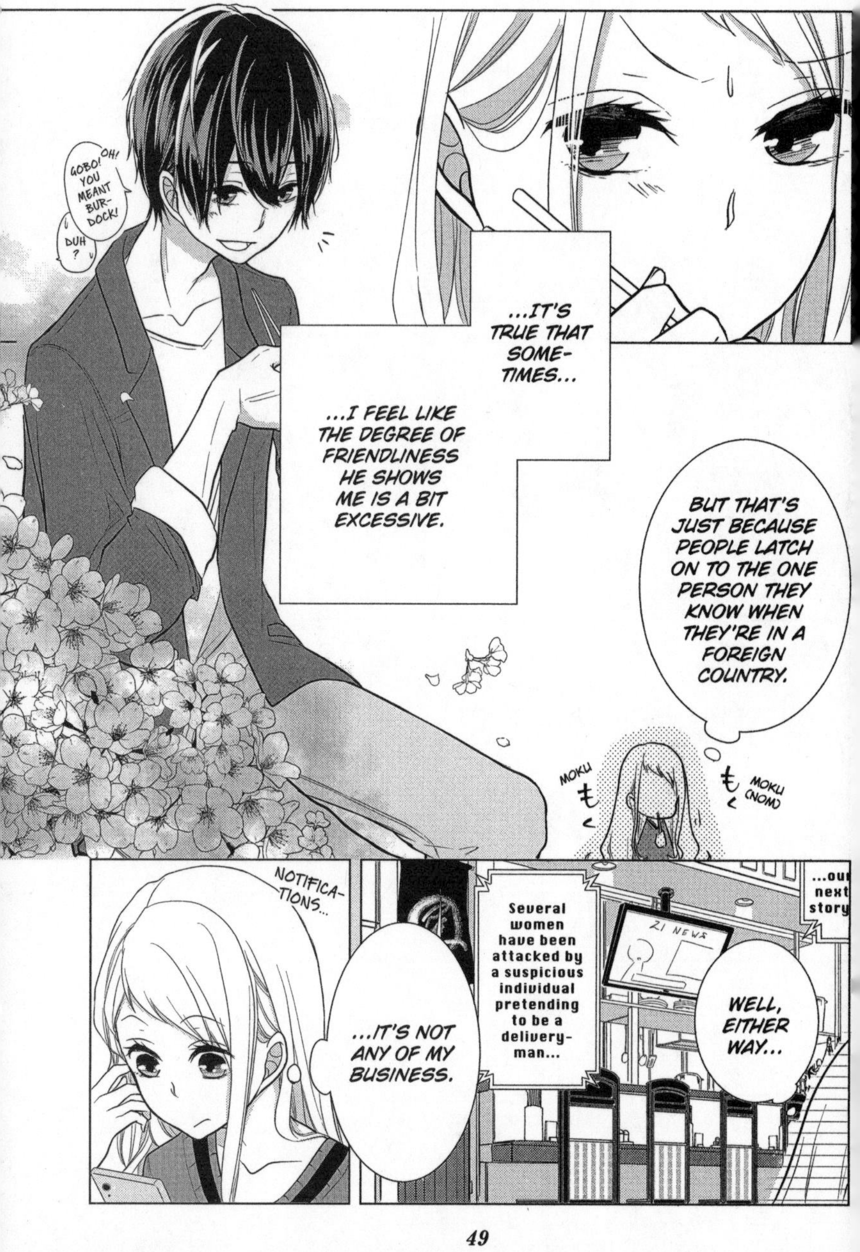

...IT'S TRUE THAT SOME-TIMES...
...I FEEL LIKE THE DEGREE OF FRIENDLINESS HE SHOWS ME IS A BIT EXCESSIVE.
OH! GOBO! YOU MEANT BUR-DOCK!
DUH?
BUT THAT'S JUST BECAUSE PEOPLE LATCH ON TO THE ONE PERSON THEY KNOW WHEN THEY'RE IN A FOREIGN COUNTRY.
MOKU (NOM)
MOKU
...our next story
ZI NEWS
Several women have been attacked by a suspicious individual pretending to be a delivery-man...
WELL, EITHER WAY...
NOTIFICA-TIONS...
...IT'S NOT ANY OF MY BUSINESS.

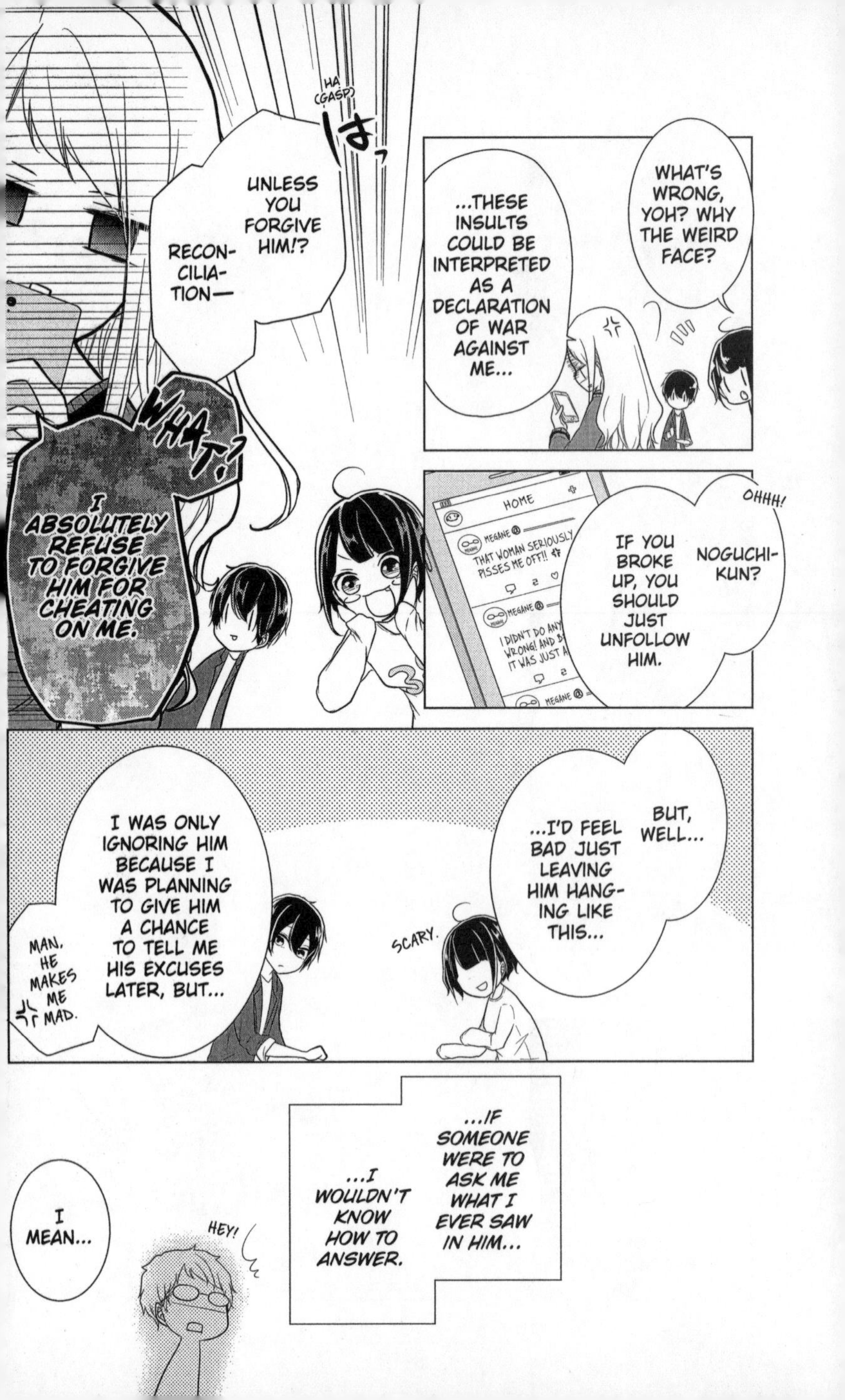
WHAT'S WRONG, YOH? WHY THE WEIRD FACE?
...THESE INSULTS COULD BE INTERPRETED AS A DECLARATION OF WAR AGAINST ME...
OHHH!
NOGUCHI-KUN?
IF YOU BROKE UP, YOU SHOULD JUST UNFOLLOW HIM.
HOME
MEGANE @
THAT WOMAN SERIOUSLY PISSES ME OFF!!
MEGANE @
MEGANE @
HA (GASP)
はっ
UNLESS YOU FORGIVE HIM!?
RECONCILIATION—
WHAT!?
I ABSOLUTELY REFUSE TO FORGIVE HIM FOR CHEATING ON ME.
BUT, WELL...
...I'D FEEL BAD JUST LEAVING HIM HANGING LIKE THIS...
SCARY.
I WAS ONLY IGNORING HIM BECAUSE I WAS PLANNING TO GIVE HIM A CHANCE TO TELL ME HIS EXCUSES LATER, BUT...
MAN, HE MAKES ME MAD.
...IF SOMEONE WERE TO ASK ME WHAT I EVER SAW IN HIM...
...I WOULDN'T KNOW HOW TO ANSWER.
HEY!
I MEAN...

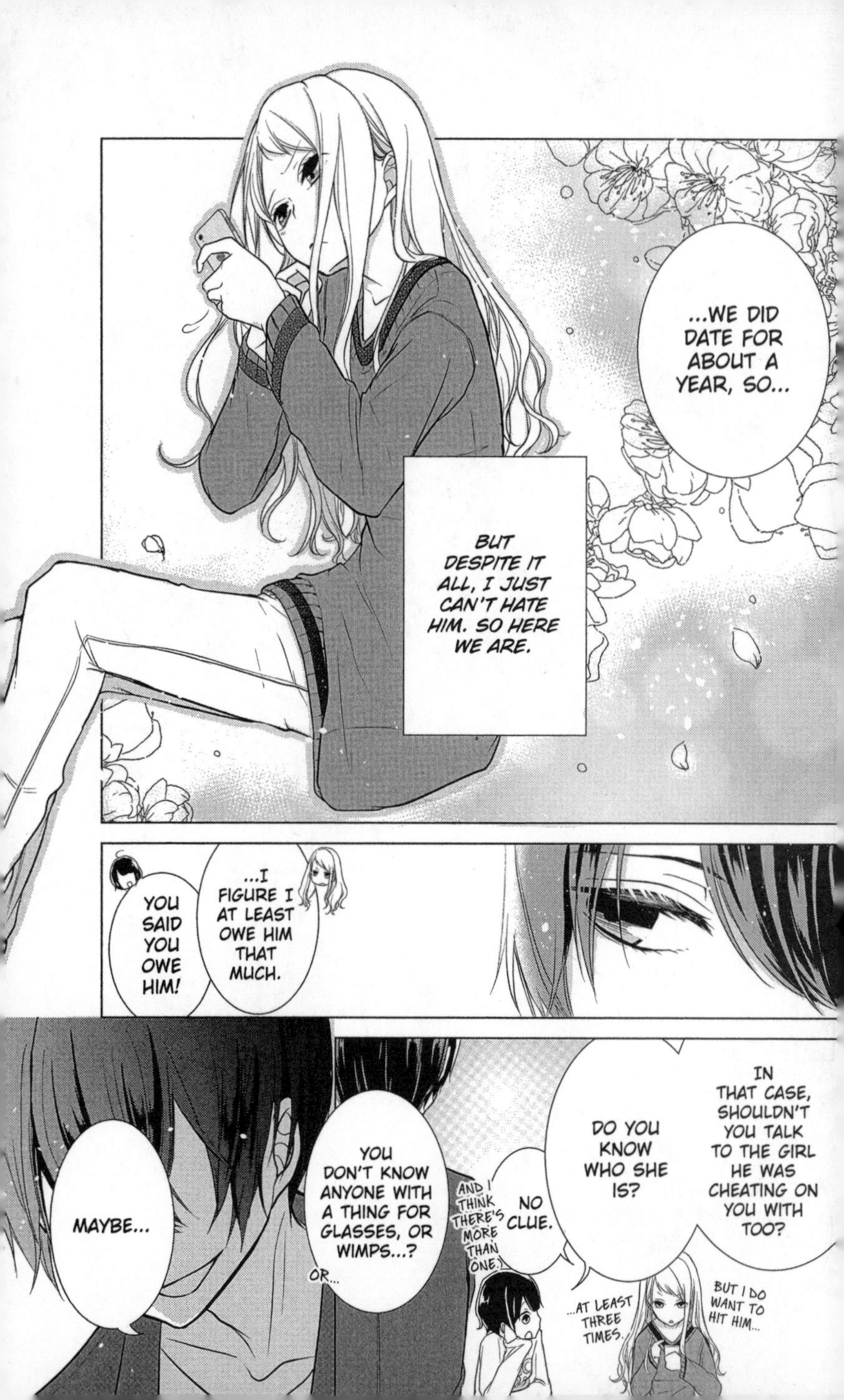
...WE DID DATE FOR ABOUT A YEAR, SO...
BUT DESPITE IT ALL, I JUST CAN'T HATE HIM. SO HERE WE ARE.
...I FIGURE I AT LEAST OWE HIM THAT MUCH.
YOU SAID YOU OWE HIM!
IN THAT CASE, SHOULDN'T YOU TALK TO THE GIRL HE WAS CHEATING ON YOU WITH TOO?
BUT I DO WANT TO HIT HIM...
DO YOU KNOW WHO SHE IS?
...AT LEAST THREE TIMES.
NO CLUE.
AND I THINK THERE'S MORE THAN ONE.
YOU DON'T KNOW ANYONE WITH A THING FOR GLASSES, OR WIMPS...?
OR...
MAYBE...

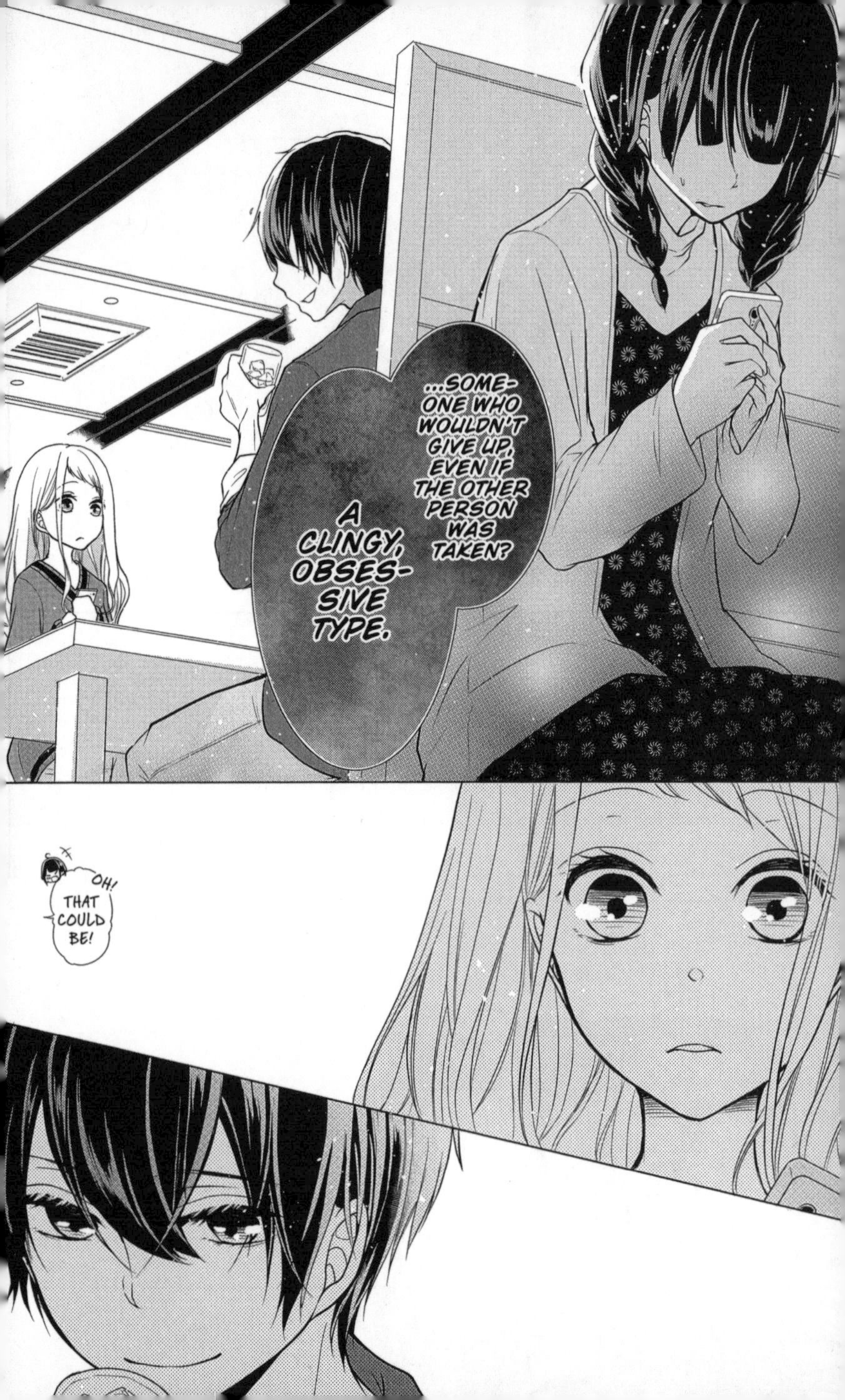
...SOMEONE WHO WOULDN'T GIVE UP, EVEN IF THE OTHER PERSON WAS TAKEN?
A CLINGY, OBSESSIVE TYPE.
OH! THAT COULD BE!

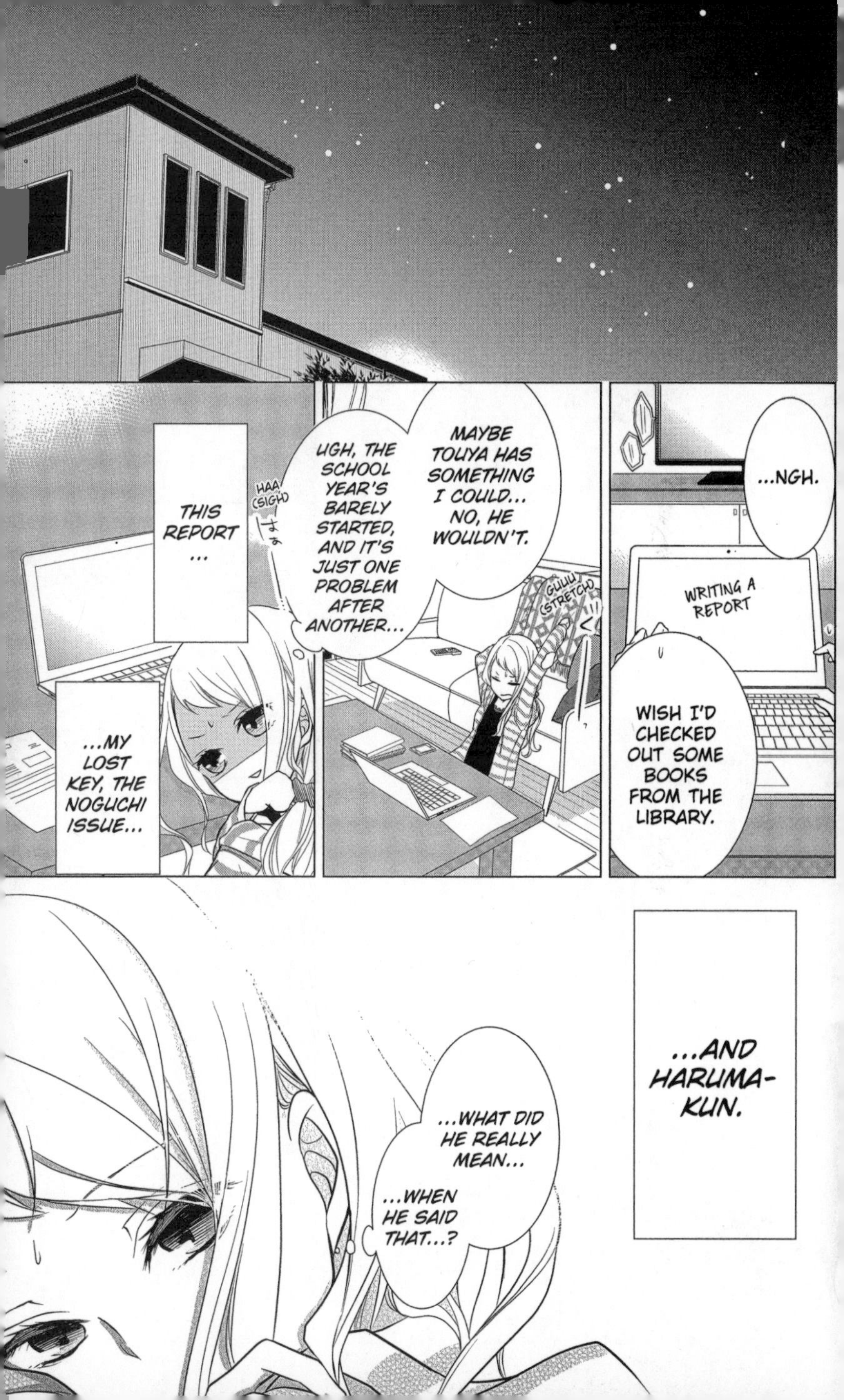
...NGH.
WRITING A REPORT
WISH I'D CHECKED OUT SOME BOOKS FROM THE LIBRARY.
MAYBE TOUYA HAS SOMETHING I COULD... NO, HE WOULDN'T.
GUUU (STRETCH)
UGH, THE SCHOOL YEAR'S BARELY STARTED, AND IT'S JUST ONE PROBLEM AFTER ANOTHER...
HAA (SIGH)
THIS REPORT...
...MY LOST KEY, THE NOGUCHI ISSUE...
...AND HARUMA-KUN.
...WHAT DID HE REALLY MEAN...
...WHEN HE SAID THAT...?

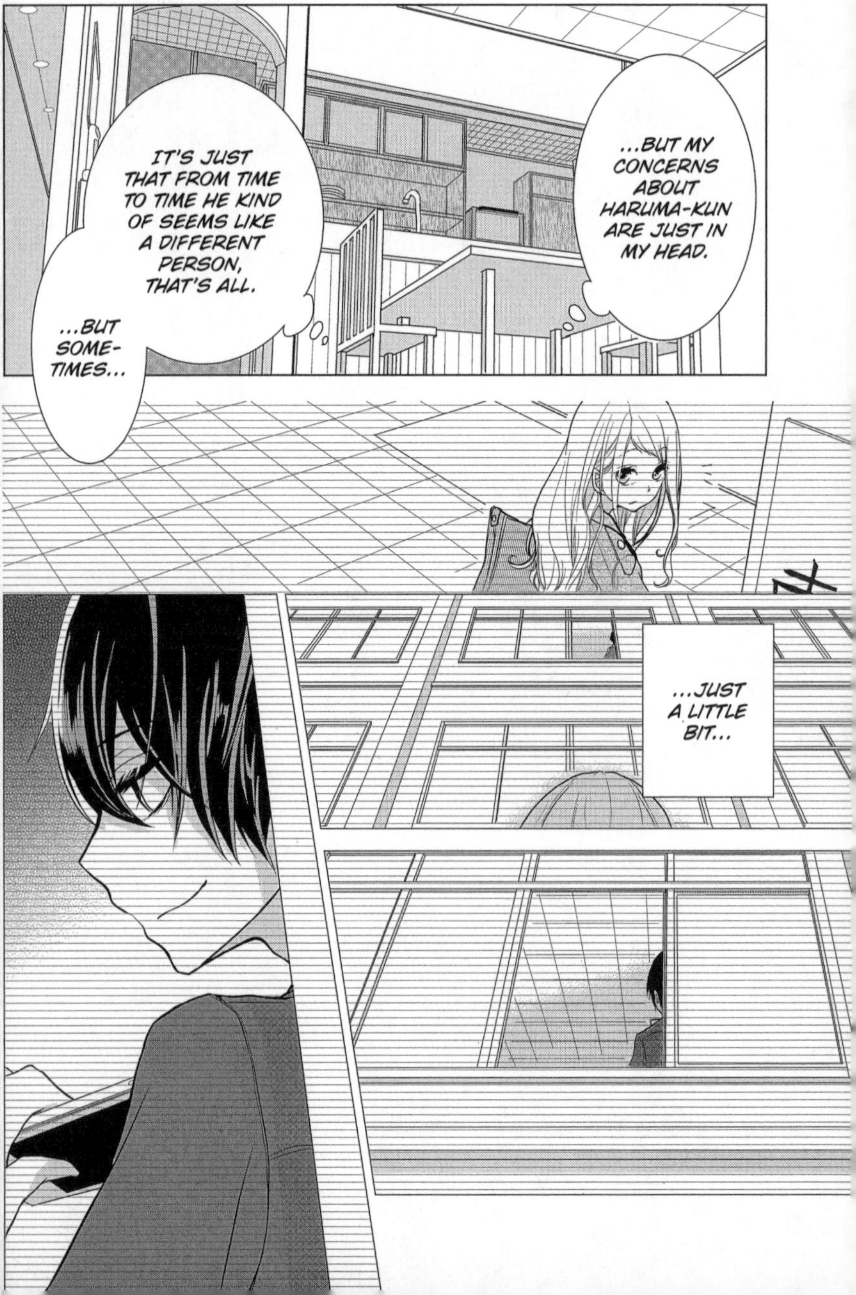
...BUT MY CONCERNS ABOUT HARUMA-KUN ARE JUST IN MY HEAD.
IT'S JUST THAT FROM TIME TO TIME HE KIND OF SEEMS LIKE A DIFFERENT PERSON, THAT'S ALL.
...BUT SOME-TIMES...
...JUST A LITTLE BIT...

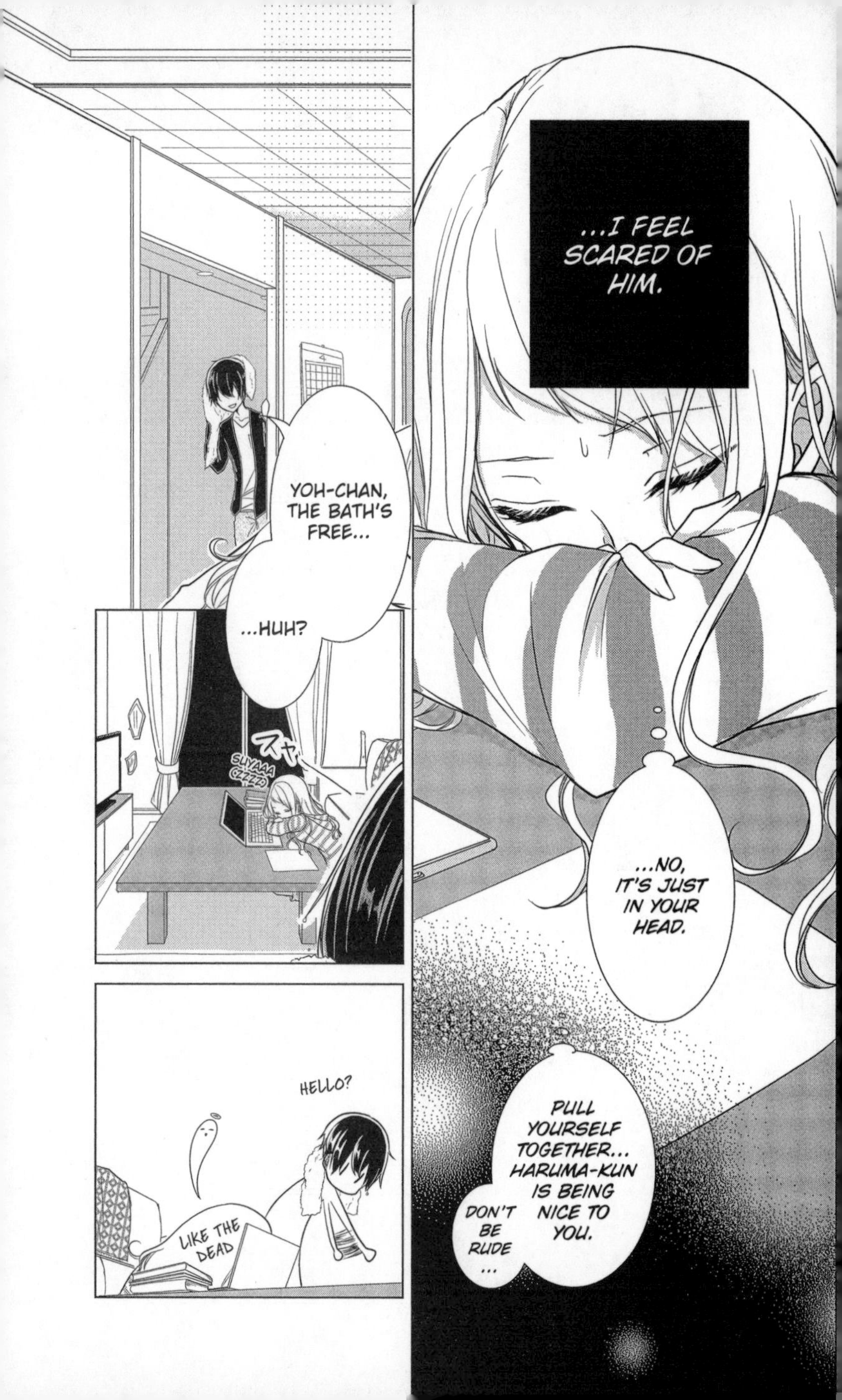
...I FEEL SCARED OF HIM.
...NO, IT'S JUST IN YOUR HEAD.
PULL YOURSELF TOGETHER... HARUMA-KUN IS BEING NICE TO YOU.
DON'T BE RUDE...
YOH-CHAN, THE BATH'S FREE...
...HUH?
スヤ
SUYAAA (ZZZZ)
HELLO?
LIKE THE DEAD

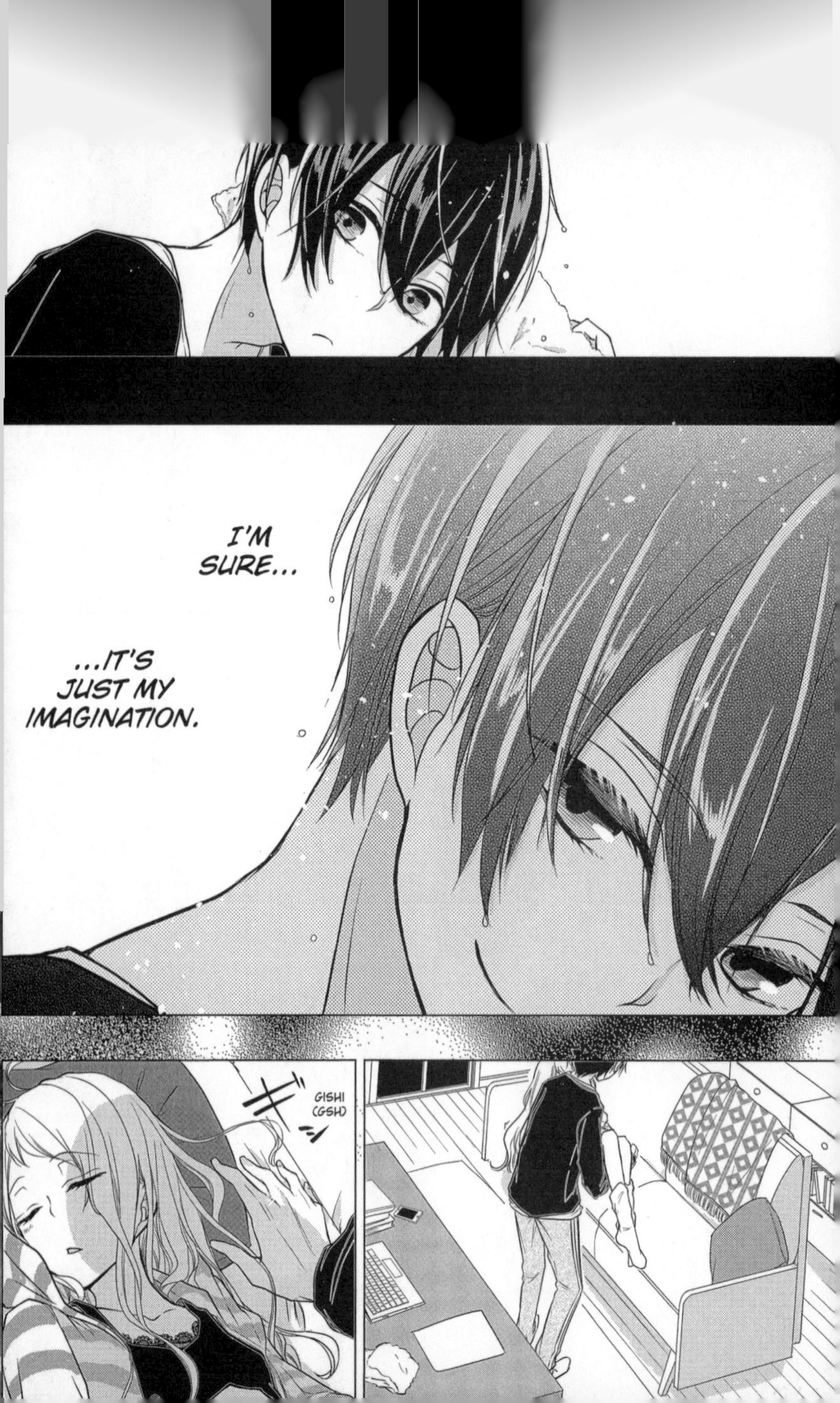
I'M SURE...
...IT'S JUST MY IMAGINATION.
GISHI (GSH)

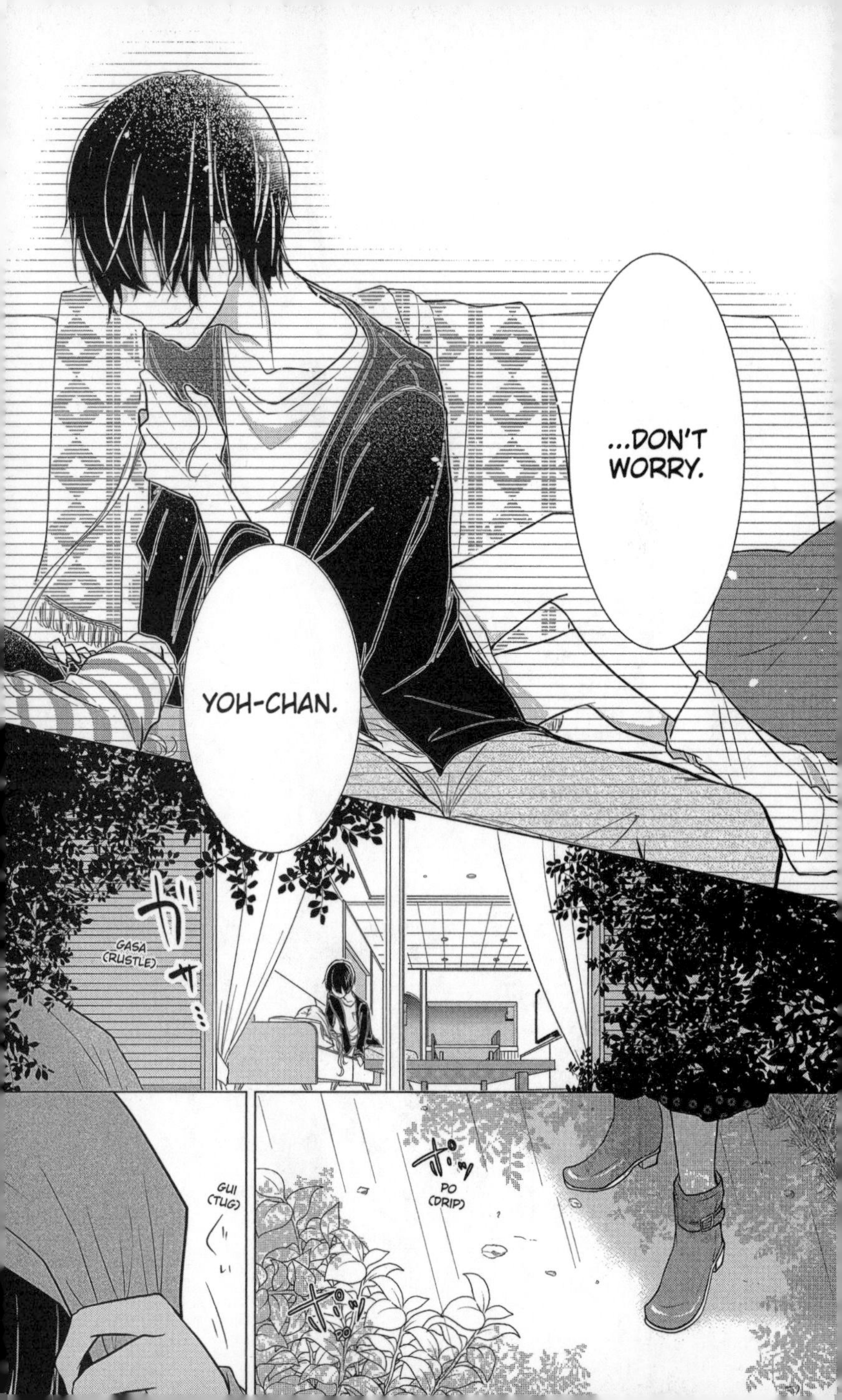
...DON'T WORRY.
YOH-CHAN.
GASA (RUSTLE)
PO (DRIP)
GUI (TUG)

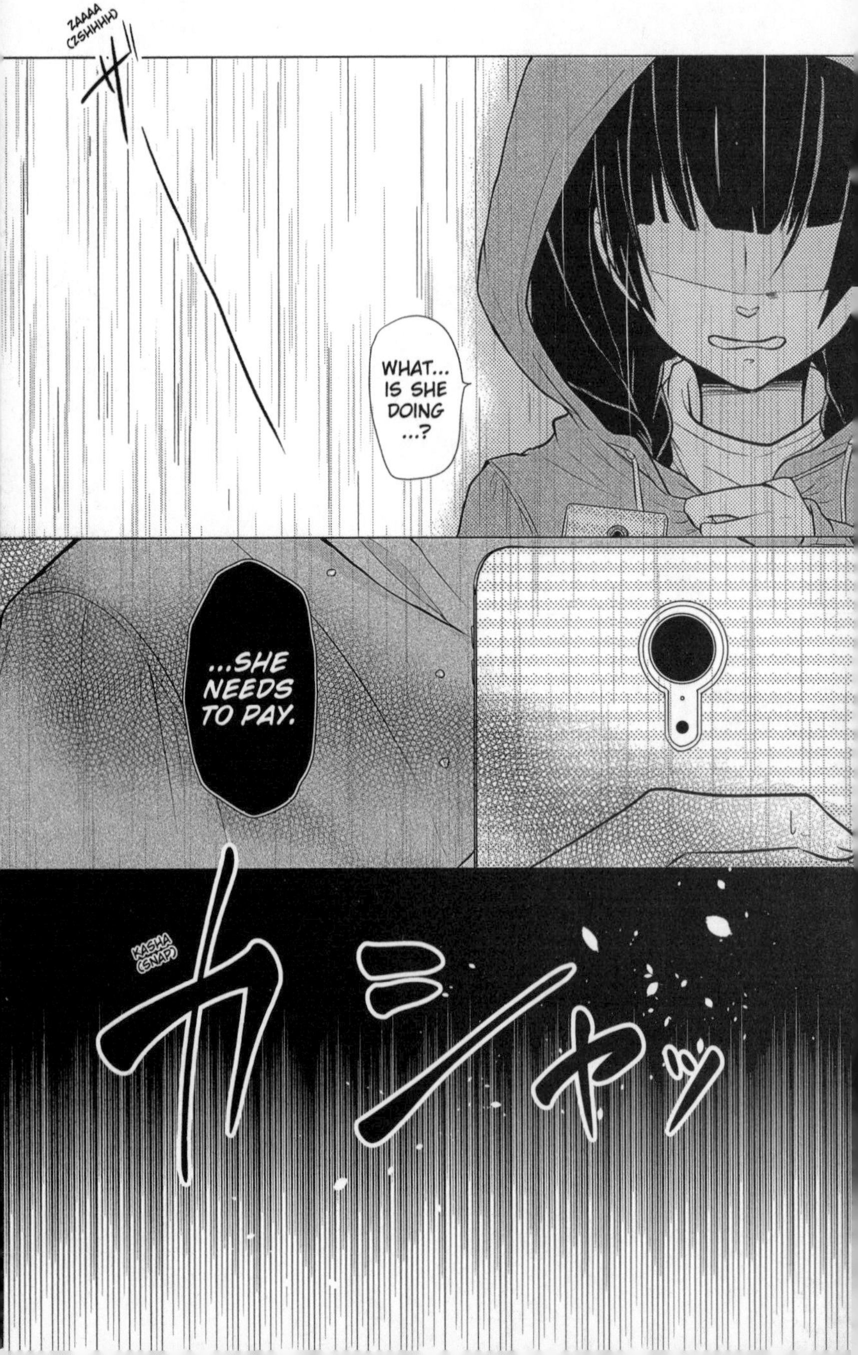
ZAAAA (ZSHHHH)
WHAT... IS SHE DOING ...?
...SHE NEEDS TO PAY.
KASHA (SNAP)
カシャッ

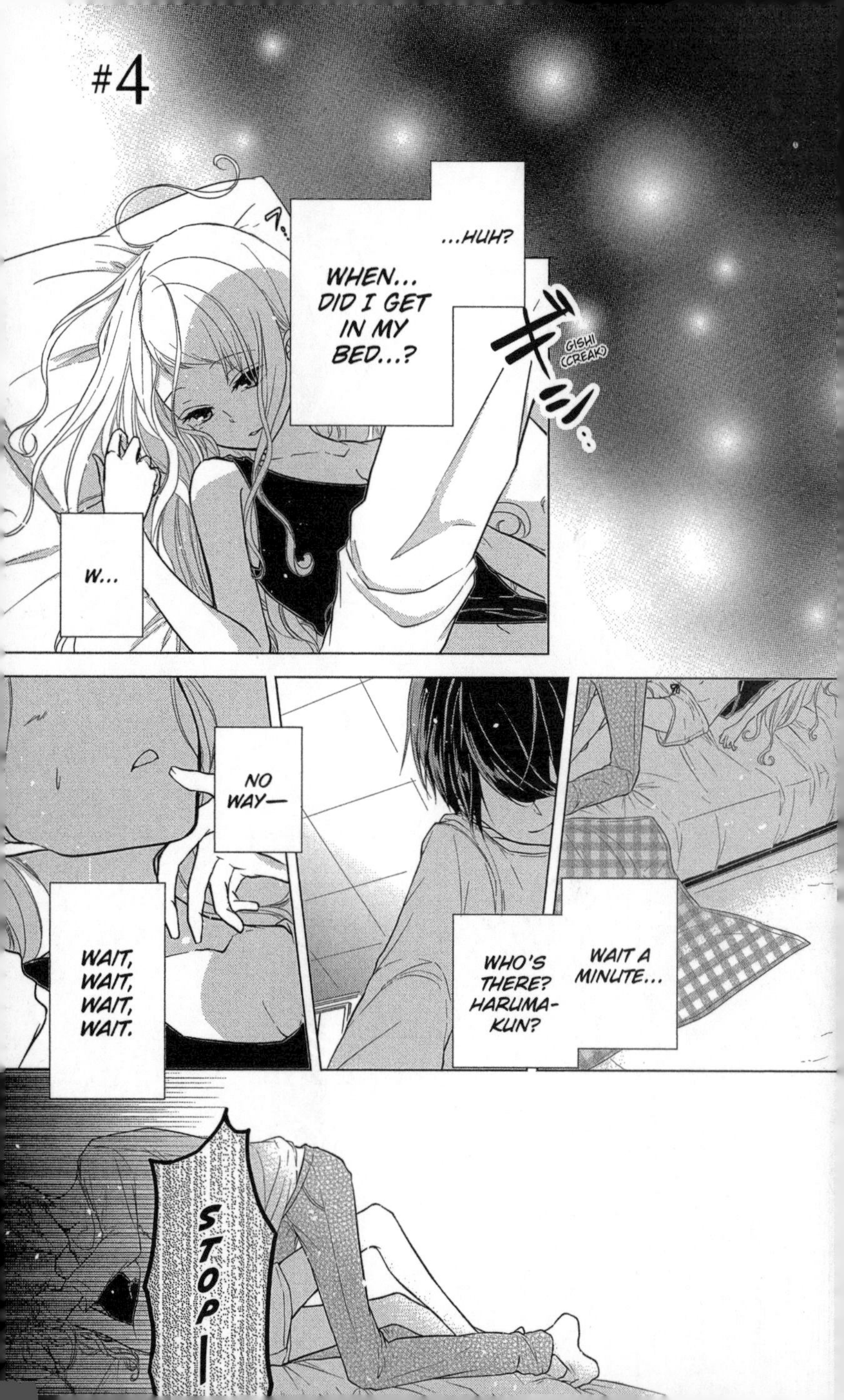
#4
...HUH?
WHEN... DID I GET IN MY BED...?
GISHI (CREAK)
W...
WAIT A MINUTE...
WHO'S THERE? HARUMA-KUN?
NO WAY—
WAIT, WAIT, WAIT, WAIT.
STOP!

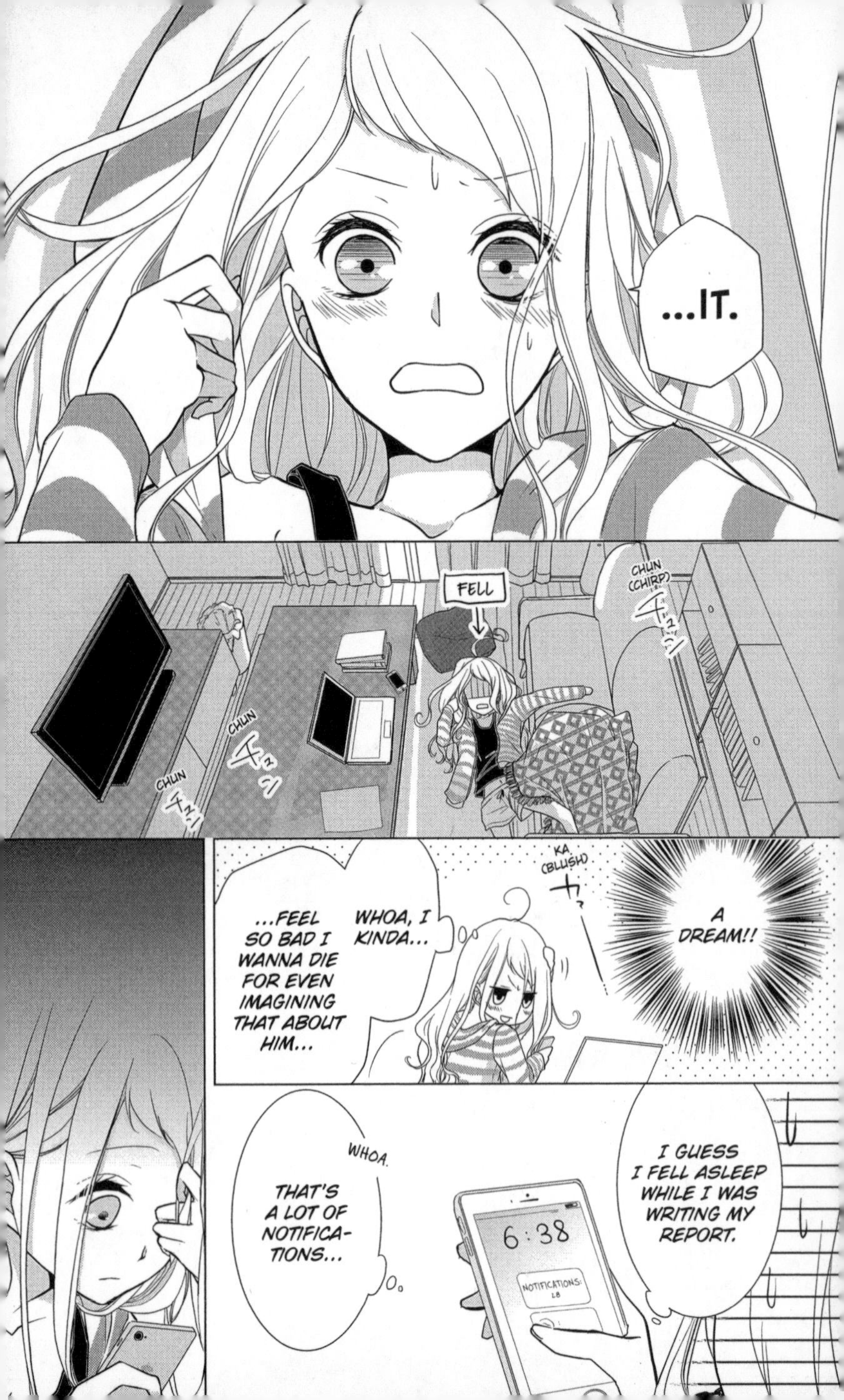
...IT.
FELL
CHUN (CHIRP)
CHUN
CHUN
A DREAM!!
KA (BLUSH)
WHOA, I KINDA...
...FEEL SO BAD I WANNA DIE FOR EVEN IMAGINING THAT ABOUT HIM...
I GUESS I FELL ASLEEP WHILE I WAS WRITING MY REPORT.
6:38
NOTIFICATIONS: 28
WHOA.
THAT'S A LOT OF NOTIFICATIONS...

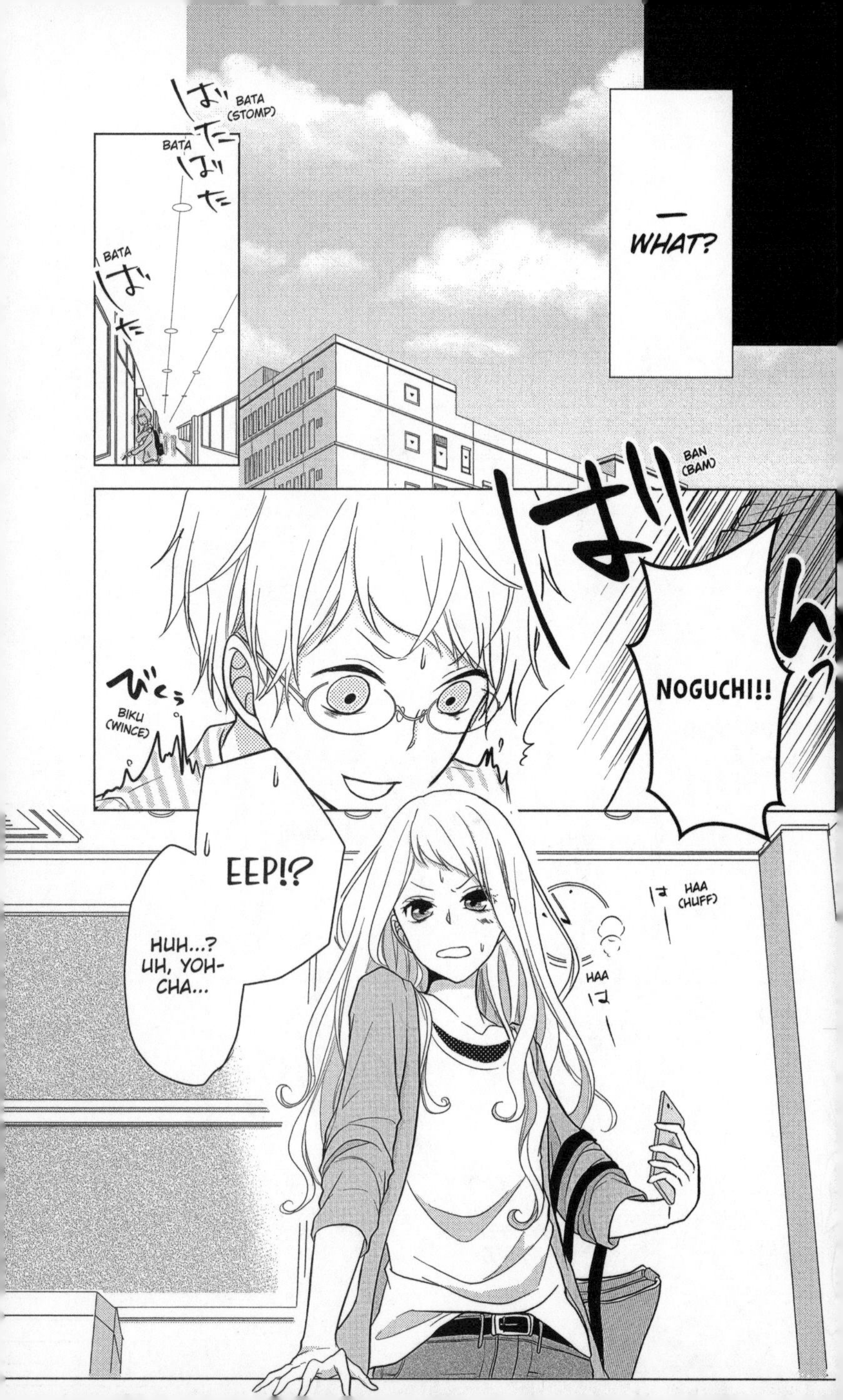
—WHAT?
ばたばた
BATA (STOMP)
BATA
ばた
BATA
ばーん
BAN (BAM)
NOGUCHI!!
びくっ
BIKU (WINCE)
EEP!?
は—
HAA (HUFF)
は—
HAA
HUH...? UH, YOH-CHA...

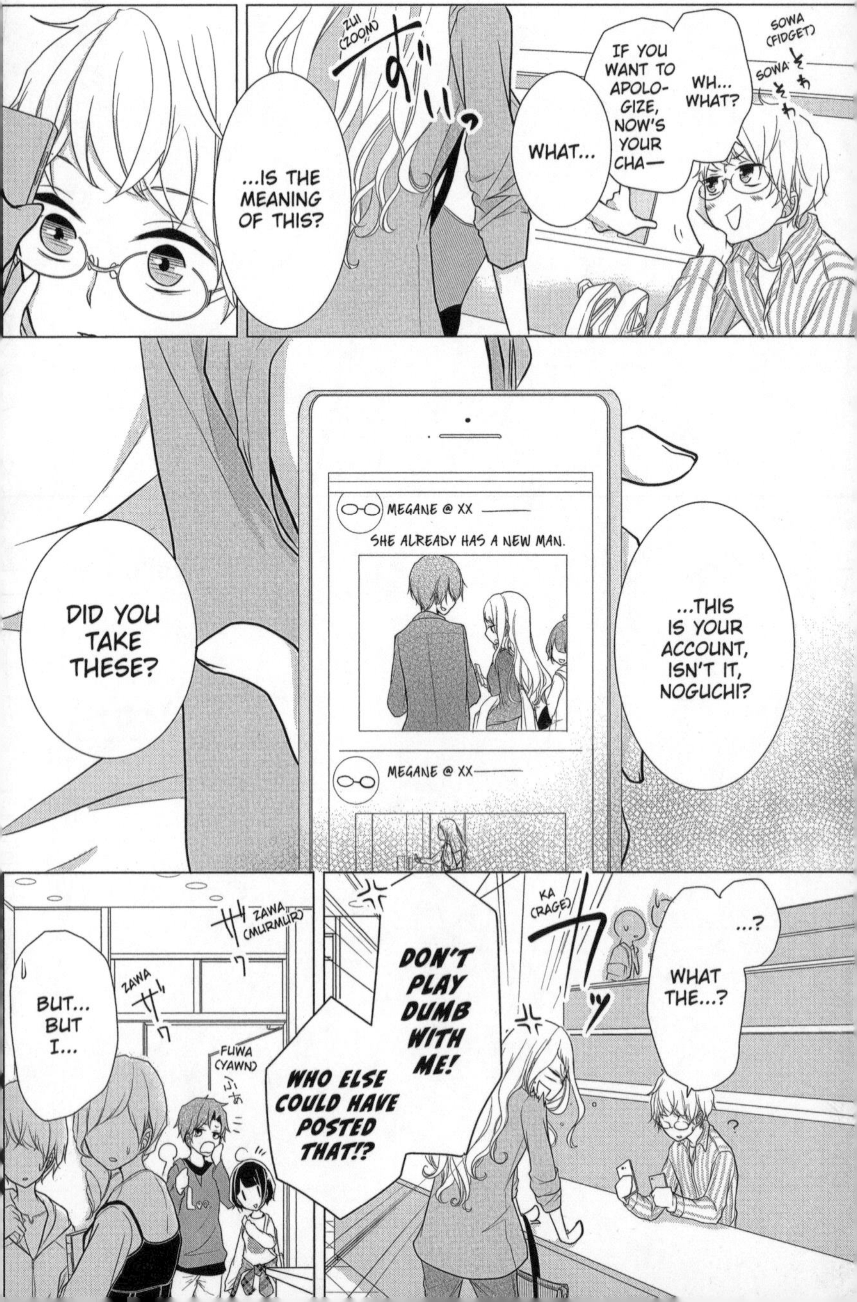

SOWA (FIDGET)
SOWA
WH... WHAT?
IF YOU WANT TO APOLOGIZE, NOW'S YOUR CHA—
WHAT...
ZUI (ZOOM)
...IS THE MEANING OF THIS?
...THIS IS YOUR ACCOUNT, ISN'T IT, NOGUCHI?
MEGANE @ XX
SHE ALREADY HAS A NEW MAN.
MEGANE @ XX
DID YOU TAKE THESE?
...?
WHAT THE...?
KA (RAGE)
DON'T PLAY DUMB WITH ME!
WHO ELSE COULD HAVE POSTED THAT!?
ZAWA (MURMUR)
ZAWA
FUWA (YAWN)
BUT... BUT I...

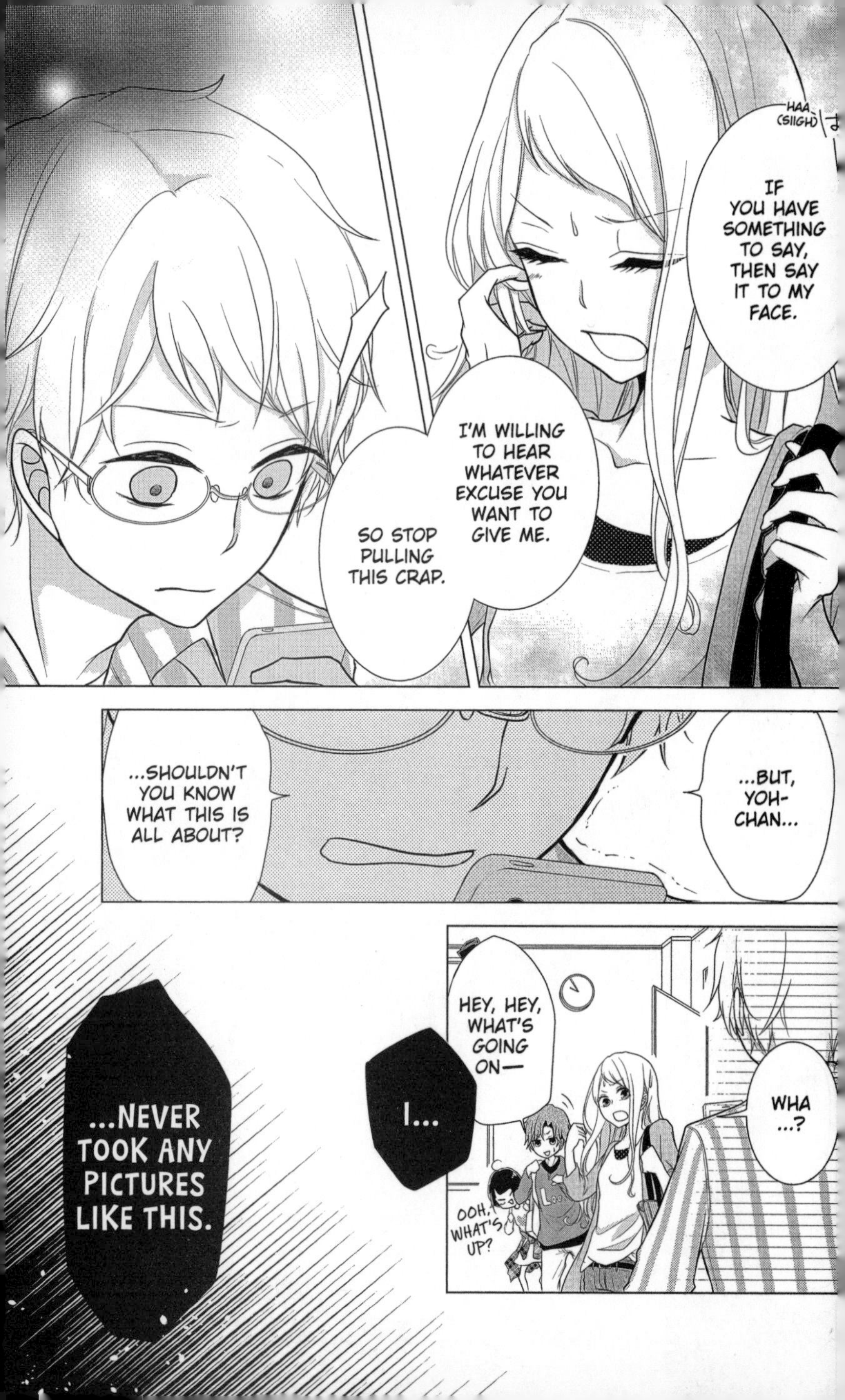
HAA (SIIGH) は
IF YOU HAVE SOMETHING TO SAY, THEN SAY IT TO MY FACE.
I'M WILLING TO HEAR WHATEVER EXCUSE YOU WANT TO GIVE ME.
SO STOP PULLING THIS CRAP.
...BUT, YOH-CHAN...
...SHOULDN'T YOU KNOW WHAT THIS IS ALL ABOUT?
WHA ...?
HEY, HEY, WHAT'S GOING ON—
OOH, WHAT'S UP?
I...
...NEVER TOOK ANY PICTURES LIKE THIS.

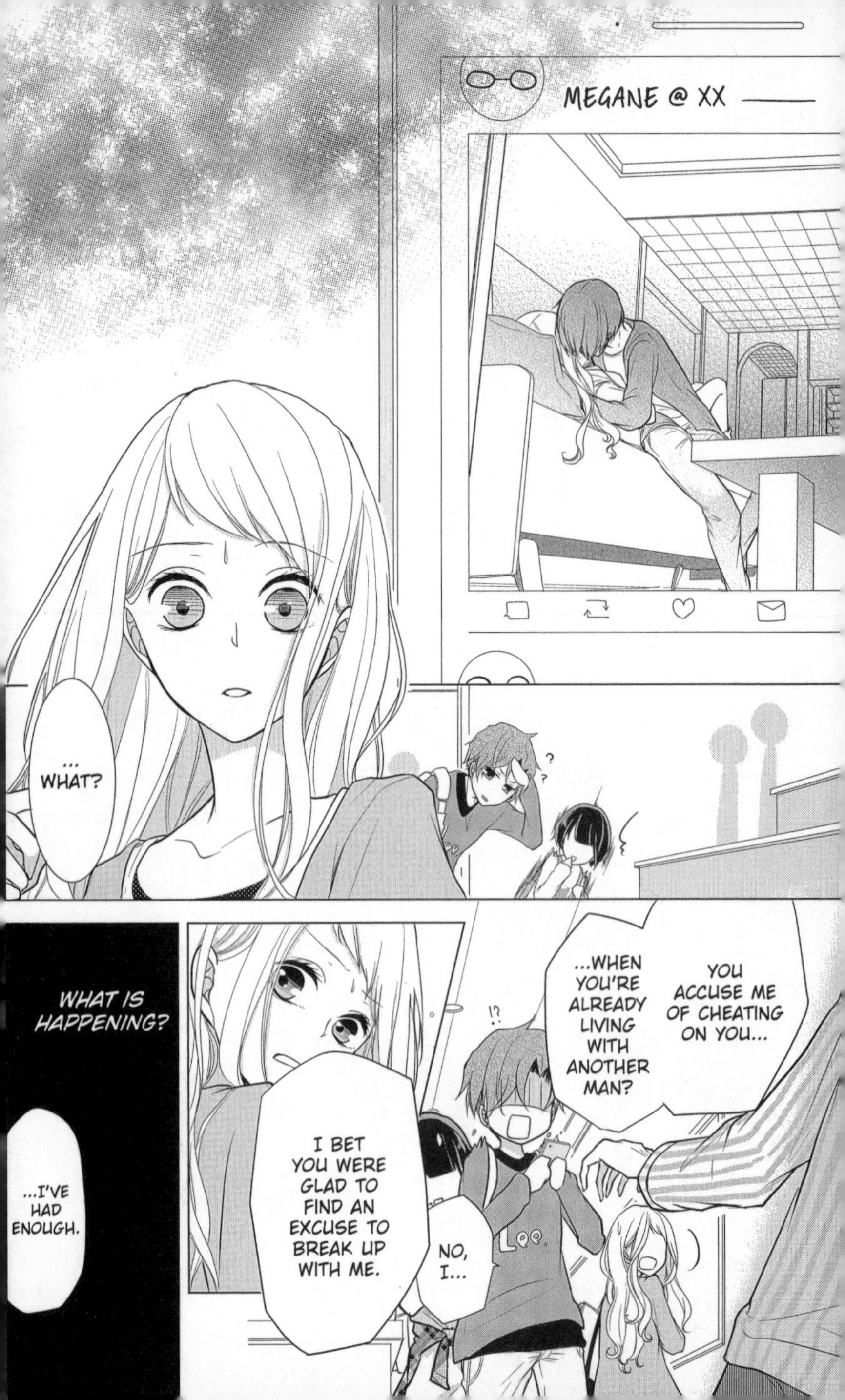
MEGANE @ XX
...WHAT?
YOU ACCUSE ME OF CHEATING ON YOU...
...WHEN YOU'RE ALREADY LIVING WITH ANOTHER MAN?
!?
NO, I...
I BET YOU WERE GLAD TO FIND AN EXCUSE TO BREAK UP WITH ME.
WHAT IS HAPPENING?
...I'VE HAD ENOUGH.

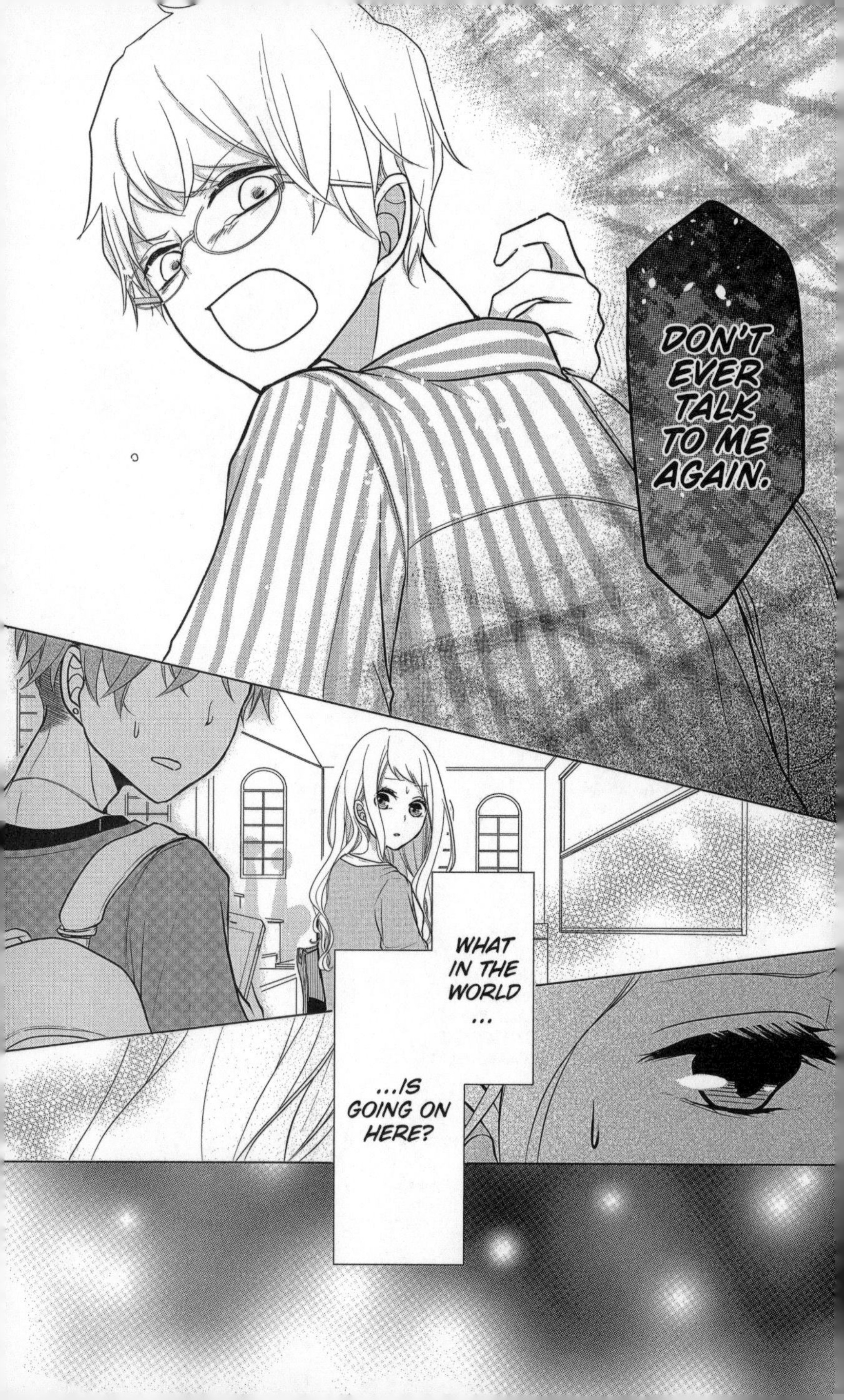
DON'T EVER TALK TO ME AGAIN.
WHAT IN THE WORLD ...
...IS GOING ON HERE?

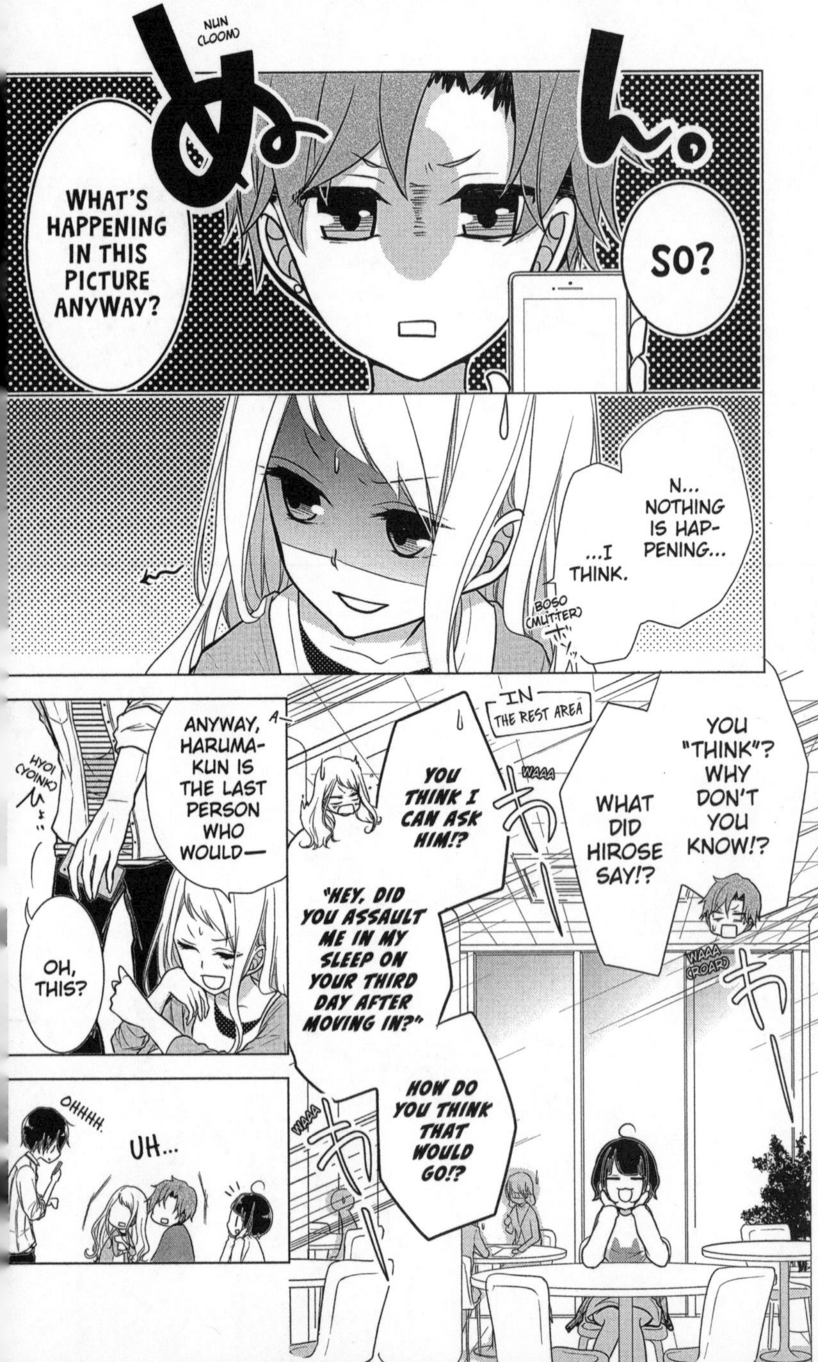
NUN (LOOM)
SO?
WHAT'S HAPPENING IN THIS PICTURE ANYWAY?
N... NOTHING IS HAP-PENING...
...I THINK.
BOSO (MUTTER)
IN THE REST AREA
YOU "THINK"? WHY DON'T YOU KNOW!?
WHAT DID HIROSE SAY!?
WAAA
YOU THINK I CAN ASK HIM!?
"HEY, DID YOU ASSAULT ME IN MY SLEEP ON YOUR THIRD DAY AFTER MOVING IN?"
WAAA (ROAR)
HOW DO YOU THINK THAT WOULD GO!?
WAAA
ANYWAY, HARUMA-KUN IS THE LAST PERSON WHO WOULD—
A-
HYOI (YOINK)
OH, THIS?
OHHHH.
UH...

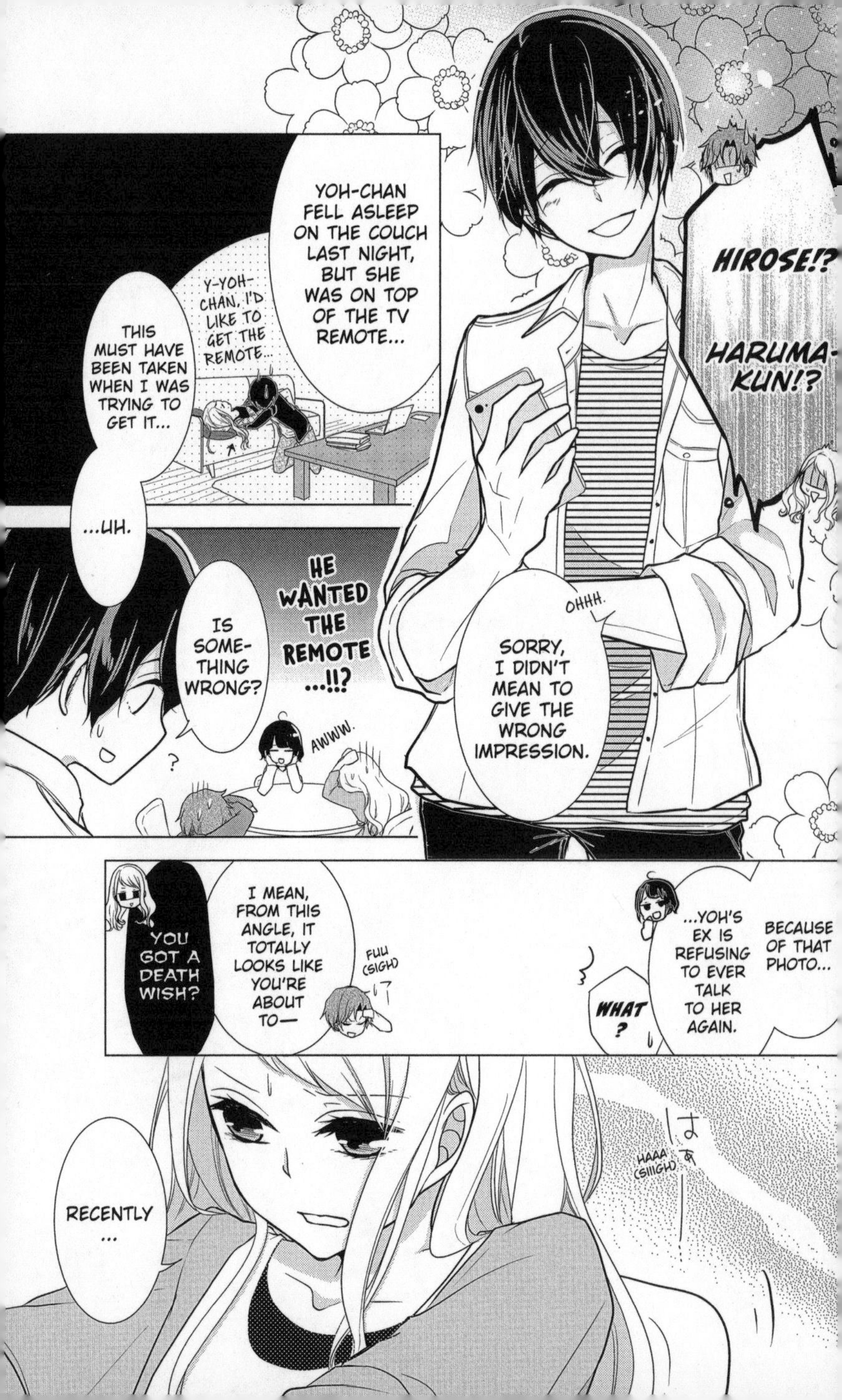

HIROSE!?
HARUMA-KUN!?
YOH-CHAN FELL ASLEEP ON THE COUCH LAST NIGHT, BUT SHE WAS ON TOP OF THE TV REMOTE...
Y-YOH-CHAN, I'D LIKE TO GET THE REMOTE...
THIS MUST HAVE BEEN TAKEN WHEN I WAS TRYING TO GET IT...
...UH.
HE WANTED THE REMOTE...!!?
IS SOMETHING WRONG?
?
AWWW.
OHHH.
SORRY, I DIDN'T MEAN TO GIVE THE WRONG IMPRESSION.
BECAUSE OF THAT PHOTO...
...YOH'S EX IS REFUSING TO EVER TALK TO HER AGAIN.
WHAT?
I MEAN, FROM THIS ANGLE, IT TOTALLY LOOKS LIKE YOU'RE ABOUT TO—
FUU (SIGH)
YOU GOT A DEATH WISH?
はあ
HAAA (SIIIGH)
RECENTLY ...

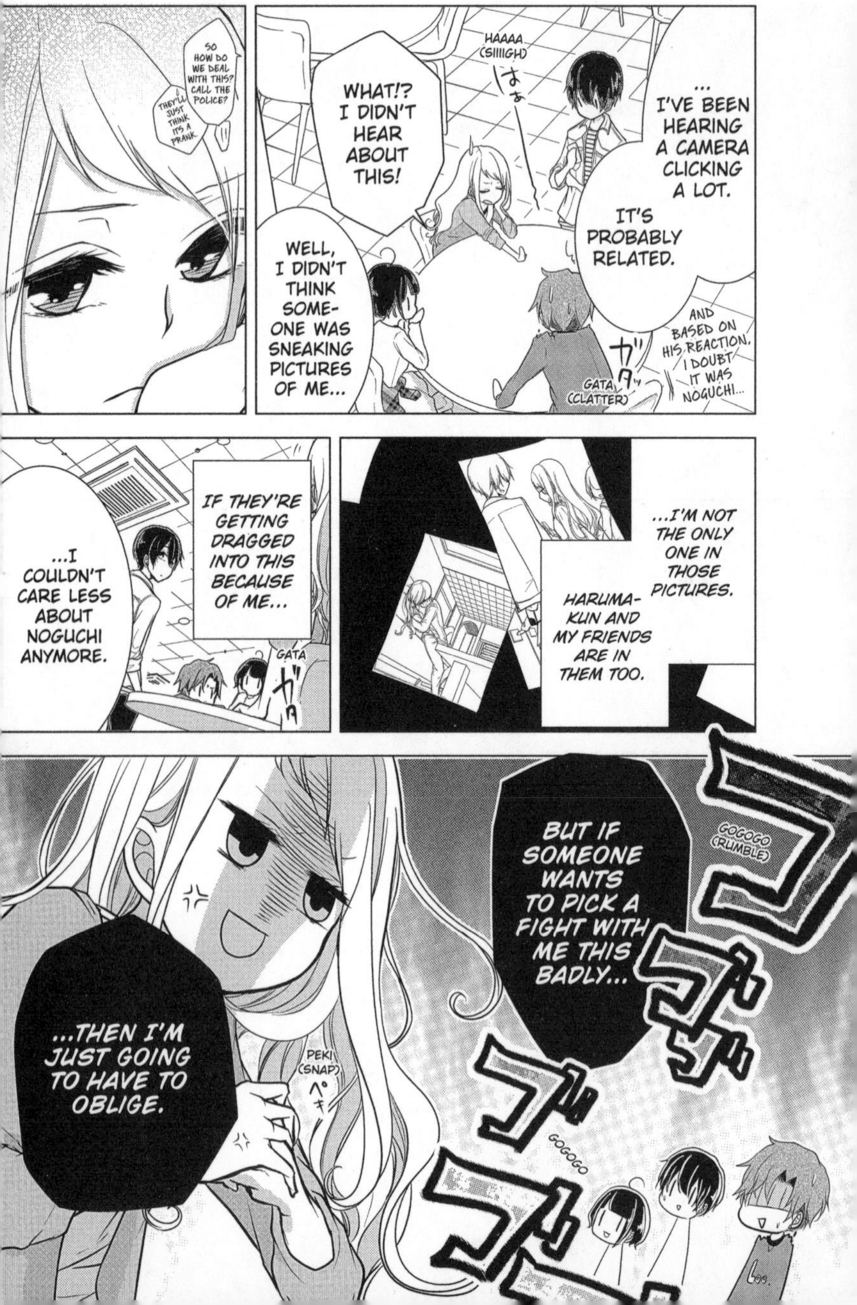
...I'VE BEEN HEARING A CAMERA CLICKING A LOT.
IT'S PROBABLY RELATED.
HAAAA (SIIIIGH)
はぁ
WHAT!? I DIDN'T HEAR ABOUT THIS!
AND BASED ON HIS REACTION, I DOUBT IT WAS NOGUCHI...
GATA (CLATTER)
WELL, I DIDN'T THINK SOMEONE WAS SNEAKING PICTURES OF ME...
SO HOW DO WE DEAL WITH THIS? CALL THE POLICE?
THEY'LL JUST THINK ITS A PRANK.
...I'M NOT THE ONLY ONE IN THOSE PICTURES.
HARUMA-KUN AND MY FRIENDS ARE IN THEM TOO.
IF THEY'RE GETTING DRAGGED INTO THIS BECAUSE OF ME...
...I COULDN'T CARE LESS ABOUT NOGUCHI ANYMORE.
GATA
GOGOGO (RUMBLE)
BUT IF SOMEONE WANTS TO PICK A FIGHT WITH ME THIS BADLY...
GOGOGO
PEKI (SNAP)
...THEN I'M JUST GOING TO HAVE TO OBLIGE.

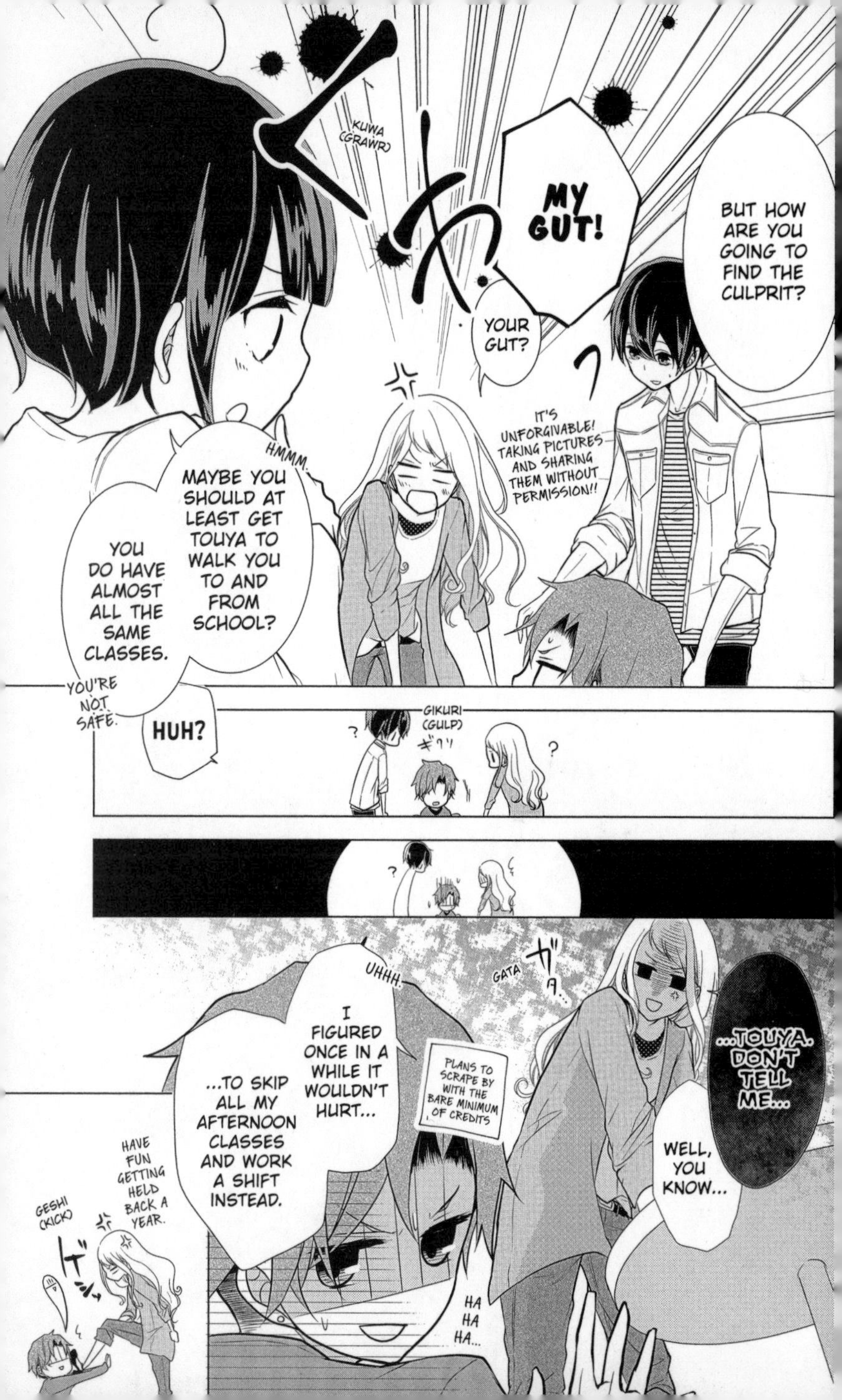

BUT HOW ARE YOU GOING TO FIND THE CULPRIT?
MY GUT!
KUWA (GRAWR)
YOUR GUT?
IT'S UNFORGIVABLE! TAKING PICTURES AND SHARING THEM WITHOUT PERMISSION!!
HMMM.
MAYBE YOU SHOULD AT LEAST GET TOUYA TO WALK YOU TO AND FROM SCHOOL?
YOU DO HAVE ALMOST ALL THE SAME CLASSES.
YOU'RE NOT SAFE.
GIKURI (GULP)
HUH?
...TOUYA. DON'T TELL ME...
GATA
WELL, YOU KNOW...
UHHH.
I FIGURED ONCE IN A WHILE IT WOULDN'T HURT...
PLANS TO SCRAPE BY WITH THE BARE MINIMUM OF CREDITS
...TO SKIP ALL MY AFTERNOON CLASSES AND WORK A SHIFT INSTEAD.
HA HA HA...
HAVE FUN GETTING HELD BACK A YEAR.
GESHI (KICK)

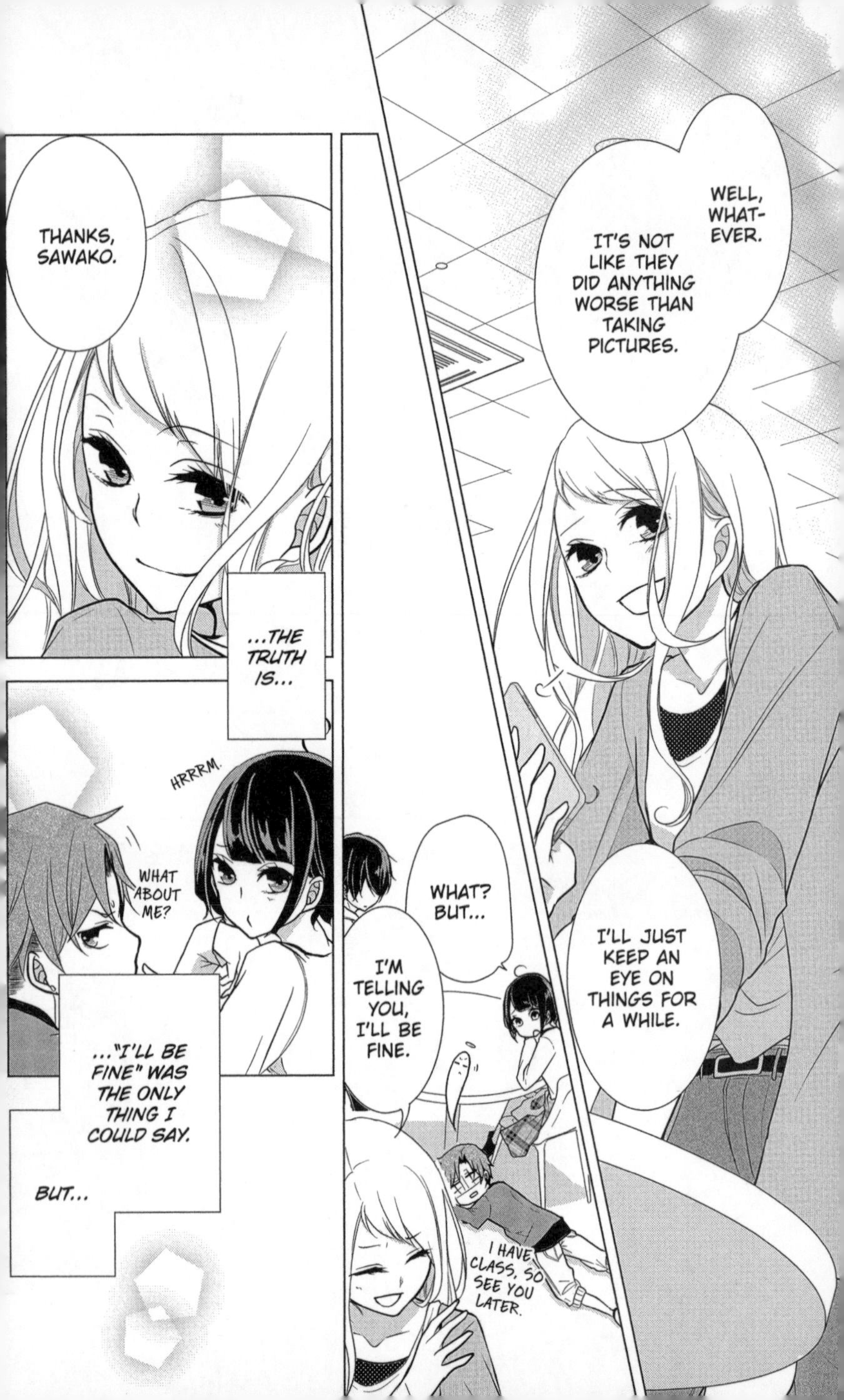
WELL, WHAT-EVER.
IT'S NOT LIKE THEY DID ANYTHING WORSE THAN TAKING PICTURES.
I'LL JUST KEEP AN EYE ON THINGS FOR A WHILE.
WHAT? BUT...
I'M TELLING YOU, I'LL BE FINE.
I HAVE CLASS, SO SEE YOU LATER.
THANKS, SAWAKO.
...THE TRUTH IS...
HRRRM.
WHAT ABOUT ME?
..."I'LL BE FINE" WAS THE ONLY THING I COULD SAY.
BUT...

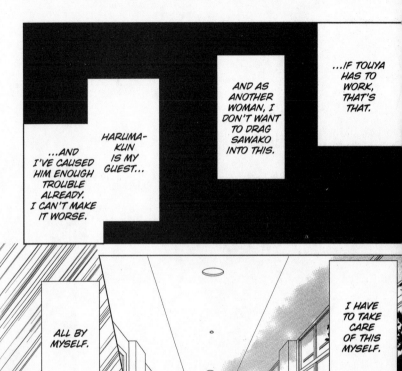

...IF TOLIYA HAS TO WORK, THAT'S THAT.

AND AS ANOTHER WOMAN, I DON'T WANT TO DRAG SAWAKO INTO THIS.

HARUMA-KUN IS MY GUEST...

...AND I'VE CAUSED HIM ENOUGH TROUBLE ALREADY. I CAN'T MAKE IT WORSE.

ALL BY MYSELF.

I HAVE TO TAKE CARE OF THIS MYSELF.

I'VE ALWAYS TAKEN CARE OF MYSELF.

ALL ON MY OWN.

GUI CYANKO

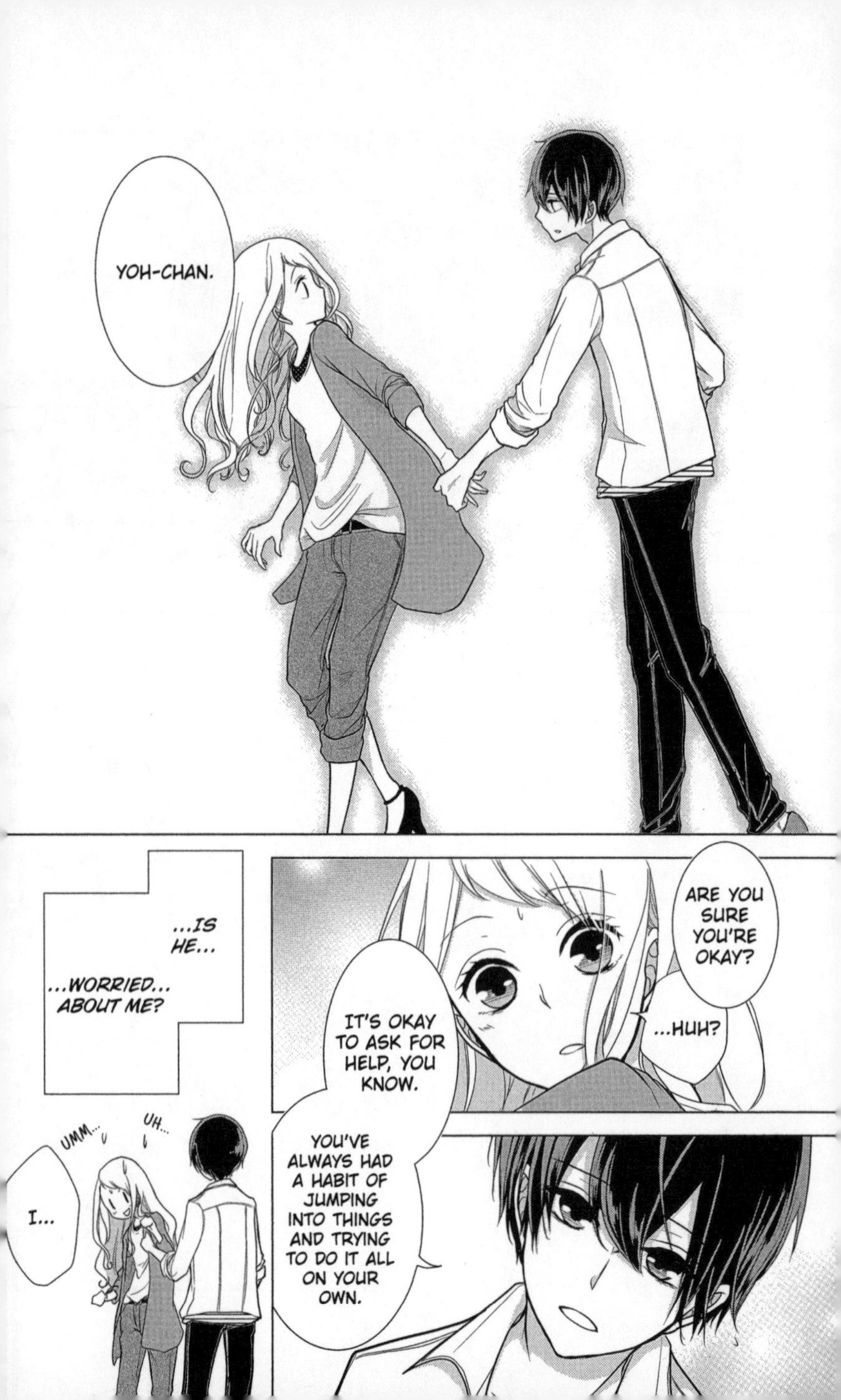
YOH-CHAN.
ARE YOU SURE YOU'RE OKAY?
...HUH?
IT'S OKAY TO ASK FOR HELP, YOU KNOW.
YOU'VE ALWAYS HAD A HABIT OF JUMPING INTO THINGS AND TRYING TO DO IT ALL ON YOUR OWN.
...IS HE...
...WORRIED... ABOUT ME?
UMM...
UH...
I...

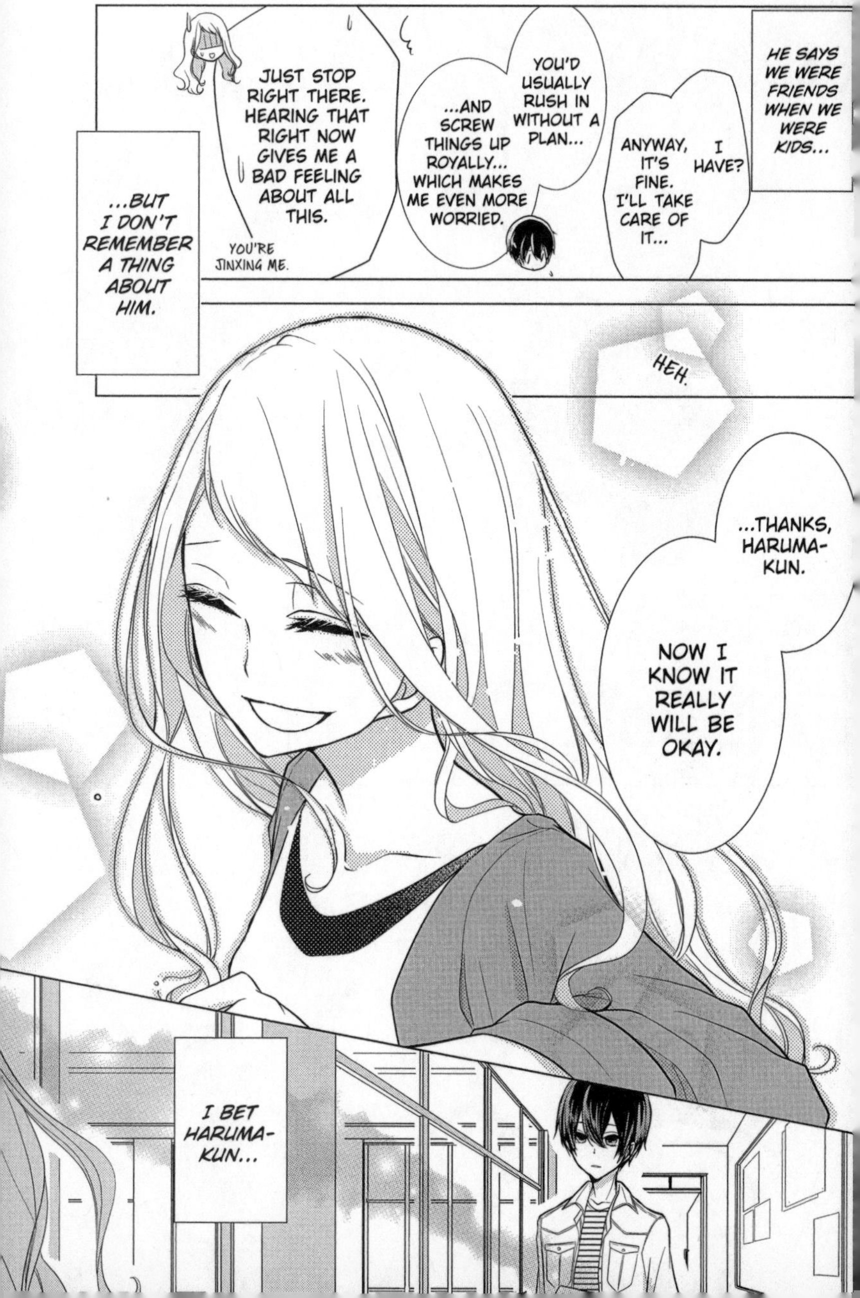
HE SAYS WE WERE FRIENDS WHEN WE WERE KIDS...
I HAVE?
ANYWAY, IT'S FINE. I'LL TAKE CARE OF IT...
YOU'D USUALLY RUSH IN WITHOUT A PLAN...
...AND SCREW THINGS UP ROYALLY... WHICH MAKES ME EVEN MORE WORRIED.
JUST STOP RIGHT THERE. HEARING THAT RIGHT NOW GIVES ME A BAD FEELING ABOUT ALL THIS.
YOU'RE JINXING ME.
...BUT I DON'T REMEMBER A THING ABOUT HIM.
HEH.
...THANKS, HARUMA-KUN.
NOW I KNOW IT REALLY WILL BE OKAY.
I BET HARUMA-KUN...

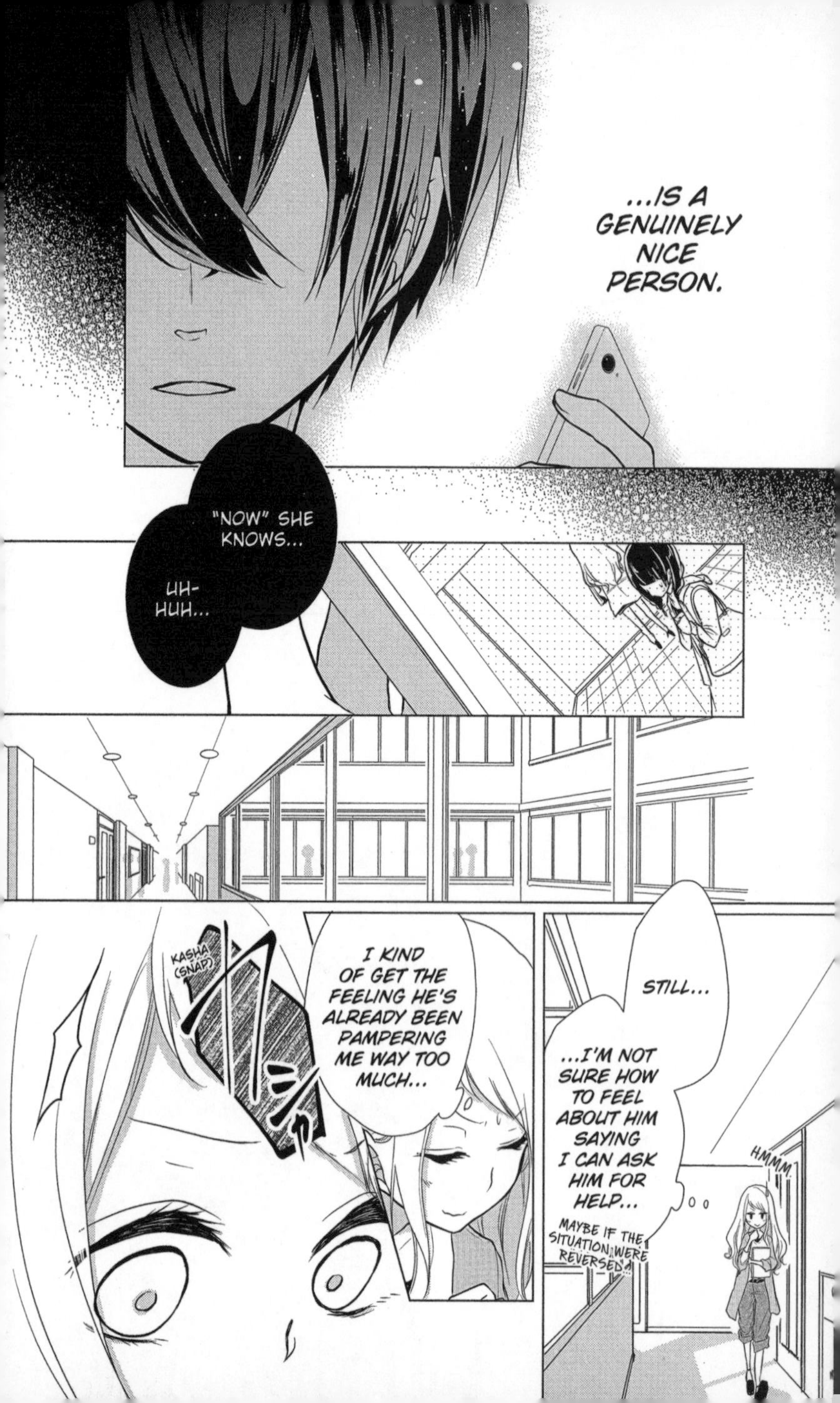
...IS A GENUINELY NICE PERSON.
"NOW" SHE KNOWS...
UH-HUH...
STILL...
...I'M NOT SURE HOW TO FEEL ABOUT HIM SAYING I CAN ASK HIM FOR HELP...
MAYBE IF THE SITUATION WERE REVERSED...
HMMM.
I KIND OF GET THE FEELING HE'S ALREADY BEEN PAMPERING ME WAY TOO MUCH...
KASHA (SNAP)

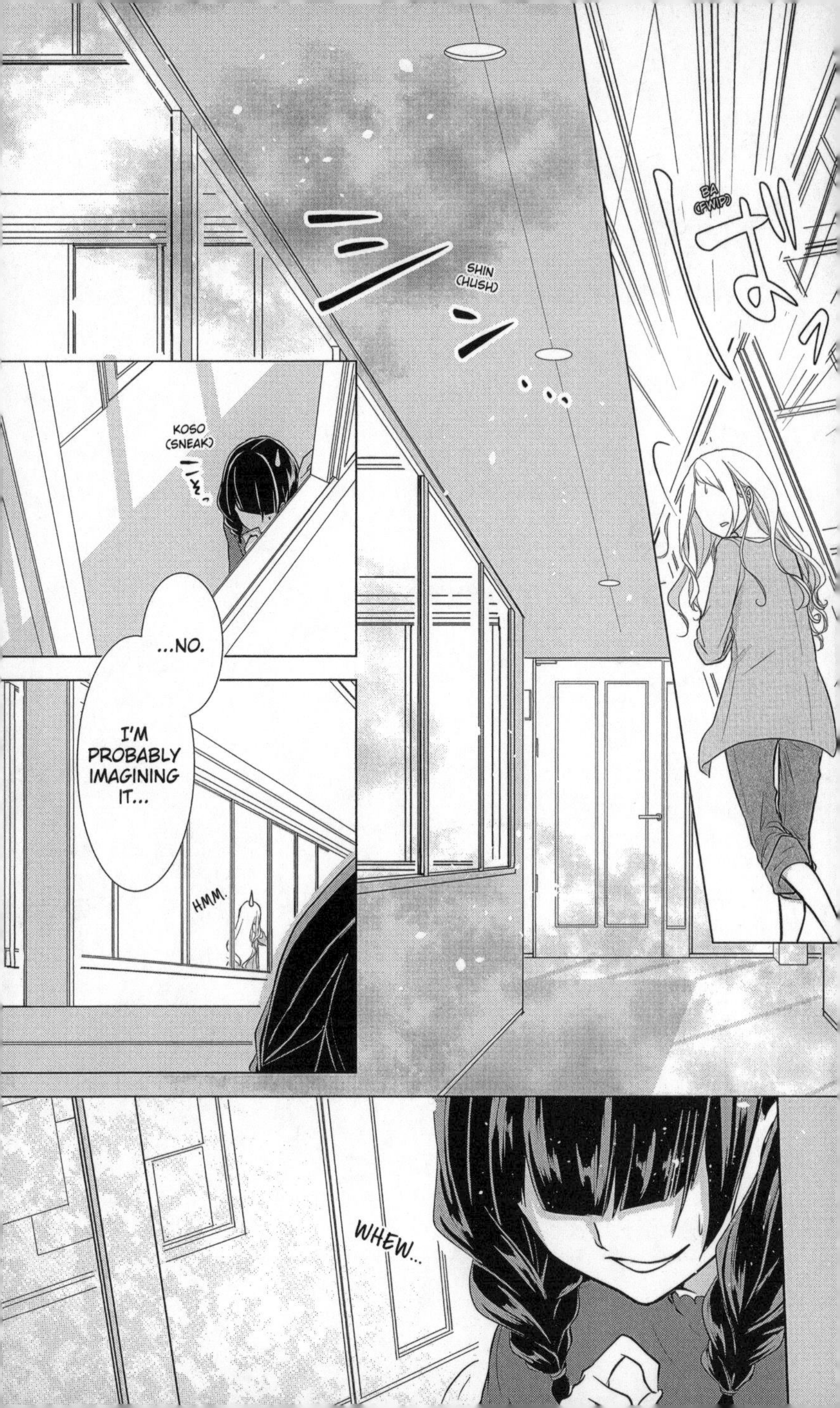
BA
(FWIP)
SHIN
(HUSH)
KOSO
(SNEAK)
...NO.
I'M PROBABLY IMAGINING IT...
HMM.
WHEW...

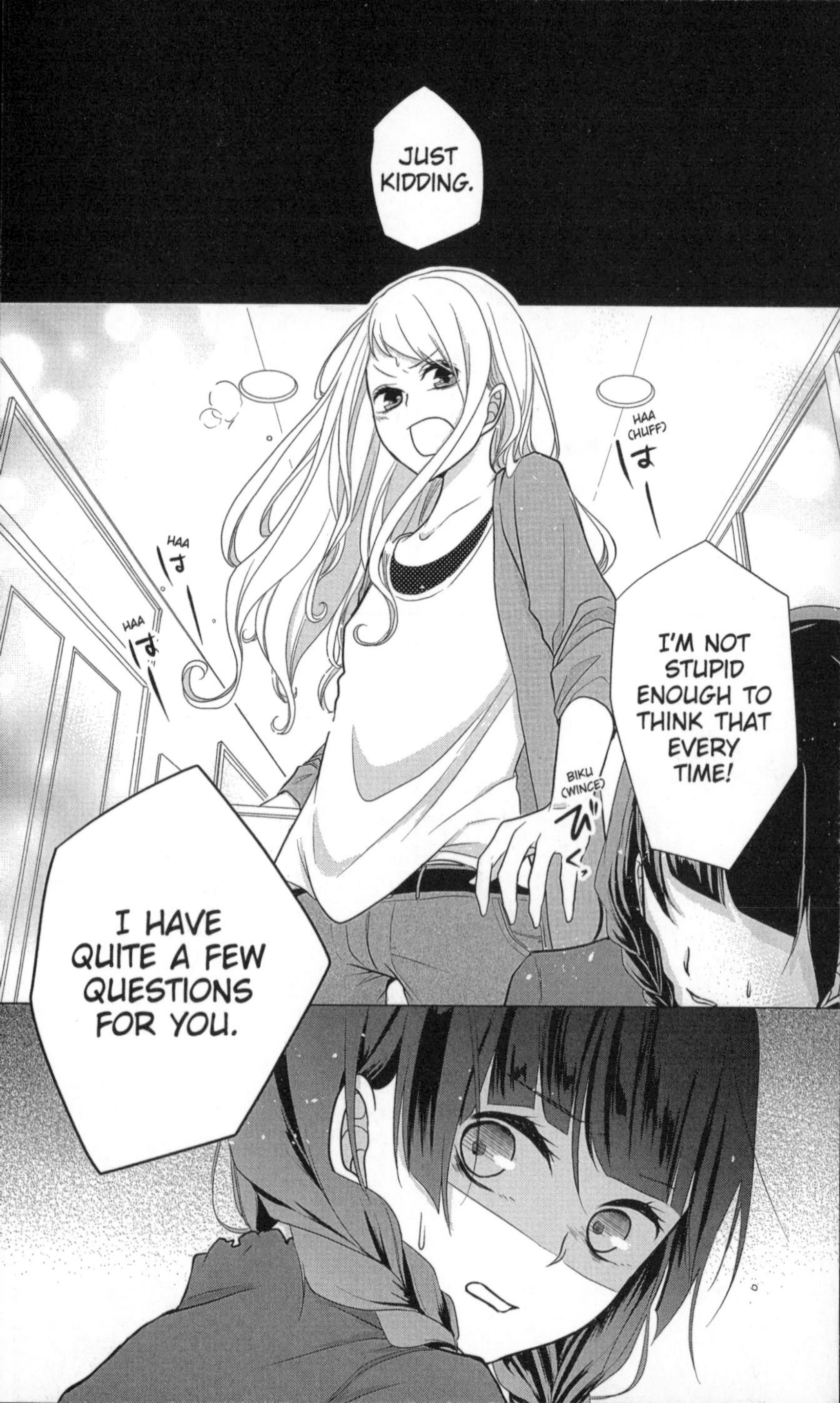

JUST KIDDING.
HAA (HUFF)
は
HAA
は
HAA
は
I'M NOT STUPID ENOUGH TO THINK THAT EVERY TIME!
BIKU (WINCE)
びく
I HAVE QUITE A FEW QUESTIONS FOR YOU.

# #5

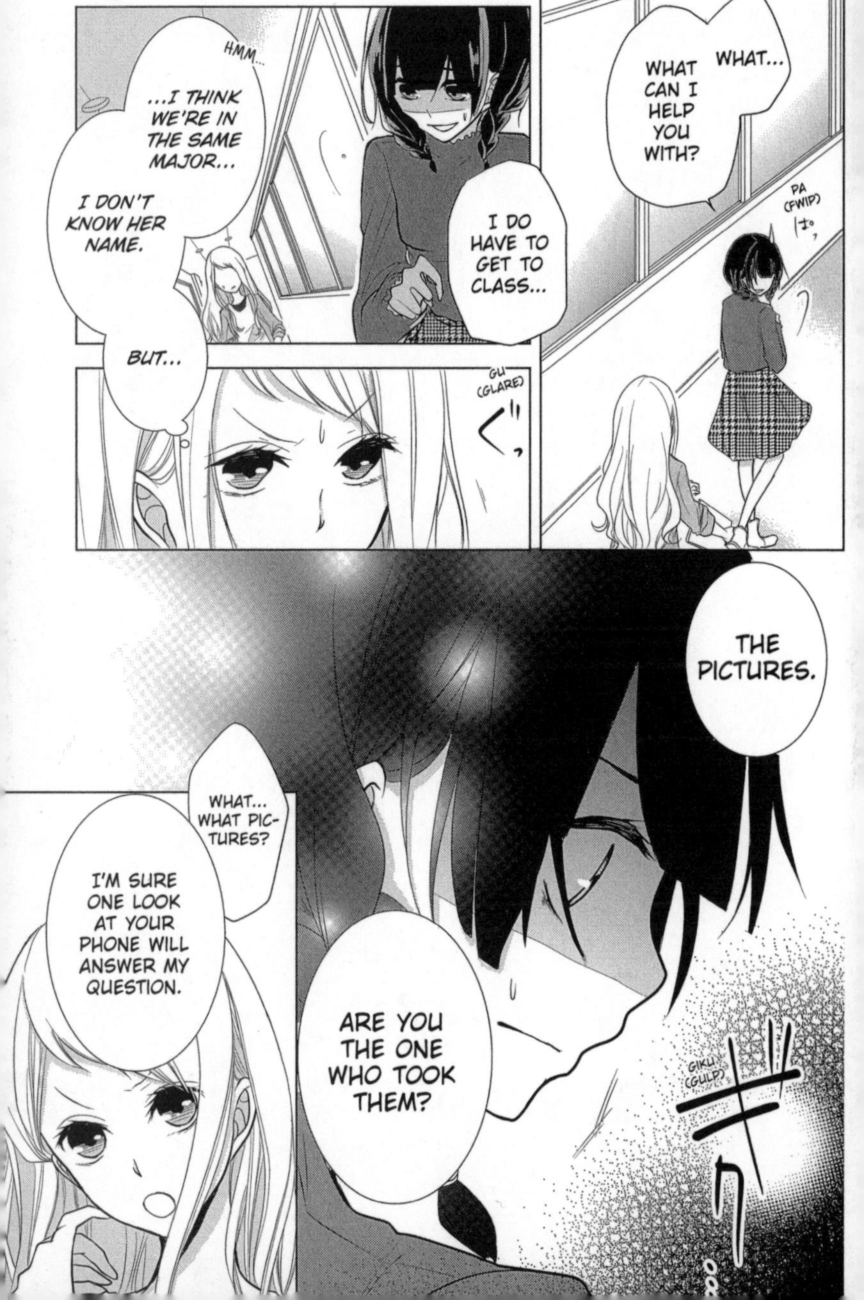
WHAT...
WHAT CAN I HELP YOU WITH?
PA (FWIP)
I DO HAVE TO GET TO CLASS...
HMM...
...I THINK WE'RE IN THE SAME MAJOR...
I DON'T KNOW HER NAME.
BUT...
GU (GLARE)
THE PICTURES.
WHAT... WHAT PIC-TURES?
ARE YOU THE ONE WHO TOOK THEM?
GIKU (GULP)
I'M SURE ONE LOOK AT YOUR PHONE WILL ANSWER MY QUESTION.

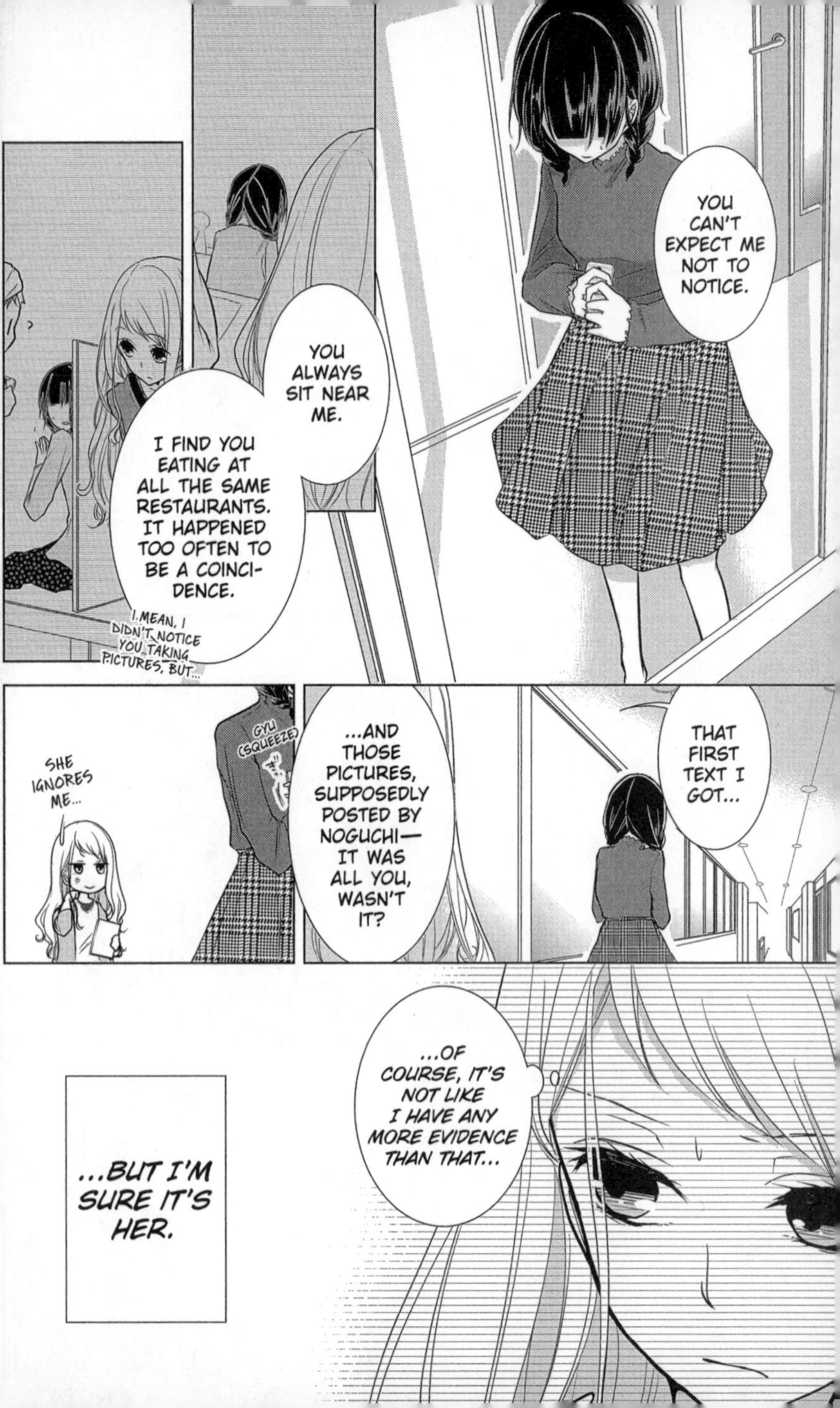
YOU CAN'T EXPECT ME NOT TO NOTICE.
YOU ALWAYS SIT NEAR ME.
I FIND YOU EATING AT ALL THE SAME RESTAURANTS. IT HAPPENED TOO OFTEN TO BE A COINCIDENCE.
I MEAN, I DIDN'T NOTICE YOU TAKING PICTURES, BUT...
THAT FIRST TEXT I GOT...
...AND THOSE PICTURES, SUPPOSEDLY POSTED BY NOGUCHI—IT WAS ALL YOU, WASN'T IT?
GYU (SQUEEZE)
SHE IGNORES ME...
...OF COURSE, IT'S NOT LIKE I HAVE ANY MORE EVIDENCE THAN THAT...
...BUT I'M SURE IT'S HER.

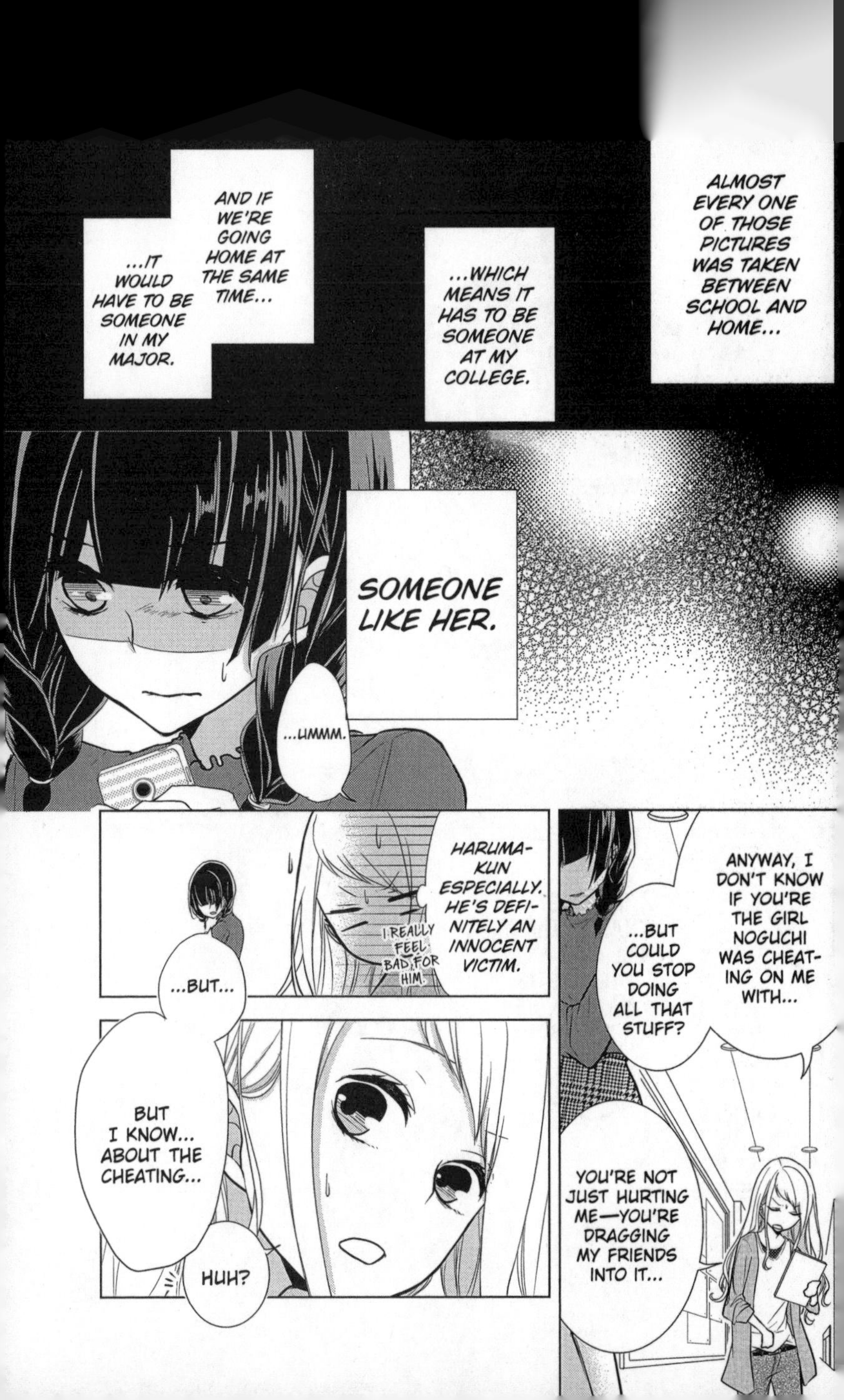
ALMOST EVERY ONE OF THOSE PICTURES WAS TAKEN BETWEEN SCHOOL AND HOME...
...WHICH MEANS IT HAS TO BE SOMEONE AT MY COLLEGE.
AND IF WE'RE GOING HOME AT THE SAME TIME...
...IT WOULD HAVE TO BE SOMEONE IN MY MAJOR.
SOMEONE LIKE HER.
...UMMM.
ANYWAY, I DON'T KNOW IF YOU'RE THE GIRL NOGUCHI WAS CHEATING ON ME WITH...
...BUT COULD YOU STOP DOING ALL THAT STUFF?
YOU'RE NOT JUST HURTING ME—YOU'RE DRAGGING MY FRIENDS INTO IT...
HARUMA-KUN ESPECIALLY. HE'S DEFINITELY AN INNOCENT VICTIM.
I REALLY FEEL BAD FOR HIM.
...BUT...
BUT I KNOW... ABOUT THE CHEATING...
HUH?

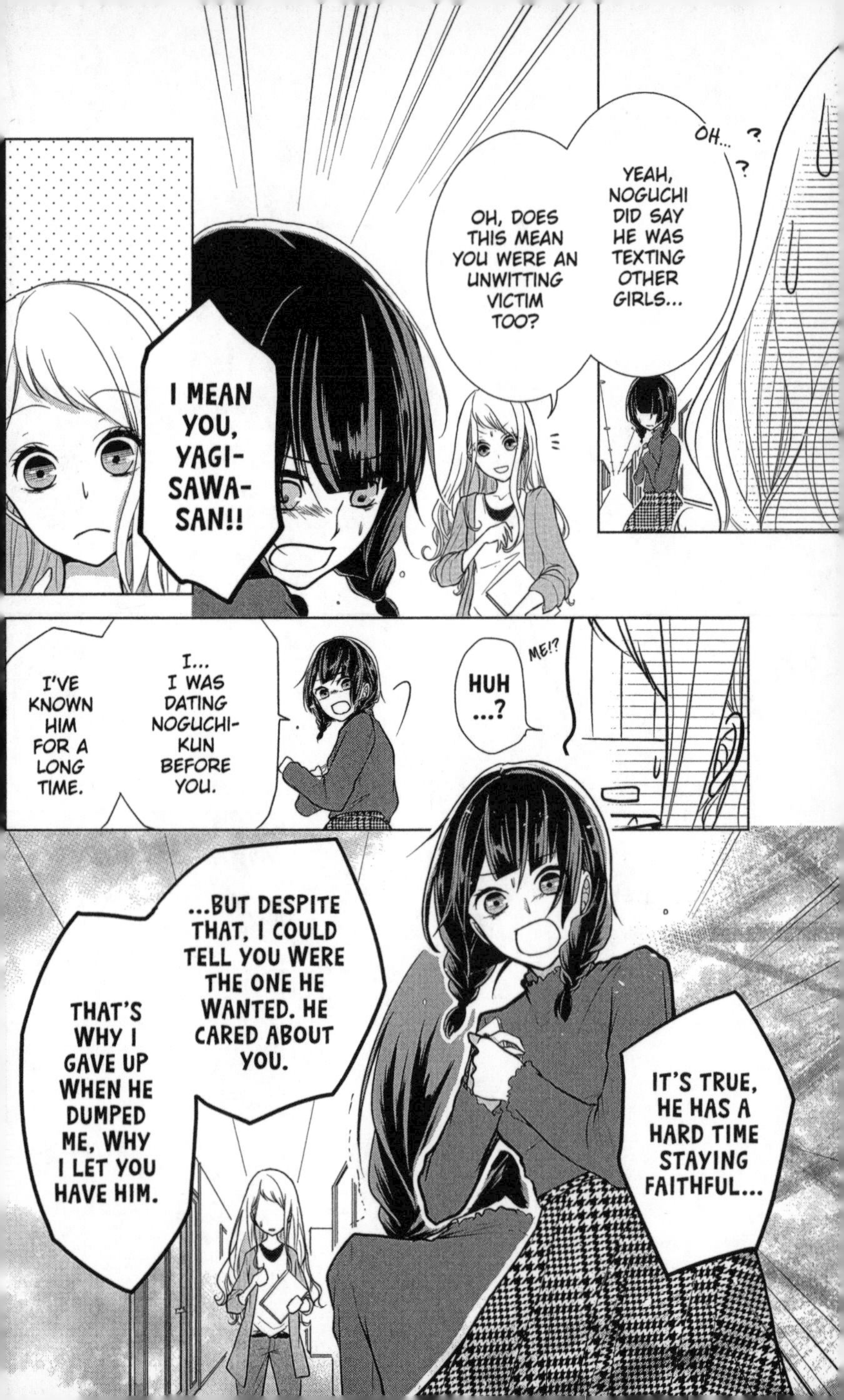
OH... ?
?
YEAH, NOGUCHI DID SAY HE WAS TEXTING OTHER GIRLS...
OH, DOES THIS MEAN YOU WERE AN UNWITTING VICTIM TOO?
I MEAN YOU, YAGI-SAWA-SAN!!
ME!?
HUH ...?
I... I WAS DATING NOGUCHI-KUN BEFORE YOU.
I'VE KNOWN HIM FOR A LONG TIME.
IT'S TRUE, HE HAS A HARD TIME STAYING FAITHFUL...
...BUT DESPITE THAT, I COULD TELL YOU WERE THE ONE HE WANTED. HE CARED ABOUT YOU.
THAT'S WHY I GAVE UP WHEN HE DUMPED ME, WHY I LET YOU HAVE HIM.

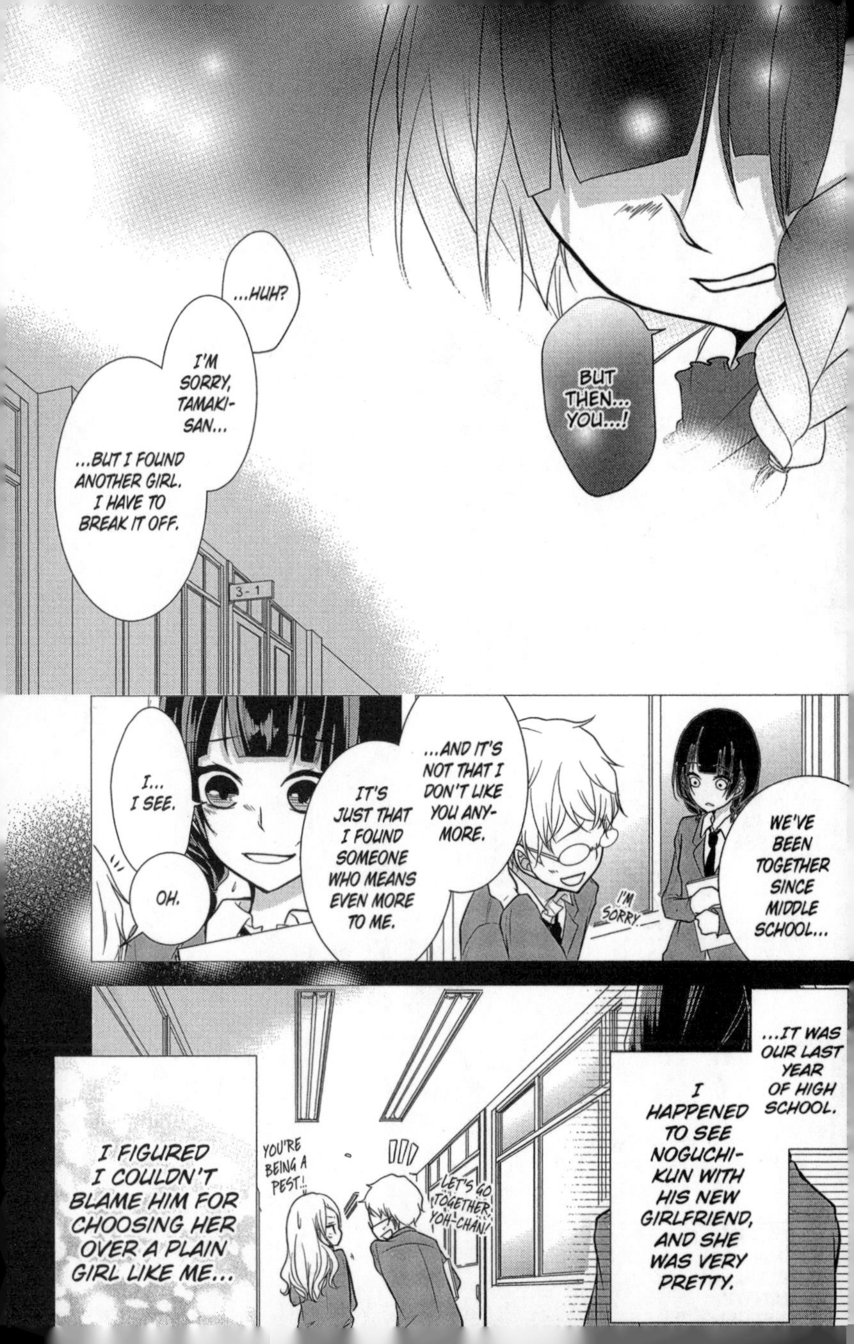
BUT THEN... YOU...!
...HUH?
I'M SORRY, TAMAKI-SAN...
...BUT I FOUND ANOTHER GIRL. I HAVE TO BREAK IT OFF.
3-1
WE'VE BEEN TOGETHER SINCE MIDDLE SCHOOL...
I'M SORRY.
...AND IT'S NOT THAT I DON'T LIKE YOU ANYMORE.
IT'S JUST THAT I FOUND SOMEONE WHO MEANS EVEN MORE TO ME.
I... I SEE.
OH.
...IT WAS OUR LAST YEAR OF HIGH SCHOOL.
I HAPPENED TO SEE NOGUCHI-KUN WITH HIS NEW GIRLFRIEND, AND SHE WAS VERY PRETTY.
LET'S GO TOGETHER, YOH-CHAN!
YOU'RE BEING A PEST!!
I FIGURED I COULDN'T BLAME HIM FOR CHOOSING HER OVER A PLAIN GIRL LIKE ME...

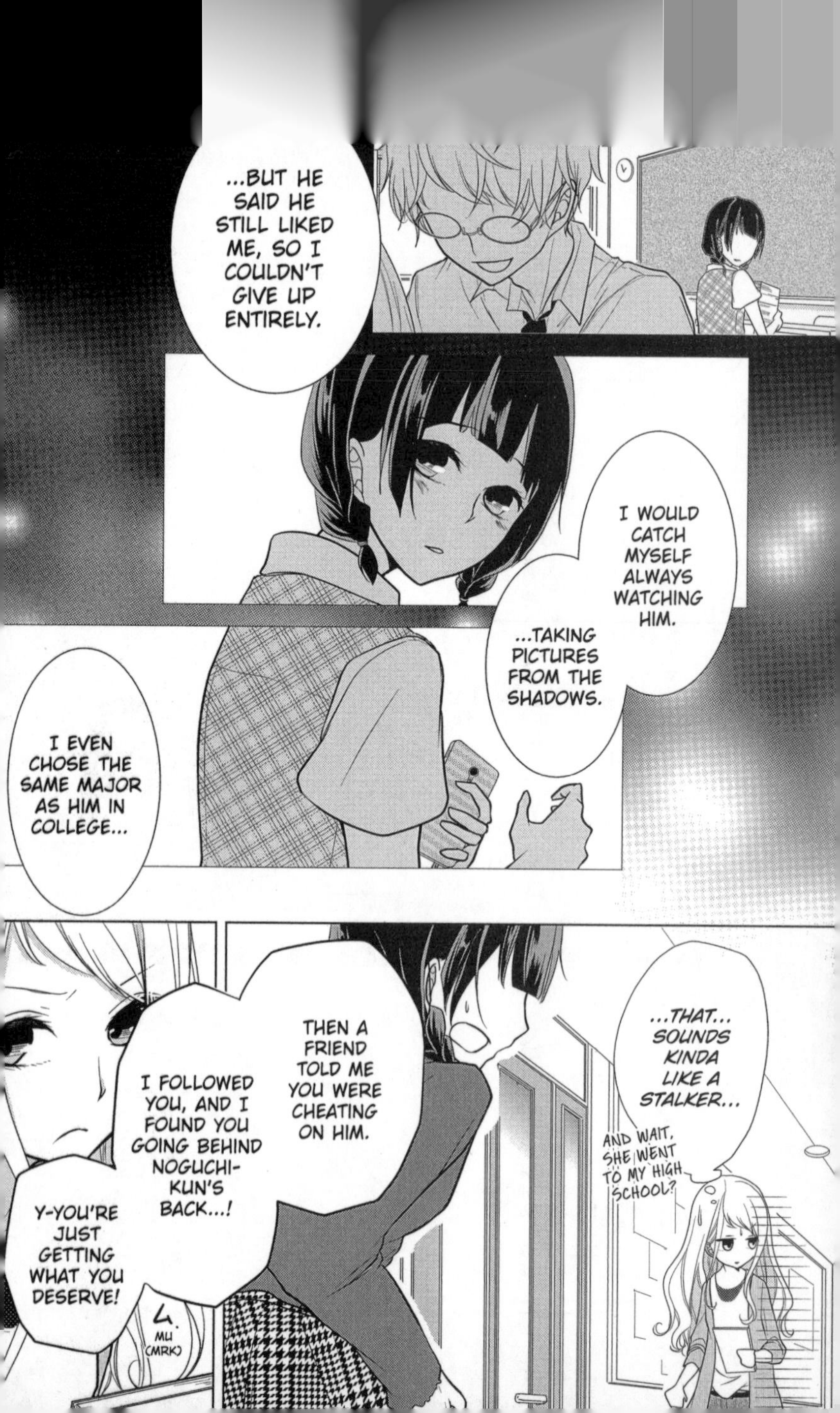
...BUT HE SAID HE STILL LIKED ME, SO I COULDN'T GIVE UP ENTIRELY.
I WOULD CATCH MYSELF ALWAYS WATCHING HIM.
...TAKING PICTURES FROM THE SHADOWS.
I EVEN CHOSE THE SAME MAJOR AS HIM IN COLLEGE...
...THAT... SOUNDS KINDA LIKE A STALKER...
AND WAIT, SHE WENT TO MY HIGH SCHOOL?
THEN A FRIEND TOLD ME YOU WERE CHEATING ON HIM.
I FOLLOWED YOU, AND I FOUND YOU GOING BEHIND NOGUCHI-KUN'S BACK...!
Y-YOU'RE JUST GETTING WHAT YOU DESERVE!
MU (MRK)

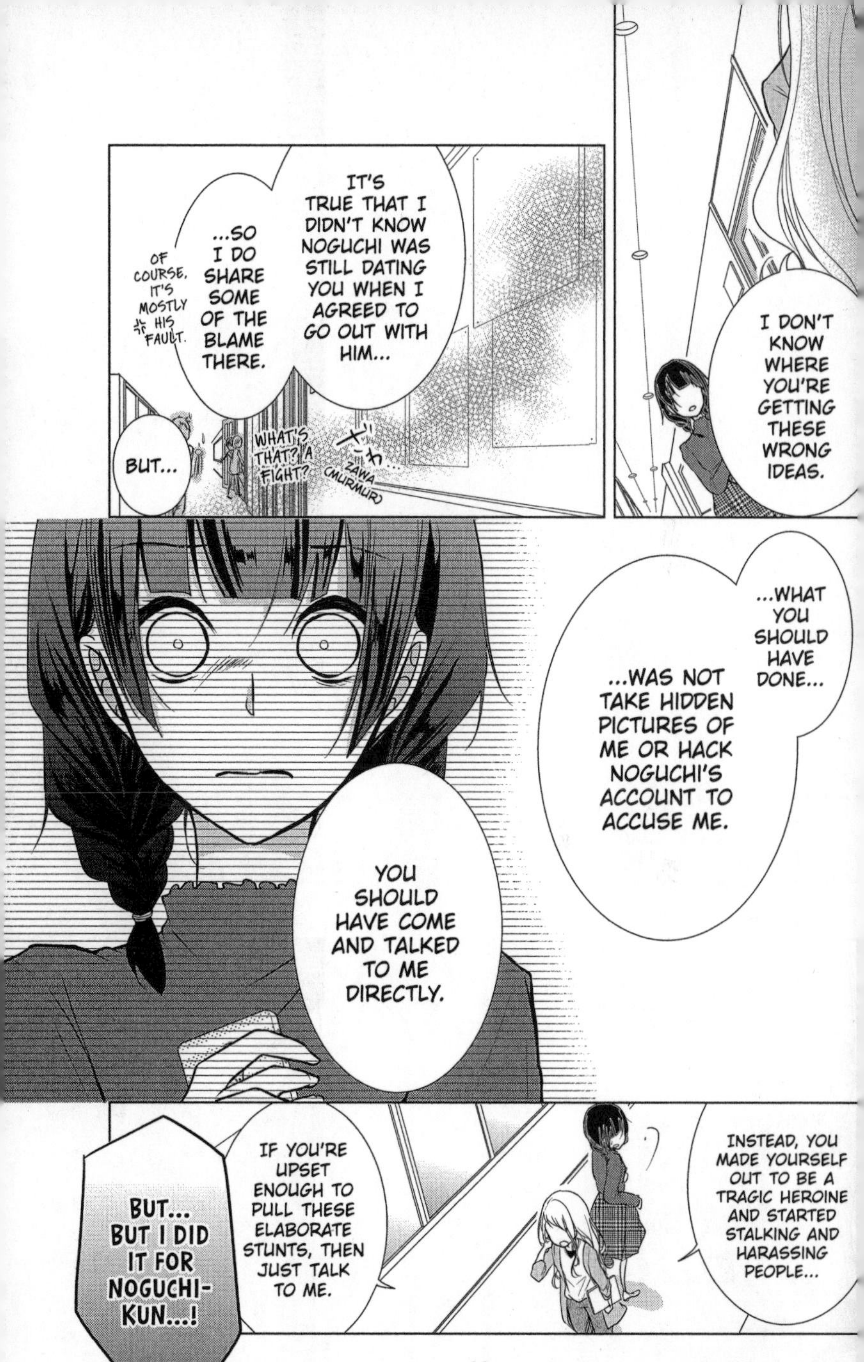

I DON'T KNOW WHERE YOU'RE GETTING THESE WRONG IDEAS.
IT'S TRUE THAT I DIDN'T KNOW NOGUCHI WAS STILL DATING YOU WHEN I AGREED TO GO OUT WITH HIM...
...SO I DO SHARE SOME OF THE BLAME THERE.
OF COURSE, IT'S MOSTLY HIS FAULT.
ZAWA (MURMUR)
WHAT'S THAT? A FIGHT?
BUT...
...WHAT YOU SHOULD HAVE DONE...
...WAS NOT TAKE HIDDEN PICTURES OF ME OR HACK NOGUCHI'S ACCOUNT TO ACCUSE ME.
YOU SHOULD HAVE COME AND TALKED TO ME DIRECTLY.
INSTEAD, YOU MADE YOURSELF OUT TO BE A TRAGIC HEROINE AND STARTED STALKING AND HARASSING PEOPLE...
IF YOU'RE UPSET ENOUGH TO PULL THESE ELABORATE STUNTS, THEN JUST TALK TO ME.
BUT... BUT I DID IT FOR NOGUCHI-KUN...!

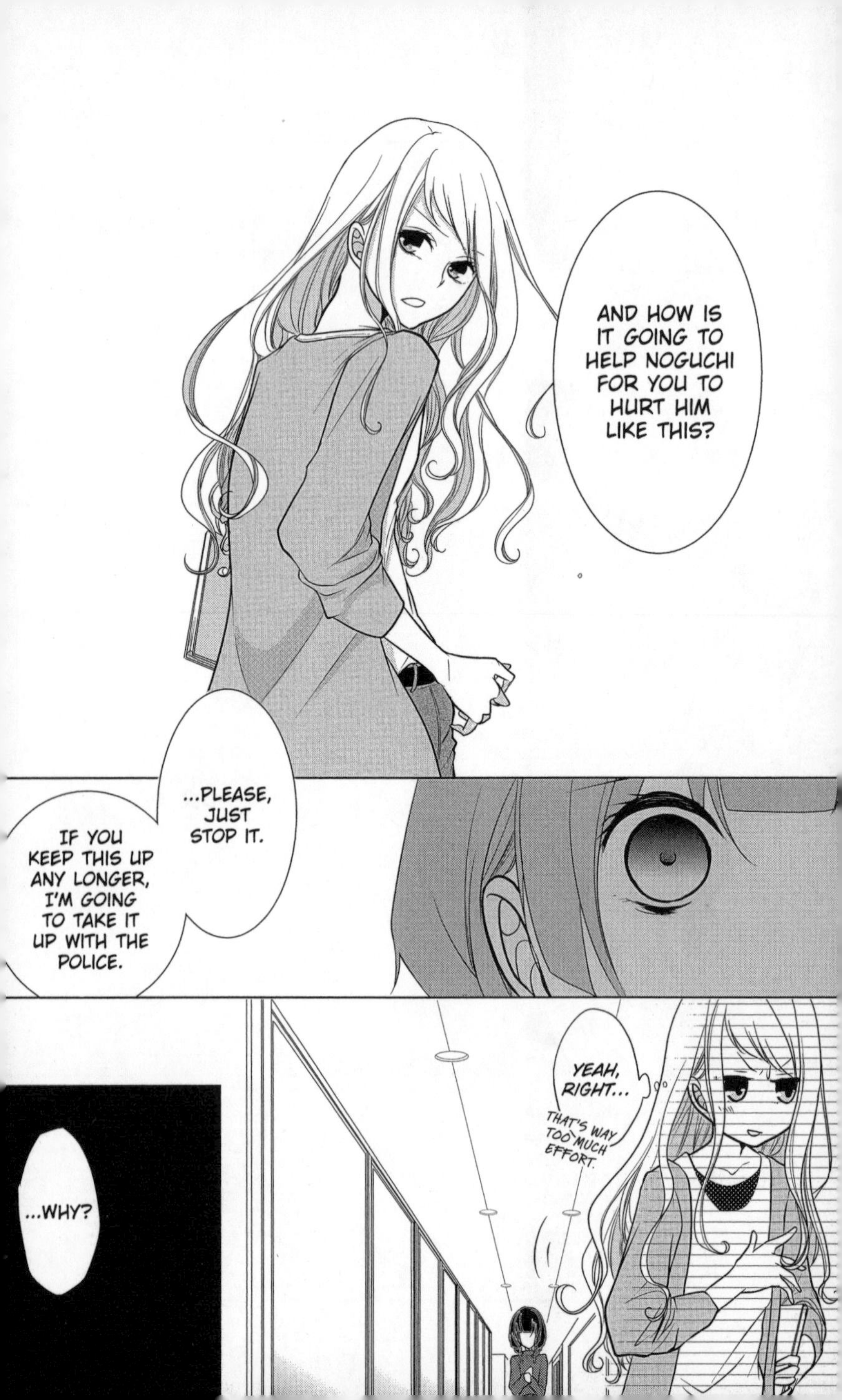
AND HOW IS IT GOING TO HELP NOGUCHI FOR YOU TO HURT HIM LIKE THIS?
...PLEASE, JUST STOP IT.
IF YOU KEEP THIS UP ANY LONGER, I'M GOING TO TAKE IT UP WITH THE POLICE.
YEAH, RIGHT...
THAT'S WAY TOO MUCH EFFORT.
...WHY?

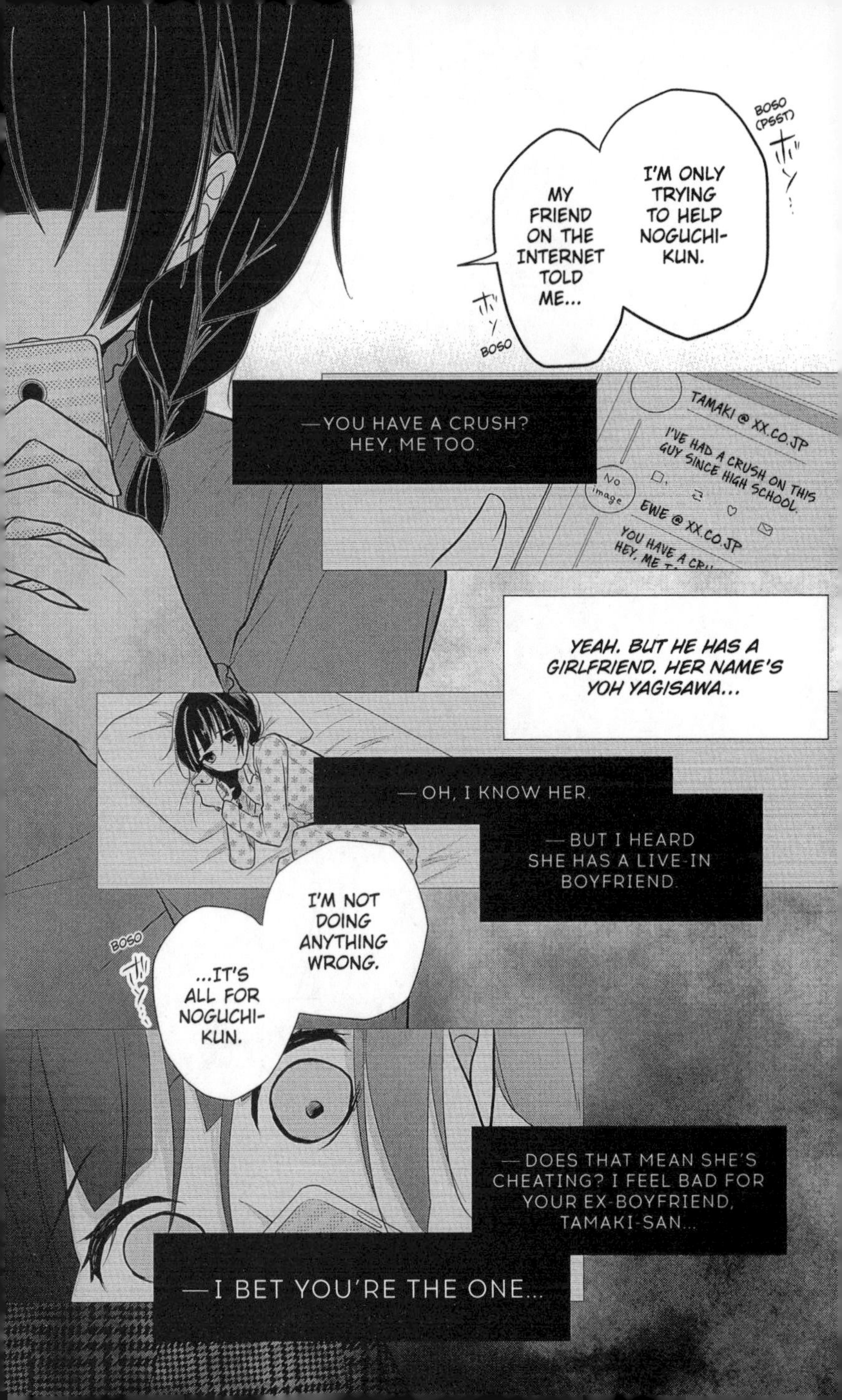
BOSO (PSST)
I'M ONLY TRYING TO HELP NOGUCHI-KUN.
MY FRIEND ON THE INTERNET TOLD ME...
BOSO
TAMAKI @ XX.CO.JP
I'VE HAD A CRUSH ON THIS GUY SINCE HIGH SCHOOL.
No image
EWE @ XX.CO.JP
—YOU HAVE A CRUSH? HEY, ME TOO.
YEAH. BUT HE HAS A GIRLFRIEND. HER NAME'S YOH YAGISAWA...
—OH, I KNOW HER.
—BUT I HEARD SHE HAS A LIVE-IN BOYFRIEND.
I'M NOT DOING ANYTHING WRONG.
...IT'S ALL FOR NOGUCHI-KUN.
BOSO
—DOES THAT MEAN SHE'S CHEATING? I FEEL BAD FOR YOUR EX-BOYFRIEND, TAMAKI-SAN...
—I BET YOU'RE THE ONE...

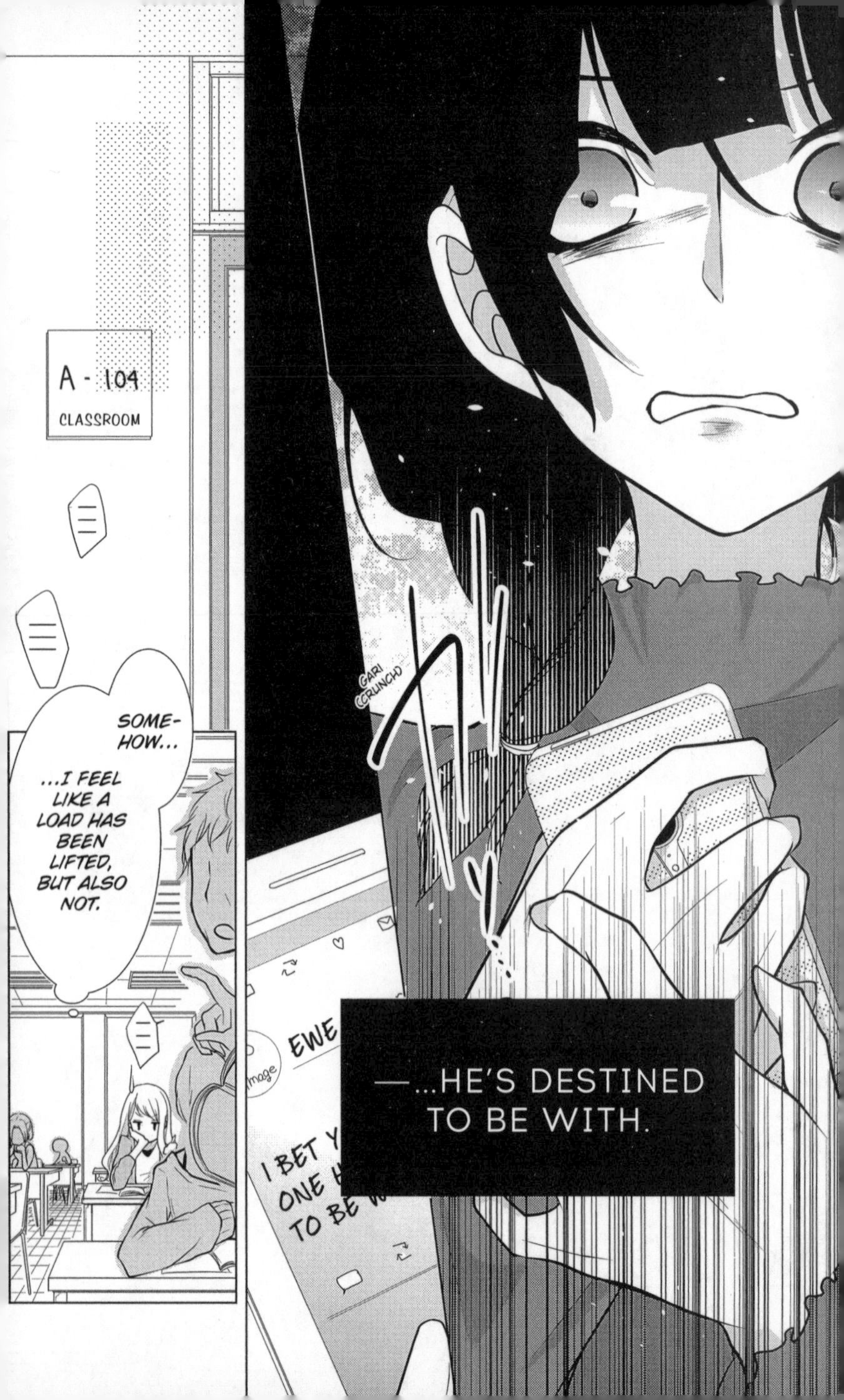
GARI (CRUNCH)
EWE
—...HE'S DESTINED TO BE WITH.
A - 104 CLASSROOM
SOMEHOW... ...I FEEL LIKE A LOAD HAS BEEN LIFTED, BUT ALSO NOT.

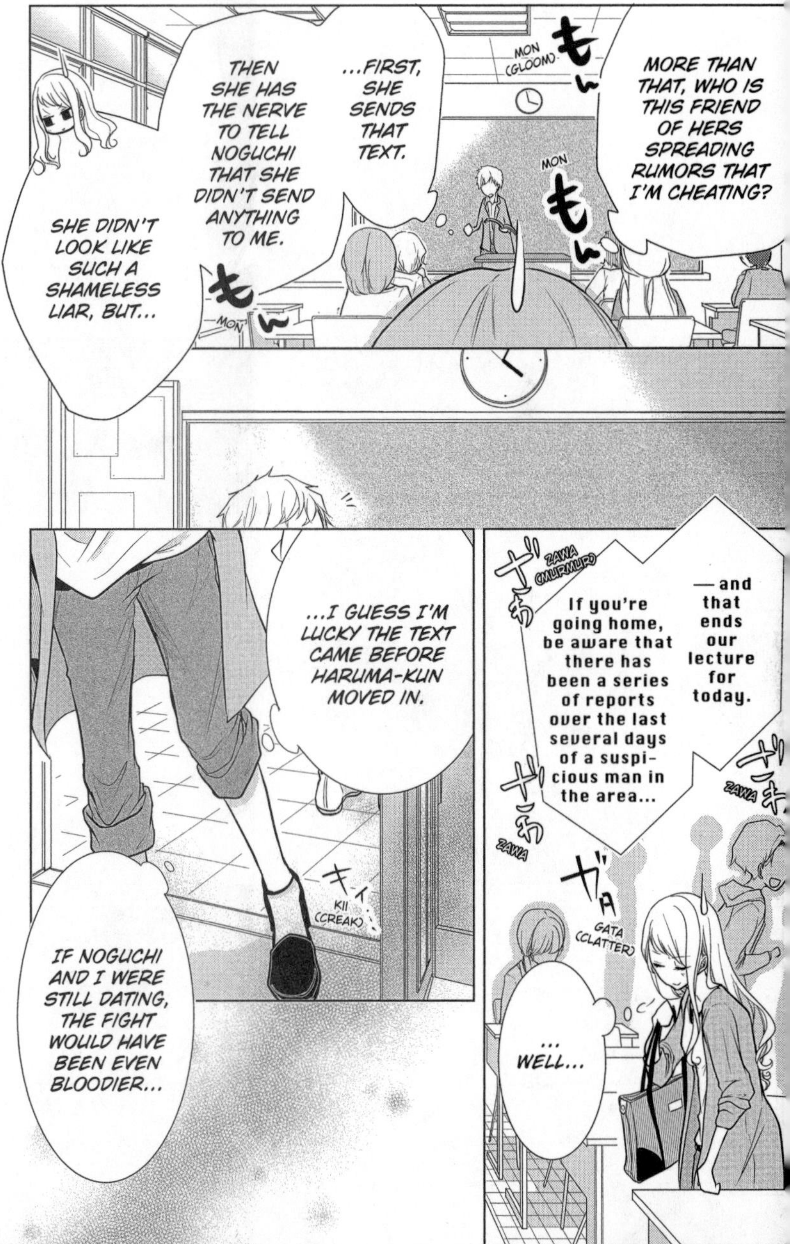
MON (GLOOM)
MON
MORE THAN THAT, WHO IS THIS FRIEND OF HERS SPREADING RUMORS THAT I'M CHEATING?
...FIRST, SHE SENDS THAT TEXT.
THEN SHE HAS THE NERVE TO TELL NOGUCHI THAT SHE DIDN'T SEND ANYTHING TO ME.
MON
SHE DIDN'T LOOK LIKE SUCH A SHAMELESS LIAR, BUT...
—and that ends our lecture for today.
If you're going home, be aware that there has been a series of reports over the last several days of a suspicious man in the area...
ZAWA (MURMUR)
ZAWA
ZAWA
GATA (CLATTER)
...WELL...
...I GUESS I'M LUCKY THE TEXT CAME BEFORE HARUMA-KUN MOVED IN.
KII (CREAK)
IF NOGUCHI AND I WERE STILL DATING, THE FIGHT WOULD HAVE BEEN EVEN BLOODIER...

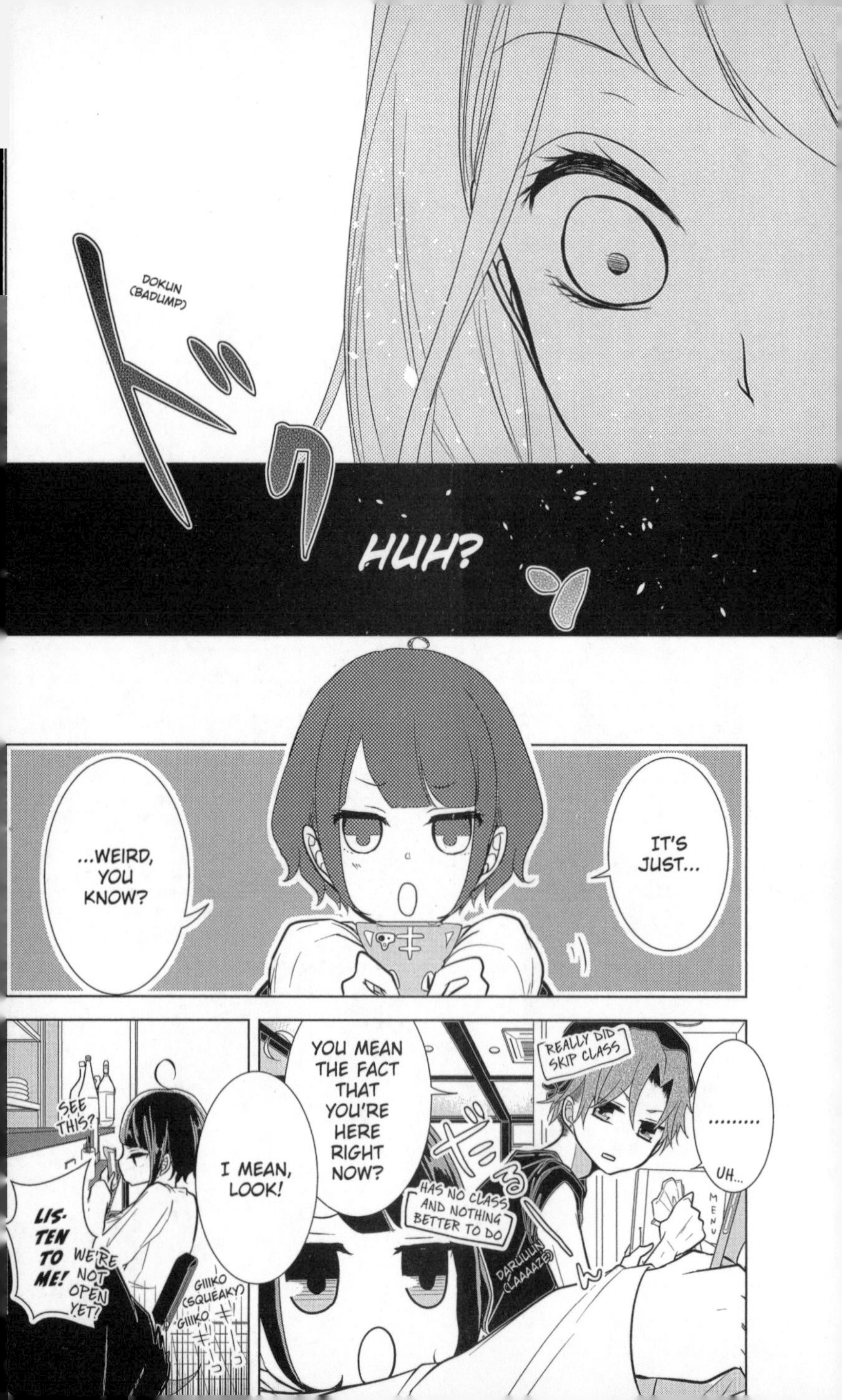
DOKUN (BADUMP)
HUH?
IT'S JUST...
...WEIRD, YOU KNOW?
REALLY DID SKIP CLASS
..........
UH...
MENU
HAS NO CLASS AND NOTHING BETTER TO DO
DARULUN (CLAAAAZE)
YOU MEAN THE FACT THAT YOU'RE HERE RIGHT NOW?
I MEAN, LOOK!
SEE THIS?
LIS-TEN TO ME!
WE'RE NOT OPEN YET!
GIIKO (SQUEAKY) GIIKO

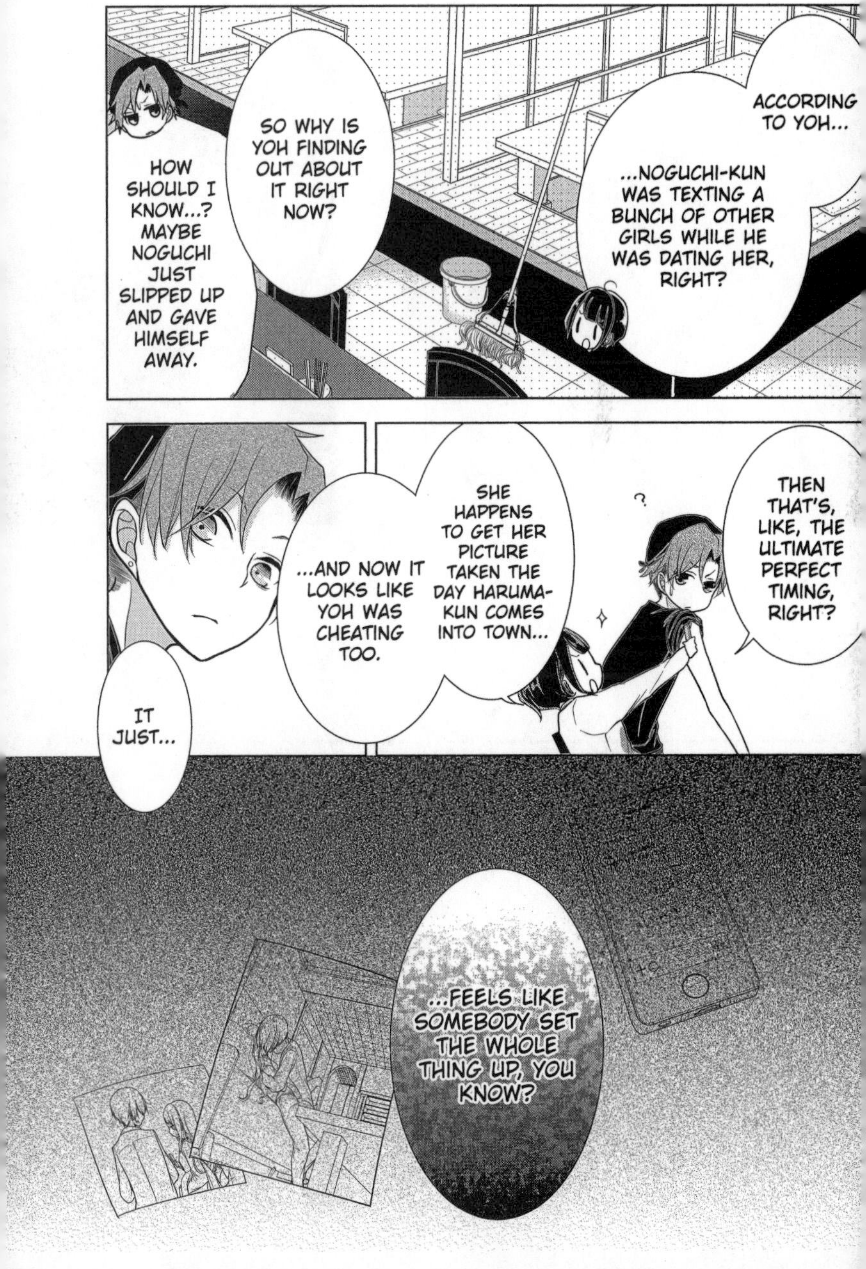
ACCORDING TO YOH...
...NOGUCHI-KUN WAS TEXTING A BUNCH OF OTHER GIRLS WHILE HE WAS DATING HER, RIGHT?
SO WHY IS YOH FINDING OUT ABOUT IT RIGHT NOW?
HOW SHOULD I KNOW...? MAYBE NOGUCHI JUST SLIPPED UP AND GAVE HIMSELF AWAY.
THEN THAT'S, LIKE, THE ULTIMATE PERFECT TIMING, RIGHT?
?
SHE HAPPENS TO GET HER PICTURE TAKEN THE DAY HARUMA-KUN COMES INTO TOWN...
...AND NOW IT LOOKS LIKE YOH WAS CHEATING TOO.
IT JUST...
...FEELS LIKE SOMEBODY SET THE WHOLE THING UP, YOU KNOW?

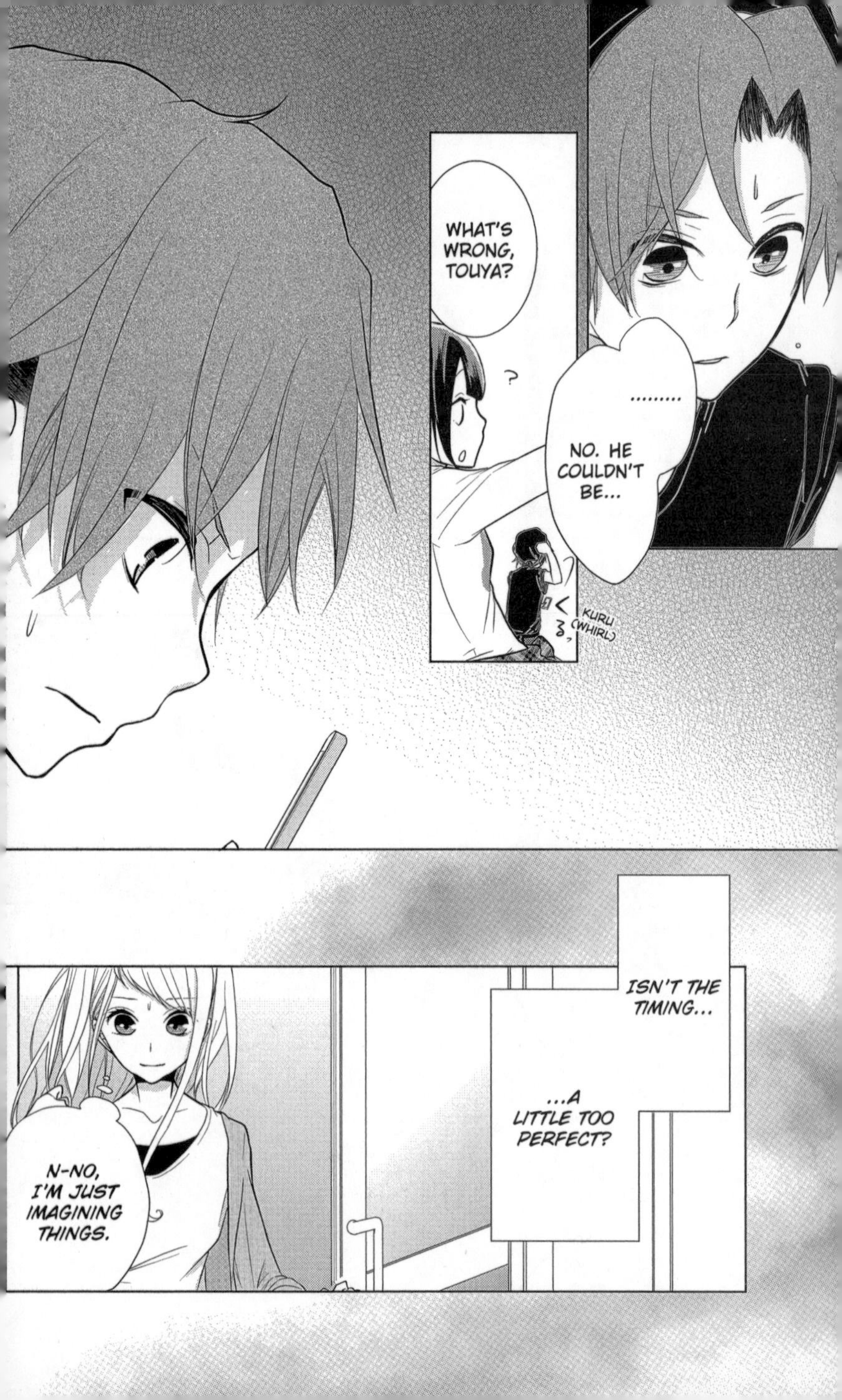
WHAT'S WRONG, TOUYA?
?
.........
NO. HE COULDN'T BE...
KURU (WHIRL)
ISN'T THE TIMING...
...A LITTLE TOO PERFECT?
N-NO, I'M JUST IMAGINING THINGS.

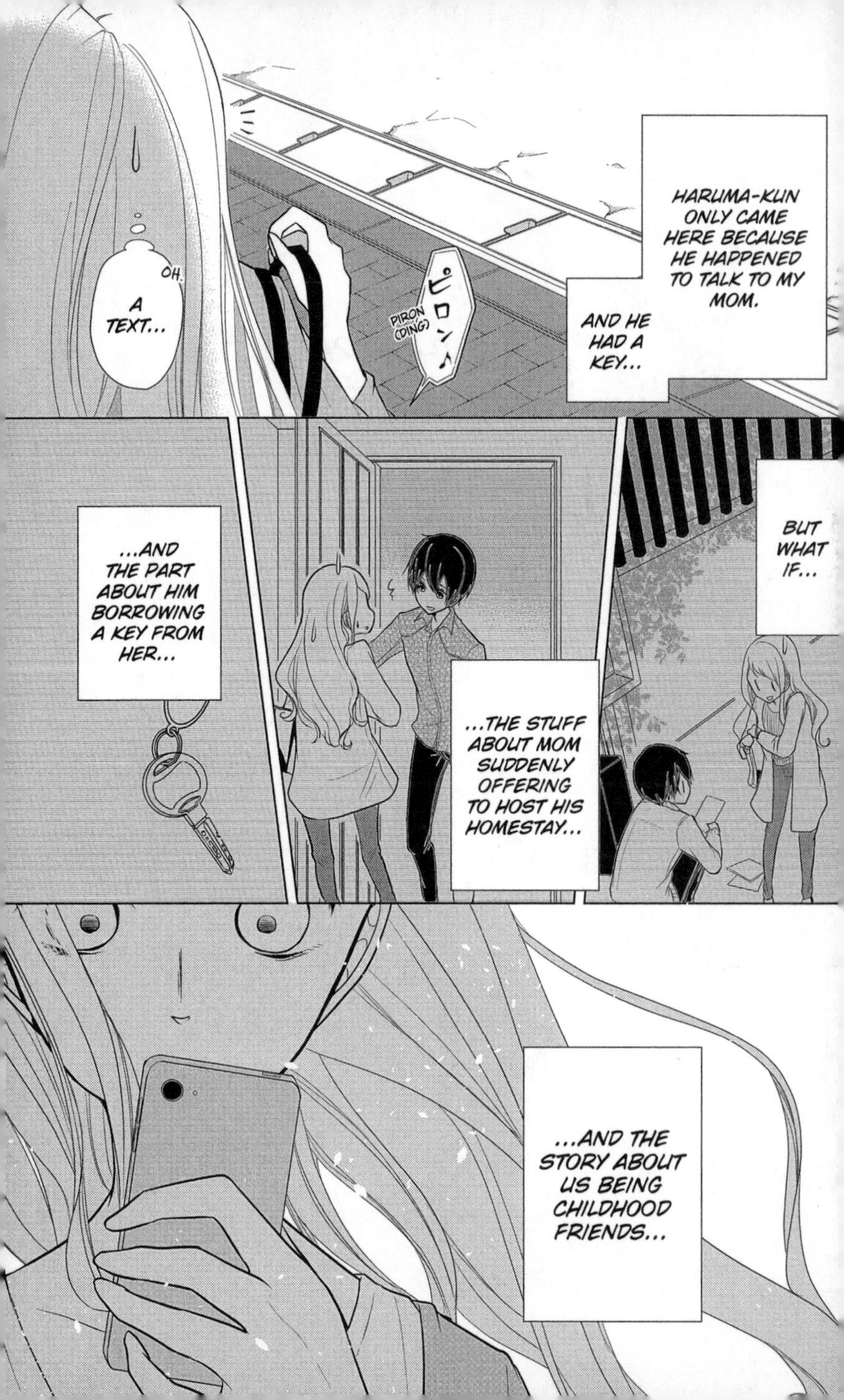
HARUMA-KUN ONLY CAME HERE BECAUSE HE HAPPENED TO TALK TO MY MOM.
AND HE HAD A KEY...
ピロン♪
PIRON (DING)
OH. A TEXT...
BUT WHAT IF...
...THE STUFF ABOUT MOM SUDDENLY OFFERING TO HOST HIS HOMESTAY...
...AND THE PART ABOUT HIM BORROWING A KEY FROM HER...
...AND THE STORY ABOUT US BEING CHILDHOOD FRIENDS...

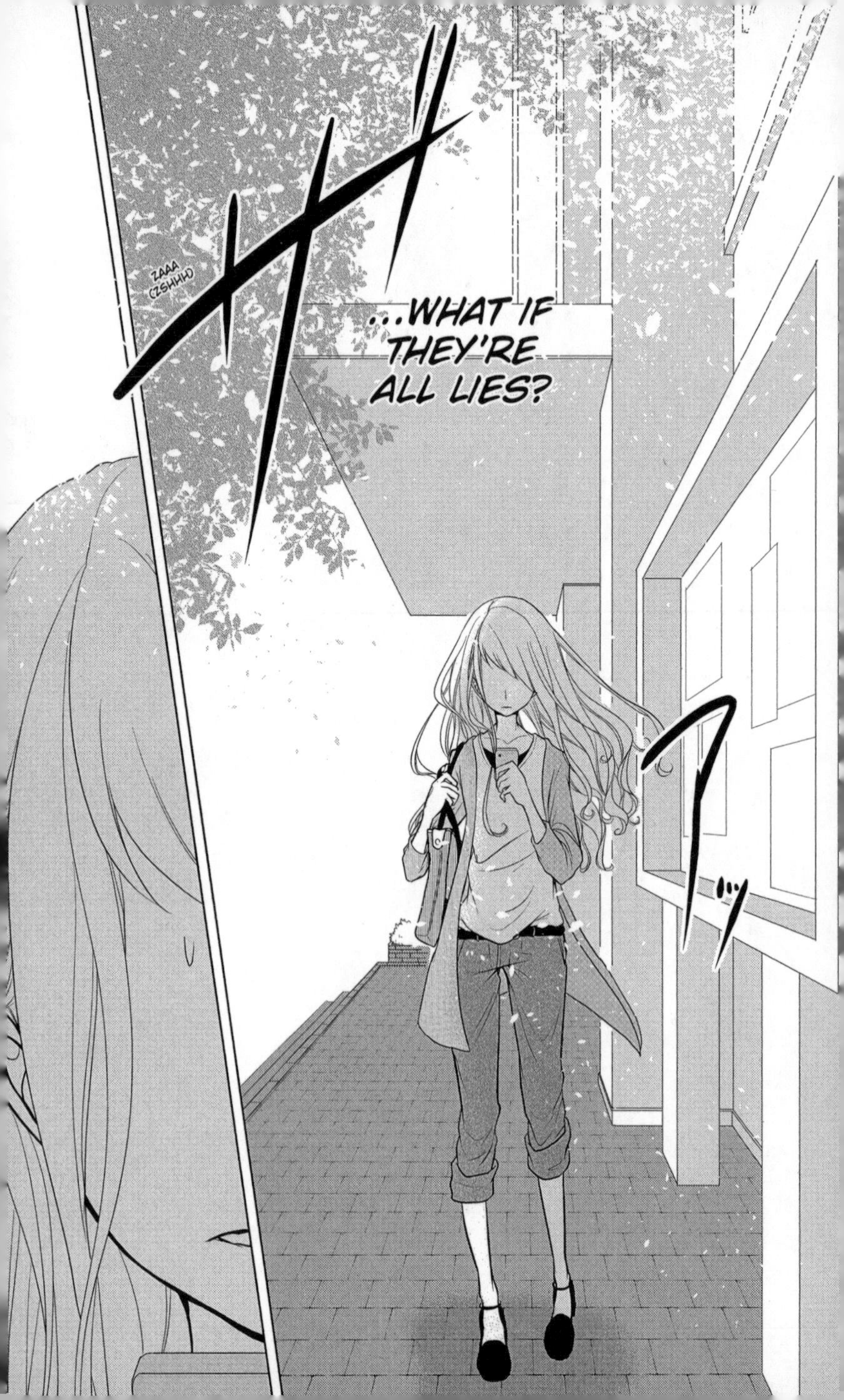
...WHAT IF THEY'RE ALL LIES?
ZAAA (ZSHHH)
アッ

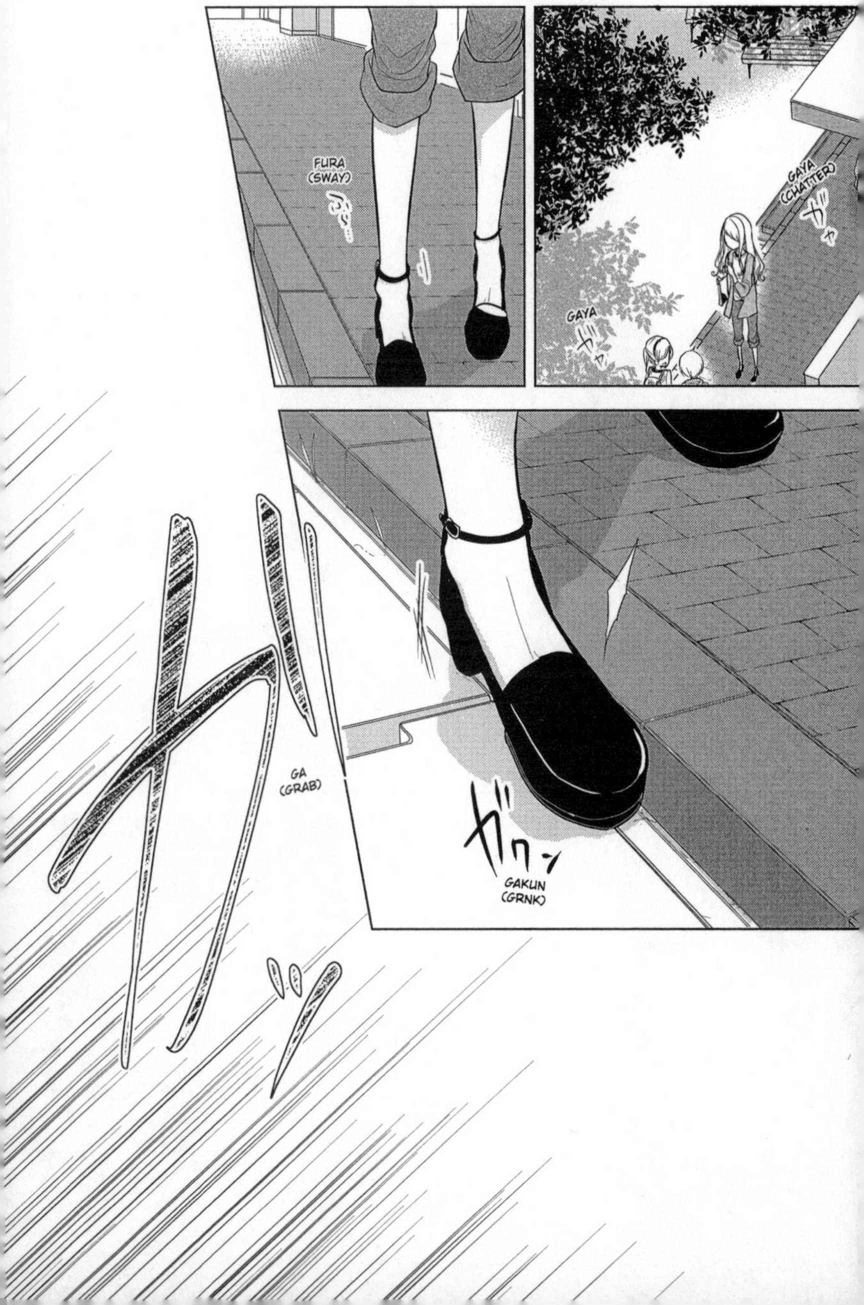
GAYA
(CHATTER)
GAYA
FURA
(SWAY)
GAKUN
(GRNK)
GA
(GRAB)

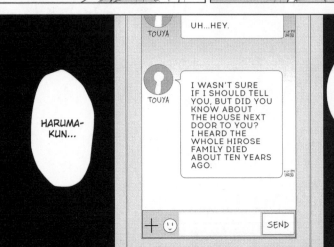

TOUYA

UH...HEY.

TOUYA

I WASN'T SURE
IF I SHOULD TELL
YOU, BUT DID YOU
KNOW ABOUT
THE HOUSE NEXT
DOOR TO YOU?
I HEARD THE
WHOLE HIROSE
FAMILY DIED
ABOUT TEN YEARS
AGO.

HARUMA-
KUN...

H...

+ ☺

SEND

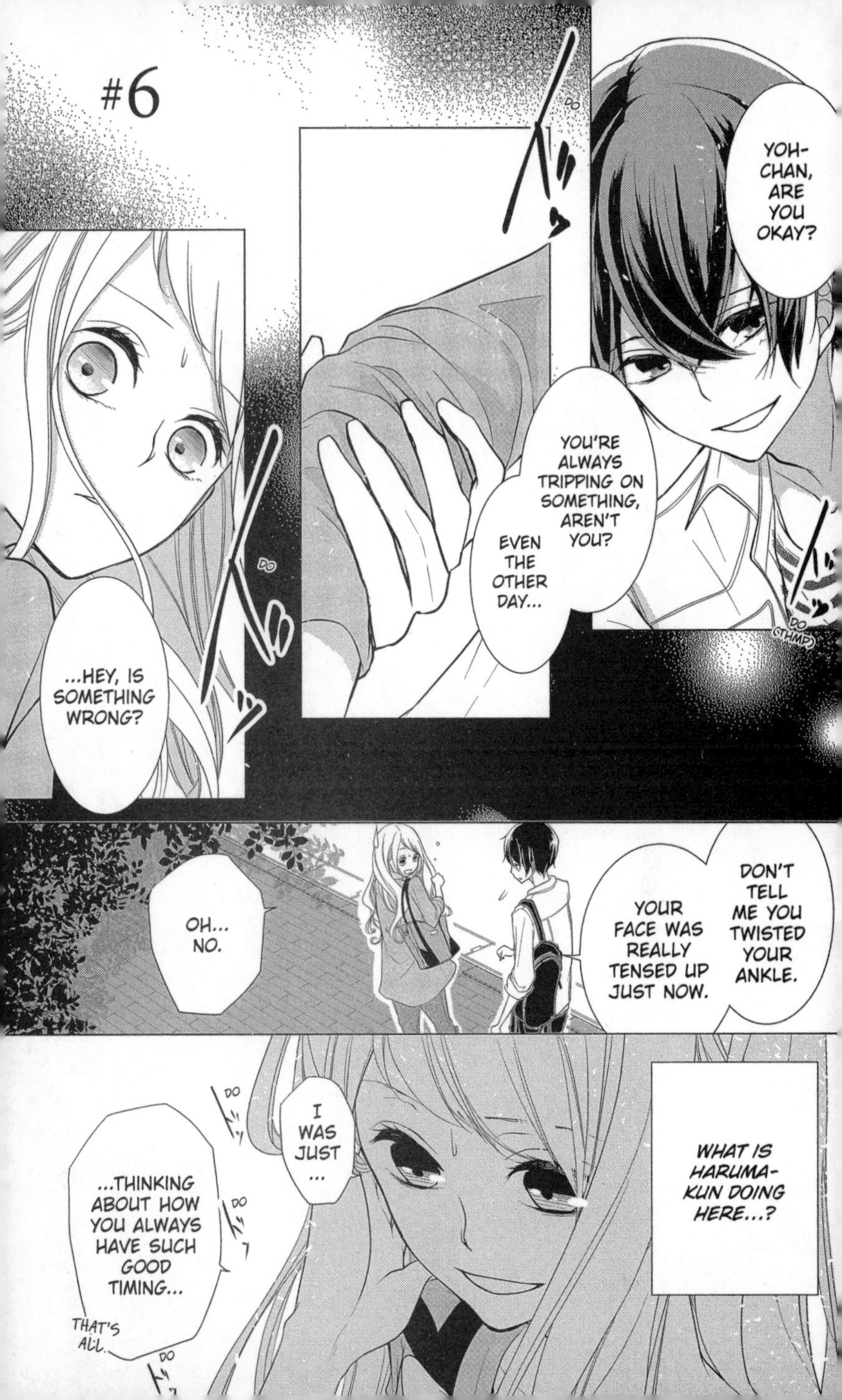
#6
DO
YOH-CHAN, ARE YOU OKAY?
YOU'RE ALWAYS TRIPPING ON SOMETHING, AREN'T YOU?
DO (THMP)
EVEN THE OTHER DAY...
DO
...HEY, IS SOMETHING WRONG?
DON'T TELL ME YOU TWISTED YOUR ANKLE.
YOUR FACE WAS REALLY TENSED UP JUST NOW.
OH... NO.
WHAT IS HARUMA-KUN DOING HERE...?
I WAS JUST ...
DO
DO
...THINKING ABOUT HOW YOU ALWAYS HAVE SUCH GOOD TIMING...
THAT'S ALL.
DO

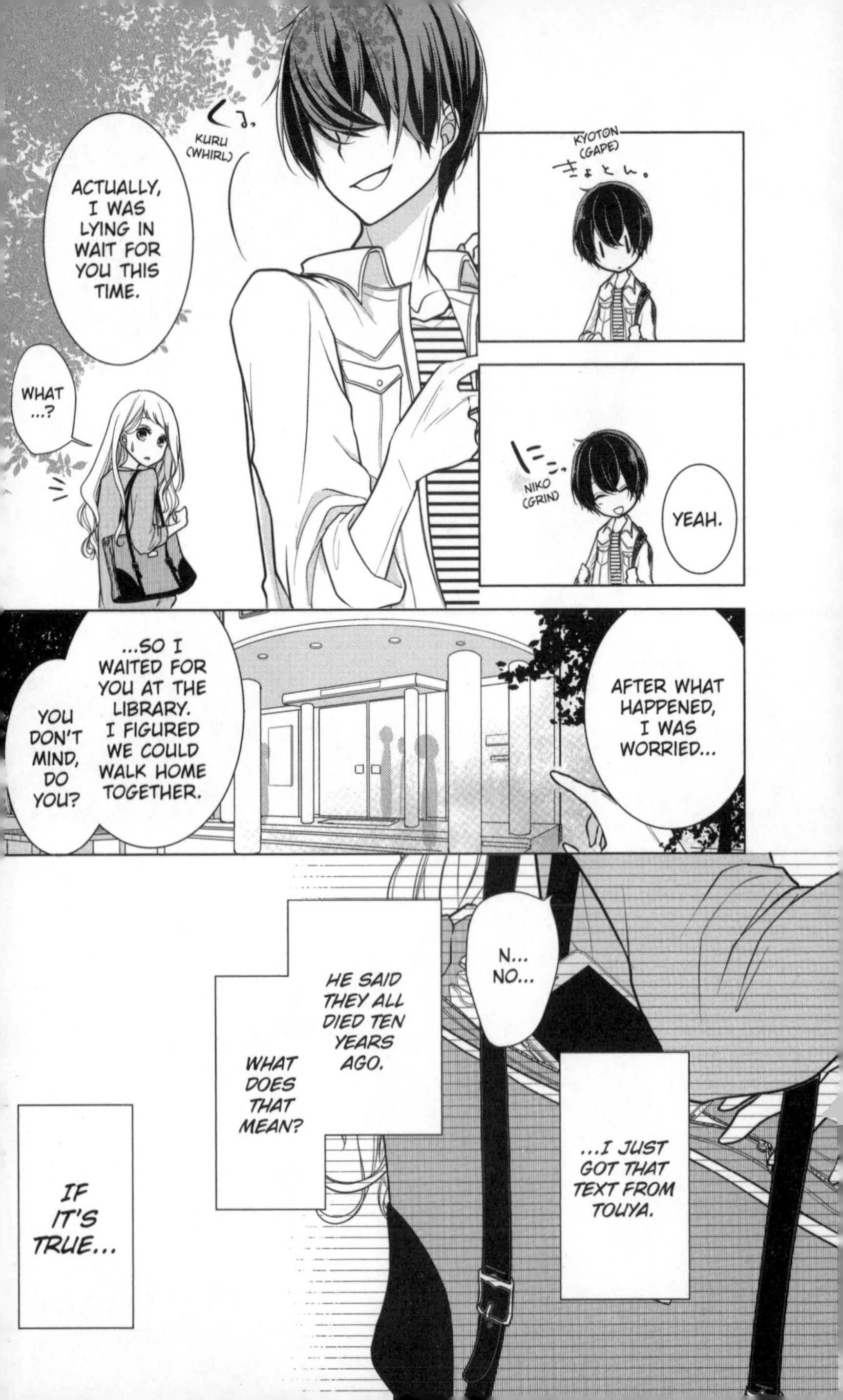
KYOTON (GAPE)
きょとん。
NIKO (GRIN)
にこ
YEAH.
KURU (WHIRL)
くる
ACTUALLY, I WAS LYING IN WAIT FOR YOU THIS TIME.
WHAT ...?
AFTER WHAT HAPPENED, I WAS WORRIED...
...SO I WAITED FOR YOU AT THE LIBRARY. I FIGURED WE COULD WALK HOME TOGETHER.
YOU DON'T MIND, DO YOU?
N... NO...
...I JUST GOT THAT TEXT FROM TOUYA.
HE SAID THEY ALL DIED TEN YEARS AGO.
WHAT DOES THAT MEAN?
IF IT'S TRUE...

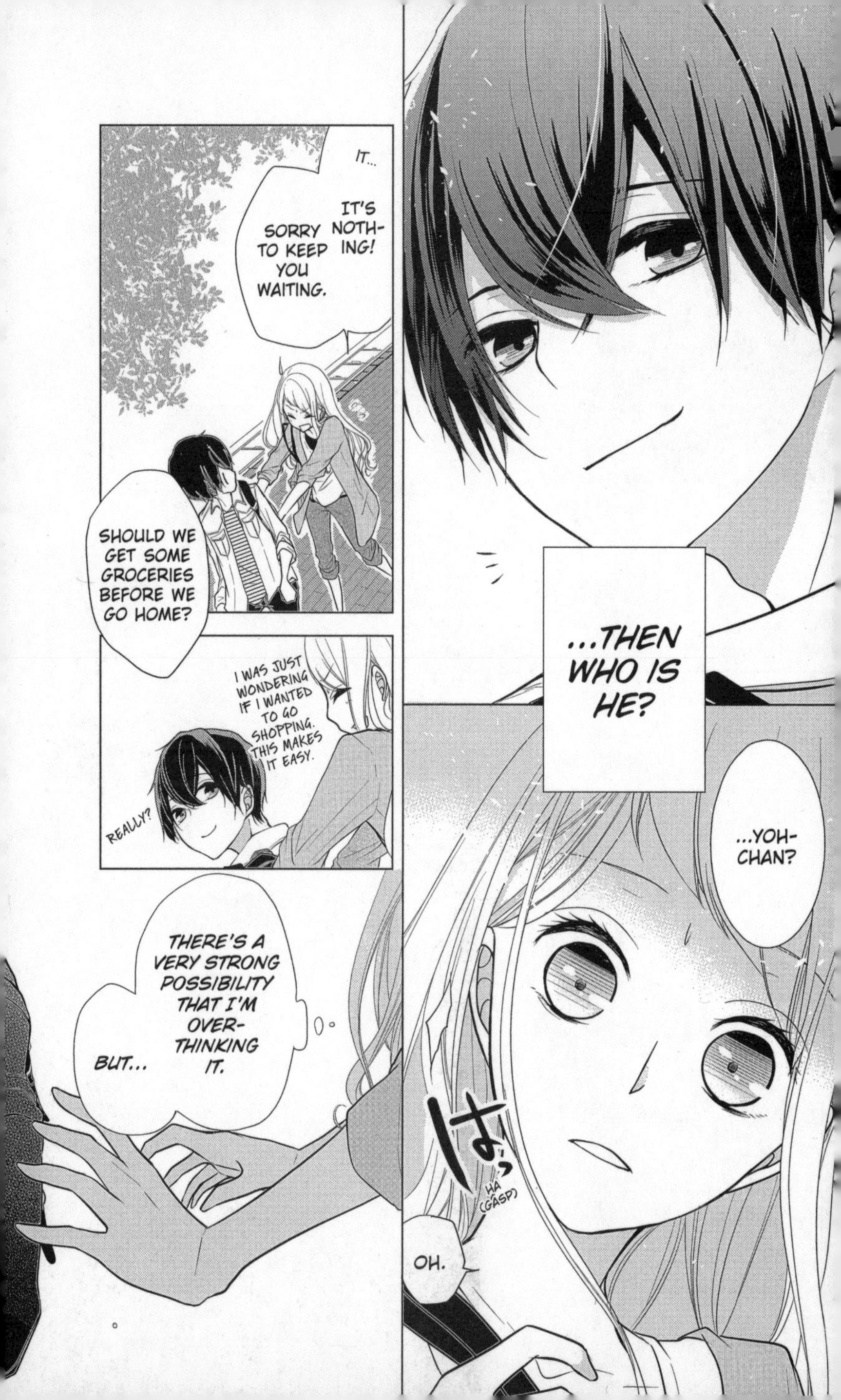
...THEN WHO IS HE?
...YOH-CHAN?
はっ
HA (GASP)
OH.
IT...
IT'S NOTHING!
SORRY TO KEEP YOU WAITING.
SHOULD WE GET SOME GROCERIES BEFORE WE GO HOME?
I WAS JUST WONDERING IF I WANTED TO GO SHOPPING. THIS MAKES IT EASY.
REALLY?
THERE'S A VERY STRONG POSSIBILITY THAT I'M OVER-THINKING IT.
BUT...

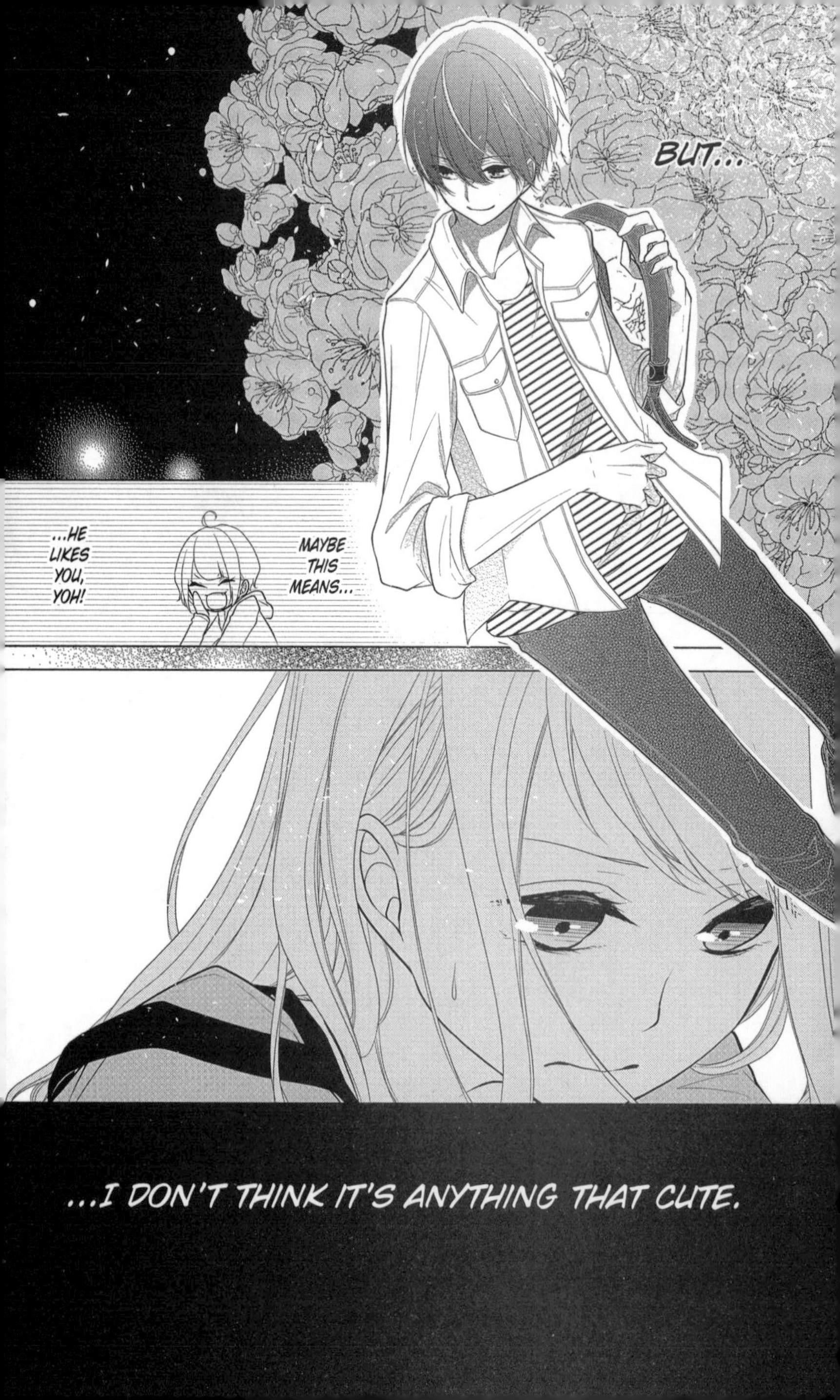
BUT...
MAYBE THIS MEANS...
...HE LIKES YOU, YOH!
...I DON'T THINK IT'S ANYTHING THAT CUTE.

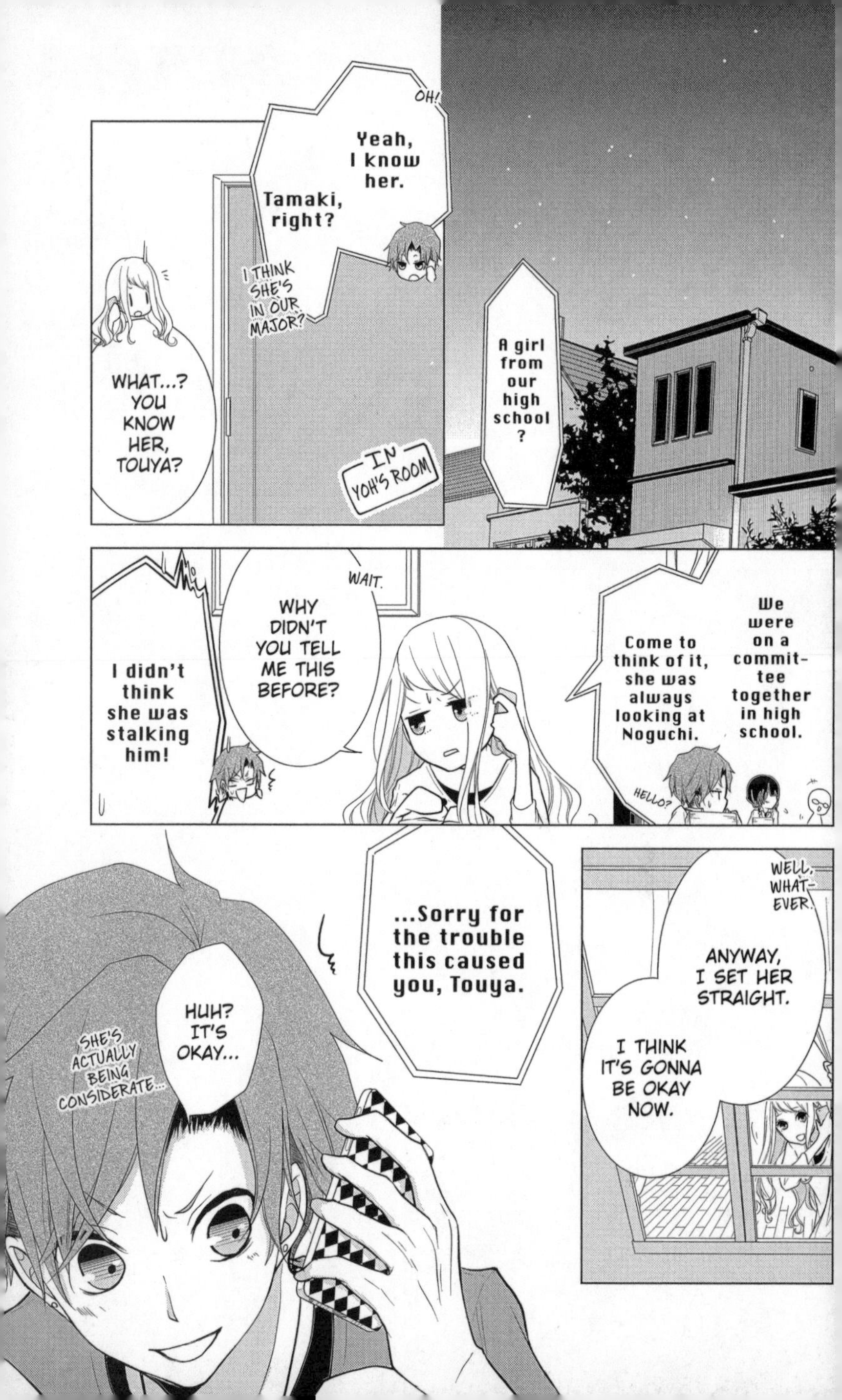
A girl from our high school?
OH!
Yeah, I know her.
Tamaki, right?
I THINK SHE'S IN OUR MAJOR?
IN YOH'S ROOM
WHAT...? YOU KNOW HER, TOUYA?
We were on a commit-tee together in high school.
Come to think of it, she was always looking at Noguchi.
HELLO?
WAIT.
WHY DIDN'T YOU TELL ME THIS BEFORE?
I didn't think she was stalking him!
WELL, WHAT-EVER.
ANYWAY, I SET HER STRAIGHT.
I THINK IT'S GONNA BE OKAY NOW.
...Sorry for the trouble this caused you, Touya.
HUH? IT'S OKAY...
SHE'S ACTUALLY BEING CONSIDERATE...

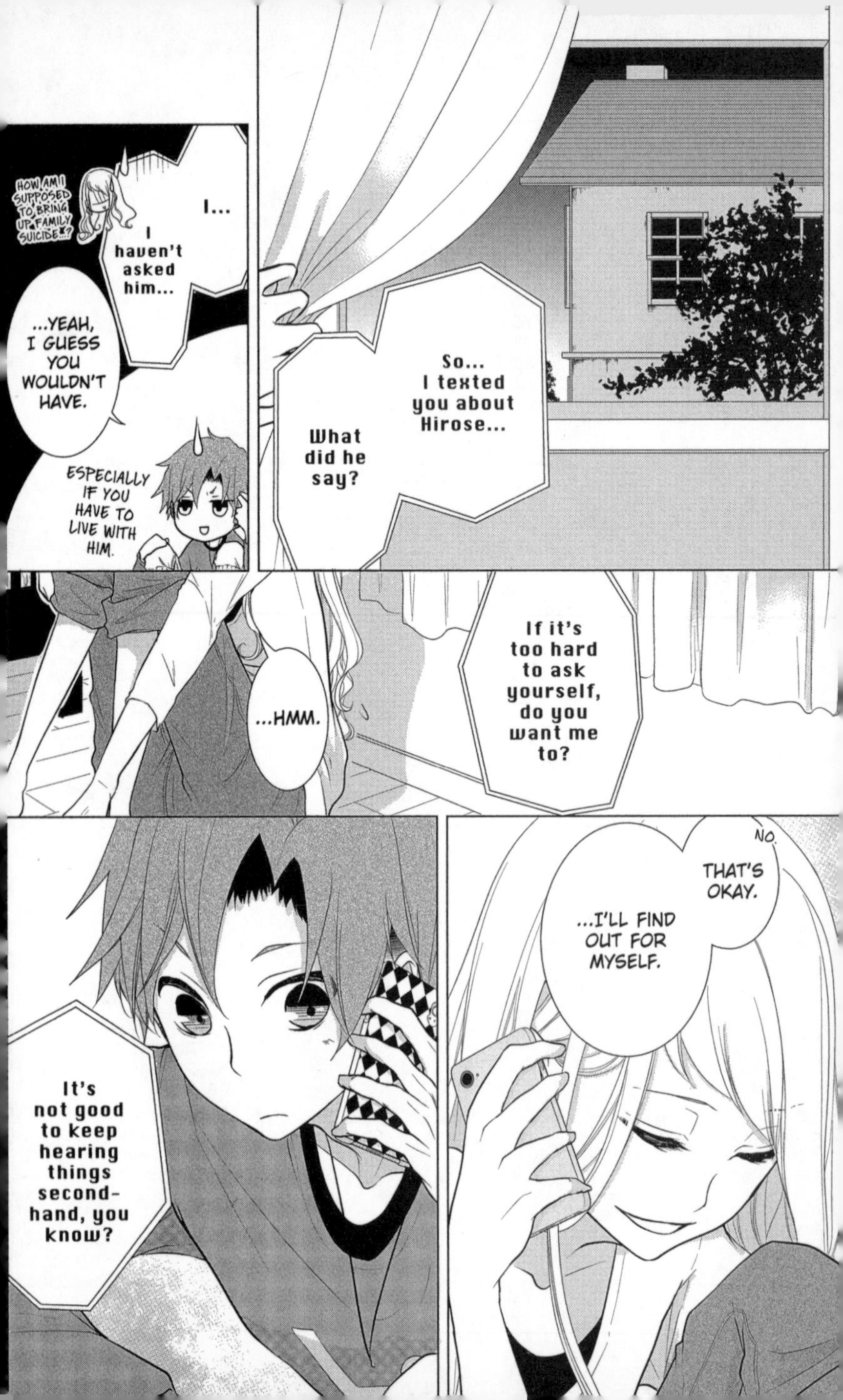
So... I texted you about Hirose...
What did he say?
I...
I haven't asked him...
HOW AM I SUPPOSED TO BRING UP FAMILY SUICIDE...?
...YEAH, I GUESS YOU WOULDN'T HAVE.
ESPECIALLY IF YOU HAVE TO LIVE WITH HIM.
If it's too hard to ask yourself, do you want me to?
...HMM.
NO.
THAT'S OKAY.
...I'LL FIND OUT FOR MYSELF.
It's not good to keep hearing things second-hand, you know?

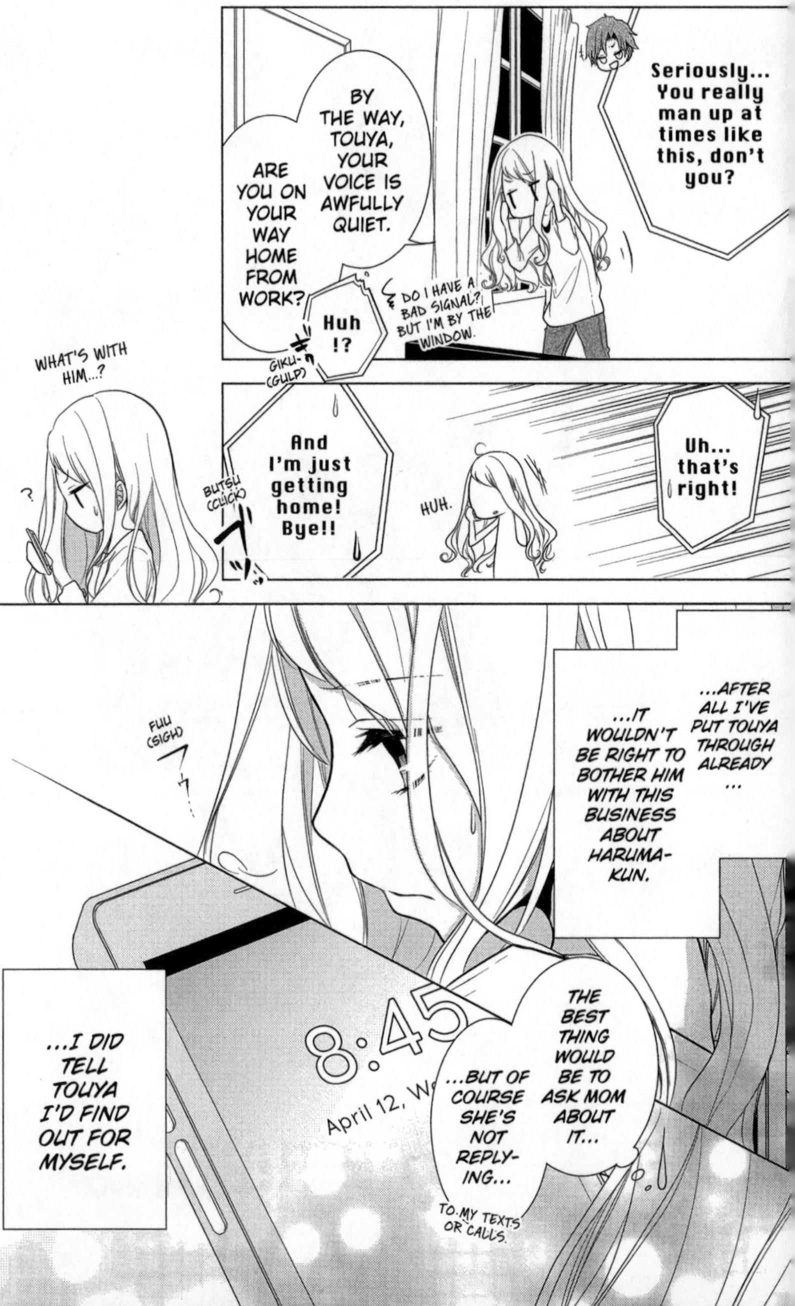
Seriously... You really man up at times like this, don't you?
BY THE WAY, TOUYA, YOUR VOICE IS AWFULLY QUIET.
ARE YOU ON YOUR WAY HOME FROM WORK?
DO I HAVE A BAD SIGNAL? BUT I'M BY THE WINDOW.
Huh!?
GIKU- (GULP)
Uh... that's right!
HUH.
And I'm just getting home! Bye!!
BUTSU (CLICK)
WHAT'S WITH HIM...?
?
...AFTER ALL I'VE PUT TOUYA THROUGH ALREADY...
...IT WOULDN'T BE RIGHT TO BOTHER HIM WITH THIS BUSINESS ABOUT HARUMA-KUN.
FUU (SIGH)
THE BEST THING WOULD BE TO ASK MOM ABOUT IT...
...BUT OF COURSE SHE'S NOT REPLYING...
TO MY TEXTS OR CALLS.
8:45
April 12,
...I DID TELL TOUYA I'D FIND OUT FOR MYSELF.

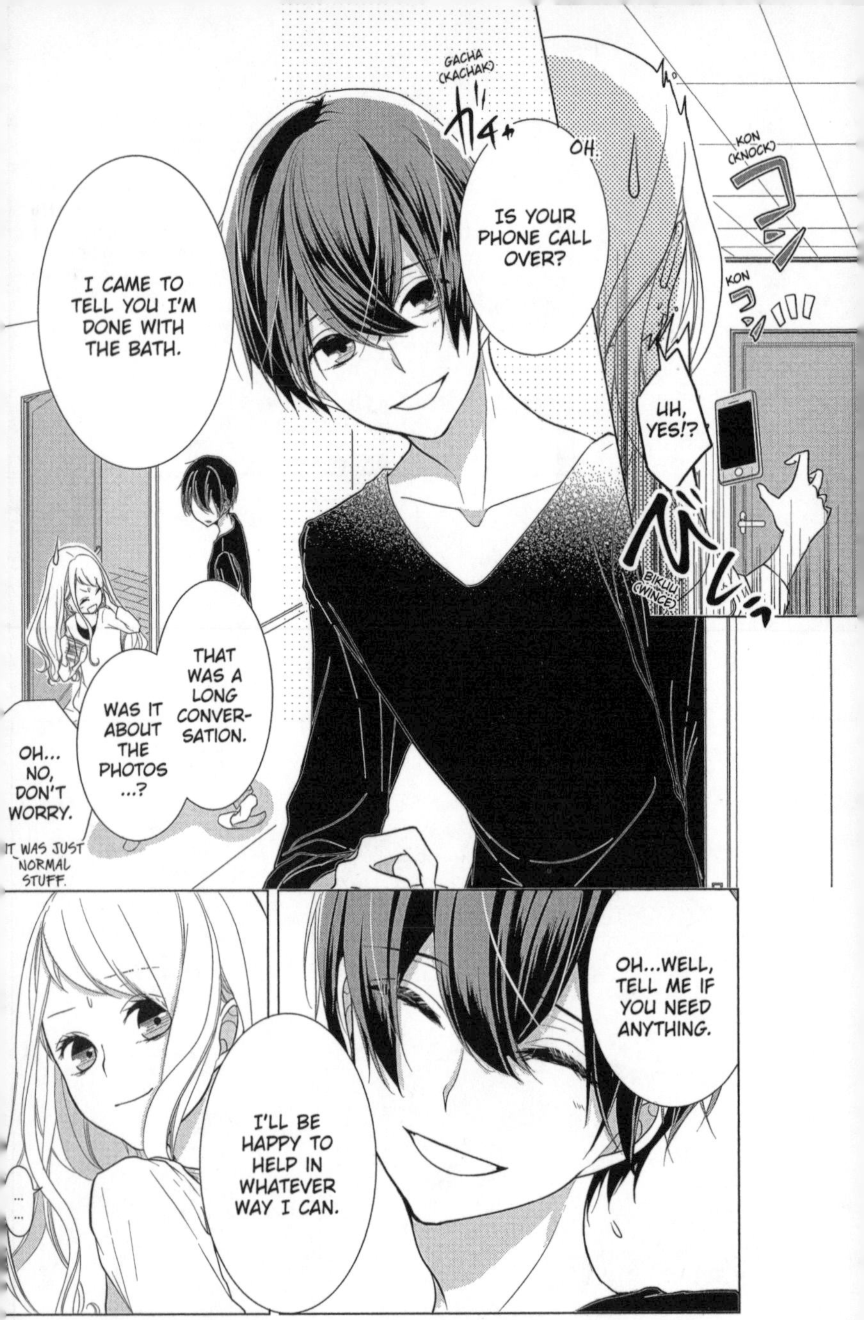
KON (KNOCK)
KON
BIKUU (WINCE)
GACHA (KACHAK)
OH.
IS YOUR PHONE CALL OVER?
UH, YES!?
I CAME TO TELL YOU I'M DONE WITH THE BATH.
THAT WAS A LONG CONVERSATION.
WAS IT ABOUT THE PHOTOS ...?
OH... NO, DON'T WORRY.
IT WAS JUST NORMAL STUFF.
OH...WELL, TELL ME IF YOU NEED ANYTHING.
I'LL BE HAPPY TO HELP IN WHATEVER WAY I CAN.
... ...

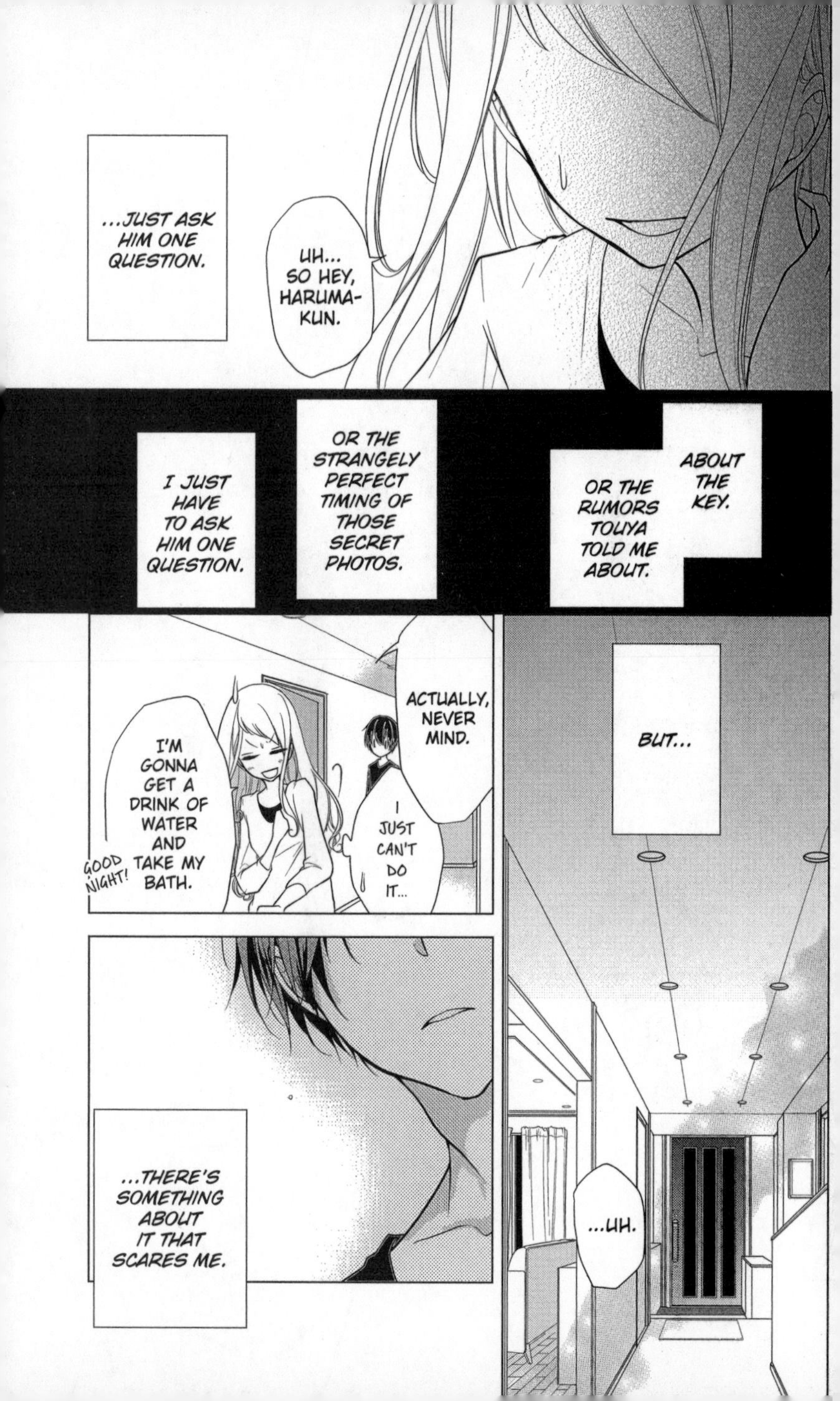
UH... SO HEY, HARUMA-KUN.
...JUST ASK HIM ONE QUESTION.
ABOUT THE KEY.
OR THE RUMORS TOUYA TOLD ME ABOUT.
OR THE STRANGELY PERFECT TIMING OF THOSE SECRET PHOTOS.
I JUST HAVE TO ASK HIM ONE QUESTION.
BUT...
...UH.
ACTUALLY, NEVER MIND.
I JUST CAN'T DO IT...
I'M GONNA GET A DRINK OF WATER AND TAKE MY BATH.
GOOD NIGHT!
...THERE'S SOMETHING ABOUT IT THAT SCARES ME.

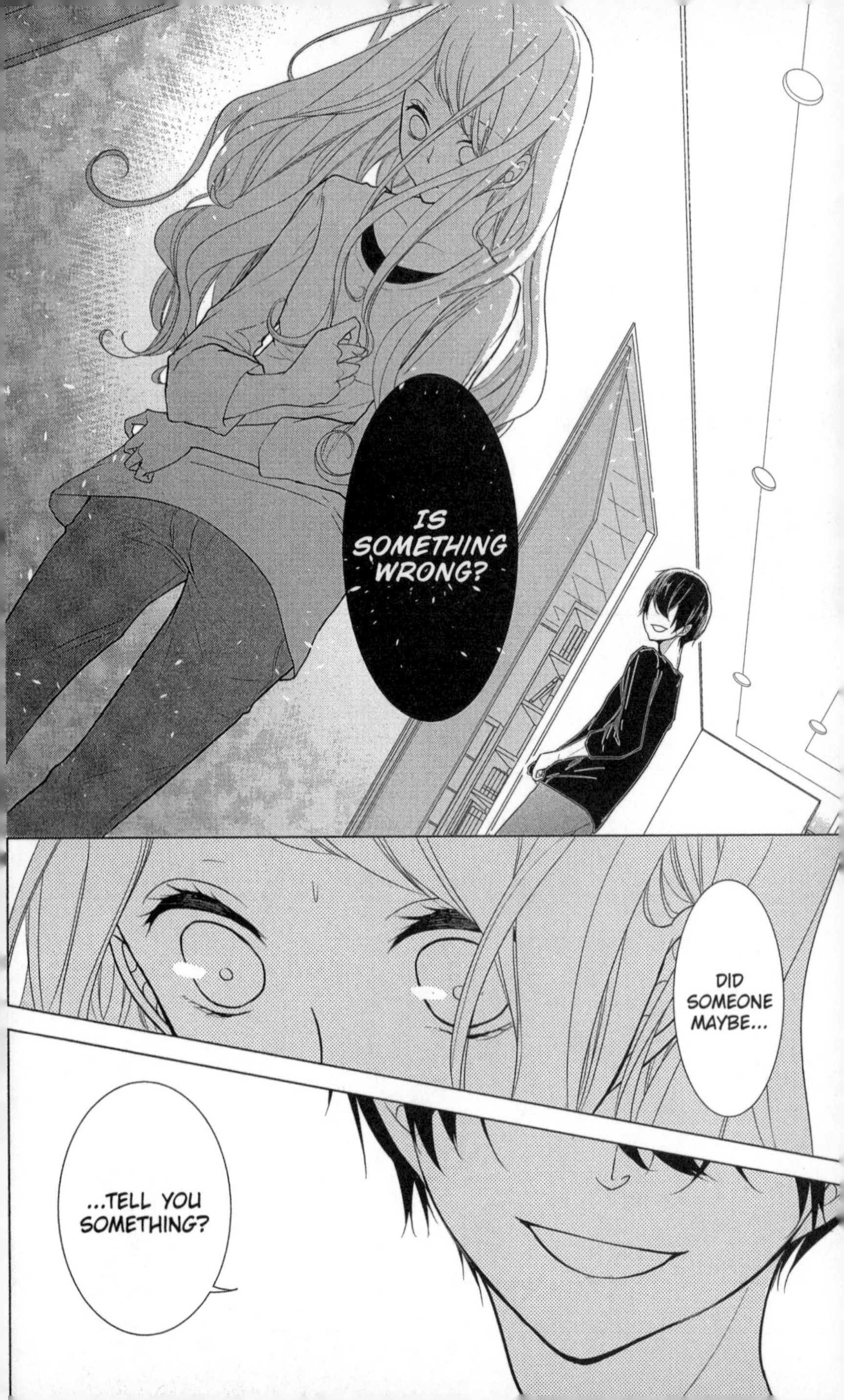
IS SOMETHING WRONG?
DID SOMEONE MAYBE...
...TELL YOU SOMETHING?

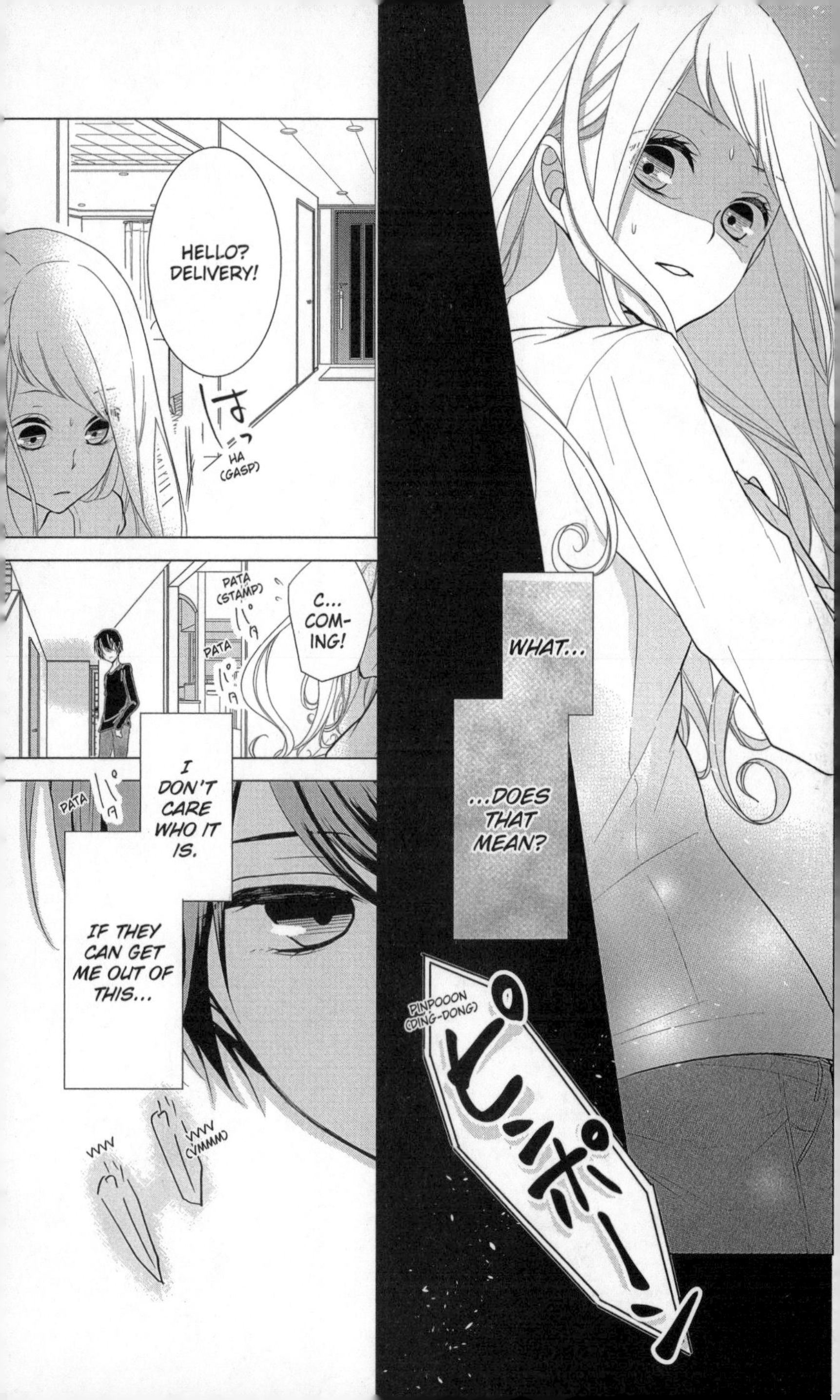
WHAT...
...DOES THAT MEAN?
PINPOOON (DING-DONG)
HELLO? DELIVERY!
HA (GASP)
C... COM-ING!
PATA (STAMP)
PATA
PATA
I DON'T CARE WHO IT IS.
IF THEY CAN GET ME OUT OF THIS...
VVV (VMMM)
VVV

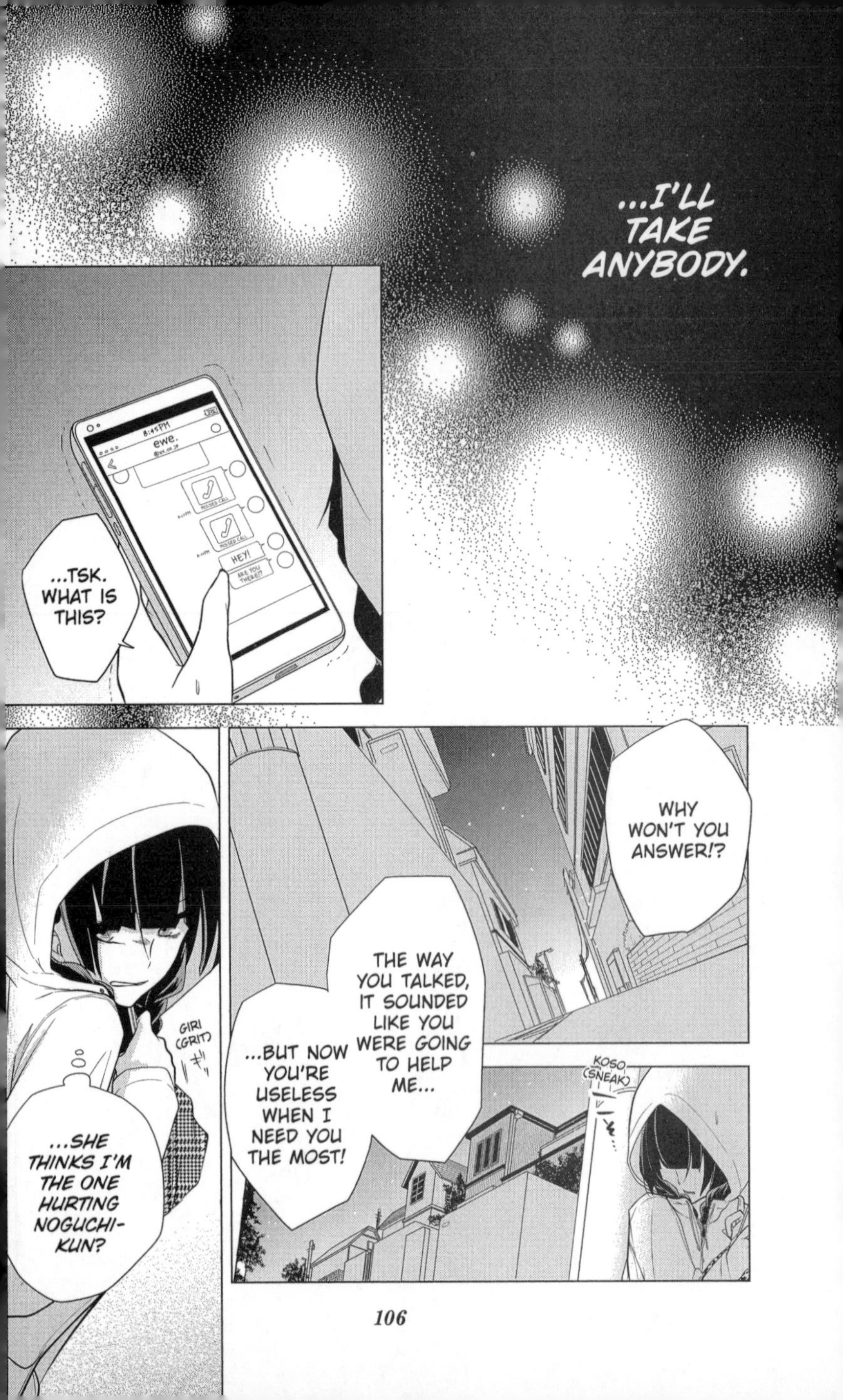
...I'LL TAKE ANYBODY.
8:45PM
ewe.
MISSED CALL
MISSED CALL
HEY!
ARE YOU THERE!?
...TSK. WHAT IS THIS?
WHY WON'T YOU ANSWER!?
THE WAY YOU TALKED, IT SOUNDED LIKE YOU WERE GOING TO HELP ME...
...BUT NOW YOU'RE USELESS WHEN I NEED YOU THE MOST!
KOSO (SNEAK)
GIRI (GRIT)
...SHE THINKS I'M THE ONE HURTING NOGUCHI-KUN?

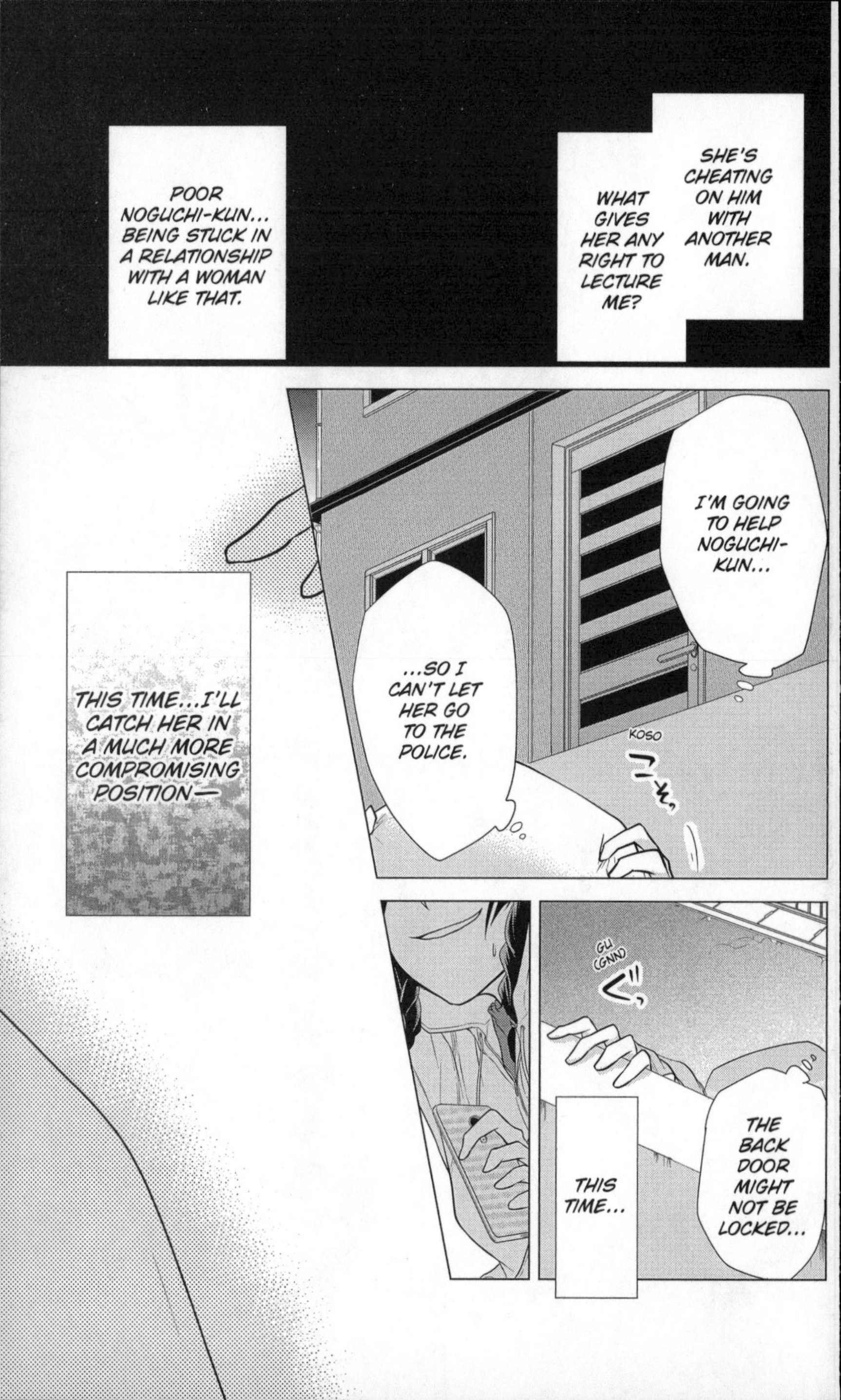
SHE'S CHEATING ON HIM WITH ANOTHER MAN.
WHAT GIVES HER ANY RIGHT TO LECTURE ME?
POOR NOGUCHI-KUN... BEING STUCK IN A RELATIONSHIP WITH A WOMAN LIKE THAT.
I'M GOING TO HELP NOGUCHI-KUN...
...SO I CAN'T LET HER GO TO THE POLICE.
KOSO
GU (GNN)
THE BACK DOOR MIGHT NOT BE LOCKED...
THIS TIME...
THIS TIME...I'LL CATCH HER IN A MUCH MORE COMPROMISING POSITION—

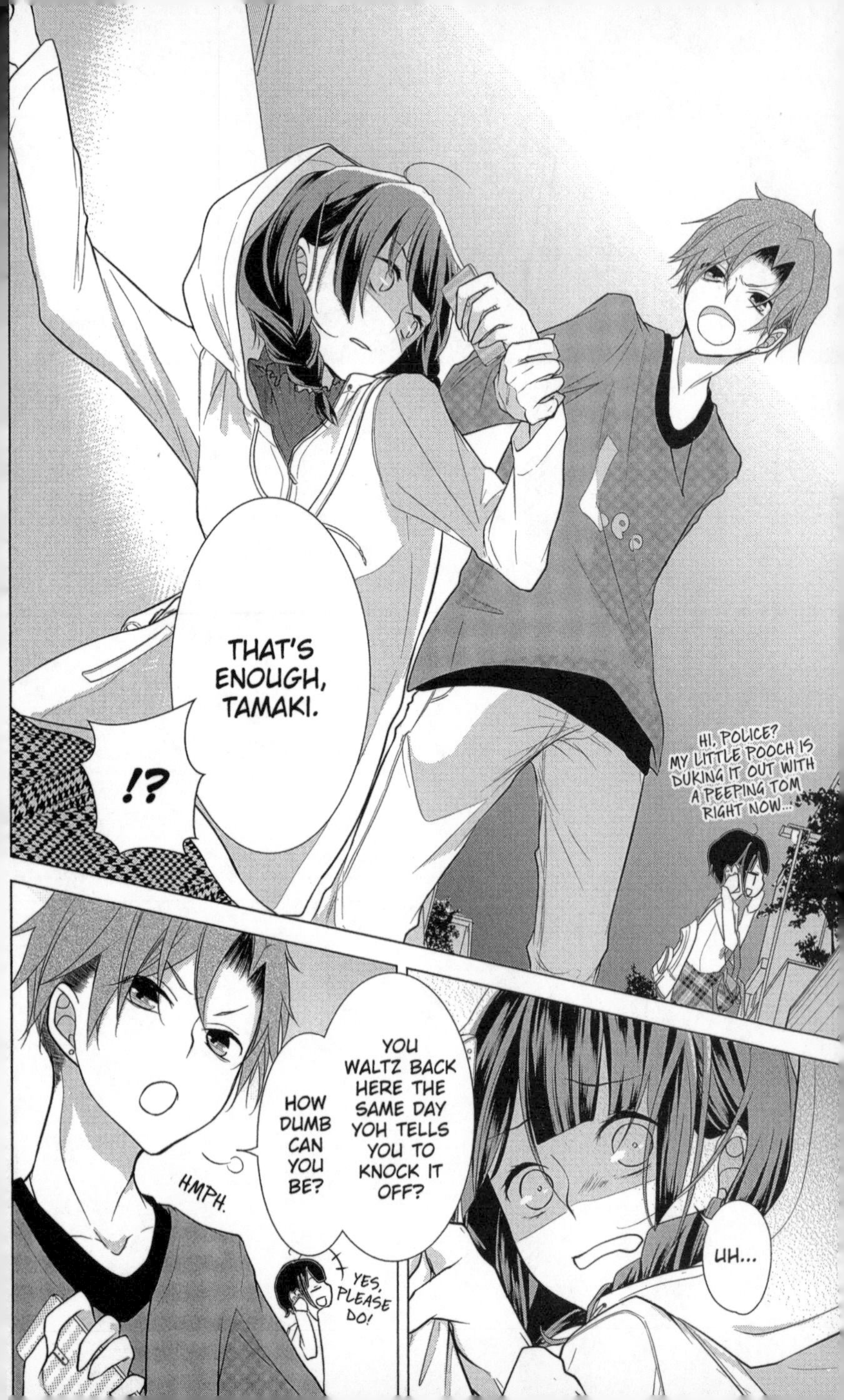
THAT'S ENOUGH, TAMAKI.
!?
HI, POLICE? MY LITTLE POOCH IS DUKING IT OUT WITH A PEEPING TOM RIGHT NOW...
YOU WALTZ BACK HERE THE SAME DAY YOH TELLS YOU TO KNOCK IT OFF?
HOW DUMB CAN YOU BE?
HMPH.
UH...
YES, PLEASE DO!

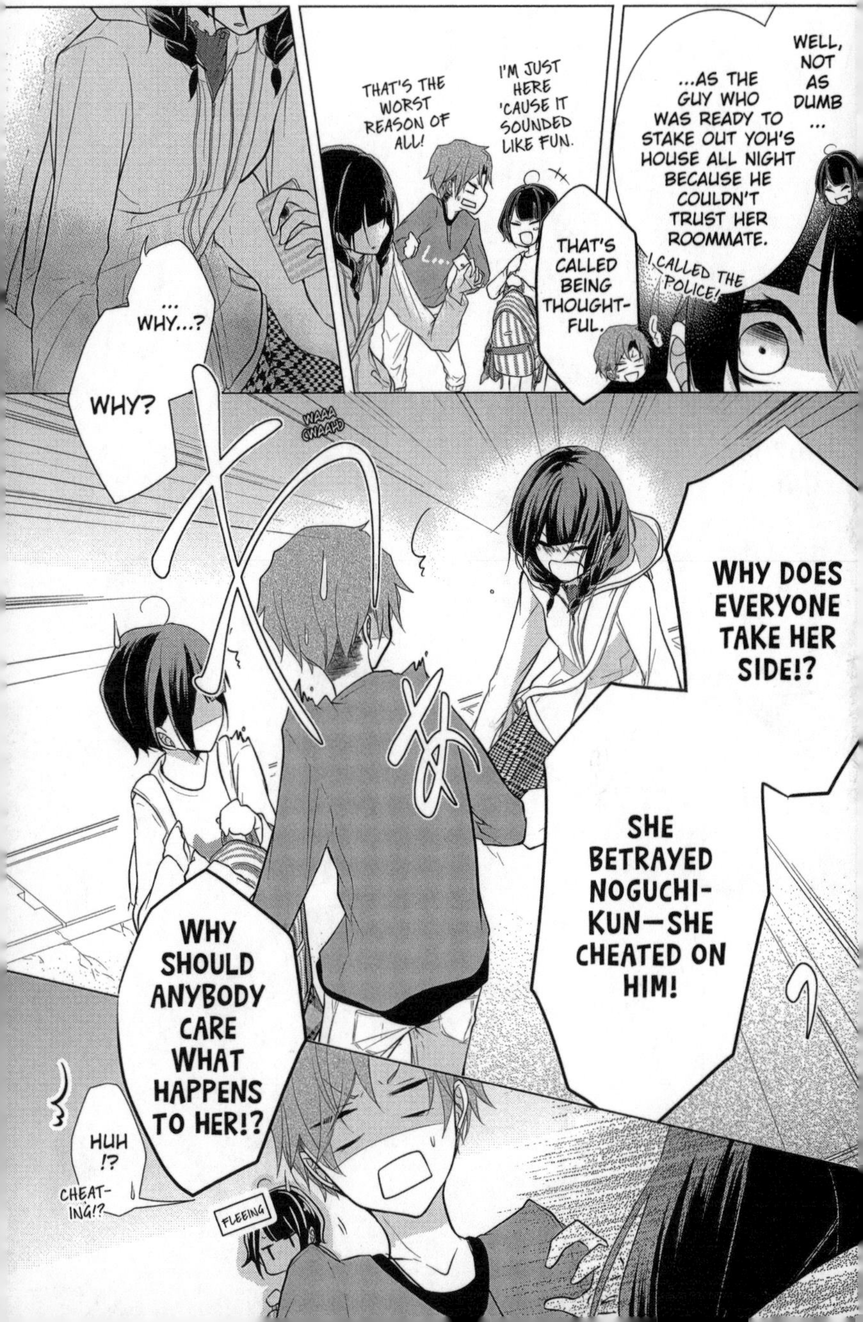
WELL, NOT AS DUMB ...
...AS THE GUY WHO WAS READY TO STAKE OUT YOH'S HOUSE ALL NIGHT BECAUSE HE COULDN'T TRUST HER ROOMMATE.
I CALLED THE POLICE!
THAT'S CALLED BEING THOUGHT-FUL.
I'M JUST HERE 'CAUSE IT SOUNDED LIKE FUN.
THAT'S THE WORST REASON OF ALL!
... WHY...?
WHY?
WHY DOES EVERYONE TAKE HER SIDE!?
WAAA WAAAH
SHE BETRAYED NOGUCHI-KUN—SHE CHEATED ON HIM!
WHY SHOULD ANYBODY CARE WHAT HAPPENS TO HER!?
HUH !?
CHEAT-ING!?
FLEEING

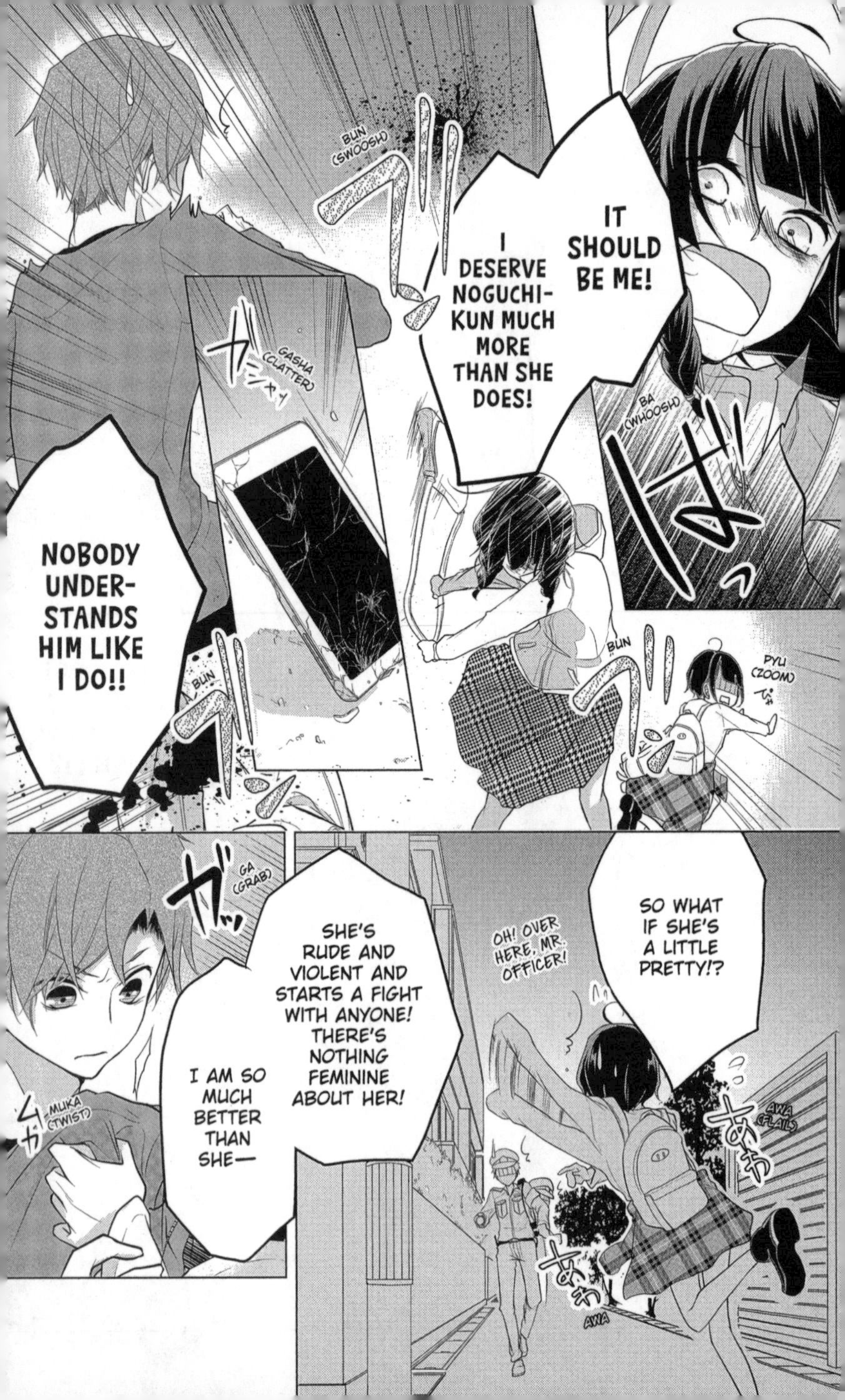
IT SHOULD BE ME!
I DESERVE NOGUCHI-KUN MUCH MORE THAN SHE DOES!
BA (WHOOSH)
BUN (SWOOSH)
GASHA (CLATTER)
NOBODY UNDER-STANDS HIM LIKE I DO!!
BUN
PYU (ZOOM)
BUN
SO WHAT IF SHE'S A LITTLE PRETTY!?
OH! OVER HERE, MR. OFFICER!
AWA (FLAIL)
AWA
GA (GRAB)
SHE'S RUDE AND VIOLENT AND STARTS A FIGHT WITH ANYONE! THERE'S NOTHING FEMININE ABOUT HER!
I AM SO MUCH BETTER THAN SHE—
MUKA (TWIST)

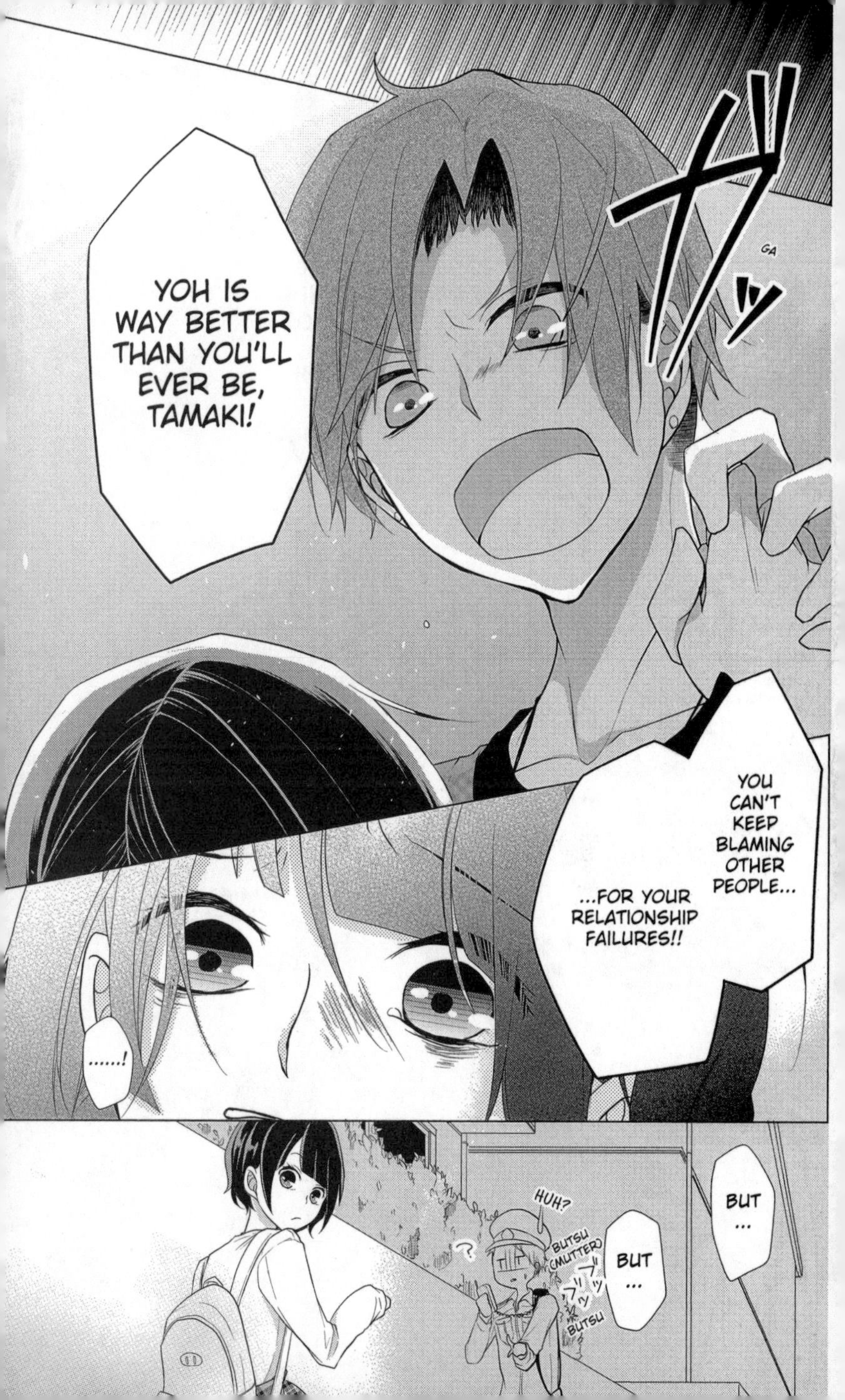
GA
YOH IS WAY BETTER THAN YOU'LL EVER BE, TAMAKI!
YOU CAN'T KEEP BLAMING OTHER PEOPLE...
...FOR YOUR RELATIONSHIP FAILURES!!
......!
BUT ...
BUT ...
HUH?
BUTSU (MUTTER) BUTSU
?

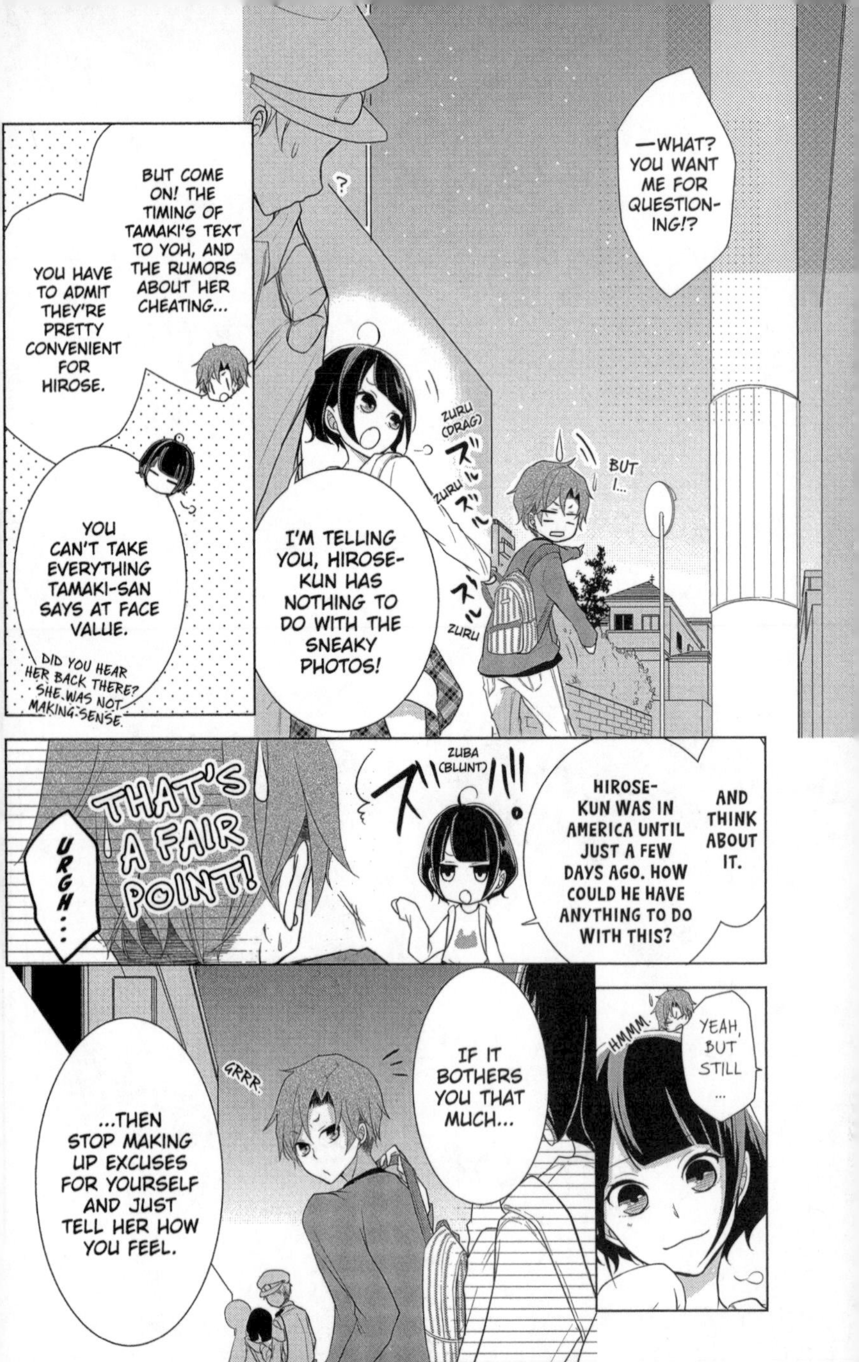
—WHAT? YOU WANT ME FOR QUESTIONING!?
?
ZURU (DRAG)
BUT I...
ZURU
I'M TELLING YOU, HIROSE-KUN HAS NOTHING TO DO WITH THE SNEAKY PHOTOS!
ZURU
BUT COME ON! THE TIMING OF TAMAKI'S TEXT TO YOH, AND THE RUMORS ABOUT HER CHEATING...
YOU HAVE TO ADMIT THEY'RE PRETTY CONVENIENT FOR HIROSE.
YOU CAN'T TAKE EVERYTHING TAMAKI-SAN SAYS AT FACE VALUE.
DID YOU HEAR HER BACK THERE? SHE WAS NOT MAKING SENSE.
AND THINK ABOUT IT.
HIROSE-KUN WAS IN AMERICA UNTIL JUST A FEW DAYS AGO. HOW COULD HE HAVE ANYTHING TO DO WITH THIS?
ZUBA (BLUNT)
THAT'S A FAIR POINT!
URGH...
YEAH, BUT STILL ...
HMMM.
IF IT BOTHERS YOU THAT MUCH...
GRRR.
...THEN STOP MAKING UP EXCUSES FOR YOURSELF AND JUST TELL HER HOW YOU FEEL.

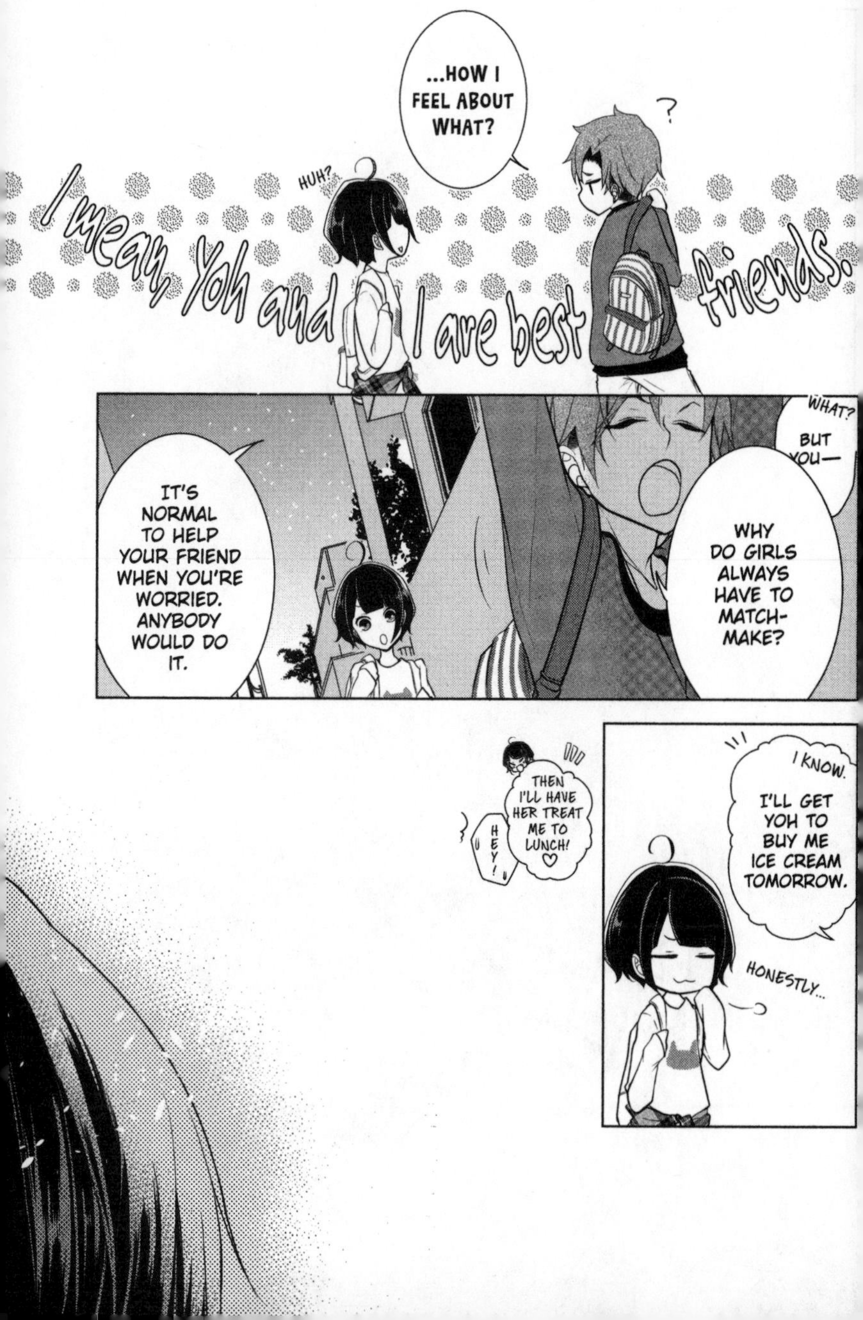
...HOW I FEEL ABOUT WHAT?
?
HUH?
I mean, Yoh and I are best friends.
WHAT? BUT YOU—
WHY DO GIRLS ALWAYS HAVE TO MATCH-MAKE?
IT'S NORMAL TO HELP YOUR FRIEND WHEN YOU'RE WORRIED. ANYBODY WOULD DO IT.
I KNOW.
I'LL GET YOH TO BUY ME ICE CREAM TOMORROW.
HONESTLY...
THEN I'LL HAVE HER TREAT ME TO LUNCH! ♡
HEY!

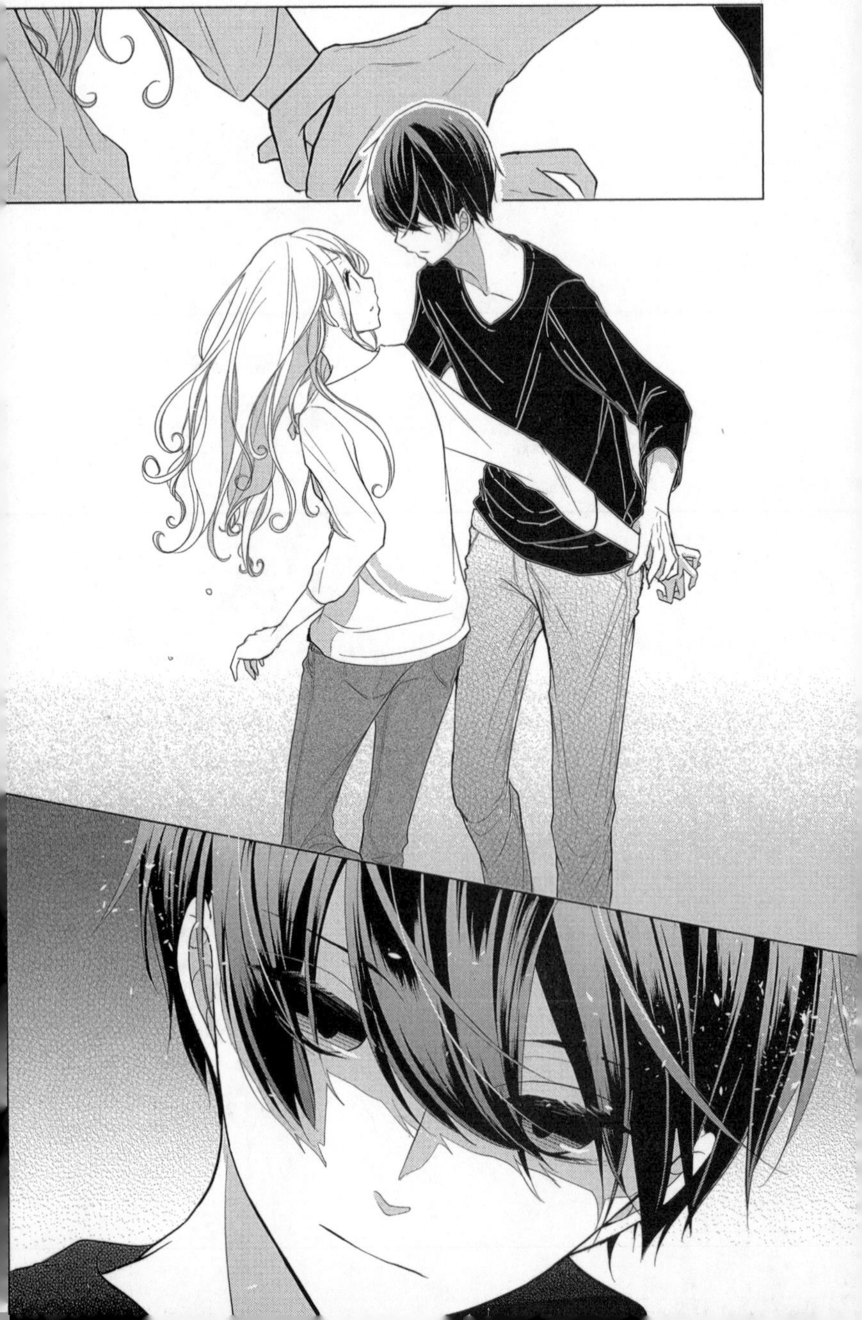

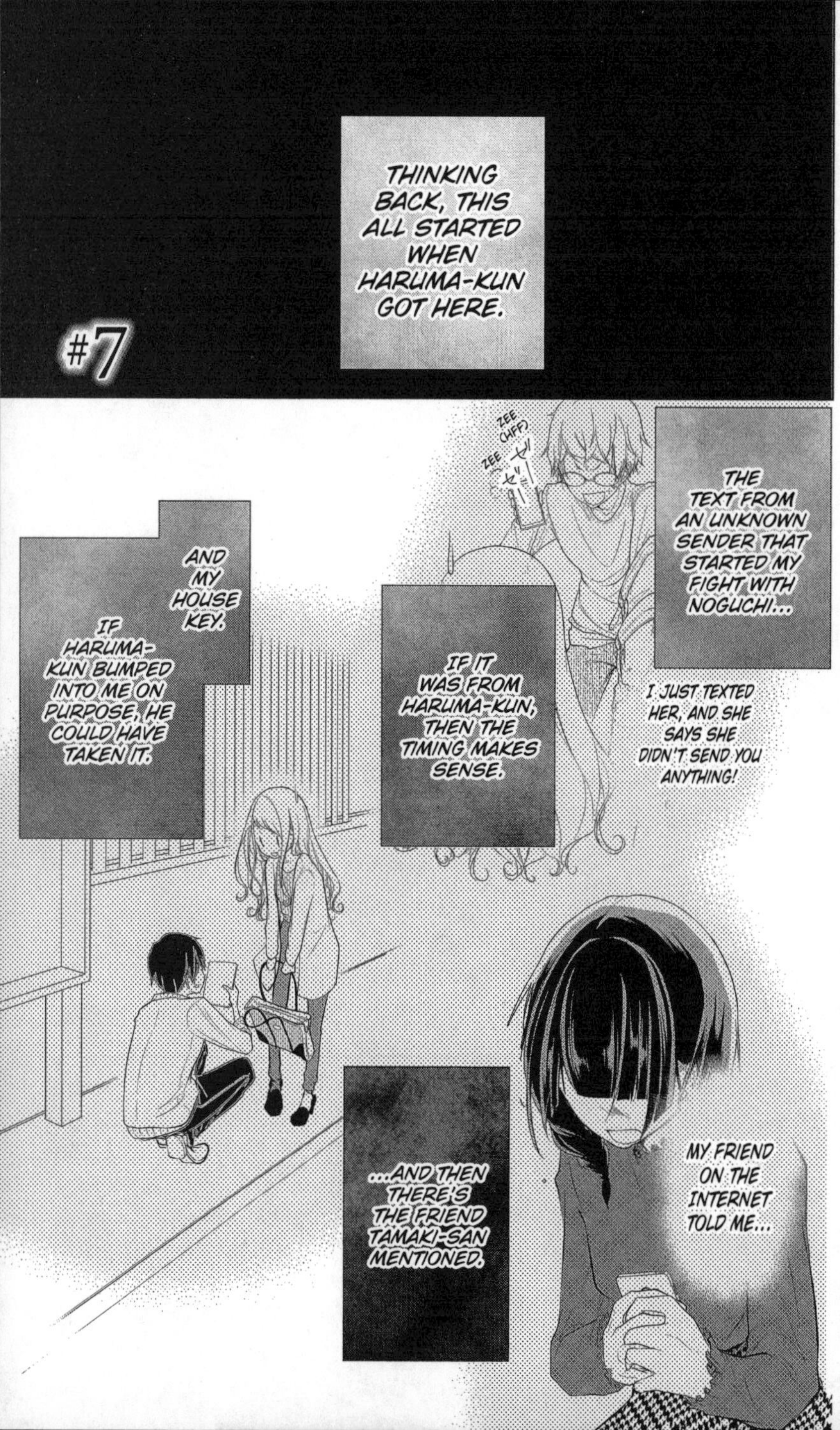
THINKING BACK, THIS ALL STARTED WHEN HARUMA-KUN GOT HERE.
#7
THE TEXT FROM AN UNKNOWN SENDER THAT STARTED MY FIGHT WITH NOGUCHI...
ZEE (HFF) ZEE
I JUST TEXTED HER, AND SHE SAYS SHE DIDN'T SEND YOU ANYTHING!
IF IT WAS FROM HARUMA-KUN, THEN THE TIMING MAKES SENSE.
AND MY HOUSE KEY.
IF HARUMA-KUN BUMPED INTO ME ON PURPOSE, HE COULD HAVE TAKEN IT.
MY FRIEND ON THE INTERNET TOLD ME...
...AND THEN THERE'S THE FRIEND TAMAKI-SAN MENTIONED.

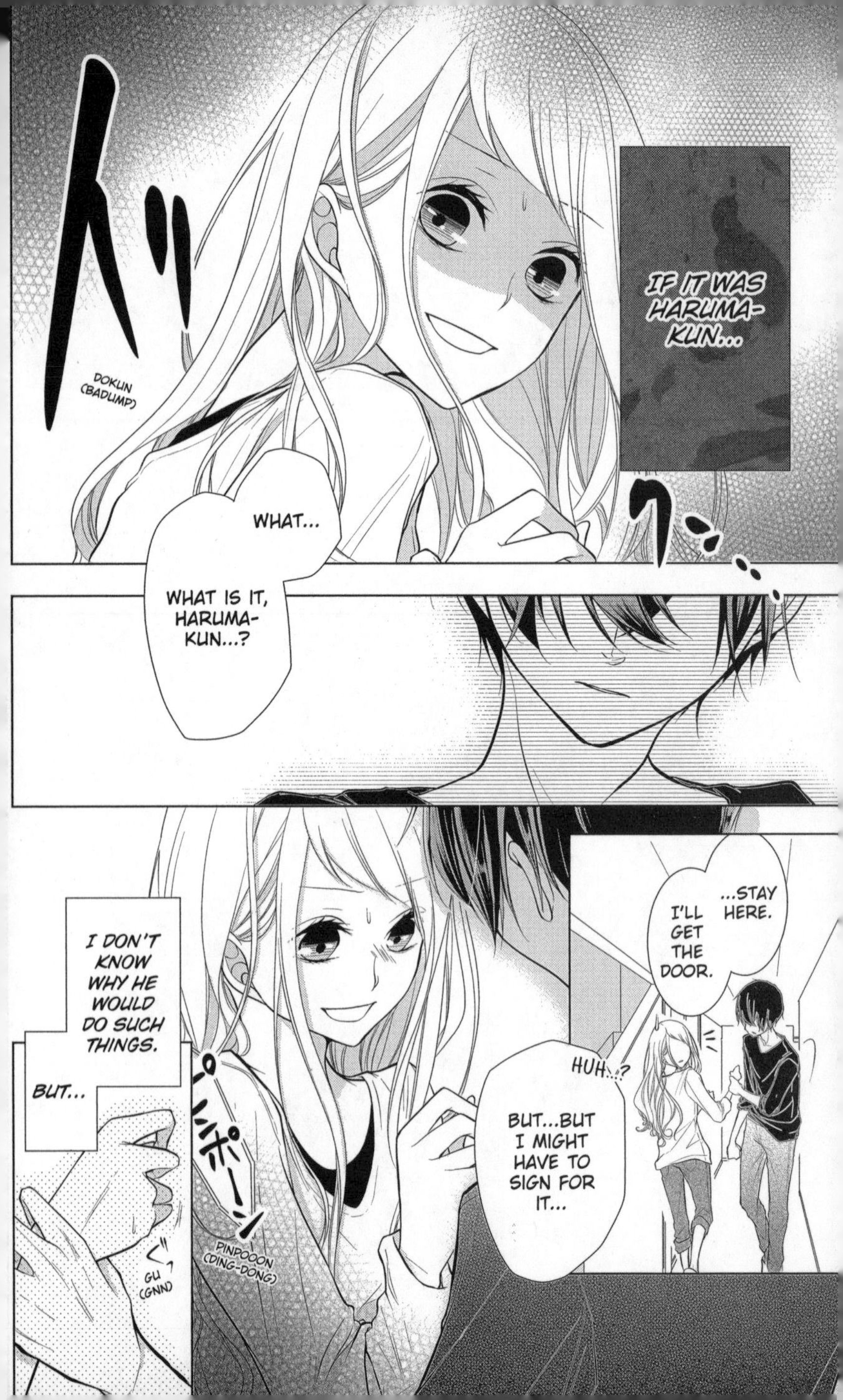
IF IT WAS HARUMA-KUN...
DOKUN (BADUMP)
WHAT...
WHAT IS IT, HARUMA-KUN...?
...STAY HERE.
I'LL GET THE DOOR.
HUH...?
BUT...BUT I MIGHT HAVE TO SIGN FOR IT...
PINPOOON (DING-DONG)
I DON'T KNOW WHY HE WOULD DO SUCH THINGS.
BUT...
GU (GNN)

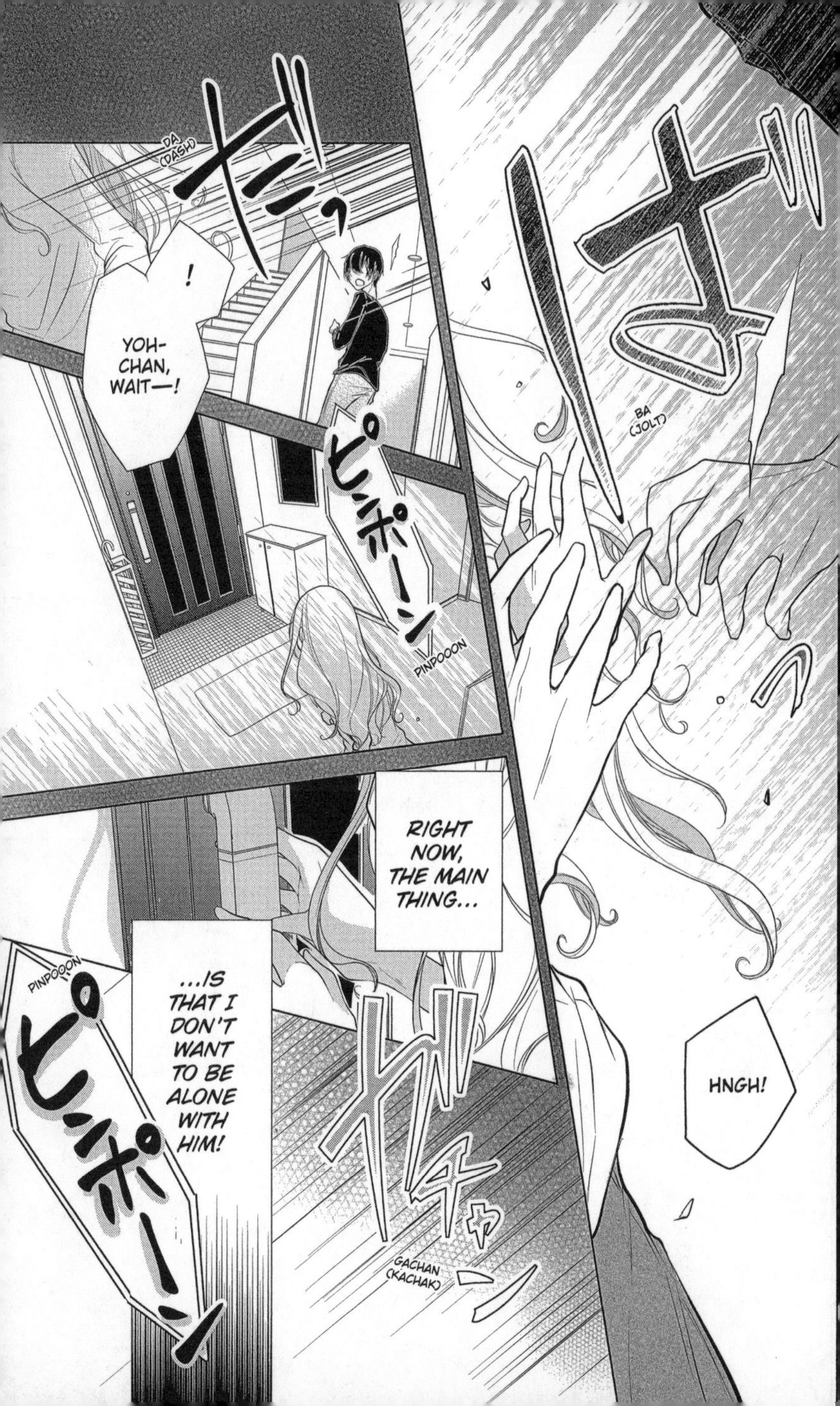
BA (JOLT)
DA (DASH)
!
YOH-CHAN, WAIT—!
PINPOOON
HNGH!
RIGHT NOW, THE MAIN THING...
...IS THAT I DON'T WANT TO BE ALONE WITH HIM!
GACHAN (KACHAK)
PINPOOON

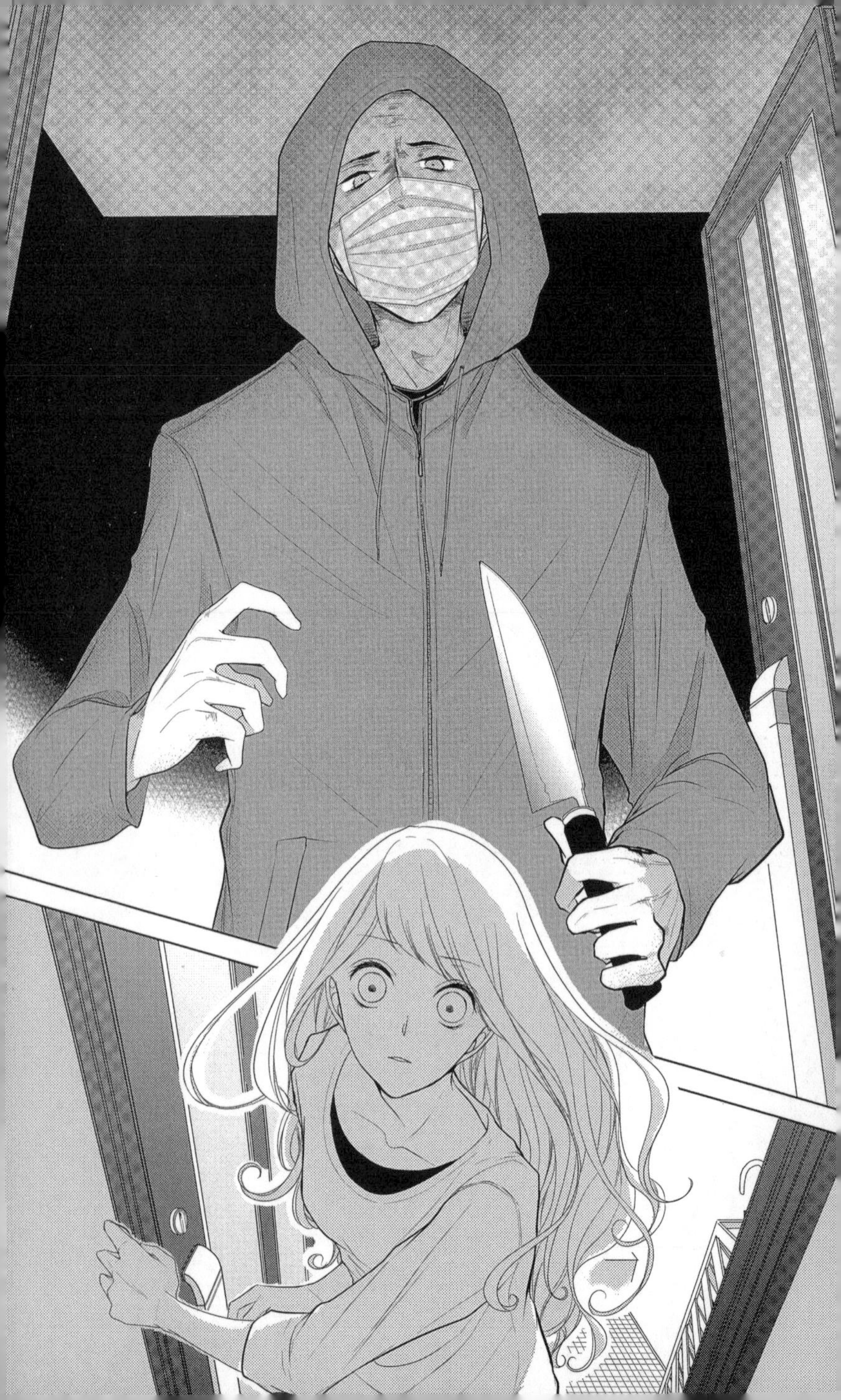

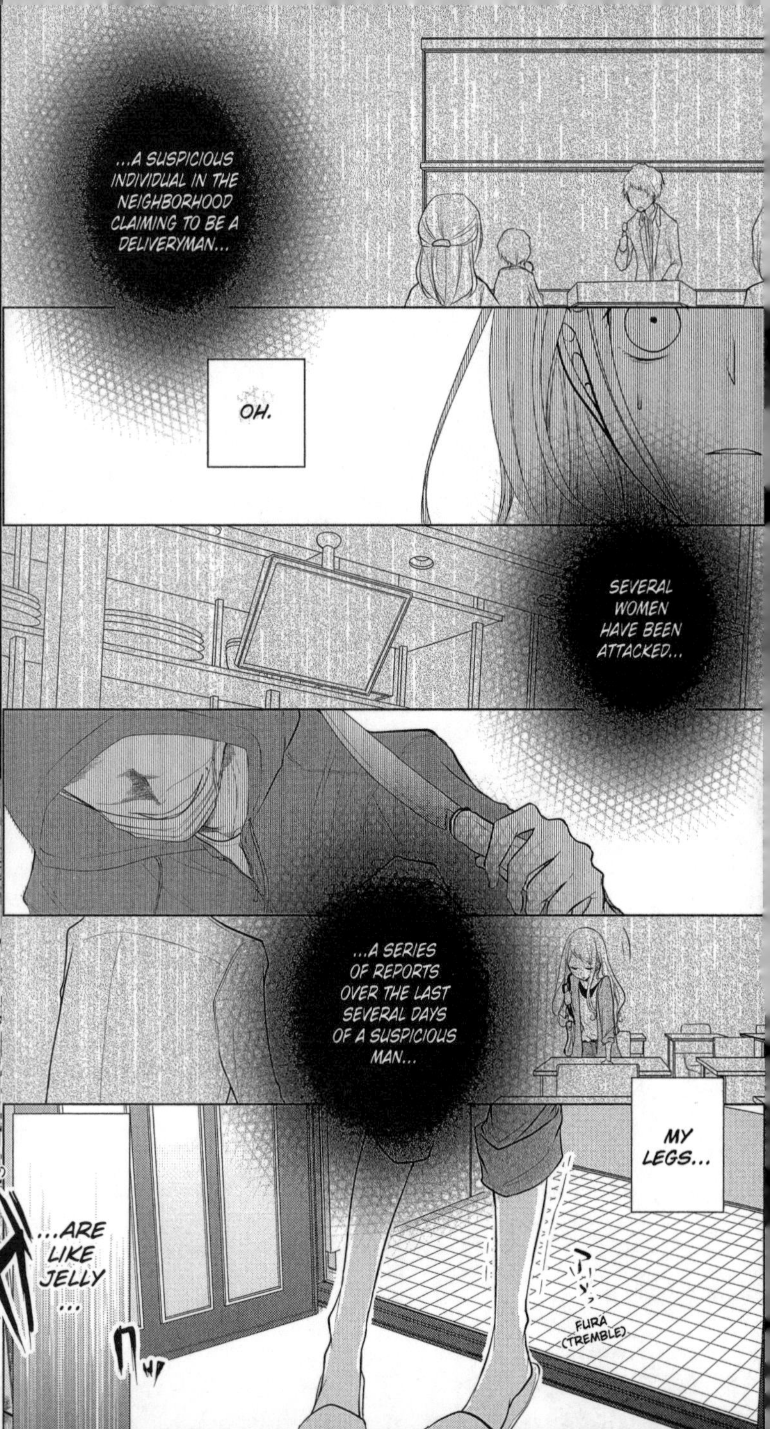
...A SUSPICIOUS INDIVIDUAL IN THE NEIGHBORHOOD CLAIMING TO BE A DELIVERYMAN...
OH.
SEVERAL WOMEN HAVE BEEN ATTACKED...
...A SERIES OF REPORTS OVER THE LAST SEVERAL DAYS OF A SUSPICIOUS MAN...
MY LEGS...
FURA (TREMBLE)
...ARE LIKE JELLY ...
GAKU (SLUMP)

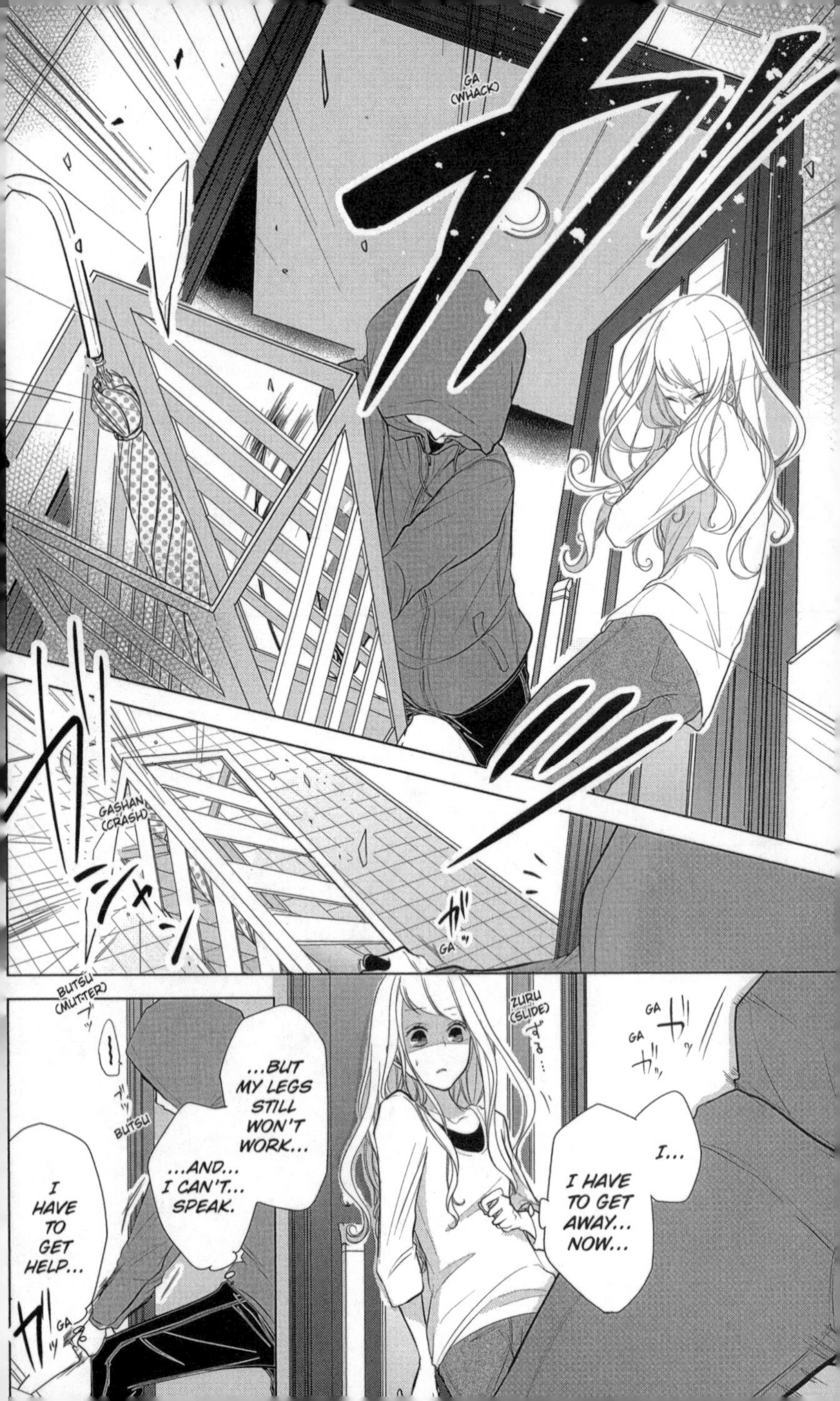
GA (WHACK)
GASHAN (CRASH)
GA
GA
GA
I...
I HAVE TO GET AWAY... NOW...
ZURU (SLIDE)
...BUT MY LEGS STILL WON'T WORK...
...AND... I CAN'T... SPEAK.
BUTSU (MUTTER)
BUTSU
I HAVE TO GET HELP...
GA

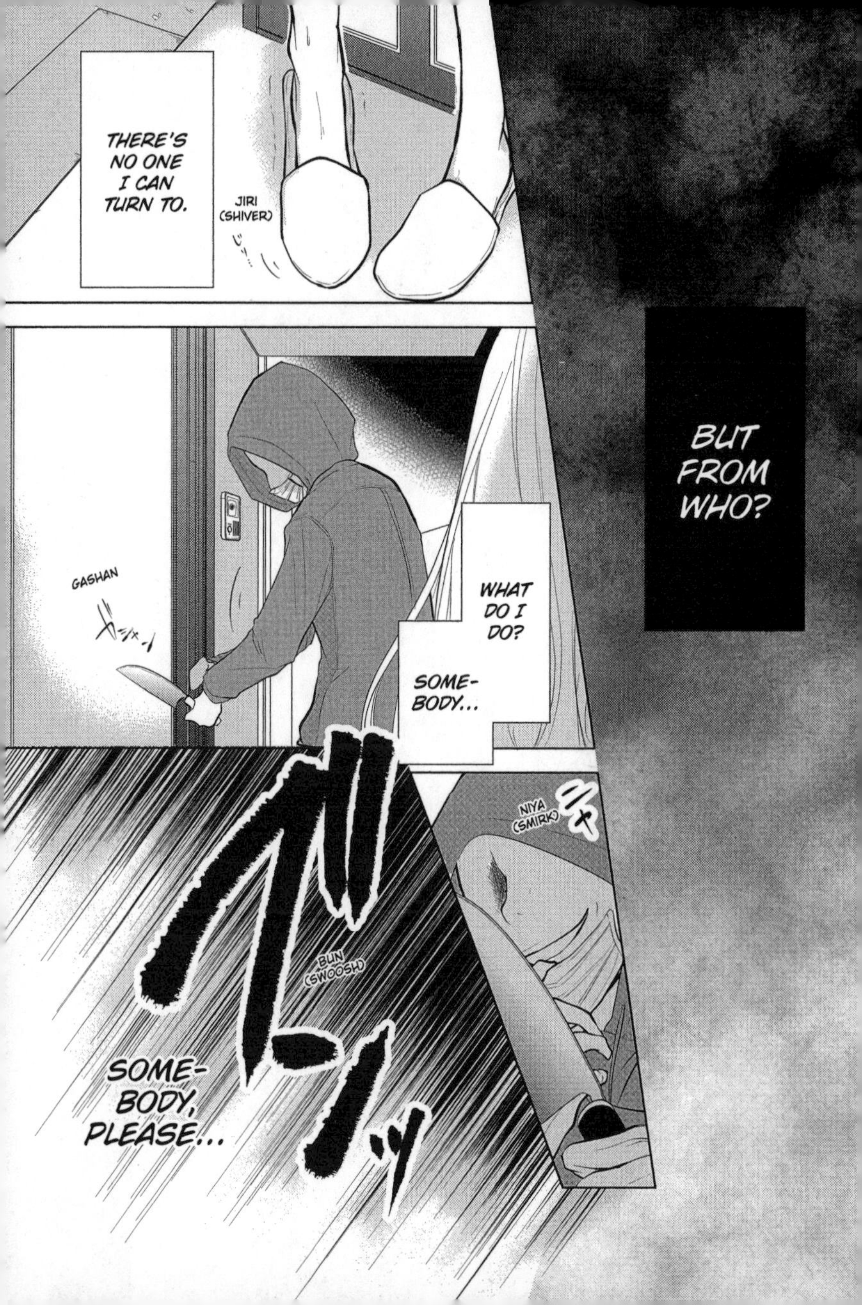
BUT FROM WHO?
THERE'S NO ONE I CAN TURN TO.
JIRI (SHIVER)
WHAT DO I DO?
SOME-BODY...
GASHAN
NIYA (SMIRK)
BUN (SWOOSH)
SOME-BODY, PLEASE...

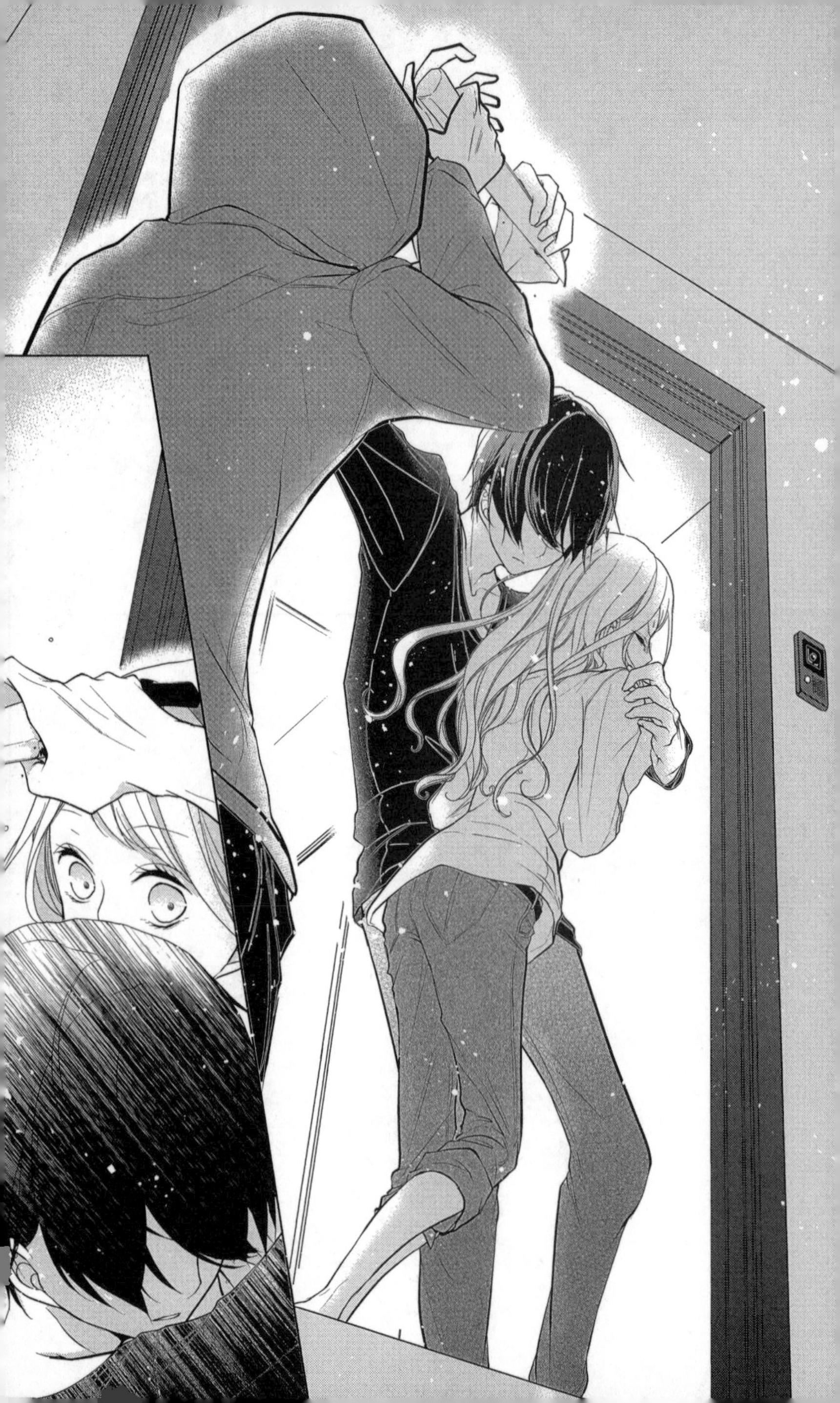

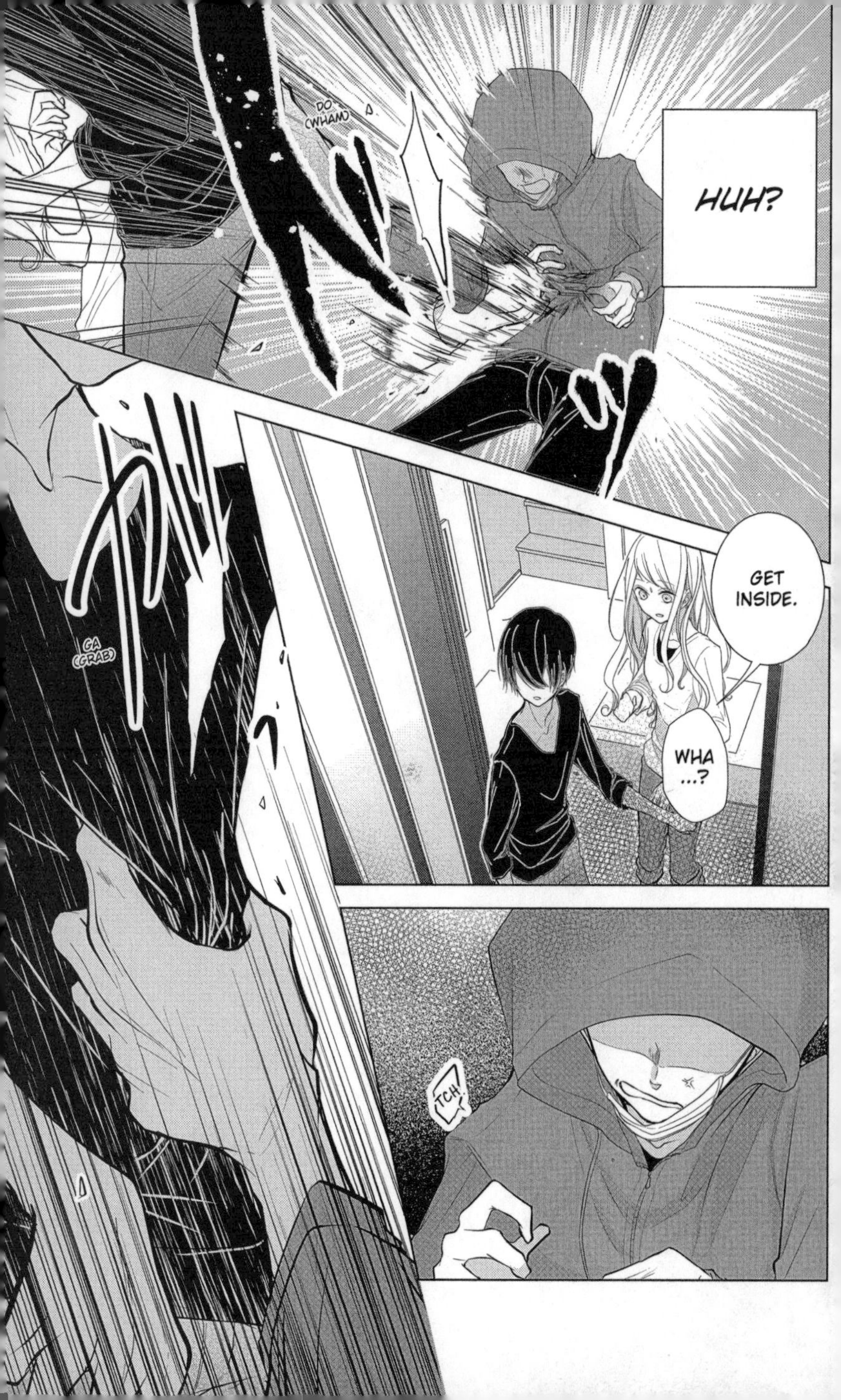
HUH?
DO (WHAM)
GET INSIDE.
WHA ...?
TCH!
GA (GRAB)

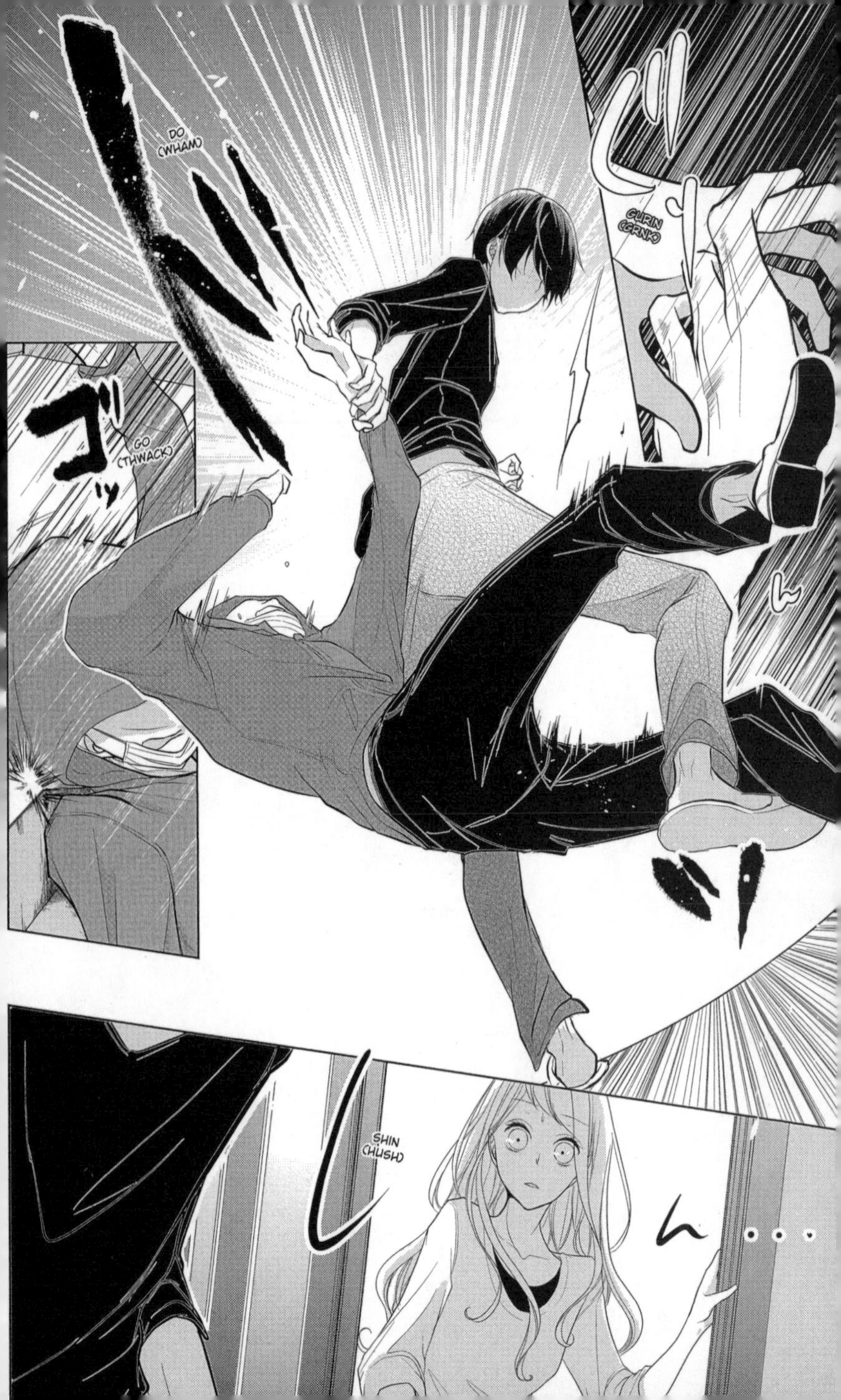
GURIN
(GRNK)
DO
(WHAM)
GO
(THWACK)
SHIN
(HUSH)
...

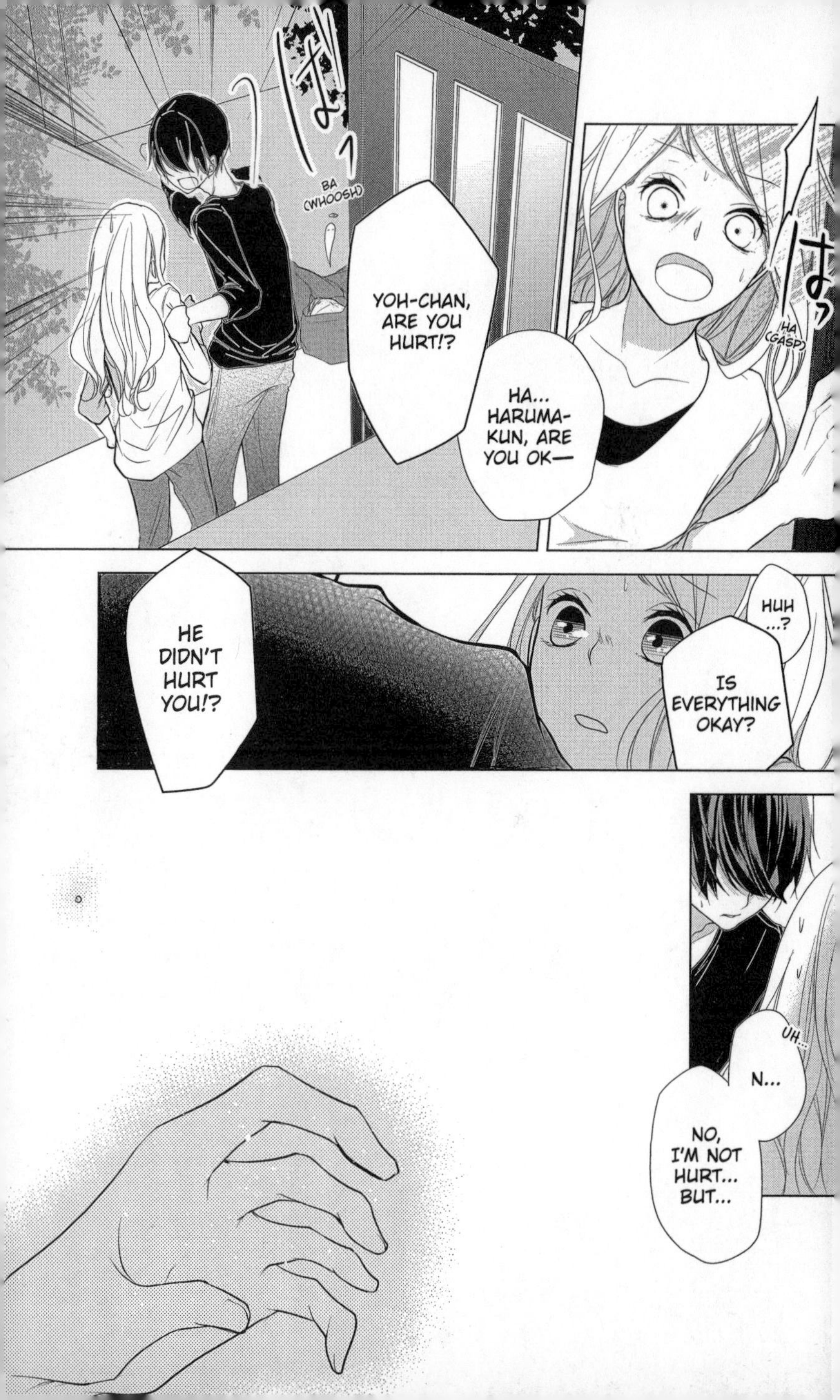
HA (GASP)
HA... HARUMA-KUN, ARE YOU OK—
BA (WHOOSH)
YOH-CHAN, ARE YOU HURT!?
HUH ...?
IS EVERYTHING OKAY?
HE DIDN'T HURT YOU!?
UH...
N...
NO, I'M NOT HURT... BUT...

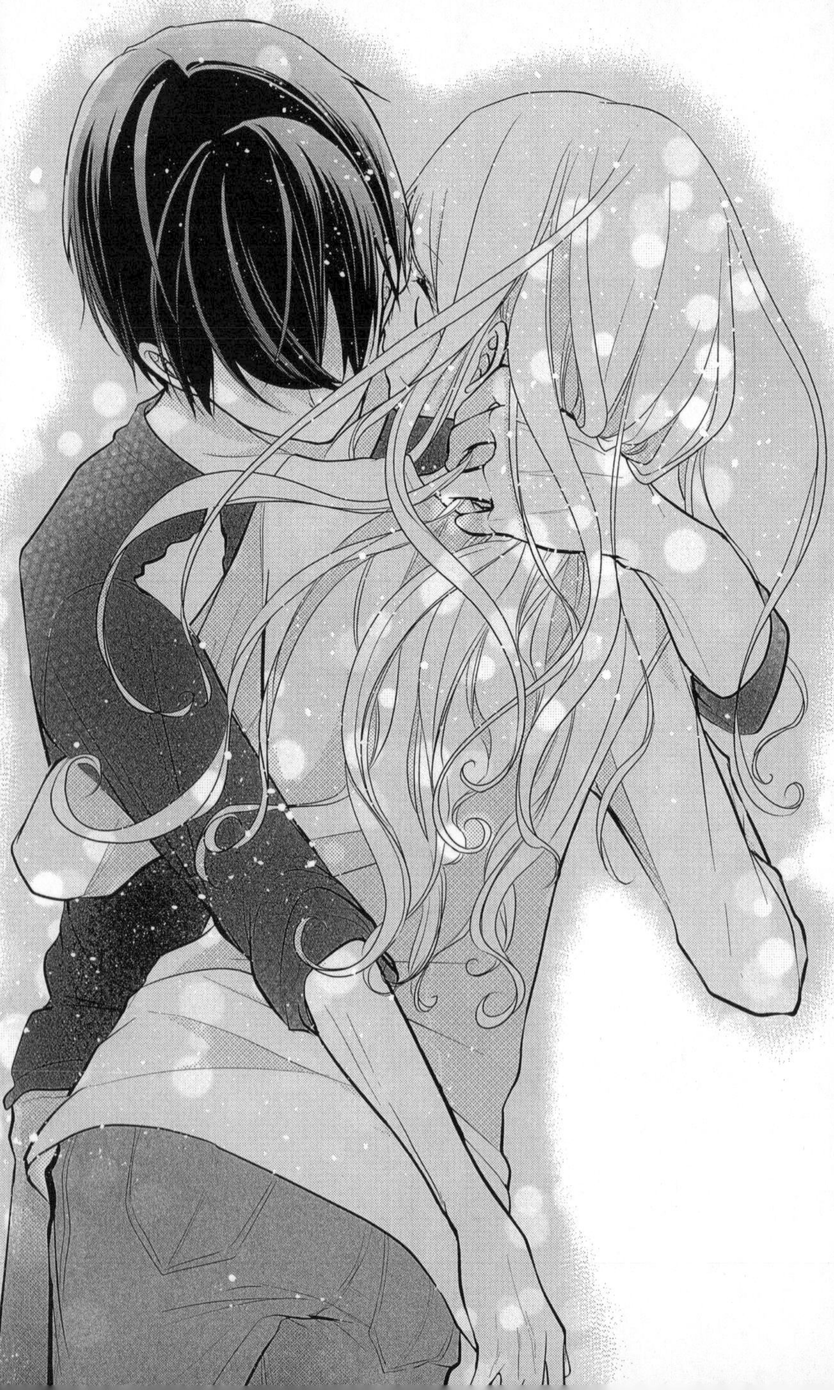

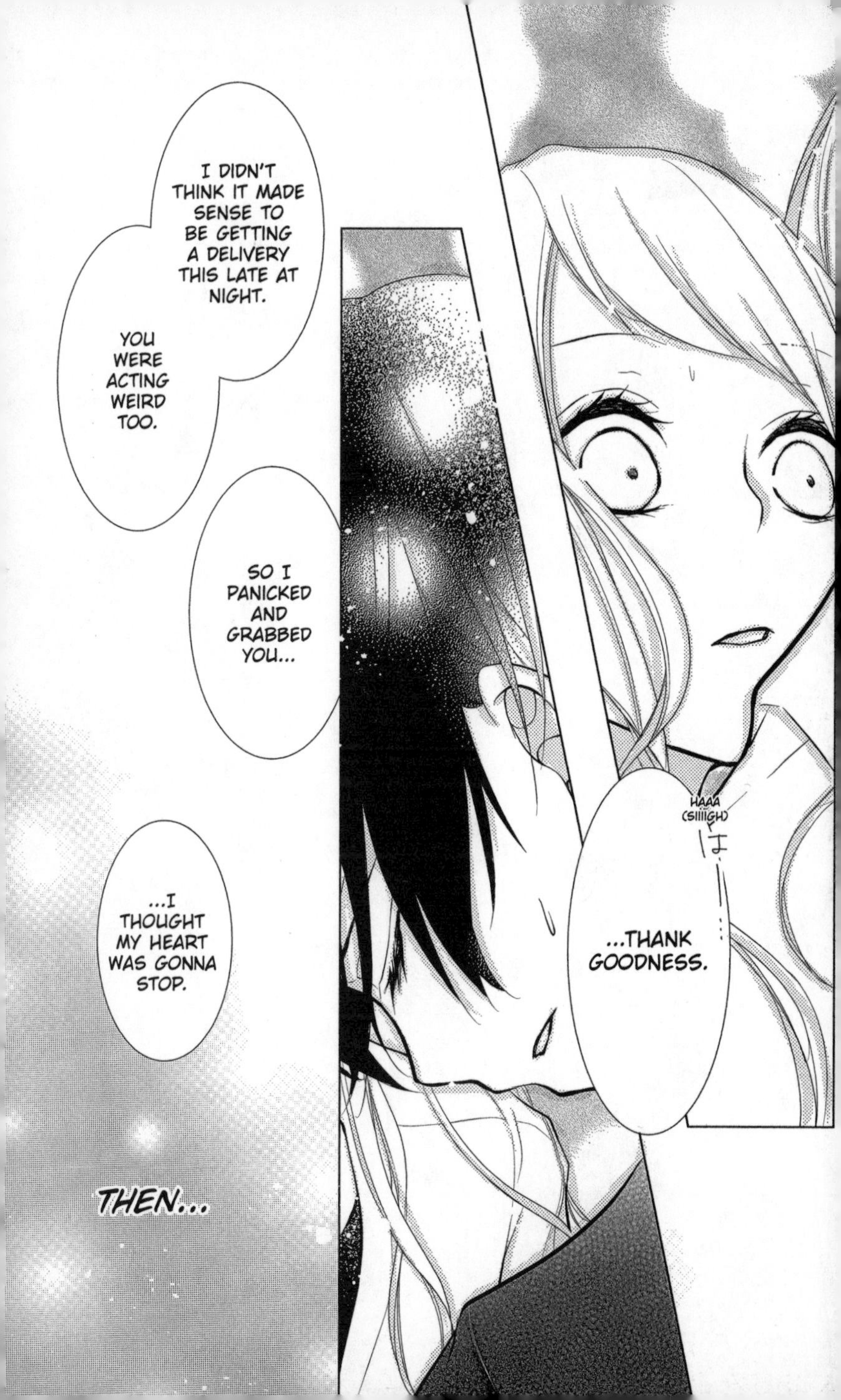
I DIDN'T THINK IT MADE SENSE TO BE GETTING A DELIVERY THIS LATE AT NIGHT.
YOU WERE ACTING WEIRD TOO.
SO I PANICKED AND GRABBED YOU...
HAAA (SIIIGH)
...THANK GOODNESS.
...I THOUGHT MY HEART WAS GONNA STOP.
THEN...

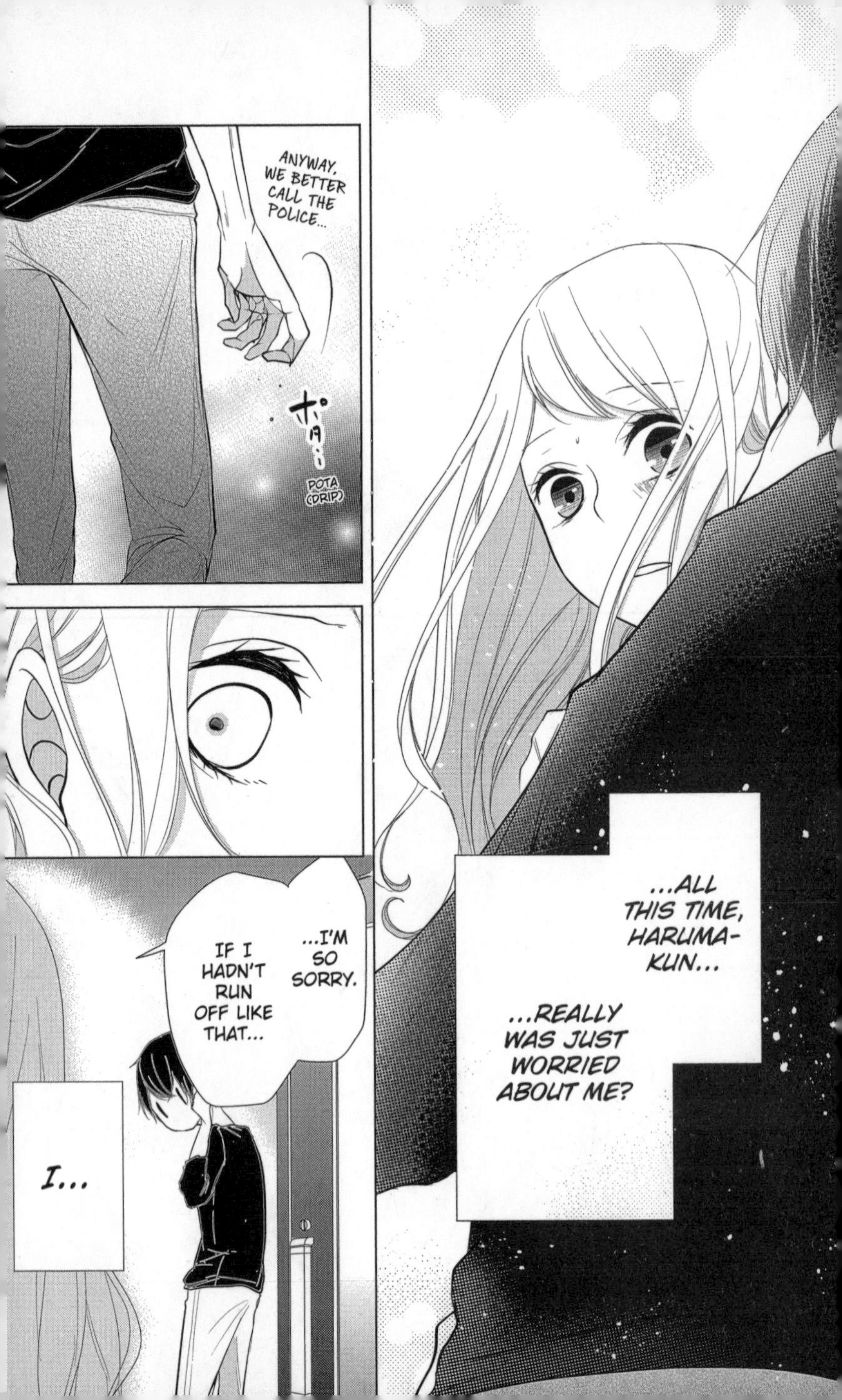
...ALL THIS TIME, HARUMA-KUN...
...REALLY WAS JUST WORRIED ABOUT ME?
ANYWAY, WE BETTER CALL THE POLICE...
ポタ
POTA (DRIP)
...I'M SO SORRY.
IF I HADN'T RUN OFF LIKE THAT...
I...

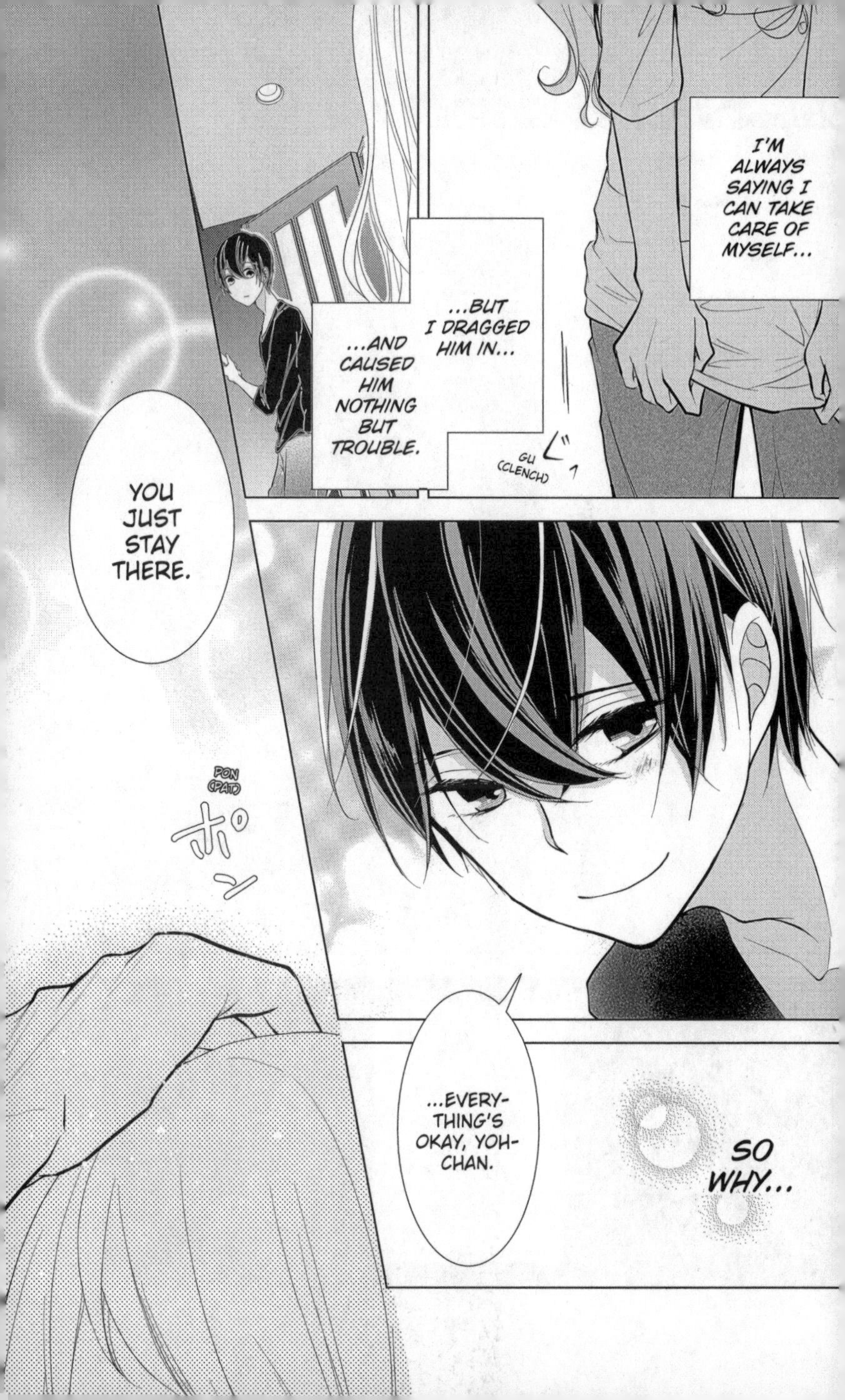
I'M ALWAYS SAYING I CAN TAKE CARE OF MYSELF...
...BUT I DRAGGED HIM IN...
...AND CAUSED HIM NOTHING BUT TROUBLE.
GU (CLENCH)
YOU JUST STAY THERE.
PON (PAT)
...EVERY-THING'S OKAY, YOH-CHAN.
SO WHY...

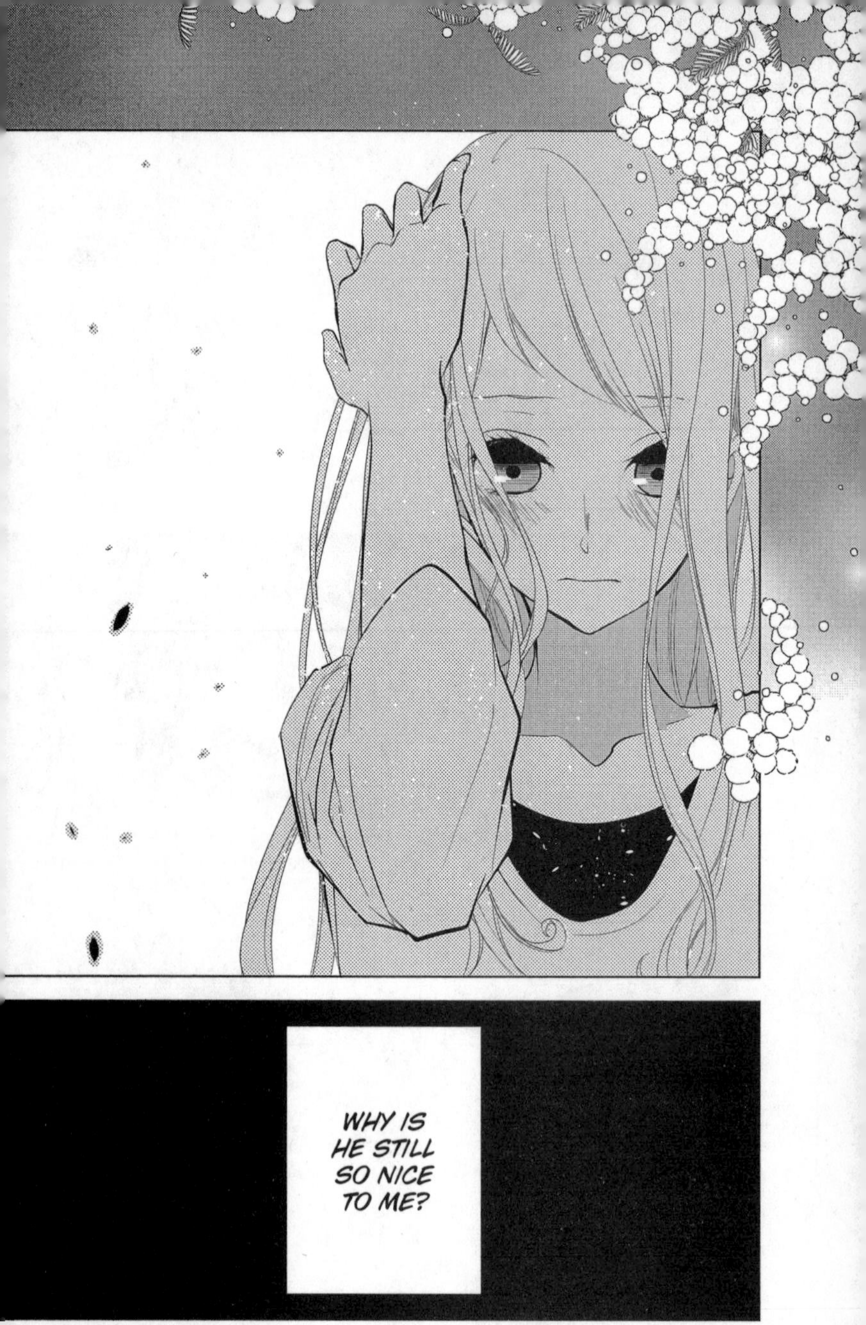
WHY IS HE STILL SO NICE TO ME?

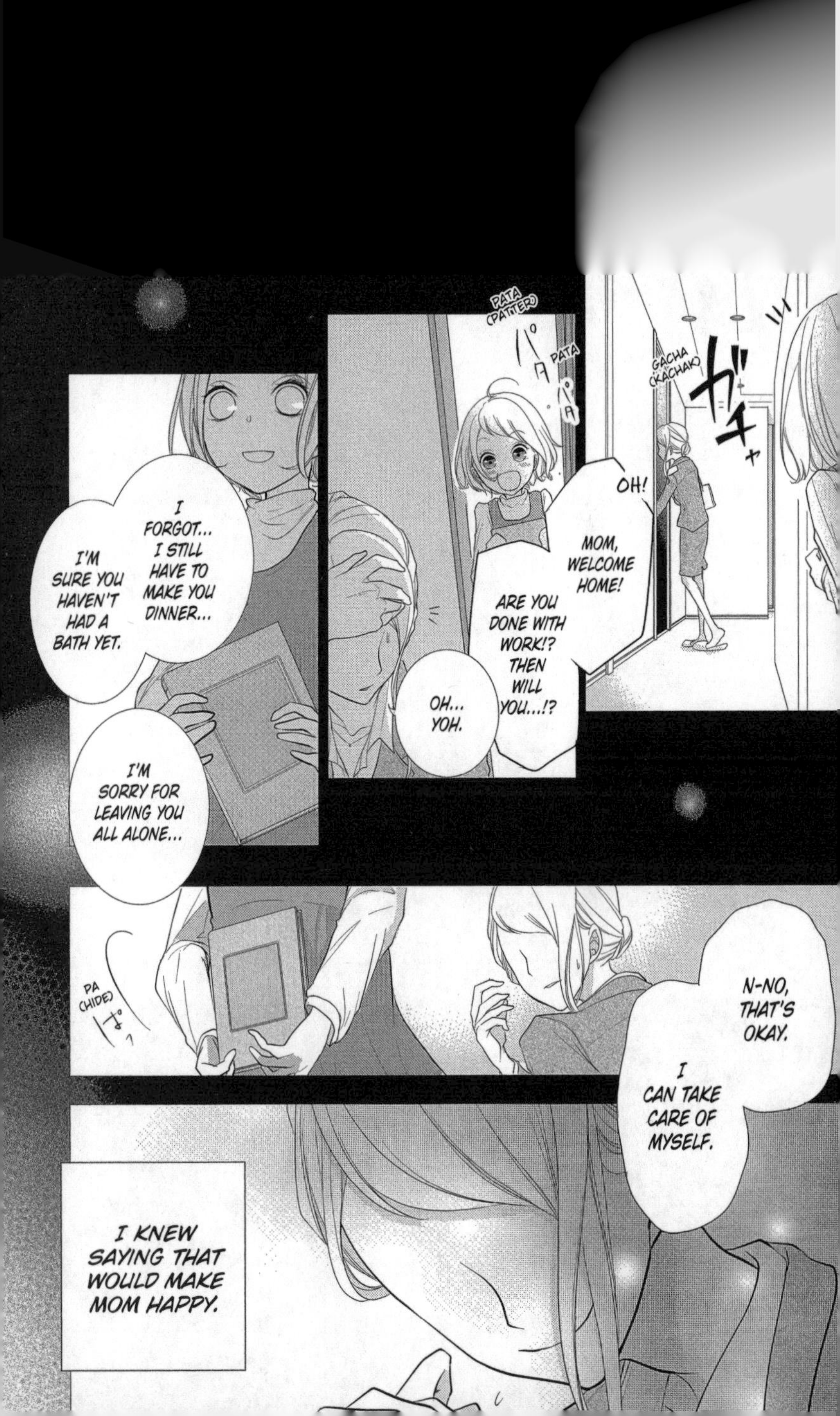
GACHA (KACHAK)
PATA (PATTER)
PATA
OH!
MOM, WELCOME HOME!
ARE YOU DONE WITH WORK!? THEN WILL YOU...!?
OH... YOH.
I FORGOT... I STILL HAVE TO MAKE YOU DINNER...
I'M SURE YOU HAVEN'T HAD A BATH YET.
I'M SORRY FOR LEAVING YOU ALL ALONE...
N-NO, THAT'S OKAY.
I CAN TAKE CARE OF MYSELF.
PA (HIDE)
I KNEW SAYING THAT WOULD MAKE MOM HAPPY.

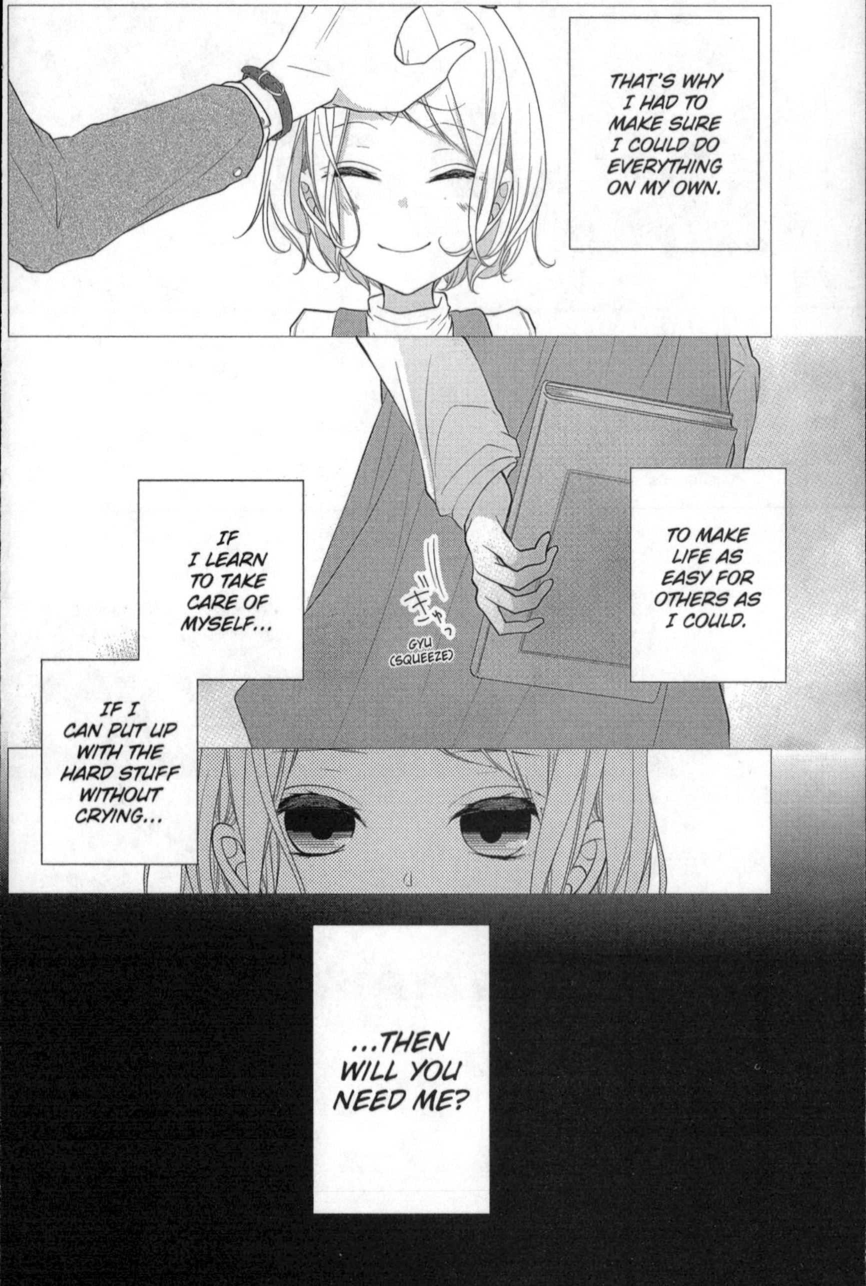
THAT'S WHY I HAD TO MAKE SURE I COULD DO EVERYTHING ON MY OWN.
TO MAKE LIFE AS EASY FOR OTHERS AS I COULD.
ぎゅっ
GYU (SQUEEZE)
IF I LEARN TO TAKE CARE OF MYSELF...
IF I CAN PUT UP WITH THE HARD STUFF WITHOUT CRYING...
...THEN WILL YOU NEED ME?

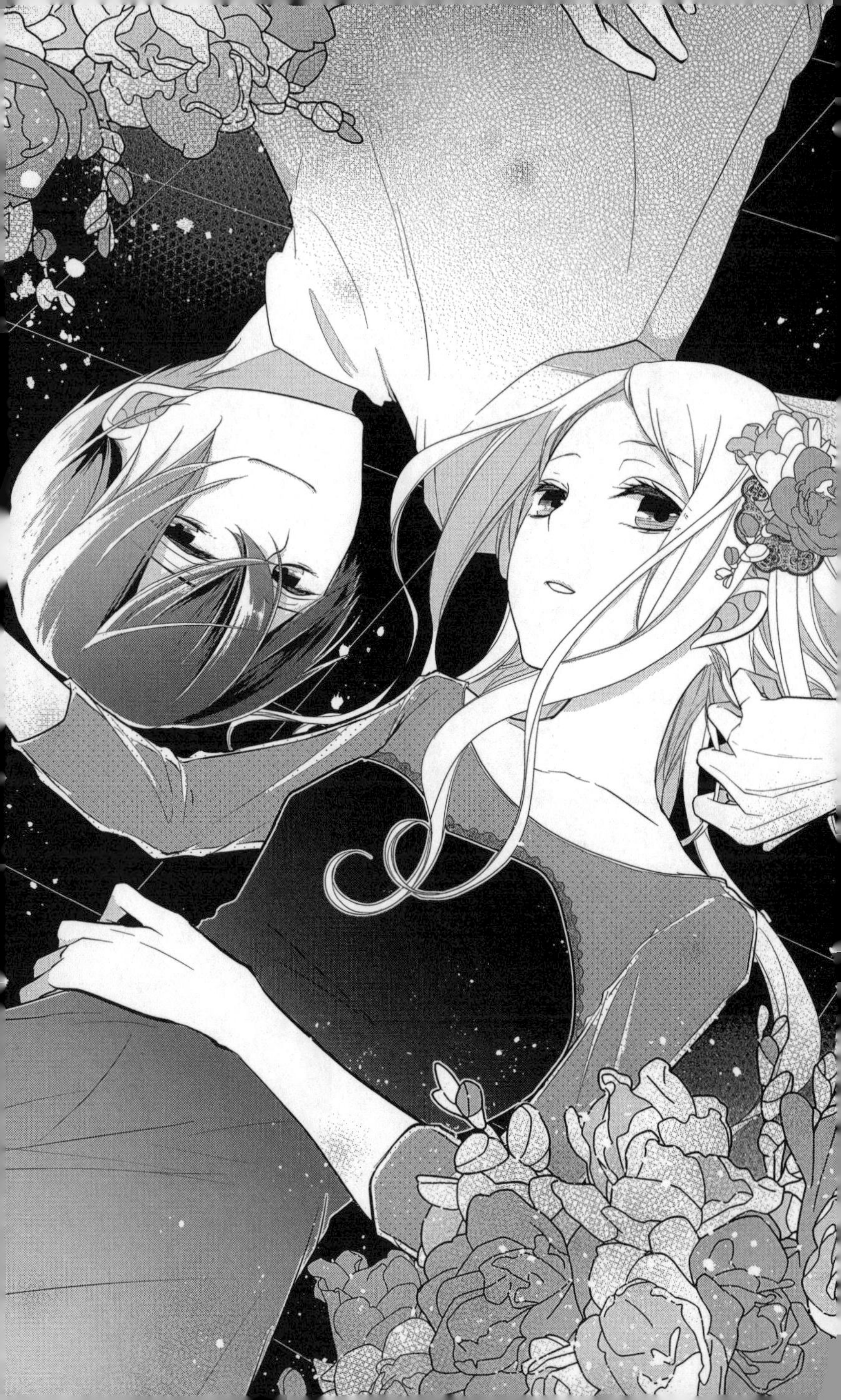

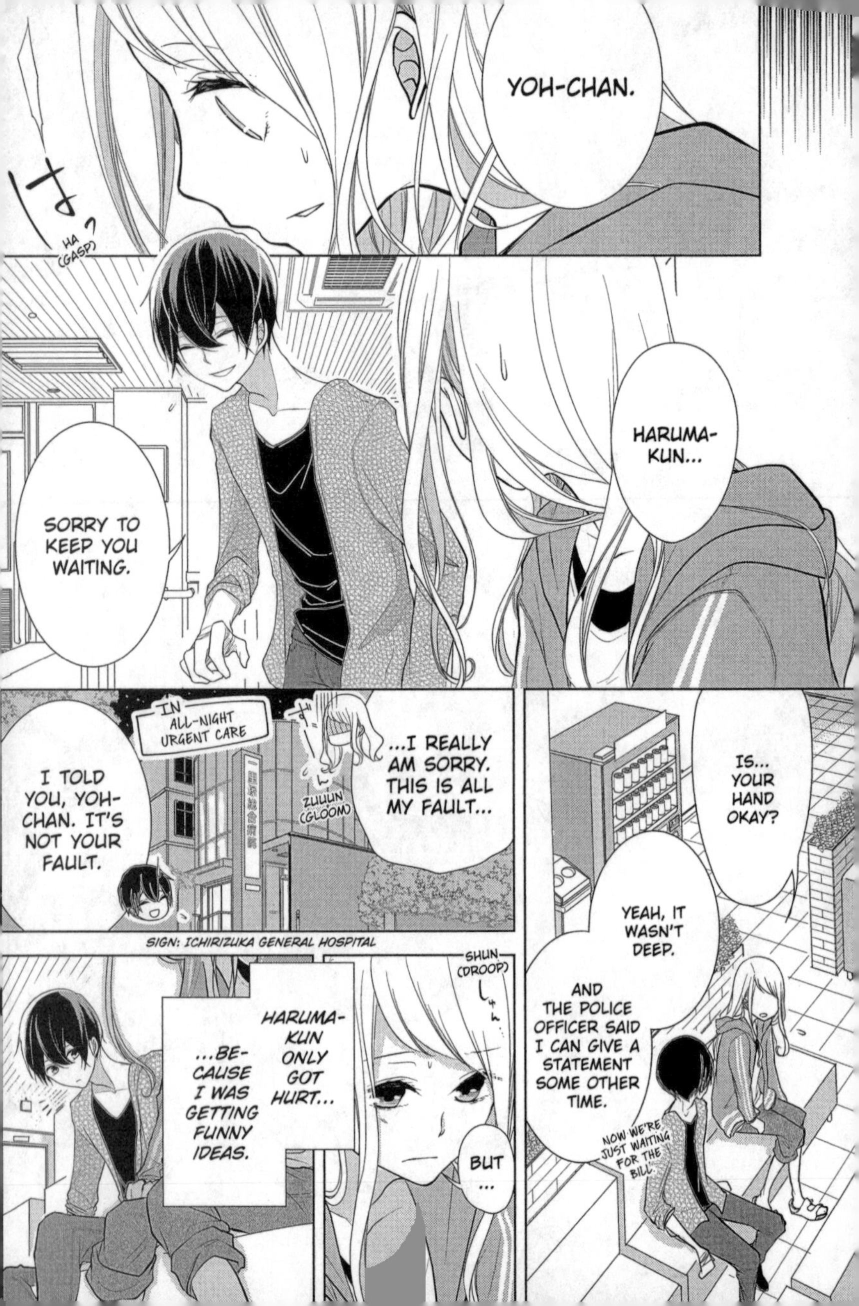
YOH-CHAN.
は
HA (GASP)
HARUMA-KUN...
SORRY TO KEEP YOU WAITING.
IS... YOUR HAND OKAY?
YEAH, IT WASN'T DEEP.
AND THE POLICE OFFICER SAID I CAN GIVE A STATEMENT SOME OTHER TIME.
NOW WE'RE JUST WAITING FOR THE BILL.
IN ALL-NIGHT URGENT CARE
...I REALLY AM SORRY. THIS IS ALL MY FAULT...
ZUUUN (GLOOM)
I TOLD YOU, YOH-CHAN. IT'S NOT YOUR FAULT.
SIGN: ICHIRIZUKA GENERAL HOSPITAL
SHUN (DROOP)
しゅん
BUT...
HARUMA-KUN ONLY GOT HURT...
...BE-CAUSE I WAS GETTING FUNNY IDEAS.

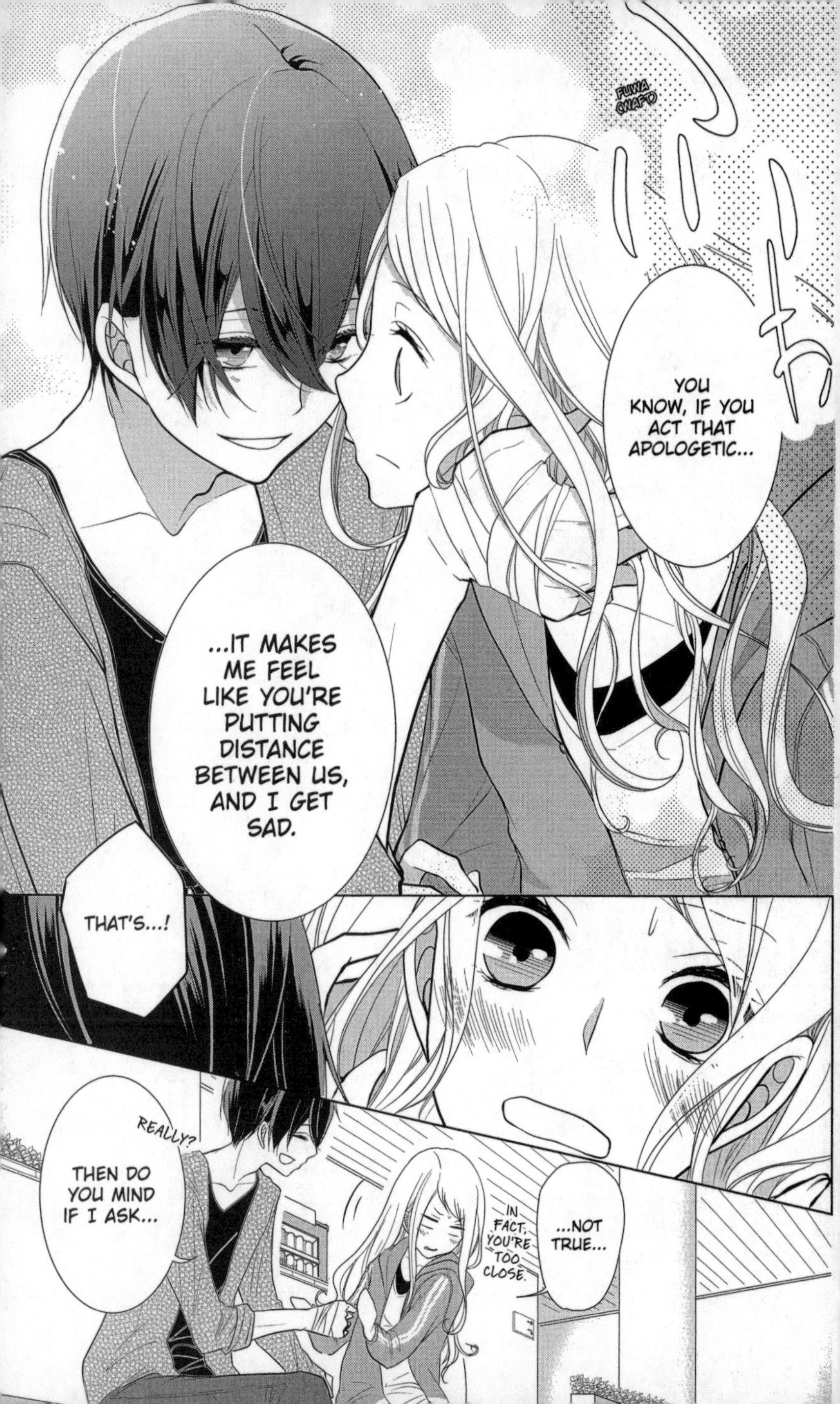
FUWA (WAFT)
YOU KNOW, IF YOU ACT THAT APOLOGETIC...
...IT MAKES ME FEEL LIKE YOU'RE PUTTING DISTANCE BETWEEN US, AND I GET SAD.
THAT'S...!
...NOT TRUE...
IN FACT, YOU'RE TOO CLOSE.
REALLY?
THEN DO YOU MIND IF I ASK...

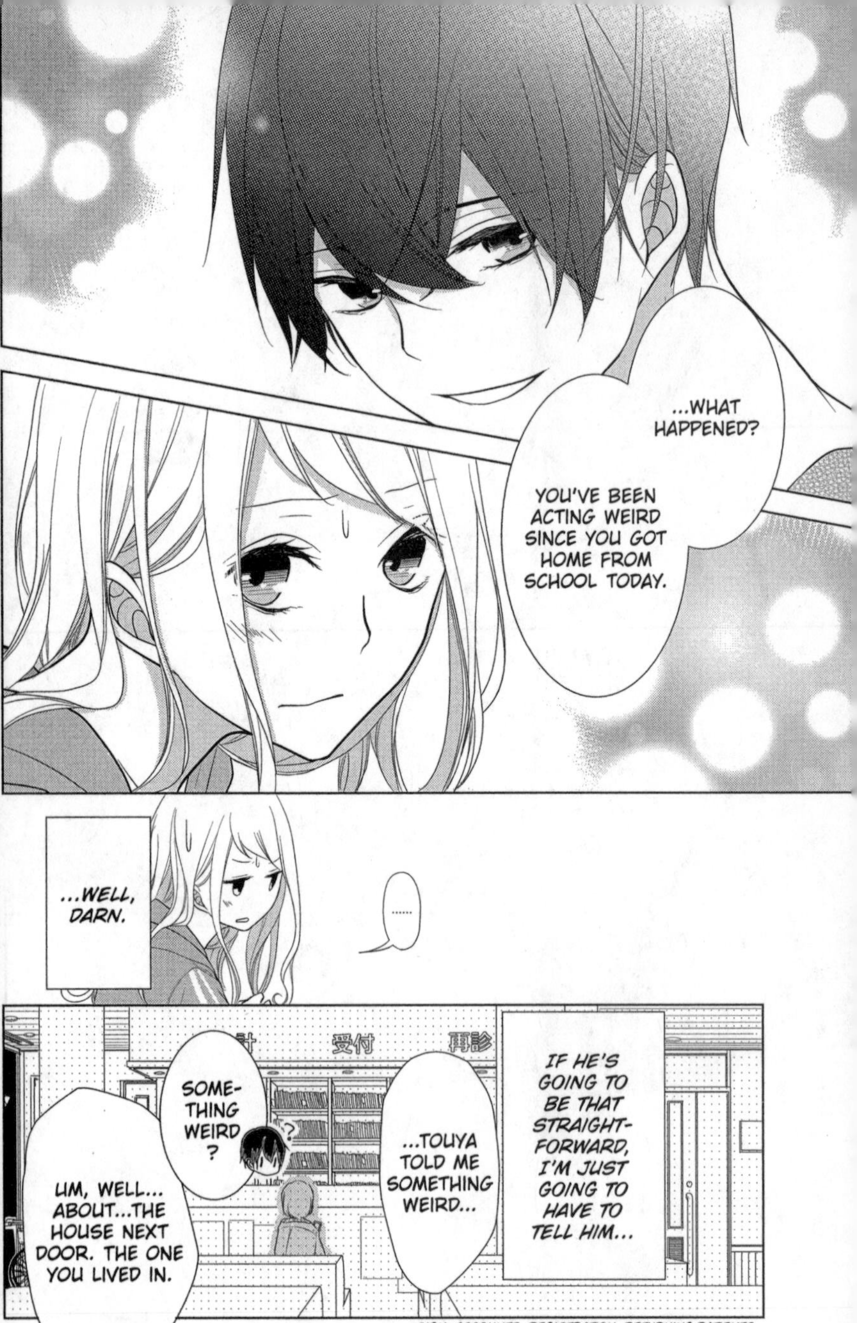
...WHAT HAPPENED?
YOU'VE BEEN ACTING WEIRD SINCE YOU GOT HOME FROM SCHOOL TODAY.
......
...WELL, DARN.
IF HE'S GOING TO BE THAT STRAIGHT-FORWARD, I'M JUST GOING TO HAVE TO TELL HIM...
...TOUYA TOLD ME SOMETHING WEIRD...
SOME-THING WEIRD?
?
UM, WELL... ABOUT...THE HOUSE NEXT DOOR. THE ONE YOU LIVED IN.
受付
再診
SIGN: ACCOUNTS, REGISTRATION, RETURNING PATIENTS

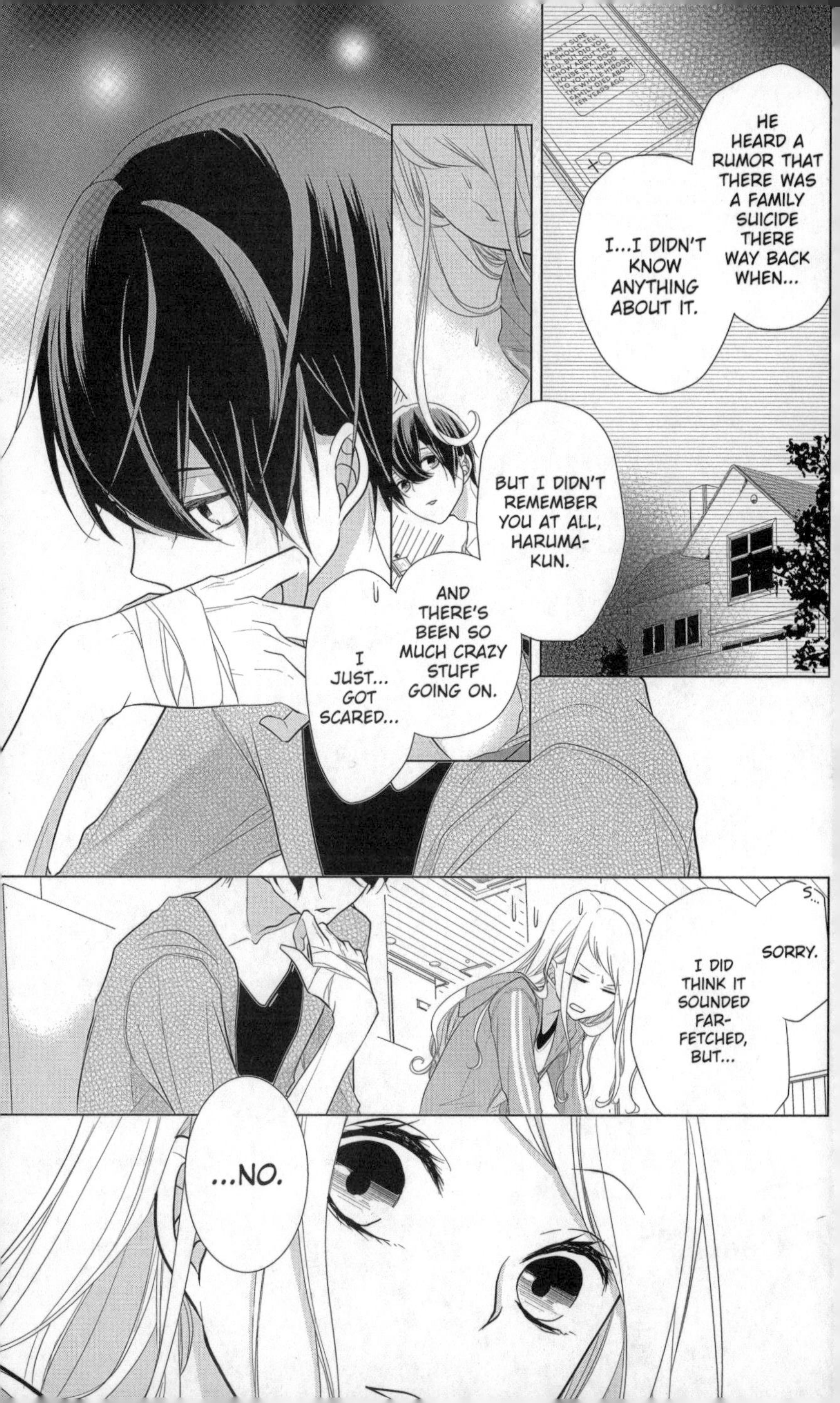
WASN'T SURE IF I SHOULD TELL YOU, BUT DID YOU KNOW ABOUT THE HOUSE NEXT DOOR TO YOU? I HEARD THE WHOLE HIROSE FAMILY DIED ABOUT TEN YEARS AGO
HE HEARD A RUMOR THAT THERE WAS A FAMILY SUICIDE THERE WAY BACK WHEN...
I...I DIDN'T KNOW ANYTHING ABOUT IT.
BUT I DIDN'T REMEMBER YOU AT ALL, HARUMA-KUN.
AND THERE'S BEEN SO MUCH CRAZY STUFF GOING ON.
I JUST... GOT SCARED...
S...
SORRY.
I DID THINK IT SOUNDED FAR-FETCHED, BUT...
...NO.

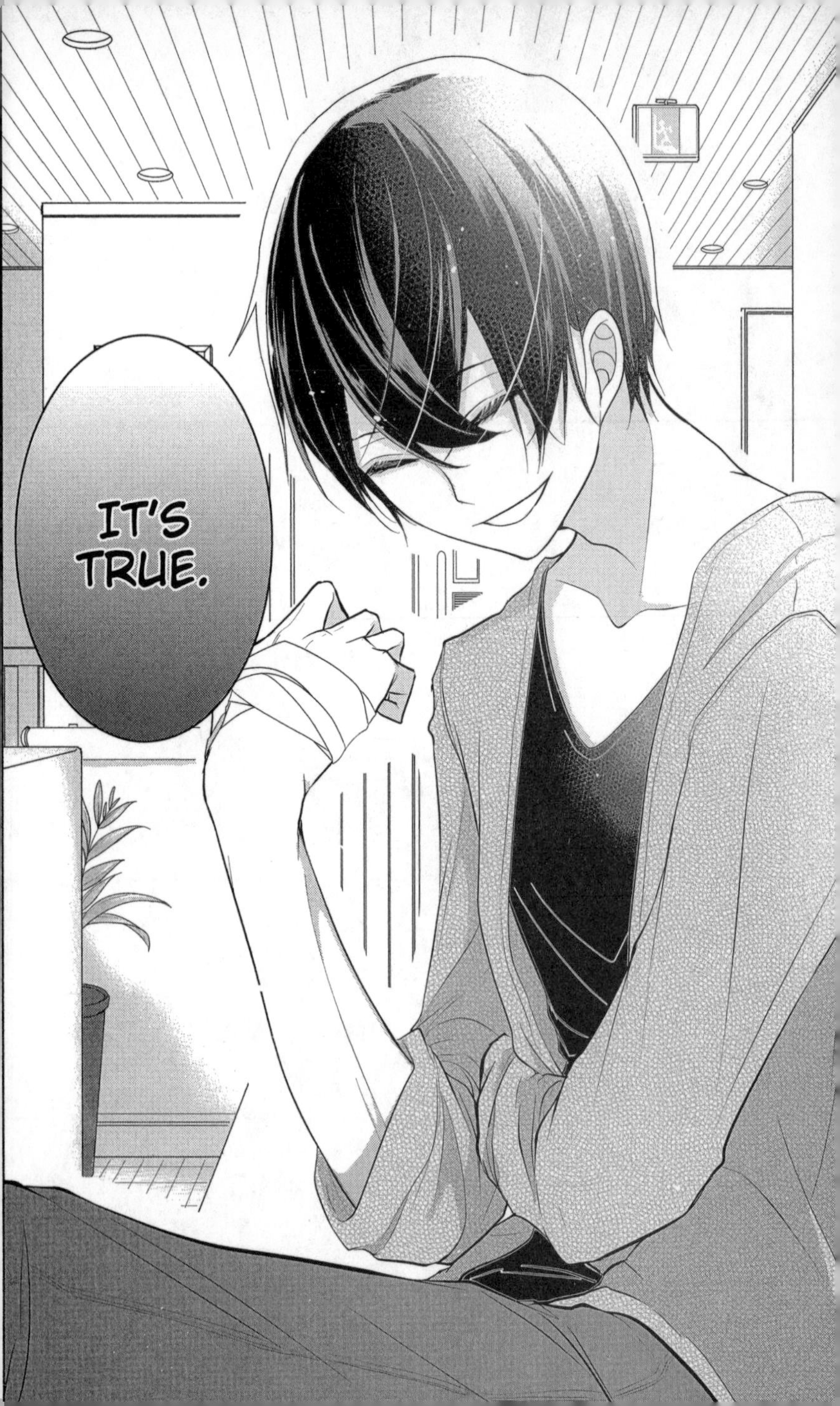
IT'S TRUE.

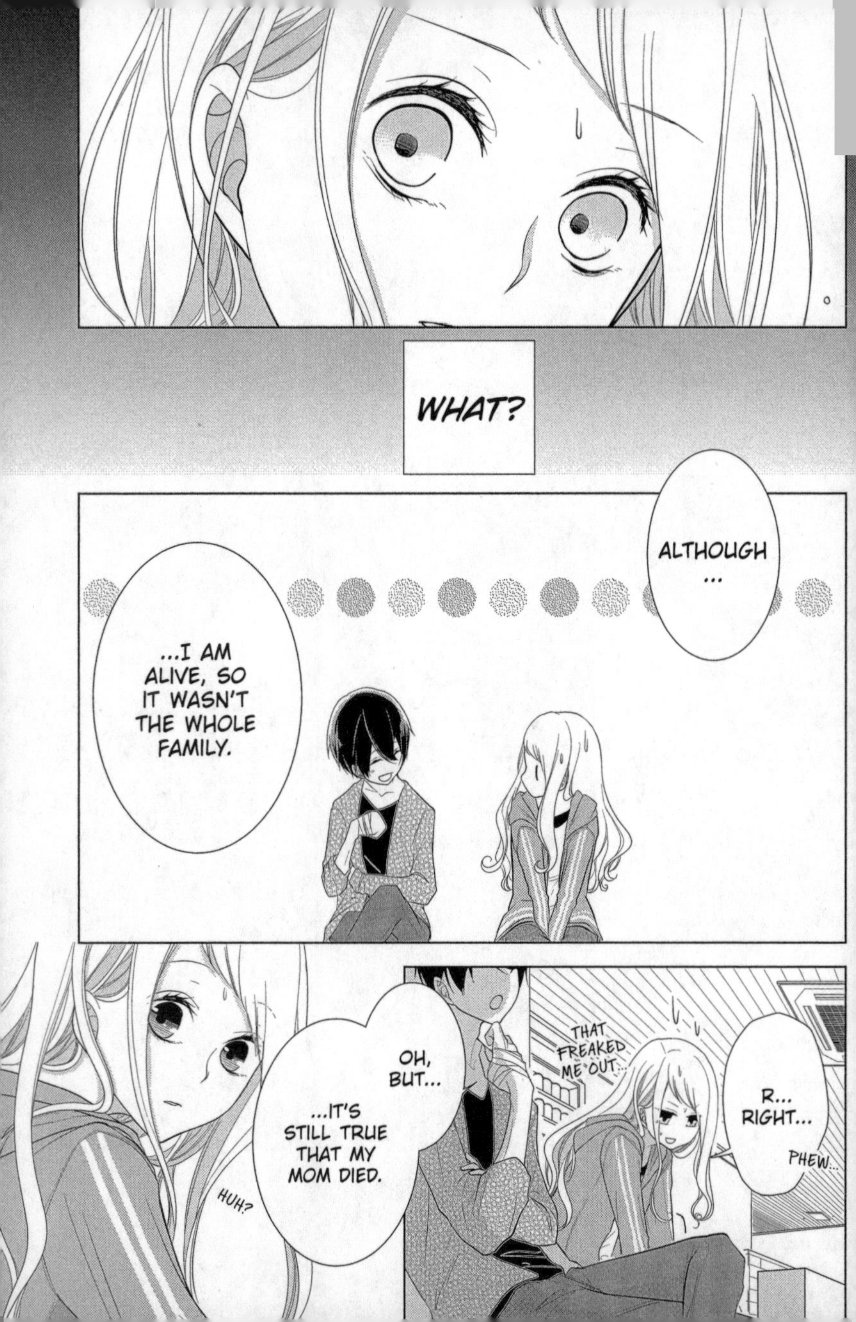
WHAT?
ALTHOUGH...
...I AM ALIVE, SO IT WASN'T THE WHOLE FAMILY.
R... RIGHT...
THAT FREAKED ME OUT...
PHEW...
OH, BUT...
...IT'S STILL TRUE THAT MY MOM DIED.
HUH?

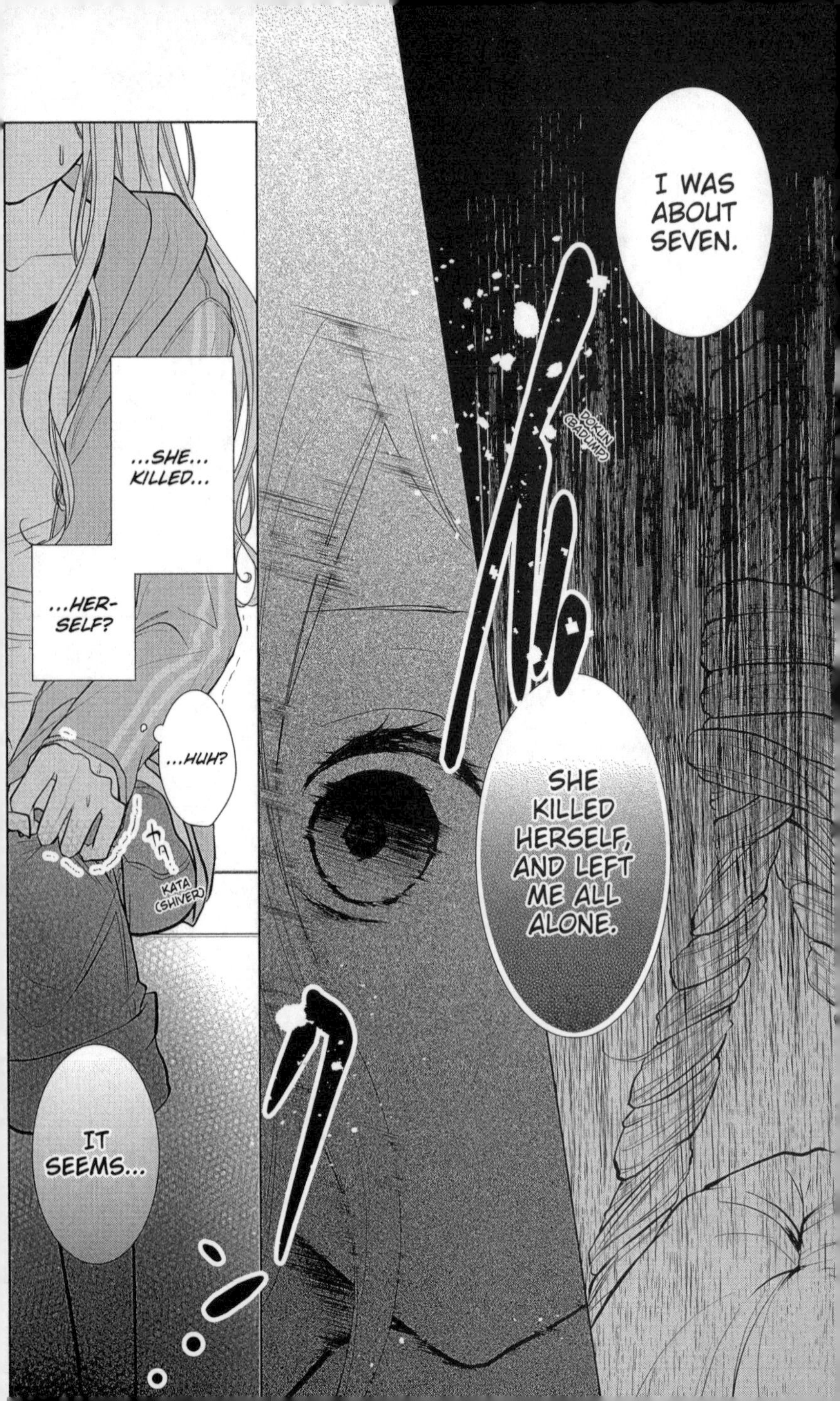
I WAS ABOUT SEVEN.
DOKUN (BADUMP)
SHE KILLED HERSELF, AND LEFT ME ALL ALONE.
...SHE... KILLED...
...HER-SELF?
...HUH?
KATA (SHIVER)
IT SEEMS...

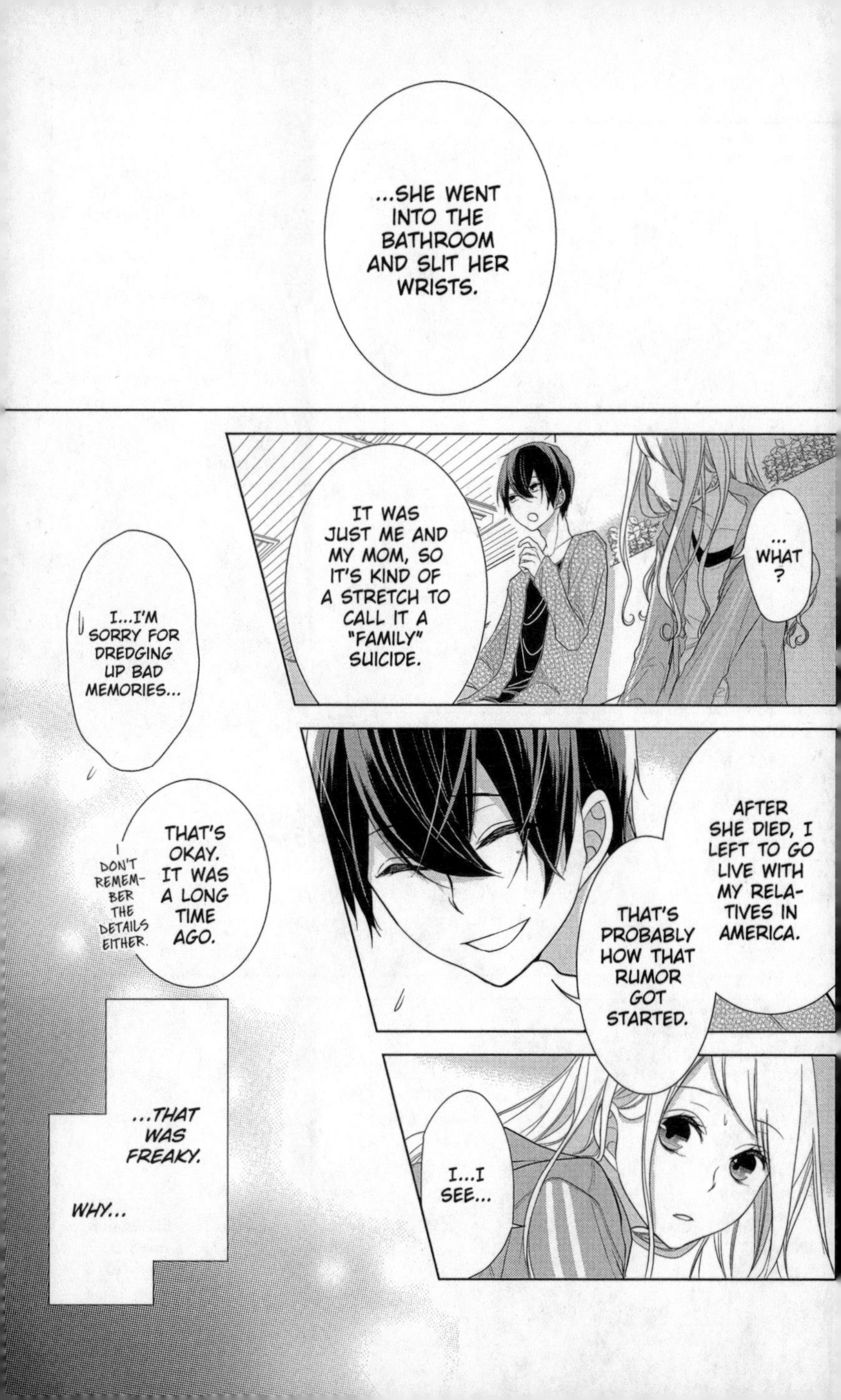
...SHE WENT INTO THE BATHROOM AND SLIT HER WRISTS.
...WHAT?
IT WAS JUST ME AND MY MOM, SO IT'S KIND OF A STRETCH TO CALL IT A "FAMILY" SUICIDE.
I...I'M SORRY FOR DREDGING UP BAD MEMORIES...
AFTER SHE DIED, I LEFT TO GO LIVE WITH MY RELA-TIVES IN AMERICA.
THAT'S PROBABLY HOW THAT RUMOR GOT STARTED.
THAT'S OKAY. IT WAS A LONG TIME AGO.
I DON'T REMEM-BER THE DETAILS EITHER.
I...I SEE...
...THAT WAS FREAKY.
WHY...

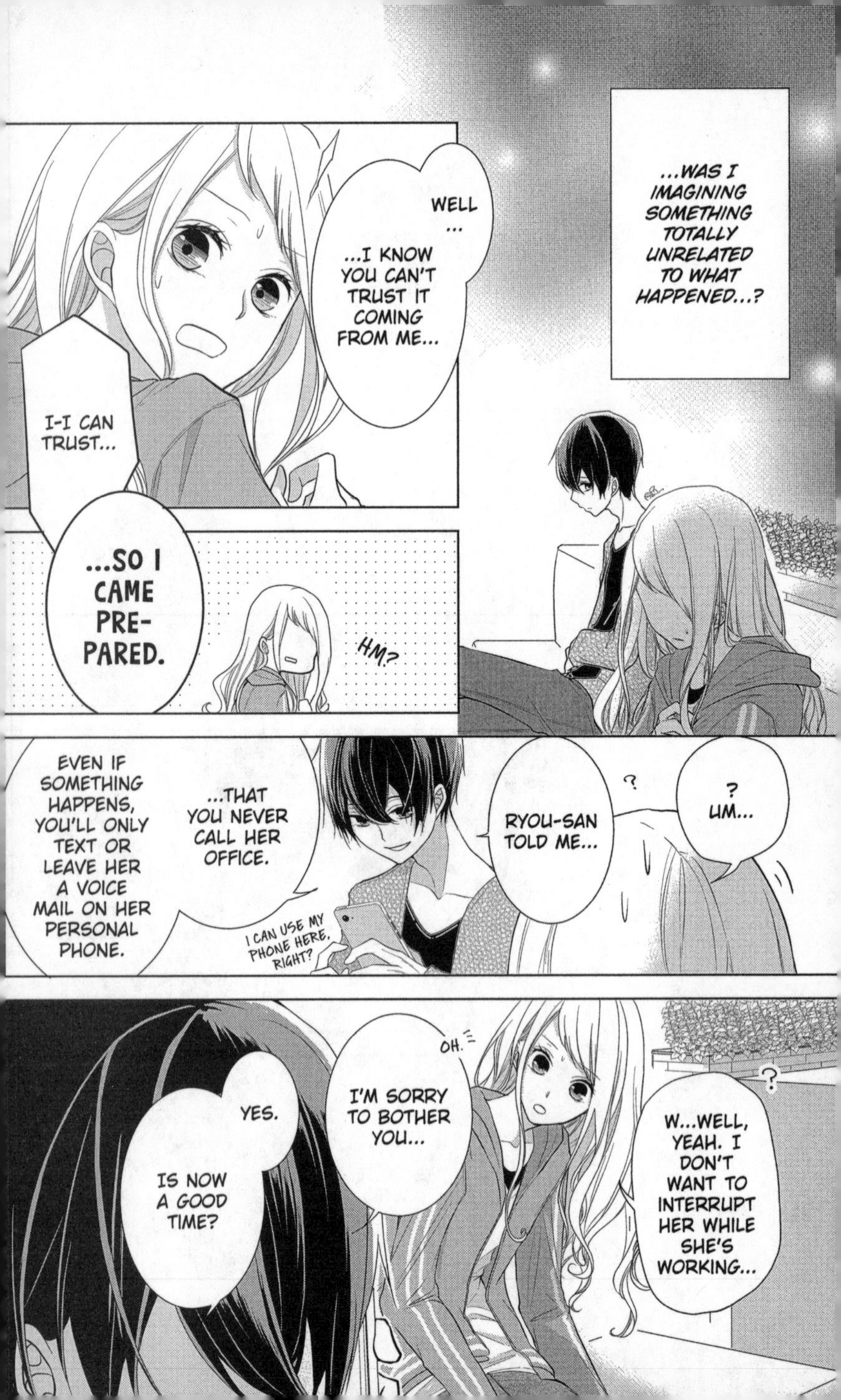

...WAS I IMAGINING SOMETHING TOTALLY UNRELATED TO WHAT HAPPENED...?
WELL ...
...I KNOW YOU CAN'T TRUST IT COMING FROM ME...
I-I CAN TRUST...
...SO I CAME PRE-PARED.
HM?
? UM...
?
RYOU-SAN TOLD ME...
...THAT YOU NEVER CALL HER OFFICE.
I CAN USE MY PHONE HERE, RIGHT?
EVEN IF SOMETHING HAPPENS, YOU'LL ONLY TEXT OR LEAVE HER A VOICE MAIL ON HER PERSONAL PHONE.
?
W...WELL, YEAH. I DON'T WANT TO INTERRUPT HER WHILE SHE'S WORKING...
OH.
I'M SORRY TO BOTHER YOU...
YES.
IS NOW A GOOD TIME?

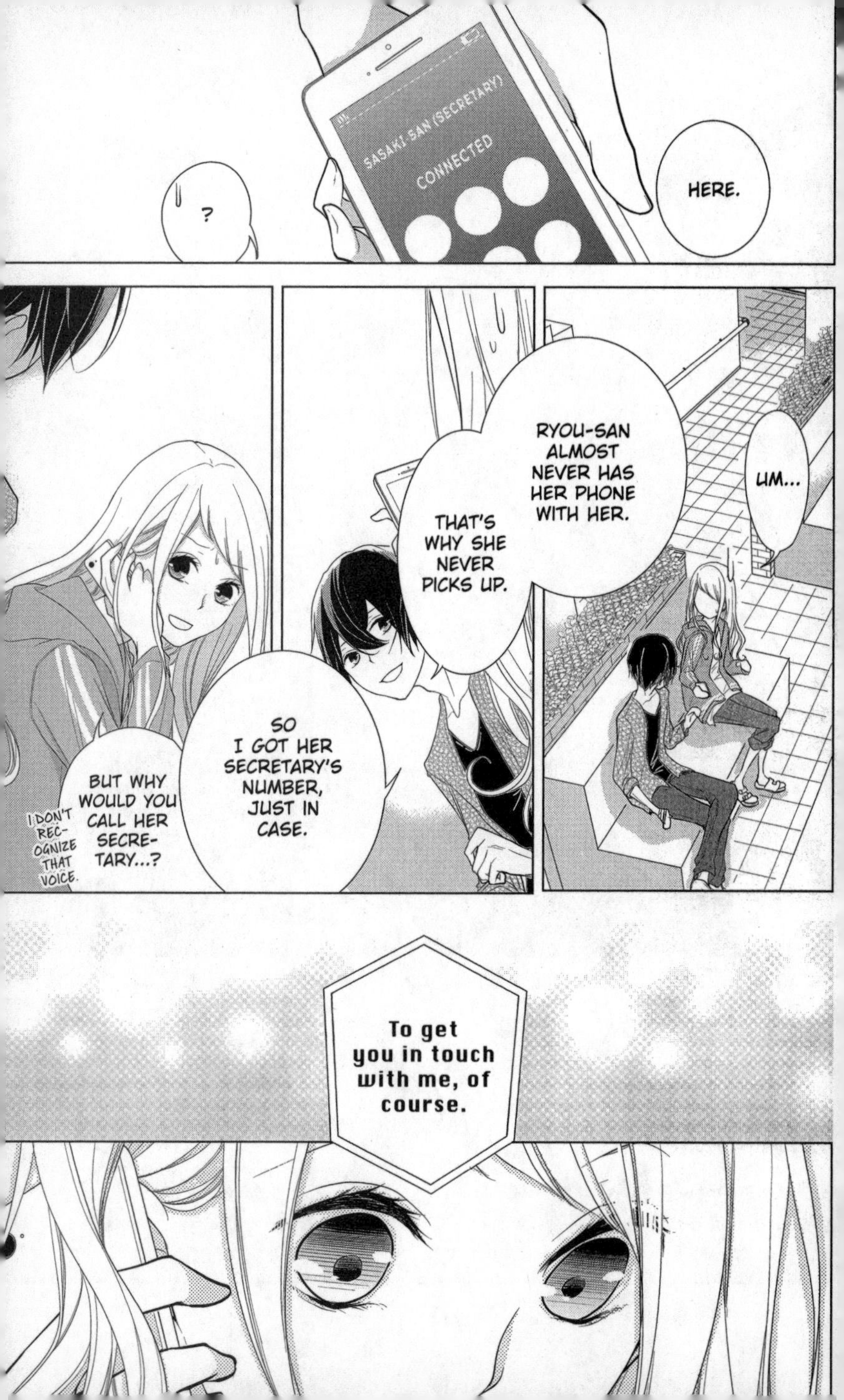
HERE.
SASAKI-SAN (SECRETARY)
CONNECTED
?
UM...
RYOU-SAN ALMOST NEVER HAS HER PHONE WITH HER.
THAT'S WHY SHE NEVER PICKS UP.
SO I GOT HER SECRETARY'S NUMBER, JUST IN CASE.
BUT WHY WOULD YOU CALL HER SECRE-TARY...?
I DON'T REC-OGNIZE THAT VOICE.
To get you in touch with me, of course.

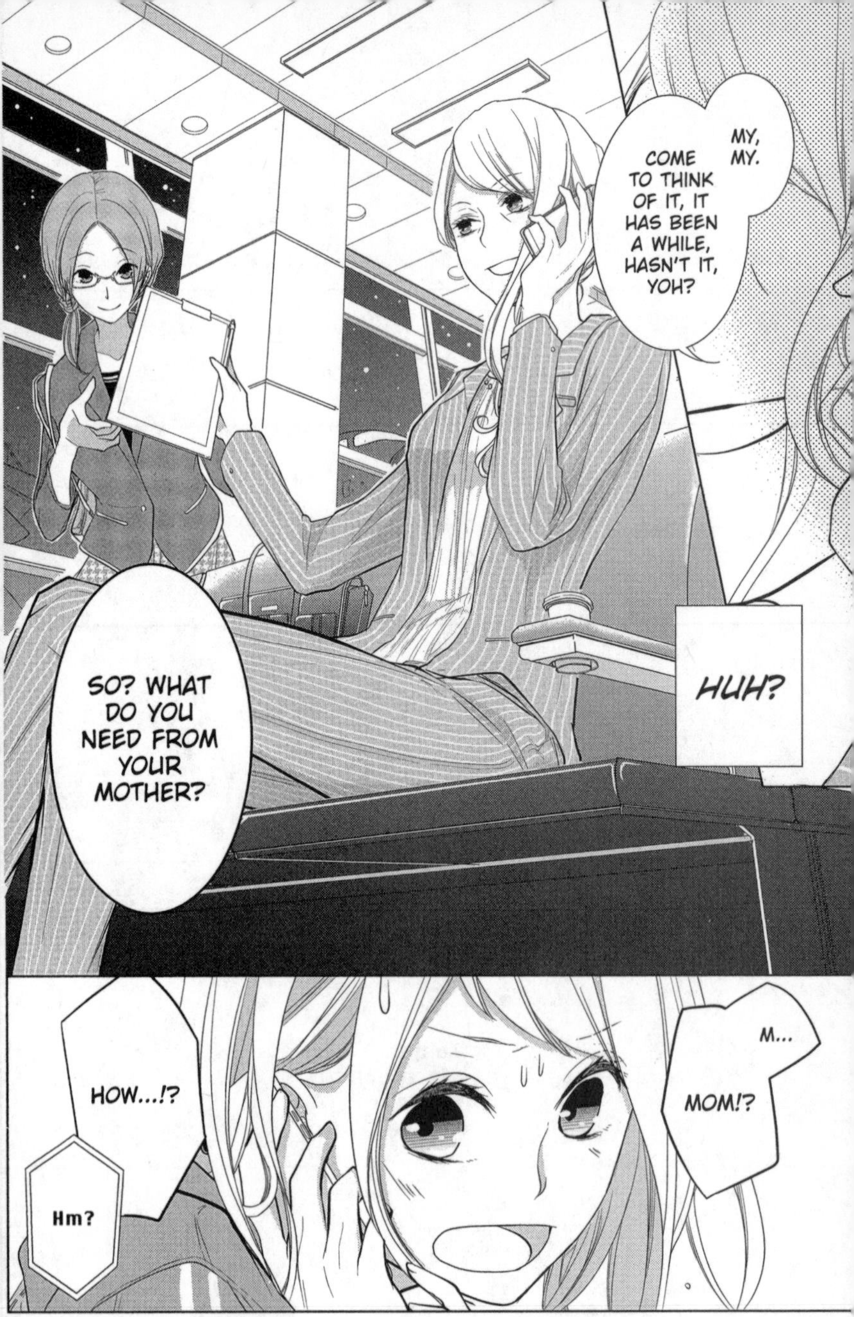
MY, MY.
COME TO THINK OF IT, IT HAS BEEN A WHILE, HASN'T IT, YOH?
SO? WHAT DO YOU NEED FROM YOUR MOTHER?
HUH?
M... MOM!?
HOW...!?
Hm?

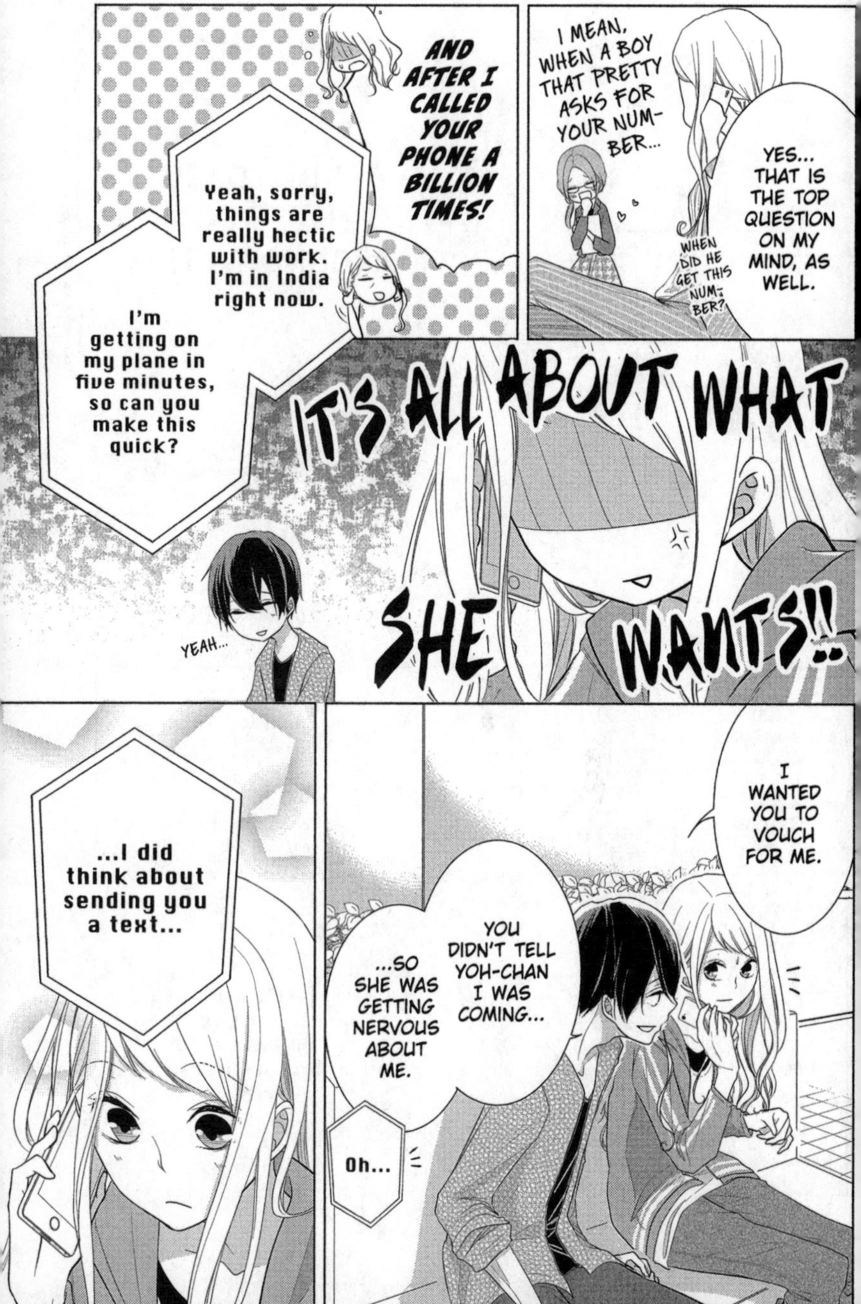
I MEAN, WHEN A BOY THAT PRETTY ASKS FOR YOUR NUMBER...
YES... THAT IS THE TOP QUESTION ON MY MIND, AS WELL.
WHEN DID HE GET THIS NUMBER?
AND AFTER I CALLED YOUR PHONE A BILLION TIMES!
Yeah, sorry, things are really hectic with work. I'm in India right now.
I'm getting on my plane in five minutes, so can you make this quick?
IT'S ALL ABOUT WHAT SHE WANTS!!
YEAH...
I WANTED YOU TO VOUCH FOR ME.
YOU DIDN'T TELL YOH-CHAN I WAS COMING...
...SO SHE WAS GETTING NERVOUS ABOUT ME.
Oh...
...I did think about sending you a text...

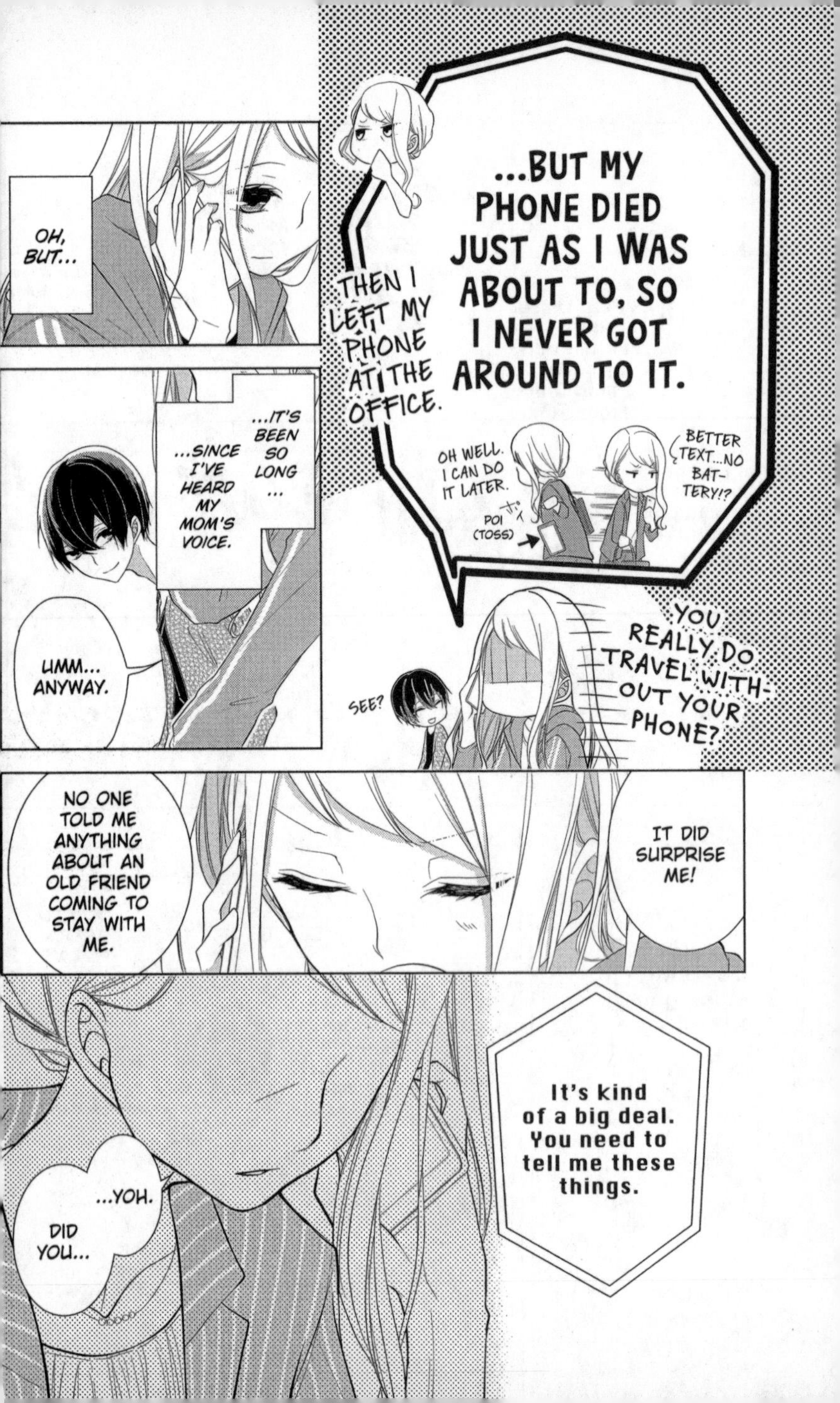
...BUT MY PHONE DIED JUST AS I WAS ABOUT TO, SO I NEVER GOT AROUND TO IT.
THEN I LEFT MY PHONE AT THE OFFICE.
BETTER TEXT...NO BATTERY!?
OH WELL. I CAN DO IT LATER.
ポイ
POI (TOSS)
YOU REALLY DO TRAVEL WITHOUT YOUR PHONE?
SEE?
OH, BUT...
...IT'S BEEN SO LONG...
...SINCE I'VE HEARD MY MOM'S VOICE.
UMM... ANYWAY.
IT DID SURPRISE ME!
NO ONE TOLD ME ANYTHING ABOUT AN OLD FRIEND COMING TO STAY WITH ME.
It's kind of a big deal. You need to tell me these things.
...YOH.
DID YOU...

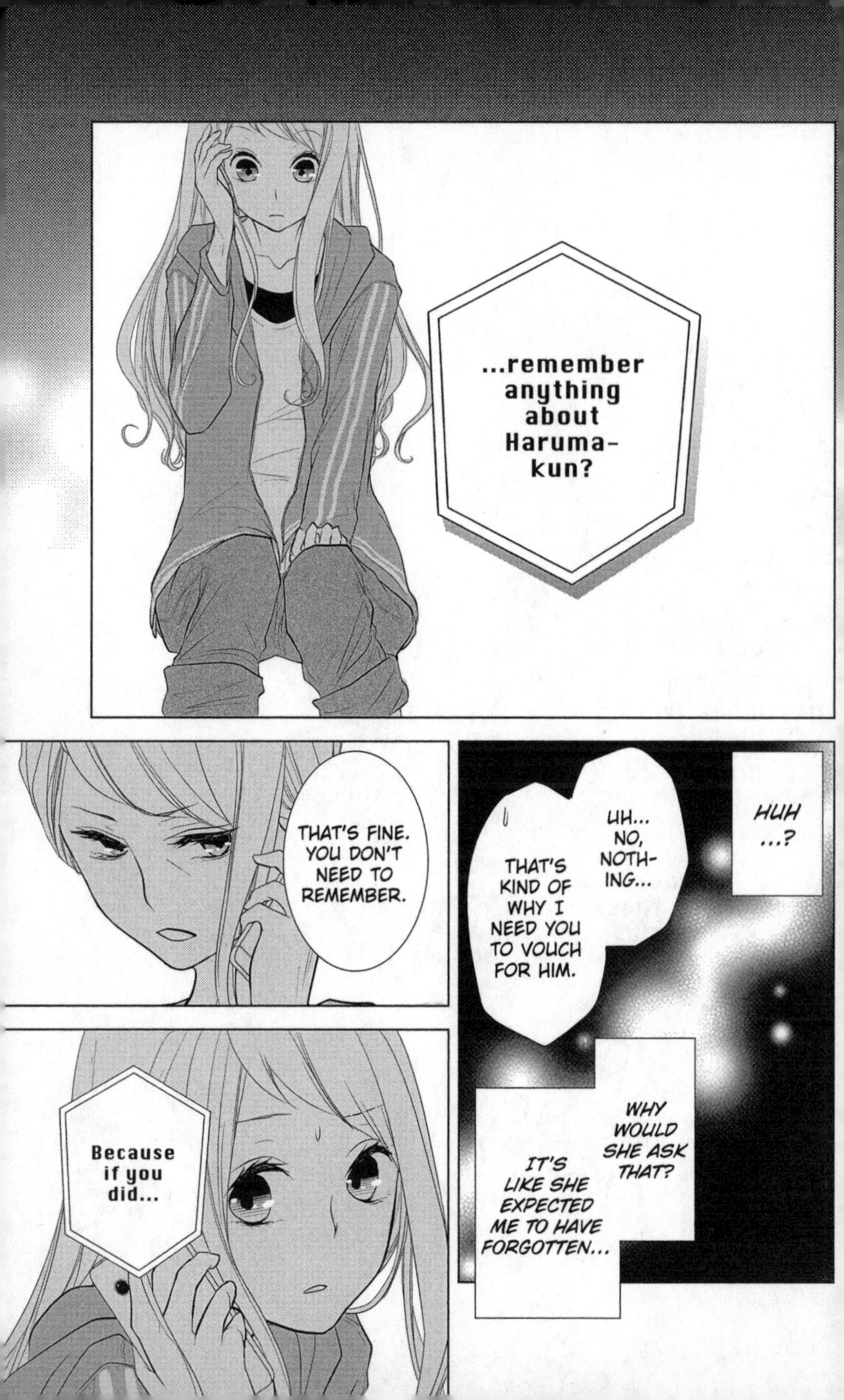
...remember anything about Haruma-kun?
HUH ...?
UH... NO, NOTH-ING...
THAT'S KIND OF WHY I NEED YOU TO VOUCH FOR HIM.
WHY WOULD SHE ASK THAT?
IT'S LIKE SHE EXPECTED ME TO HAVE FORGOTTEN...
THAT'S FINE. YOU DON'T NEED TO REMEMBER.
Because if you did...

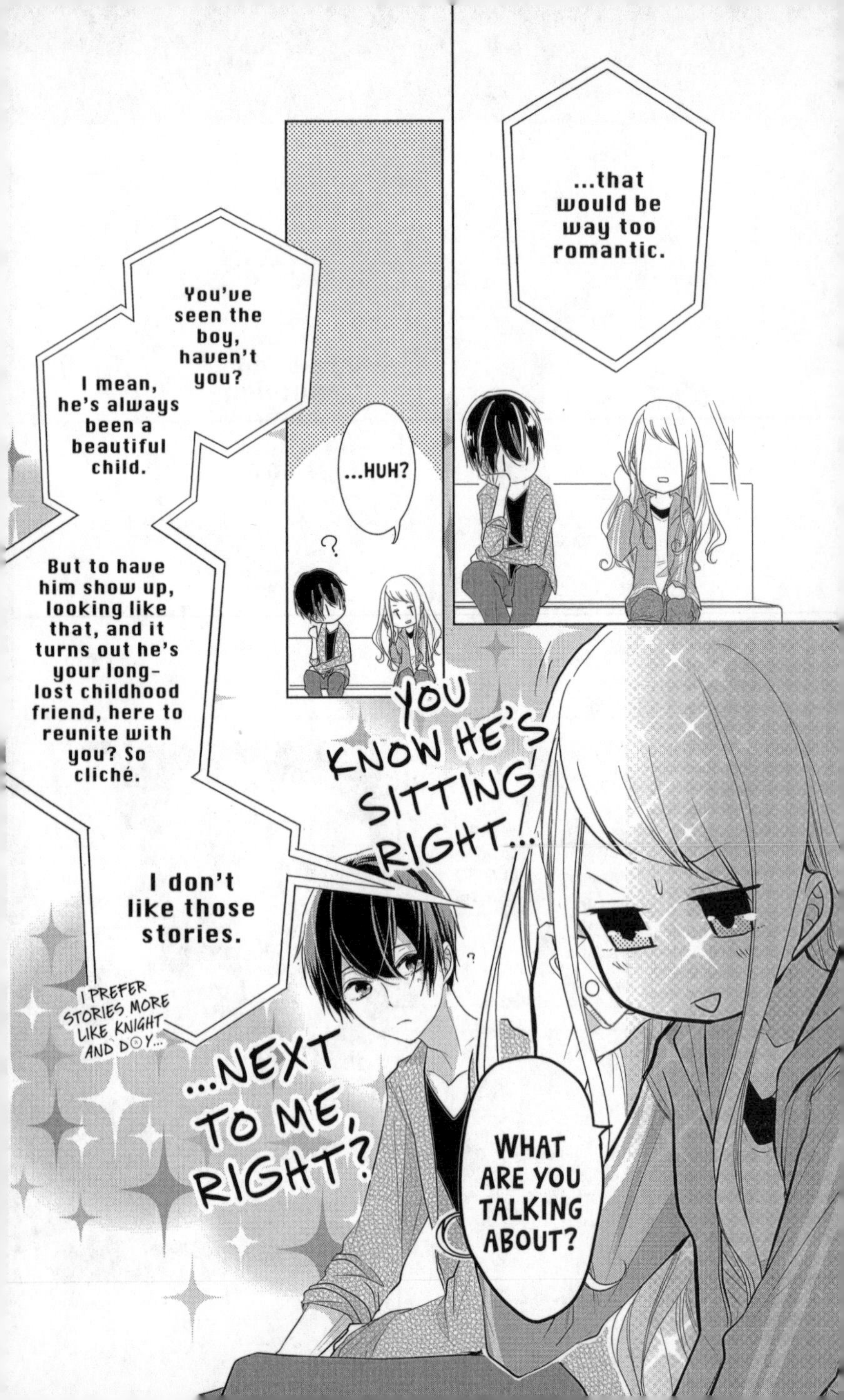
...that would be way too romantic.
...HUH?
You've seen the boy, haven't you?
I mean, he's always been a beautiful child.
But to have him show up, looking like that, and it turns out he's your long-lost childhood friend, here to reunite with you? So cliché.
I don't like those stories.
I PREFER STORIES MORE LIKE KNIGHT AND D◎Y...
YOU KNOW HE'S SITTING RIGHT...
WHAT ARE YOU TALKING ABOUT?
...NEXT TO ME, RIGHT?

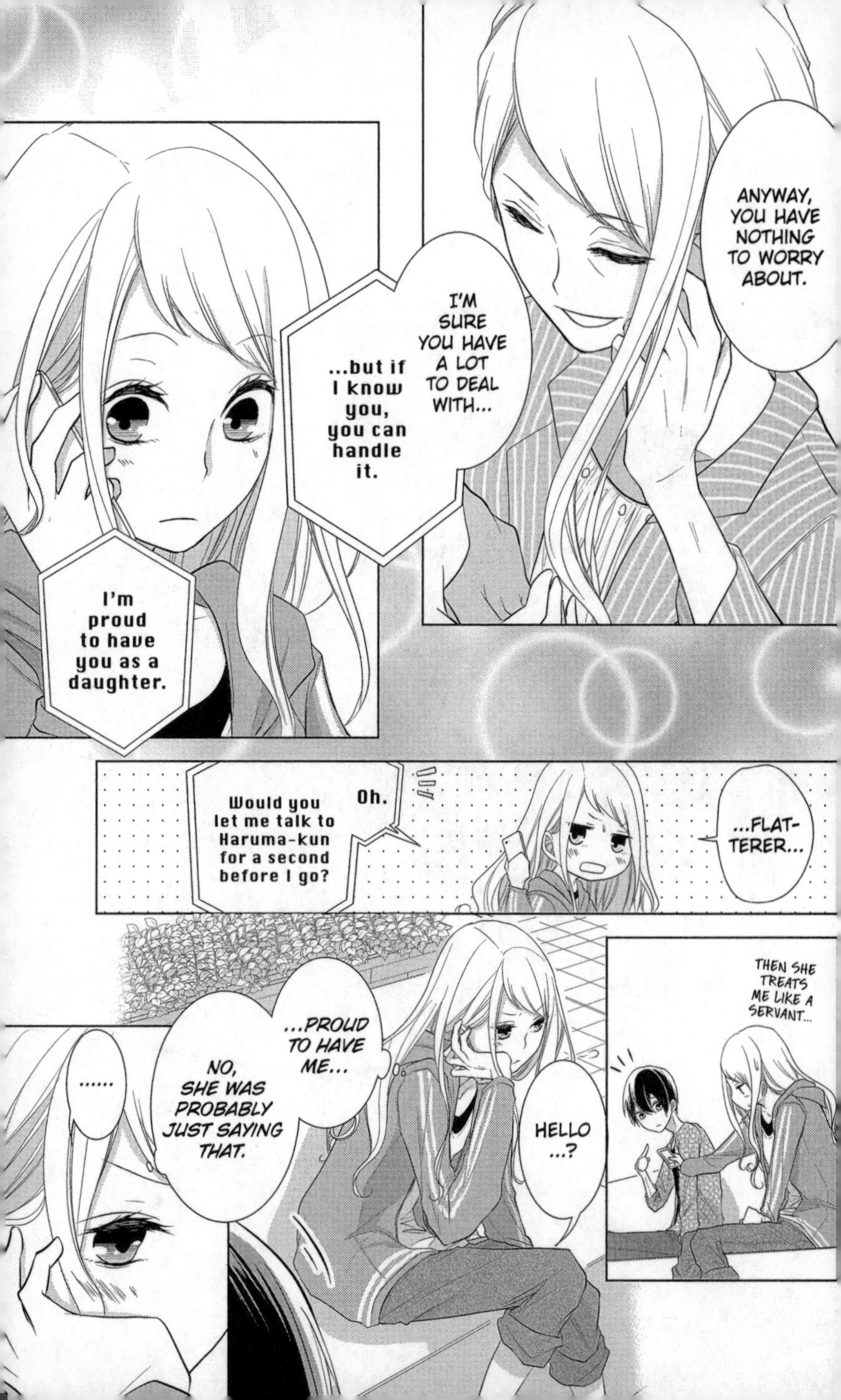
ANYWAY, YOU HAVE NOTHING TO WORRY ABOUT.
I'M SURE YOU HAVE A LOT TO DEAL WITH...
...but if I know you, you can handle it.
I'm proud to have you as a daughter.
...FLAT-TERER...
Oh.
Would you let me talk to Haruma-kun for a second before I go?
THEN SHE TREATS ME LIKE A SERVANT...
HELLO ...?
...PROUD TO HAVE ME...
NO, SHE WAS PROBABLY JUST SAYING THAT.
......

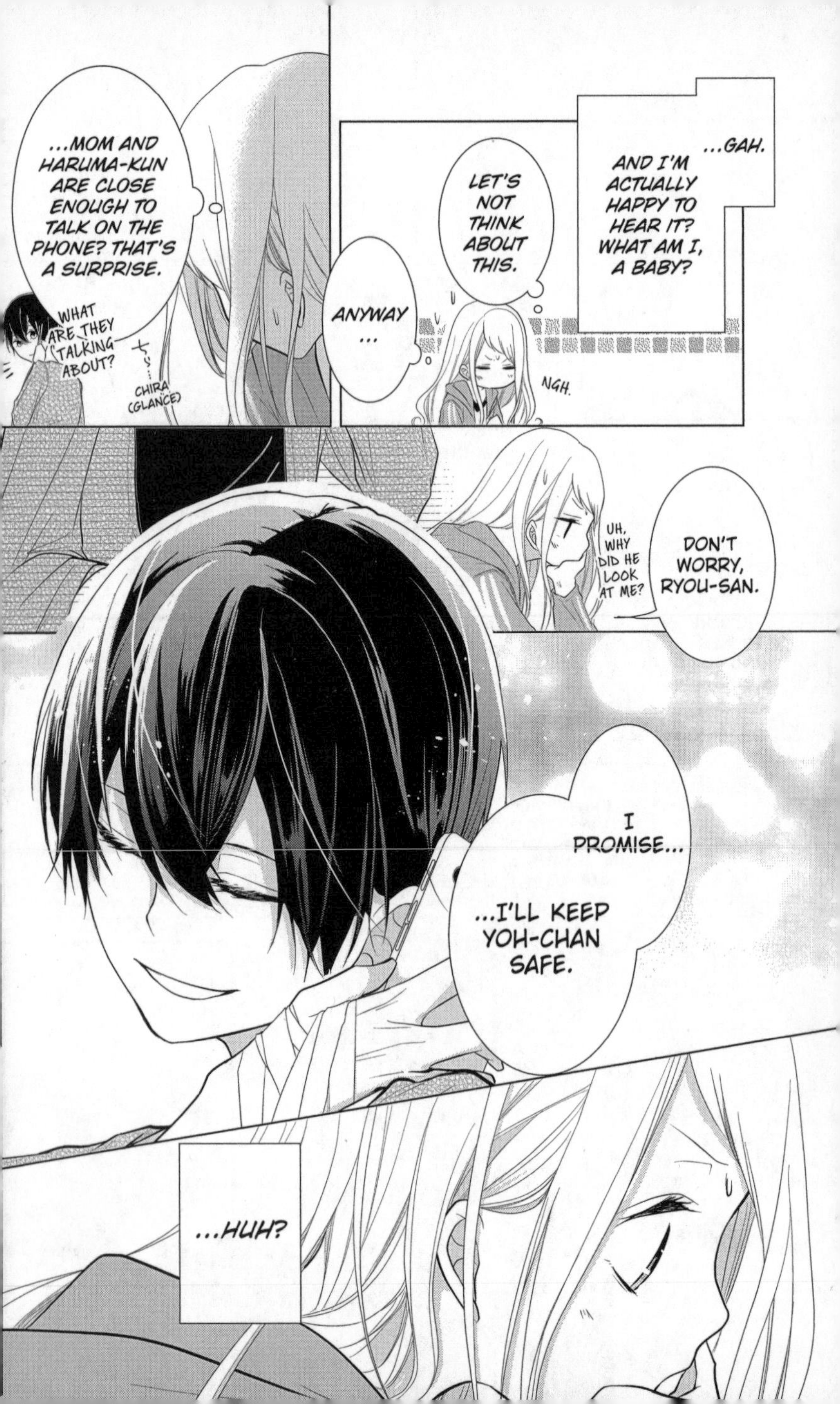
...GAH.
AND I'M ACTUALLY HAPPY TO HEAR IT? WHAT AM I, A BABY?
LET'S NOT THINK ABOUT THIS.
ANYWAY...
NGH.
...MOM AND HARUMA-KUN ARE CLOSE ENOUGH TO TALK ON THE PHONE? THAT'S A SURPRISE.
CHIRA (GLANCE)
WHAT ARE THEY TALKING ABOUT?
DON'T WORRY, RYOU-SAN.
UH, WHY DID HE LOOK AT ME?
I PROMISE...
...I'LL KEEP YOH-CHAN SAFE.
...HUH?

# #10

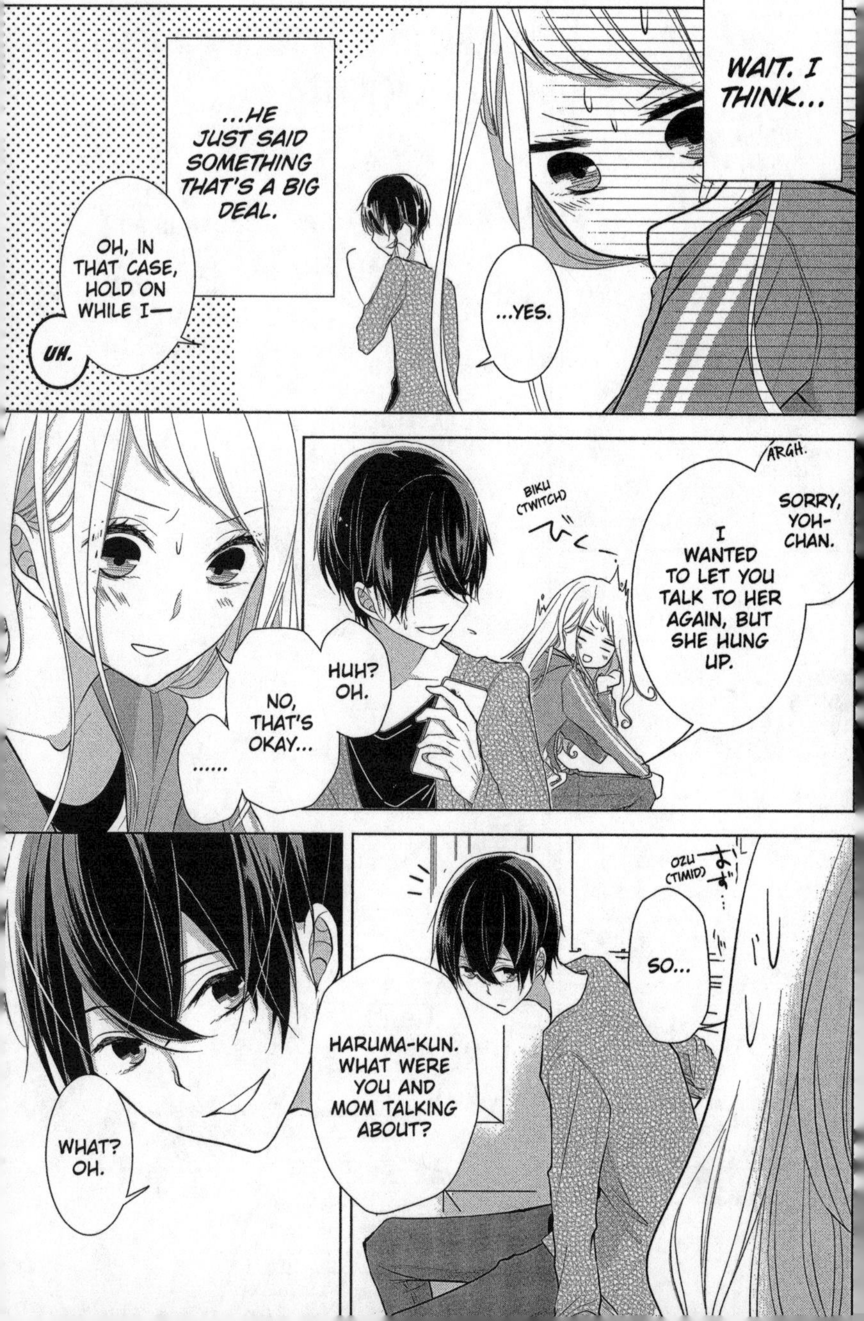

WAIT. I THINK...
...HE JUST SAID SOMETHING THAT'S A BIG DEAL.
...YES.
OH, IN THAT CASE, HOLD ON WHILE I—
UH.
ARGH.
SORRY, YOH-CHAN.
I WANTED TO LET YOU TALK TO HER AGAIN, BUT SHE HUNG UP.
BIKU (TWITCH)
びくーっ
HUH? OH.
NO, THAT'S OKAY...
......
OZU (TIMID)
おず…
SO...
HARUMA-KUN. WHAT WERE YOU AND MOM TALKING ABOUT?
WHAT? OH.

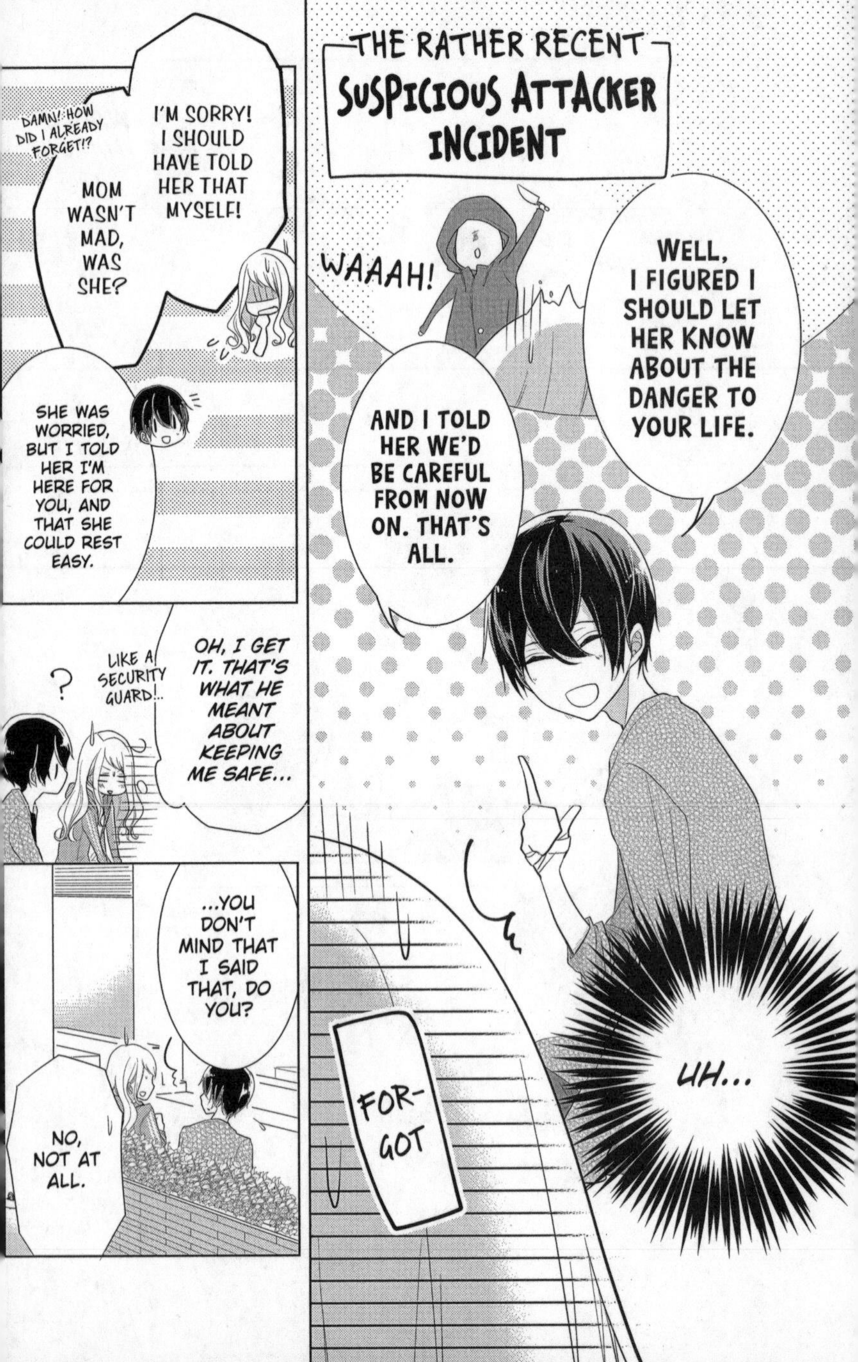
THE RATHER RECENT SUSPICIOUS ATTACKER INCIDENT
WAAAH!
WELL, I FIGURED I SHOULD LET HER KNOW ABOUT THE DANGER TO YOUR LIFE.
AND I TOLD HER WE'D BE CAREFUL FROM NOW ON. THAT'S ALL.
UH...
FOR-GOT
I'M SORRY! I SHOULD HAVE TOLD HER THAT MYSELF!
MOM WASN'T MAD, WAS SHE?
DAMN!! HOW DID I ALREADY FORGET!?
SHE WAS WORRIED, BUT I TOLD HER I'M HERE FOR YOU, AND THAT SHE COULD REST EASY.
OH, I GET IT. THAT'S WHAT HE MEANT ABOUT KEEPING ME SAFE...
LIKE A SECURITY GUARD!...
?
...YOU DON'T MIND THAT I SAID THAT, DO YOU?
NO, NOT AT ALL.

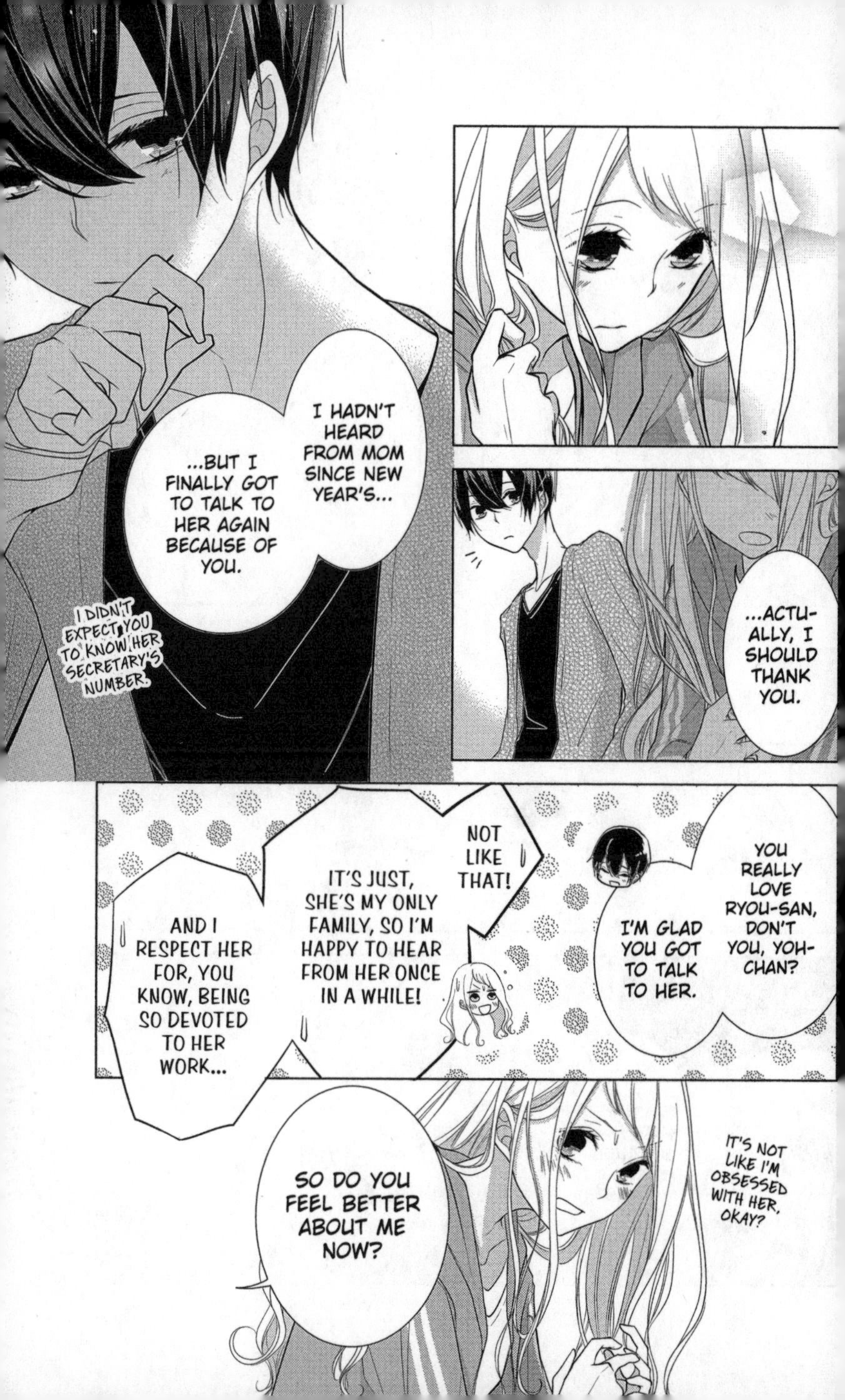
...ACTUALLY, I SHOULD THANK YOU.
I HADN'T HEARD FROM MOM SINCE NEW YEAR'S...
...BUT I FINALLY GOT TO TALK TO HER AGAIN BECAUSE OF YOU.
I DIDN'T EXPECT YOU TO KNOW HER SECRETARY'S NUMBER.
YOU REALLY LOVE RYOU-SAN, DON'T YOU, YOH-CHAN?
I'M GLAD YOU GOT TO TALK TO HER.
NOT LIKE THAT!
IT'S JUST, SHE'S MY ONLY FAMILY, SO I'M HAPPY TO HEAR FROM HER ONCE IN A WHILE!
AND I RESPECT HER FOR, YOU KNOW, BEING SO DEVOTED TO HER WORK...
IT'S NOT LIKE I'M OBSESSED WITH HER, OKAY?
SO DO YOU FEEL BETTER ABOUT ME NOW?

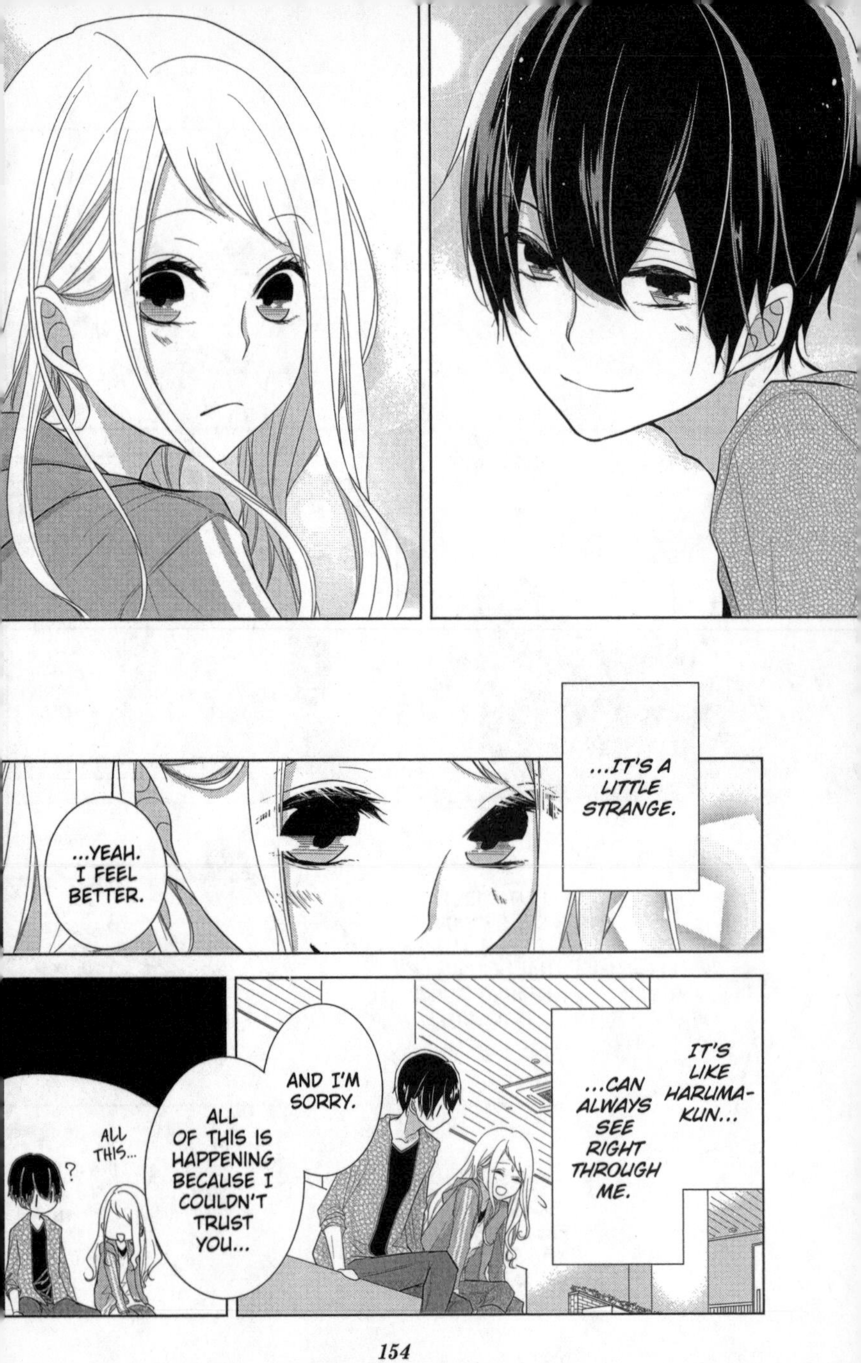
...IT'S A LITTLE STRANGE.
...YEAH. I FEEL BETTER.
IT'S LIKE HARUMA-KUN...
...CAN ALWAYS SEE RIGHT THROUGH ME.
AND I'M SORRY.
ALL OF THIS IS HAPPENING BECAUSE I COULDN'T TRUST YOU...
ALL THIS...
?

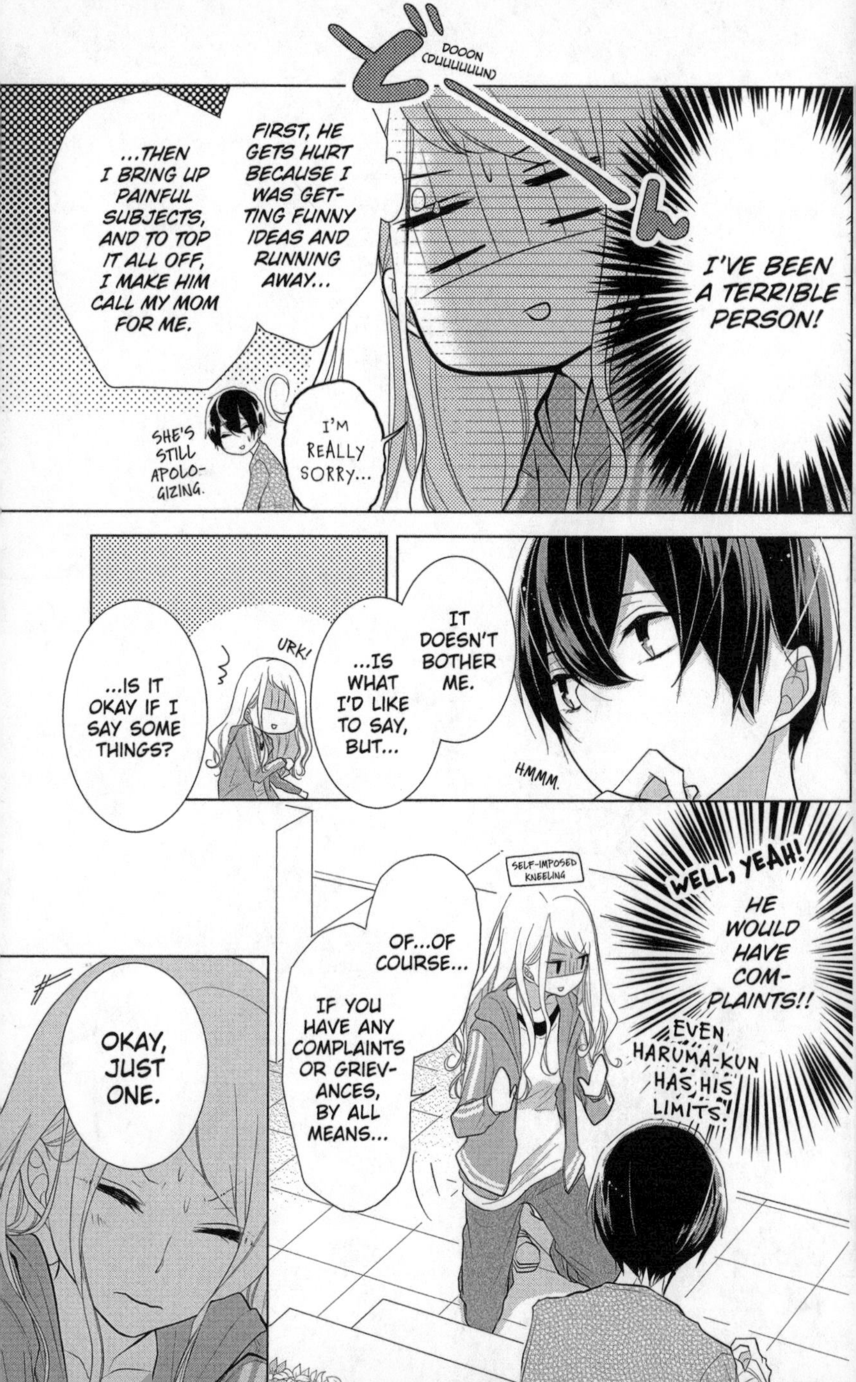
DOOON (DUUUUUUN)
I'VE BEEN A TERRIBLE PERSON!
FIRST, HE GETS HURT BECAUSE I WAS GETTING FUNNY IDEAS AND RUNNING AWAY...
...THEN I BRING UP PAINFUL SUBJECTS, AND TO TOP IT ALL OFF, I MAKE HIM CALL MY MOM FOR ME.
I'M REALLY SORRY...
SHE'S STILL APOLOGIZING.
IT DOESN'T BOTHER ME.
...IS WHAT I'D LIKE TO SAY, BUT...
HMMM.
URK!
...IS IT OKAY IF I SAY SOME THINGS?
WELL, YEAH! HE WOULD HAVE COMPLAINTS!!
EVEN HARUMA-KUN HAS HIS LIMITS!
SELF-IMPOSED KNEELING
OF...OF COURSE...
IF YOU HAVE ANY COMPLAINTS OR GRIEVANCES, BY ALL MEANS...
OKAY, JUST ONE.

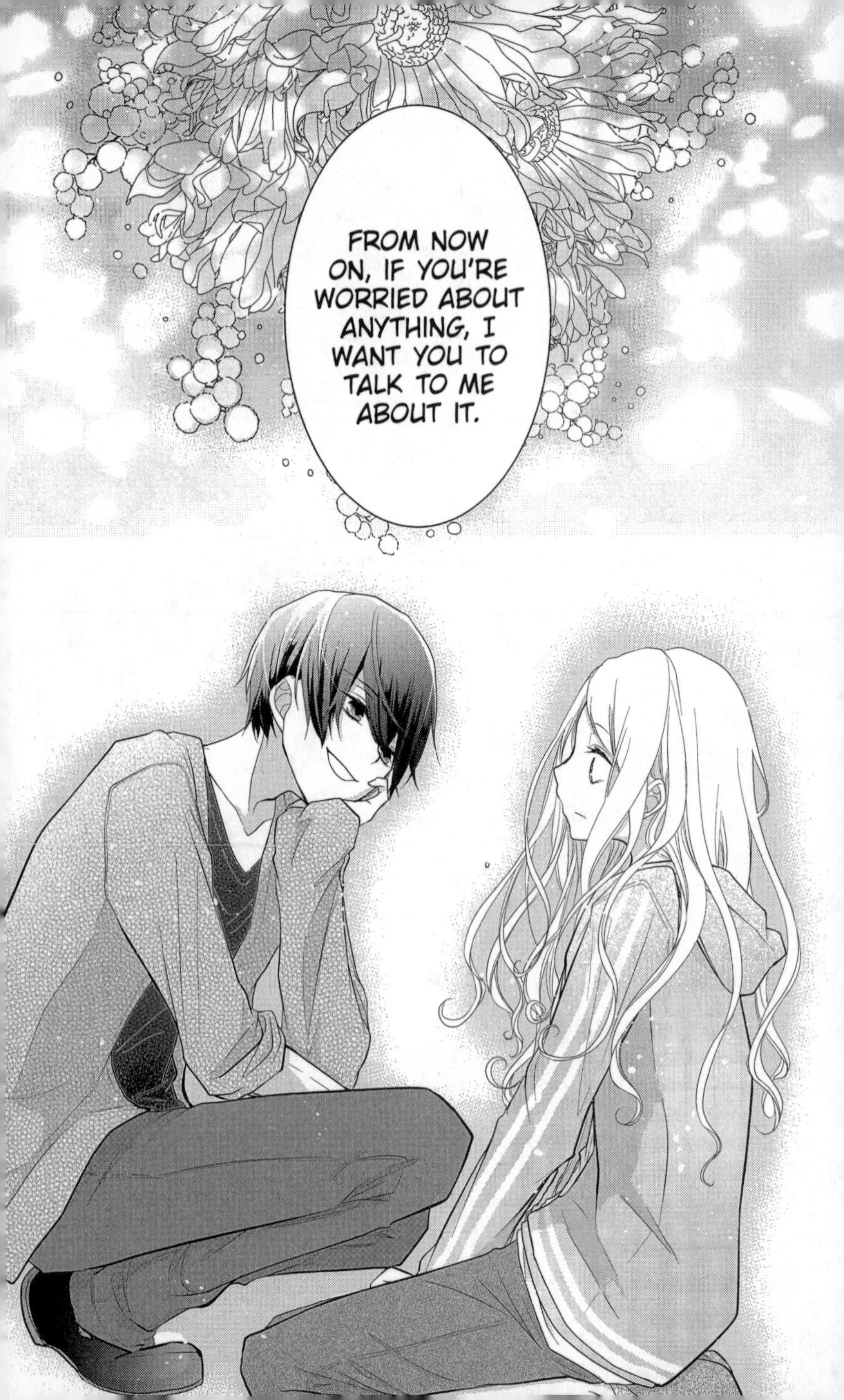
FROM NOW ON, IF YOU'RE WORRIED ABOUT ANYTHING, I WANT YOU TO TALK TO ME ABOUT IT.

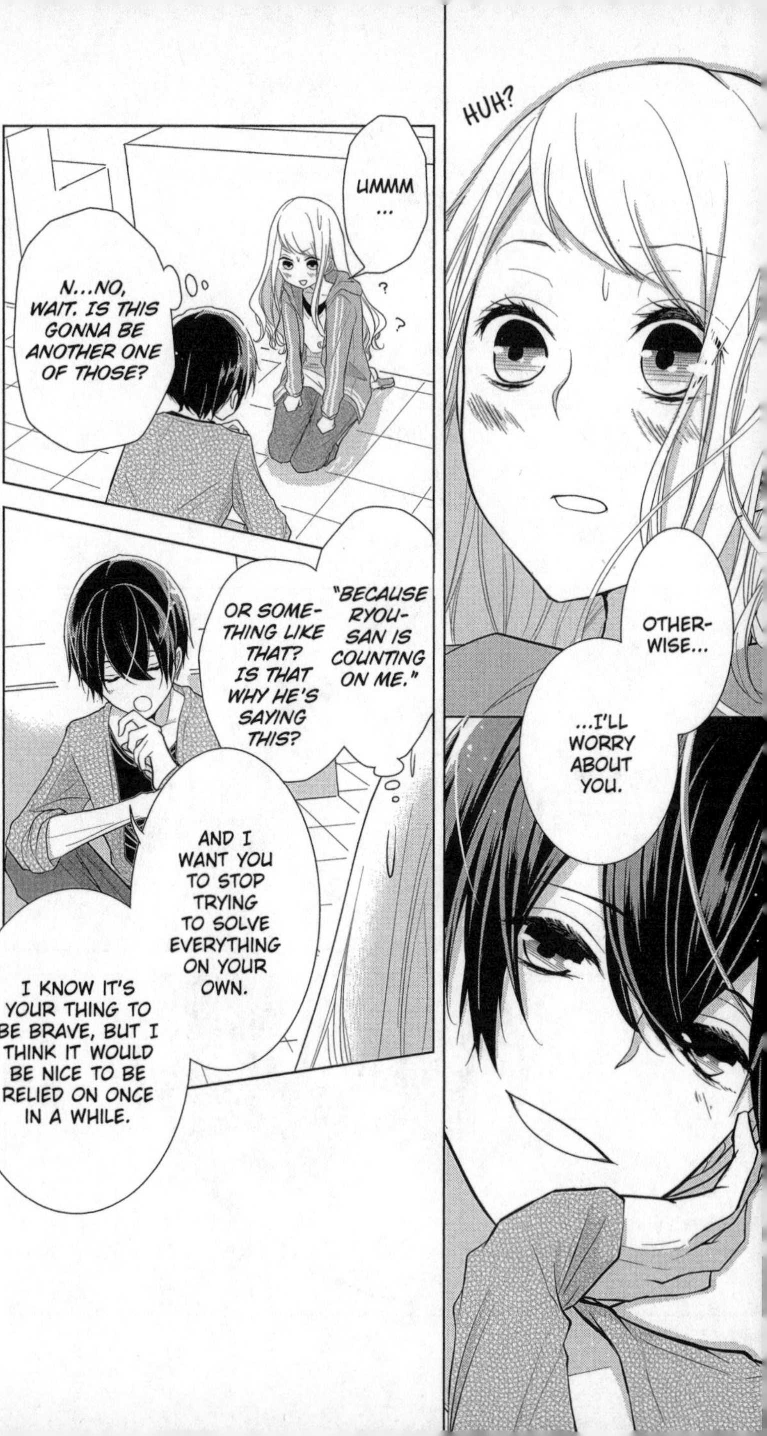
UMMM ...
N...NO, WAIT. IS THIS GONNA BE ANOTHER ONE OF THOSE?
"BECAUSE RYOU-SAN IS COUNTING ON ME."
OR SOME-THING LIKE THAT? IS THAT WHY HE'S SAYING THIS?
AND I WANT YOU TO STOP TRYING TO SOLVE EVERYTHING ON YOUR OWN.
I KNOW IT'S YOUR THING TO BE BRAVE, BUT I THINK IT WOULD BE NICE TO BE RELIED ON ONCE IN A WHILE.
HUH?
OTHER-WISE...
...I'LL WORRY ABOUT YOU.

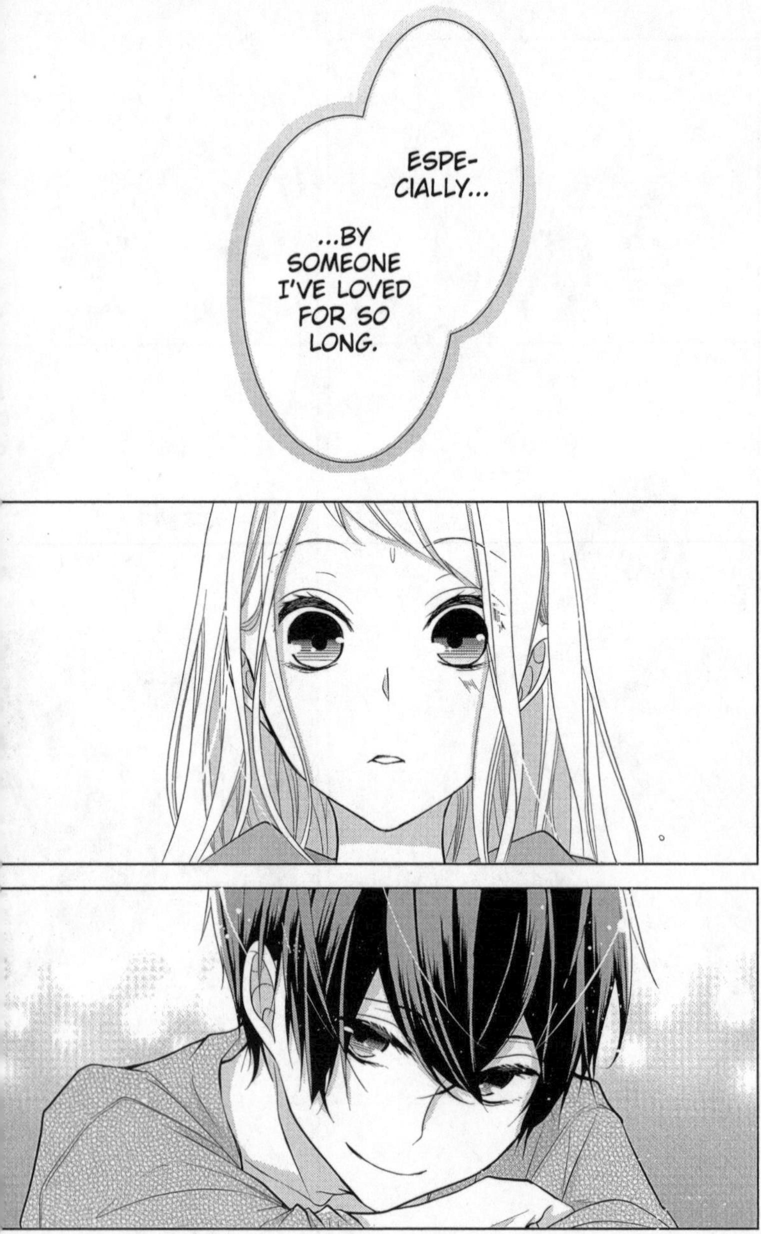
ESPE-
CIALLY...
...BY SOMEONE I'VE LOVED FOR SO LONG.

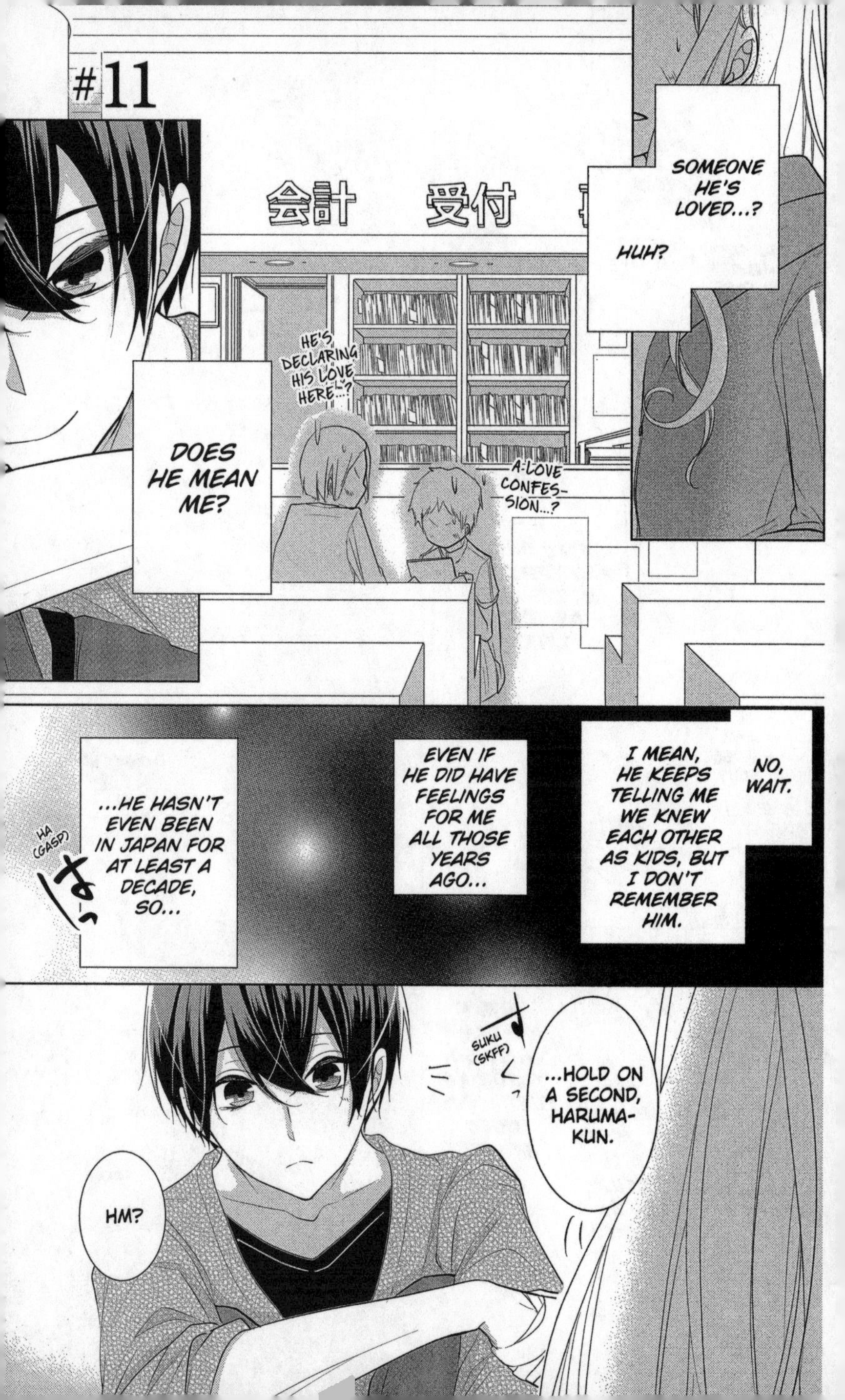
#11
SOMEONE HE'S LOVED...?
HUH?
会計 受付
A-LOVE CONFESSION...?
HE'S DECLARING HIS LOVE HERE...?
DOES HE MEAN ME?
NO, WAIT.
I MEAN, HE KEEPS TELLING ME WE KNEW EACH OTHER AS KIDS, BUT I DON'T REMEMBER HIM.
EVEN IF HE DID HAVE FEELINGS FOR ME ALL THOSE YEARS AGO...
...HE HASN'T EVEN BEEN IN JAPAN FOR AT LEAST A DECADE, SO...
HA (GASP)
SUKU (SKFF)
...HOLD ON A SECOND, HARUMA-KUN.
HM?

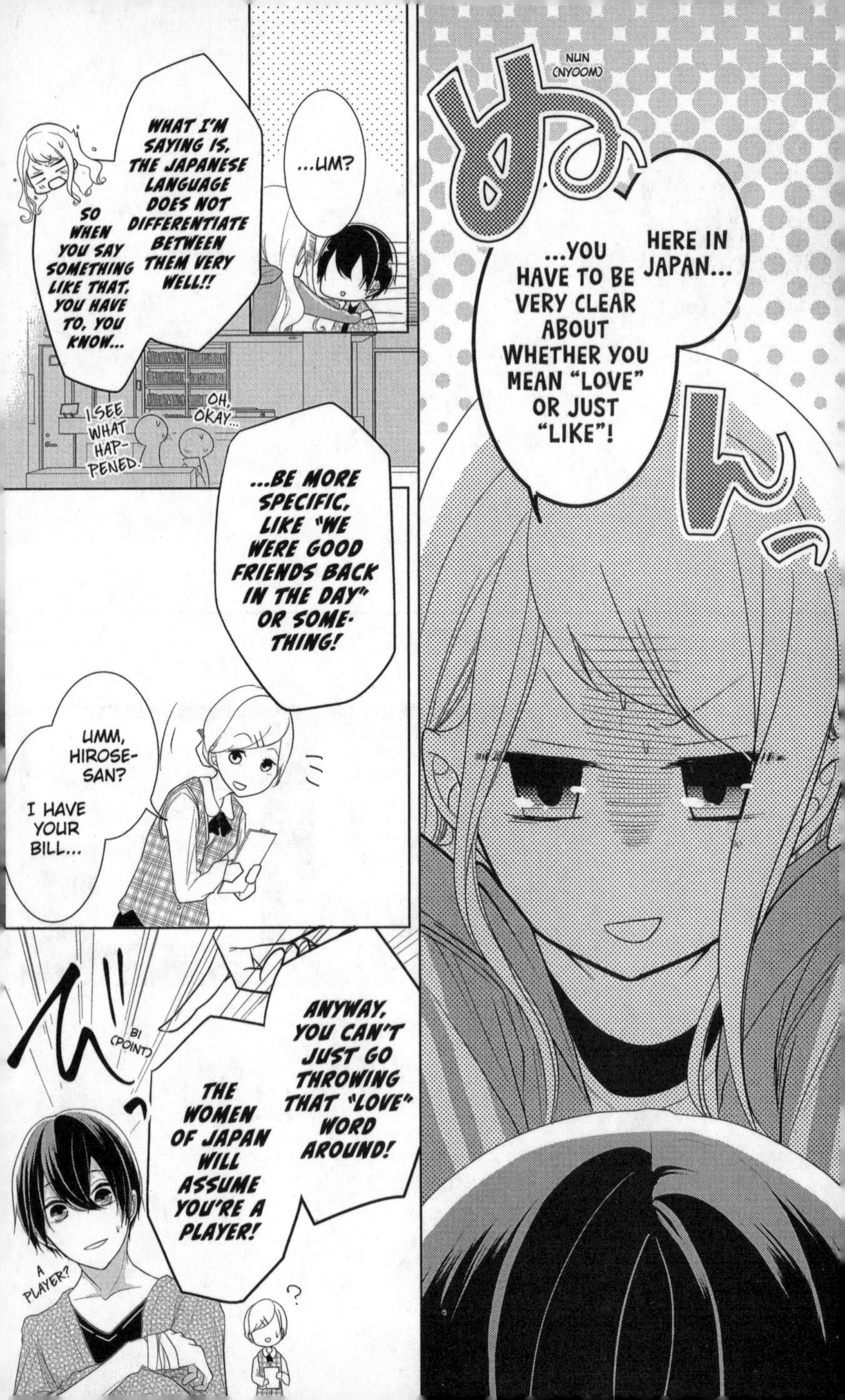
NUN (NYOOM)
HERE IN JAPAN...
...YOU HAVE TO BE VERY CLEAR ABOUT WHETHER YOU MEAN "LOVE" OR JUST "LIKE"!
...UM?
WHAT I'M SAYING IS, THE JAPANESE LANGUAGE DOES NOT DIFFERENTIATE BETWEEN THEM VERY WELL!!
SO WHEN YOU SAY SOMETHING LIKE THAT, YOU HAVE TO, YOU KNOW...
OH, OKAY...
I SEE WHAT HAP-PENED.
...BE MORE SPECIFIC, LIKE "WE WERE GOOD FRIENDS BACK IN THE DAY" OR SOME-THING!
UMM, HIROSE-SAN?
I HAVE YOUR BILL...
ANYWAY, YOU CAN'T JUST GO THROWING THAT "LOVE" WORD AROUND!
THE WOMEN OF JAPAN WILL ASSUME YOU'RE A PLAYER!
BI (POINT)
A PLAYER?
?

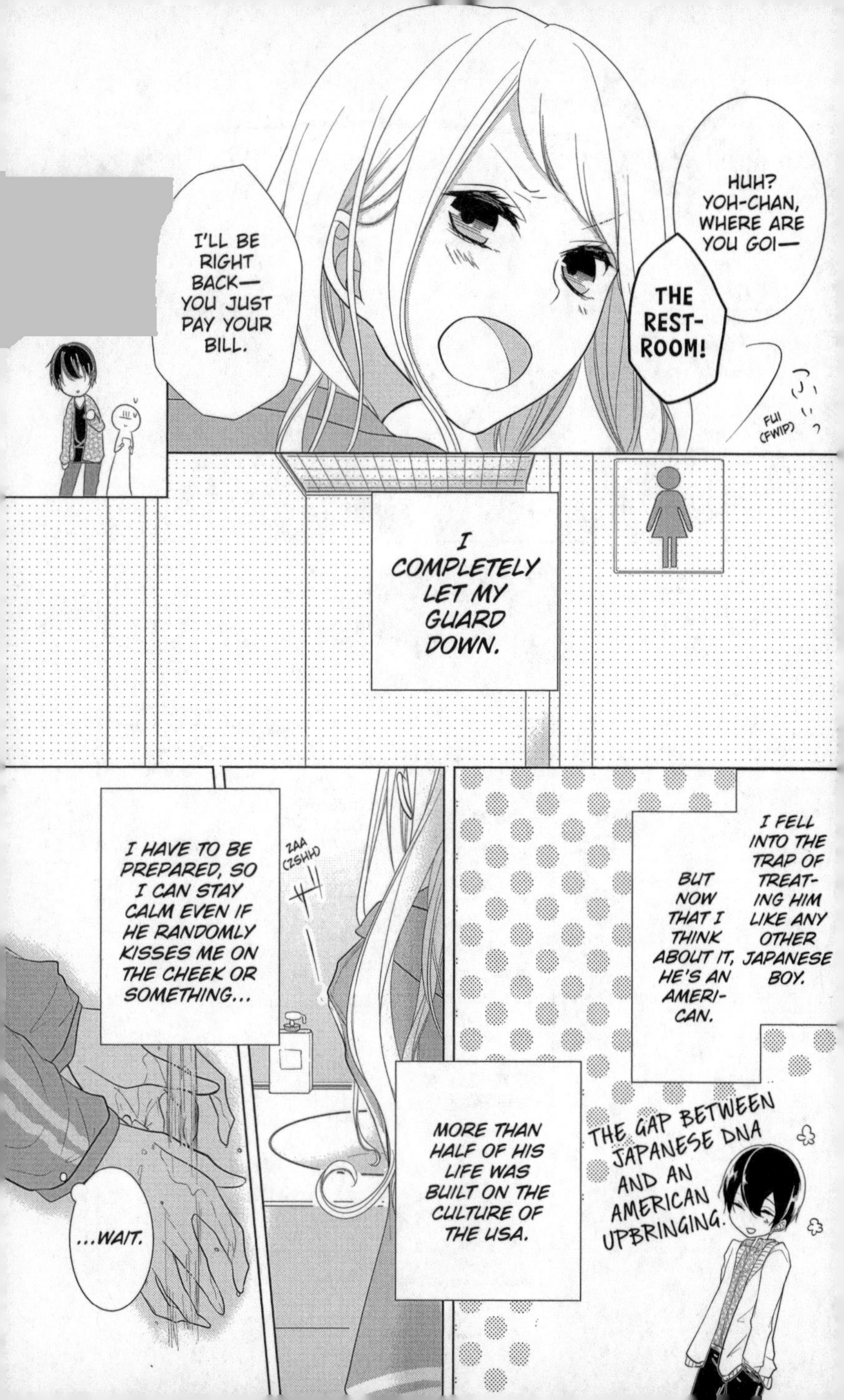

HUH? YOH-CHAN, WHERE ARE YOU GOI—
THE REST-ROOM!
FUI (FWIP)
I'LL BE RIGHT BACK—YOU JUST PAY YOUR BILL.
I COMPLETELY LET MY GUARD DOWN.
I FELL INTO THE TRAP OF TREATING HIM LIKE ANY OTHER JAPANESE BOY.
BUT NOW THAT I THINK ABOUT IT, HE'S AN AMERICAN.
MORE THAN HALF OF HIS LIFE WAS BUILT ON THE CULTURE OF THE USA.
THE GAP BETWEEN JAPANESE DNA AND AN AMERICAN UPBRINGING.
ZAA (ZSHH)
I HAVE TO BE PREPARED, SO I CAN STAY CALM EVEN IF HE RANDOMLY KISSES ME ON THE CHEEK OR SOMETHING...
...WAIT.

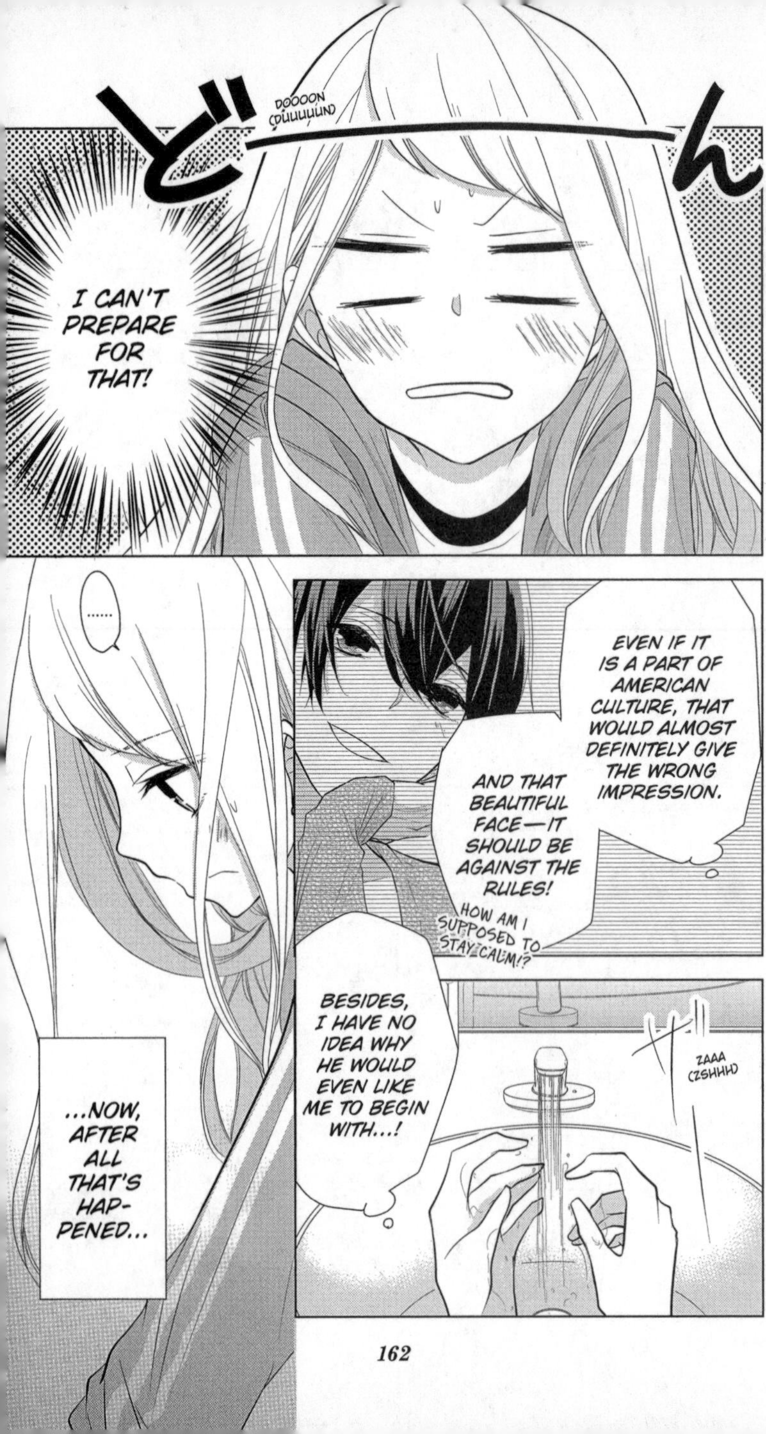

どーん
DOOOON (DUUUUUN)
I CAN'T PREPARE FOR THAT!
EVEN IF IT IS A PART OF AMERICAN CULTURE, THAT WOULD ALMOST DEFINITELY GIVE THE WRONG IMPRESSION.
AND THAT BEAUTIFUL FACE—IT SHOULD BE AGAINST THE RULES!
HOW AM I SUPPOSED TO STAY CALM!?
ZAAA (ZSHHH)
BESIDES, I HAVE NO IDEA WHY HE WOULD EVEN LIKE ME TO BEGIN WITH...!
......
...NOW, AFTER ALL THAT'S HAP-PENED...

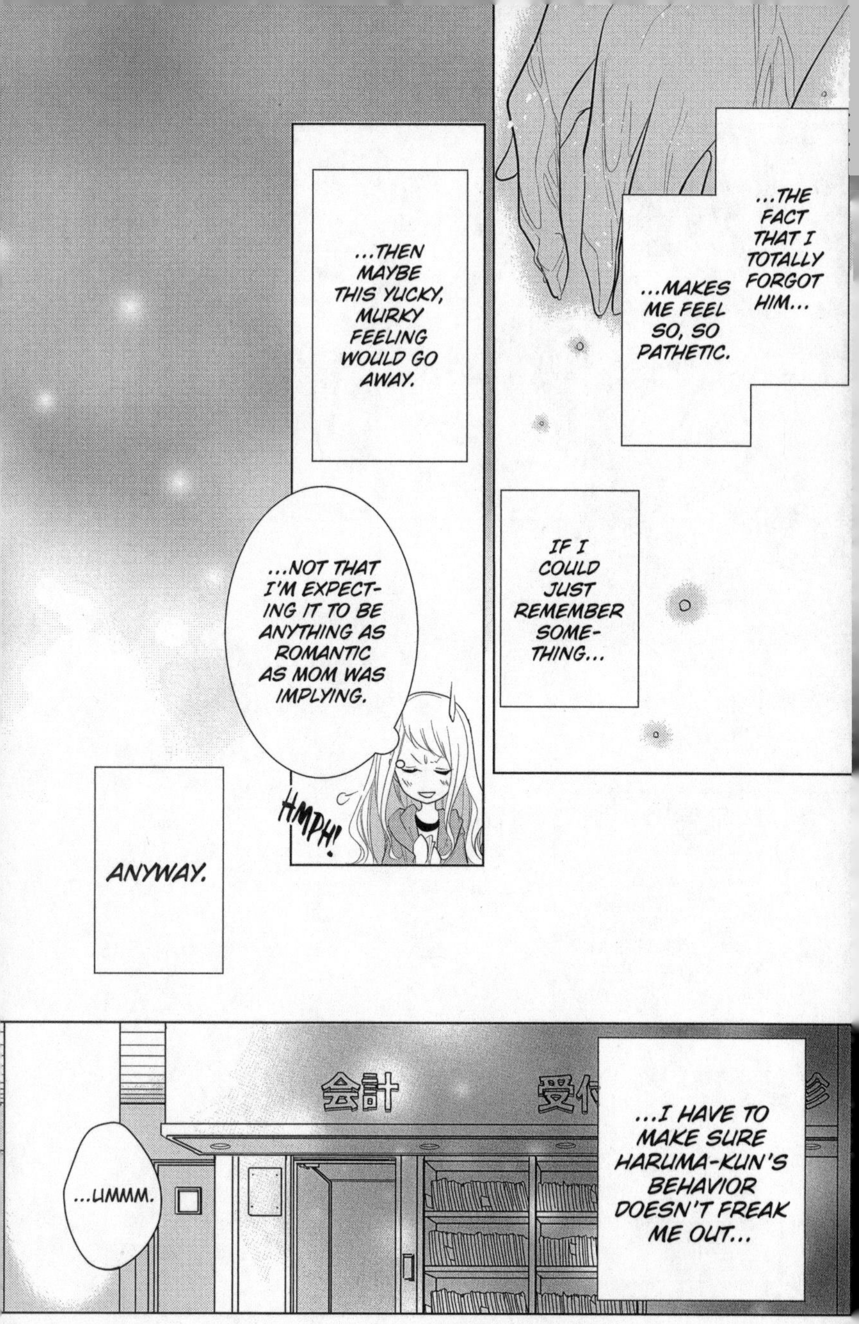

...THE FACT THAT I TOTALLY FORGOT HIM...
...MAKES ME FEEL SO, SO PATHETIC.
IF I COULD JUST REMEMBER SOME-THING...
...THEN MAYBE THIS YUCKY, MURKY FEELING WOULD GO AWAY.
...NOT THAT I'M EXPECT-ING IT TO BE ANYTHING AS ROMANTIC AS MOM WAS IMPLYING.
HMPH!
ANYWAY.
...I HAVE TO MAKE SURE HARUMA-KUN'S BEHAVIOR DOESN'T FREAK ME OUT...
会計
...UMMM.

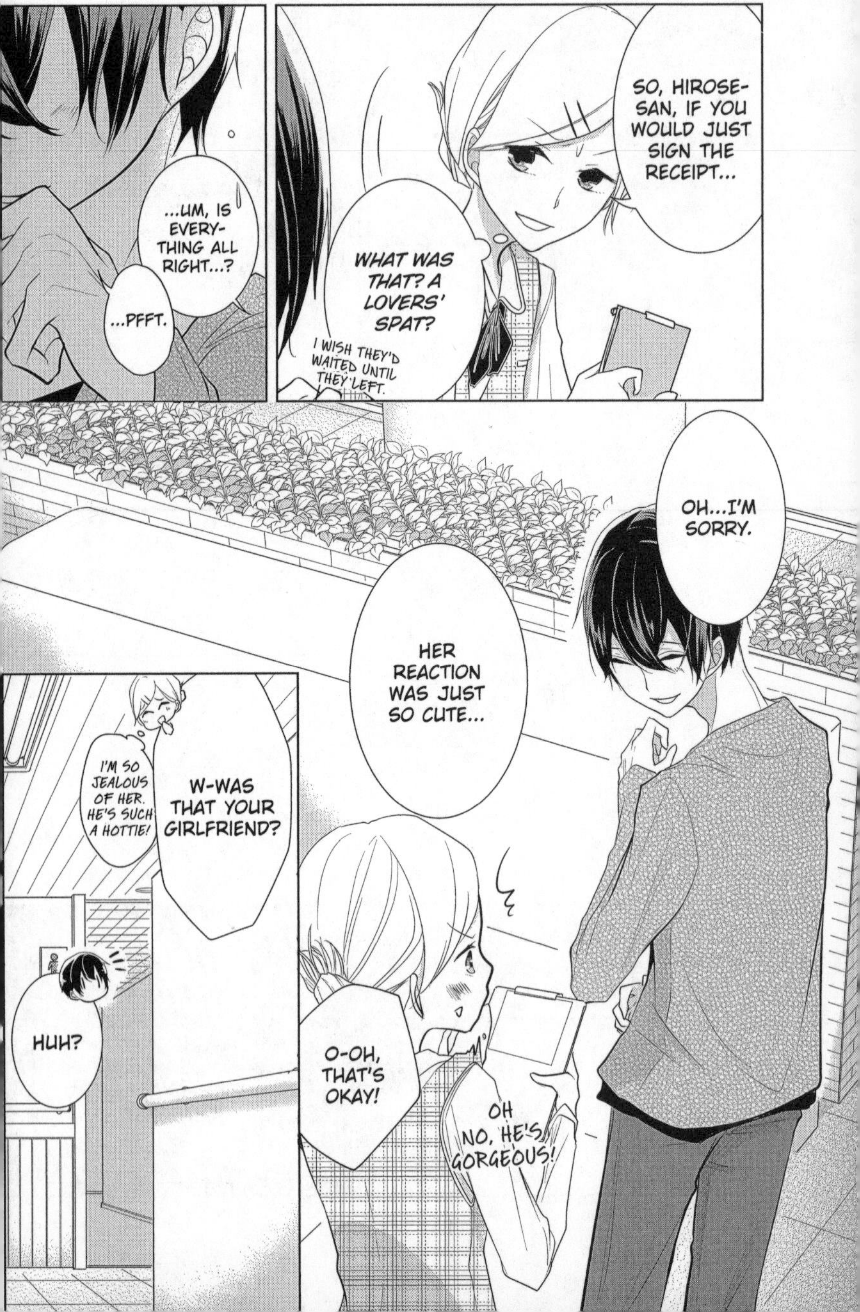

SO, HIROSE-SAN, IF YOU WOULD JUST SIGN THE RECEIPT...
WHAT WAS THAT? A LOVERS' SPAT?
I WISH THEY'D WAITED UNTIL THEY LEFT.
...UM, IS EVERYTHING ALL RIGHT...?
...PFFT.
OH...I'M SORRY.
HER REACTION WAS JUST SO CUTE...
O-OH, THAT'S OKAY!
OH NO, HE'S GORGEOUS!
W-WAS THAT YOUR GIRLFRIEND?
I'M SO JEALOUS OF HER. HE'S SUCH A HOTTIE!
HUH?

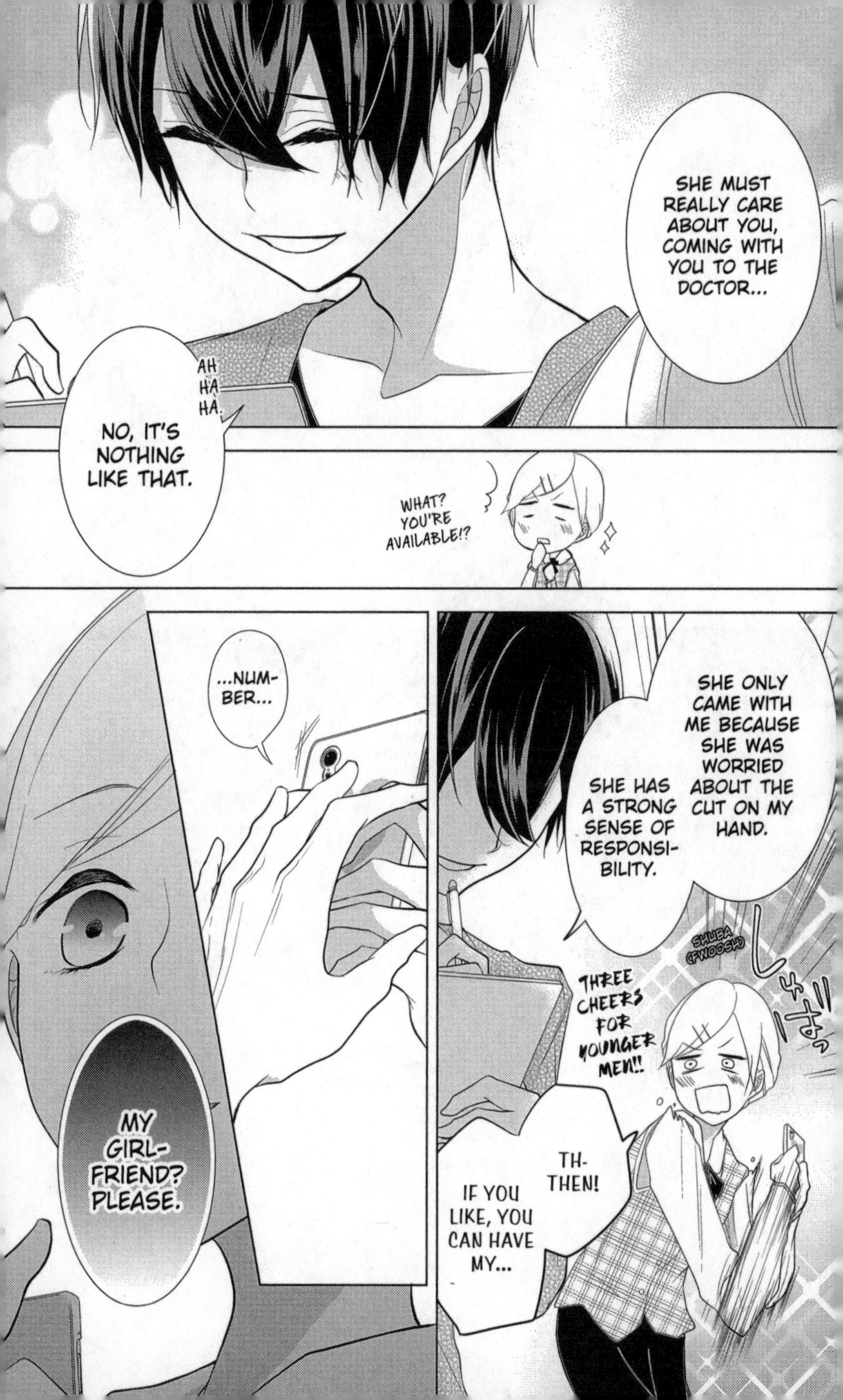
SHE MUST REALLY CARE ABOUT YOU, COMING WITH YOU TO THE DOCTOR...
AH HA HA.
NO, IT'S NOTHING LIKE THAT.
WHAT? YOU'RE AVAILABLE!?
SHE ONLY CAME WITH ME BECAUSE SHE WAS WORRIED ABOUT THE CUT ON MY HAND.
SHE HAS A STRONG SENSE OF RESPONSI-BILITY.
SHUBA (FWOOSH)
THREE CHEERS FOR YOUNGER MEN!!
TH-THEN!
IF YOU LIKE, YOU CAN HAVE MY...
...NUM-BER...
MY GIRL-FRIEND? PLEASE.

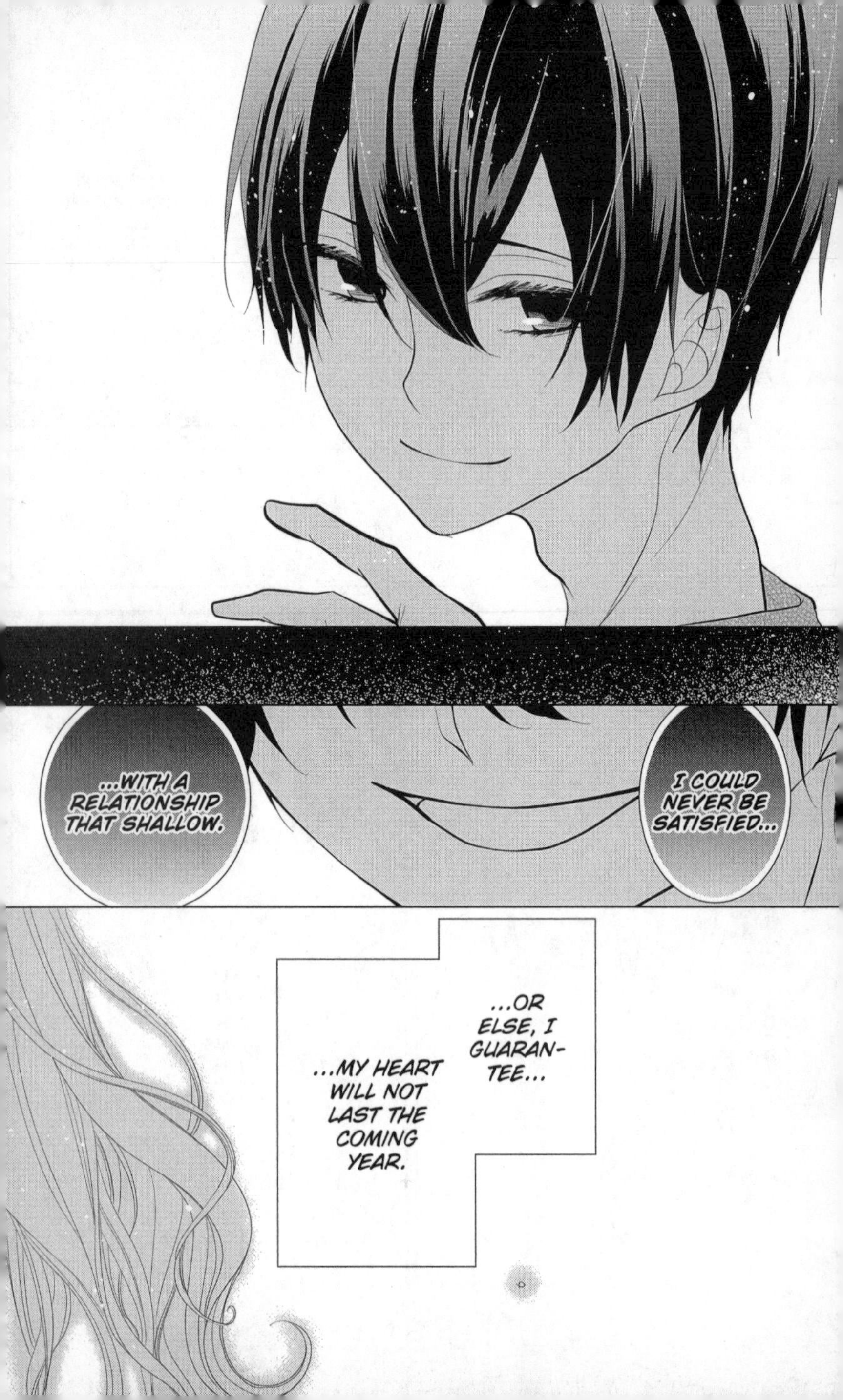
I COULD NEVER BE SATISFIED...
...WITH A RELATIONSHIP THAT SHALLOW.
...OR ELSE, I GUARAN-TEE...
...MY HEART WILL NOT LAST THE COMING YEAR.

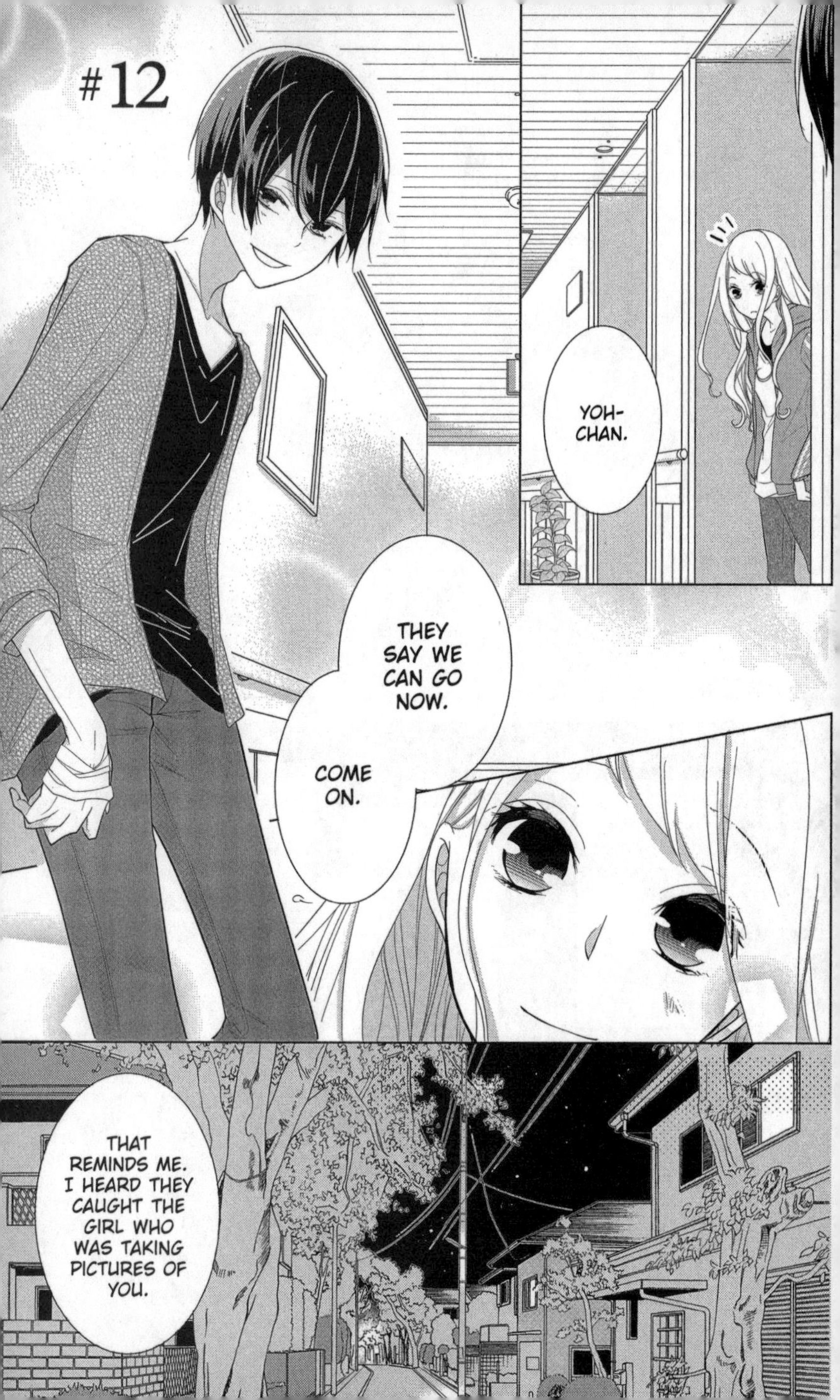
#12
YOH-CHAN.
THEY SAY WE CAN GO NOW.
COME ON.
THAT REMINDS ME. I HEARD THEY CAUGHT THE GIRL WHO WAS TAKING PICTURES OF YOU.

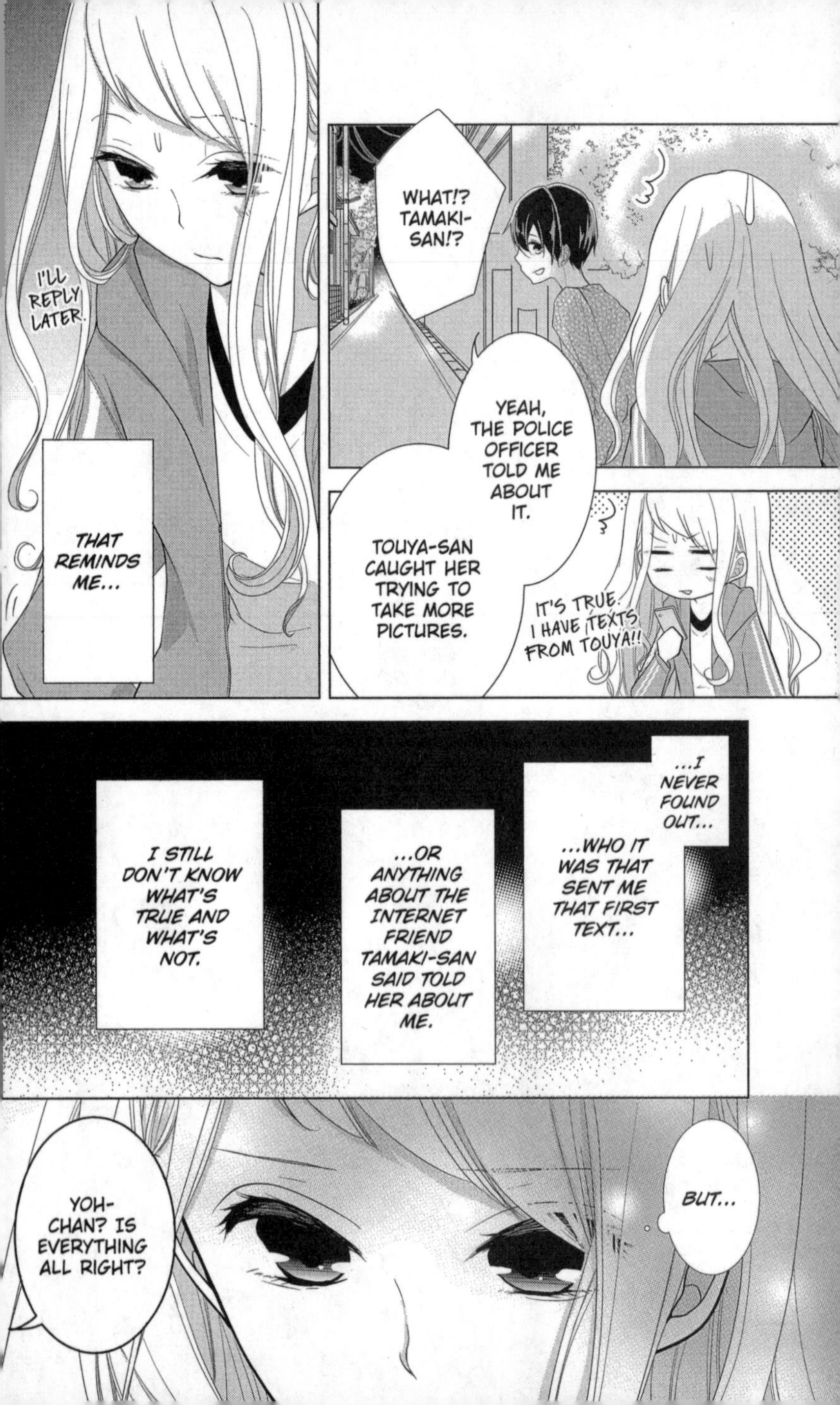
WHAT!? TAMAKI-SAN!?
YEAH, THE POLICE OFFICER TOLD ME ABOUT IT.
TOUYA-SAN CAUGHT HER TRYING TO TAKE MORE PICTURES.
IT'S TRUE. I HAVE TEXTS FROM TOUYA!!
I'LL REPLY LATER.
THAT REMINDS ME...
...I NEVER FOUND OUT...
...WHO IT WAS THAT SENT ME THAT FIRST TEXT...
...OR ANYTHING ABOUT THE INTERNET FRIEND TAMAKI-SAN SAID TOLD HER ABOUT ME.
I STILL DON'T KNOW WHAT'S TRUE AND WHAT'S NOT.
BUT...
YOH-CHAN? IS EVERYTHING ALL RIGHT?

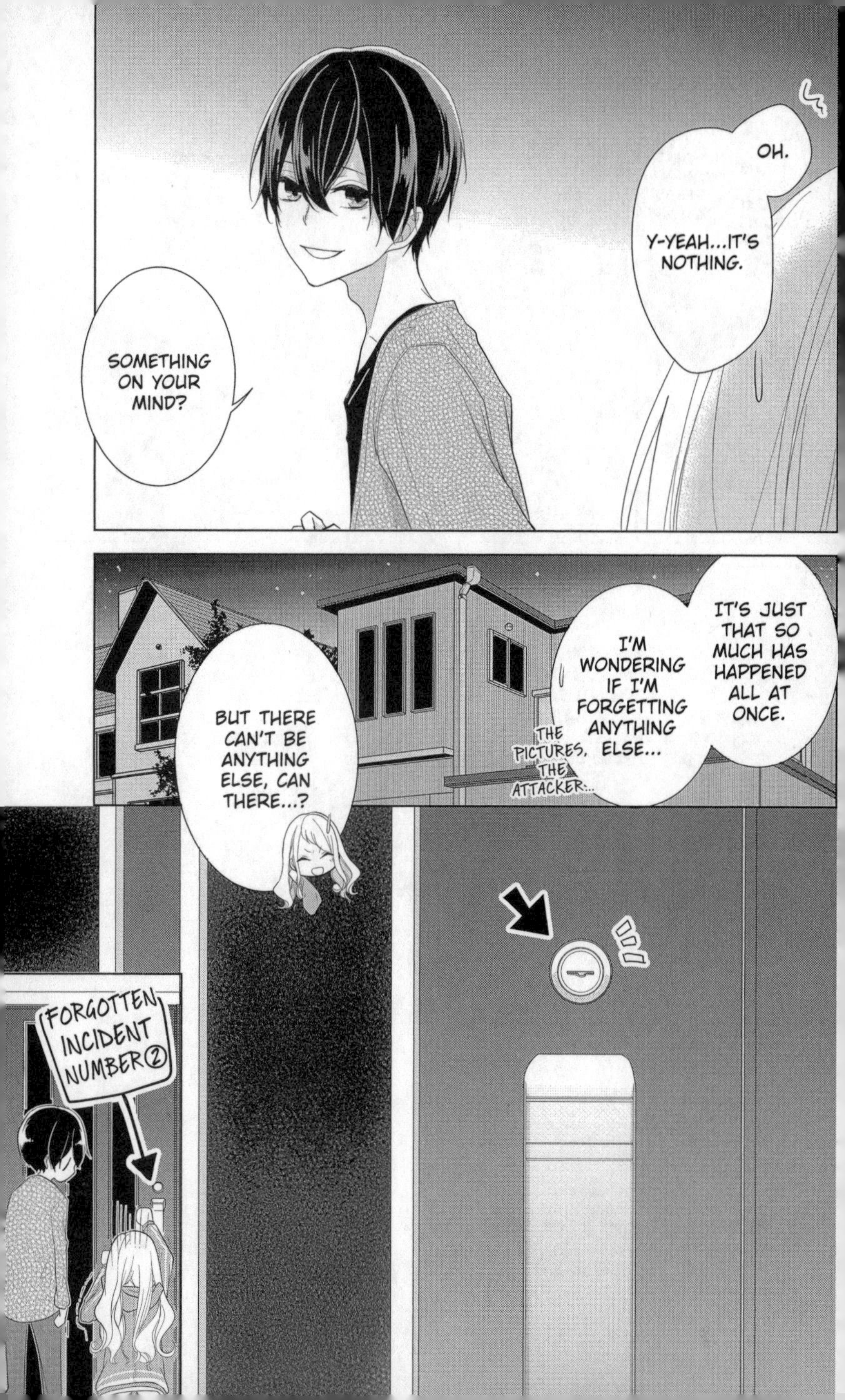
OH.
Y-YEAH...IT'S NOTHING.
SOMETHING ON YOUR MIND?
IT'S JUST THAT SO MUCH HAS HAPPENED ALL AT ONCE.
I'M WONDERING IF I'M FORGETTING ANYTHING ELSE...
THE PICTURES, THE ATTACKER...
BUT THERE CAN'T BE ANYTHING ELSE, CAN THERE...?
FORGOTTEN INCIDENT NUMBER ②

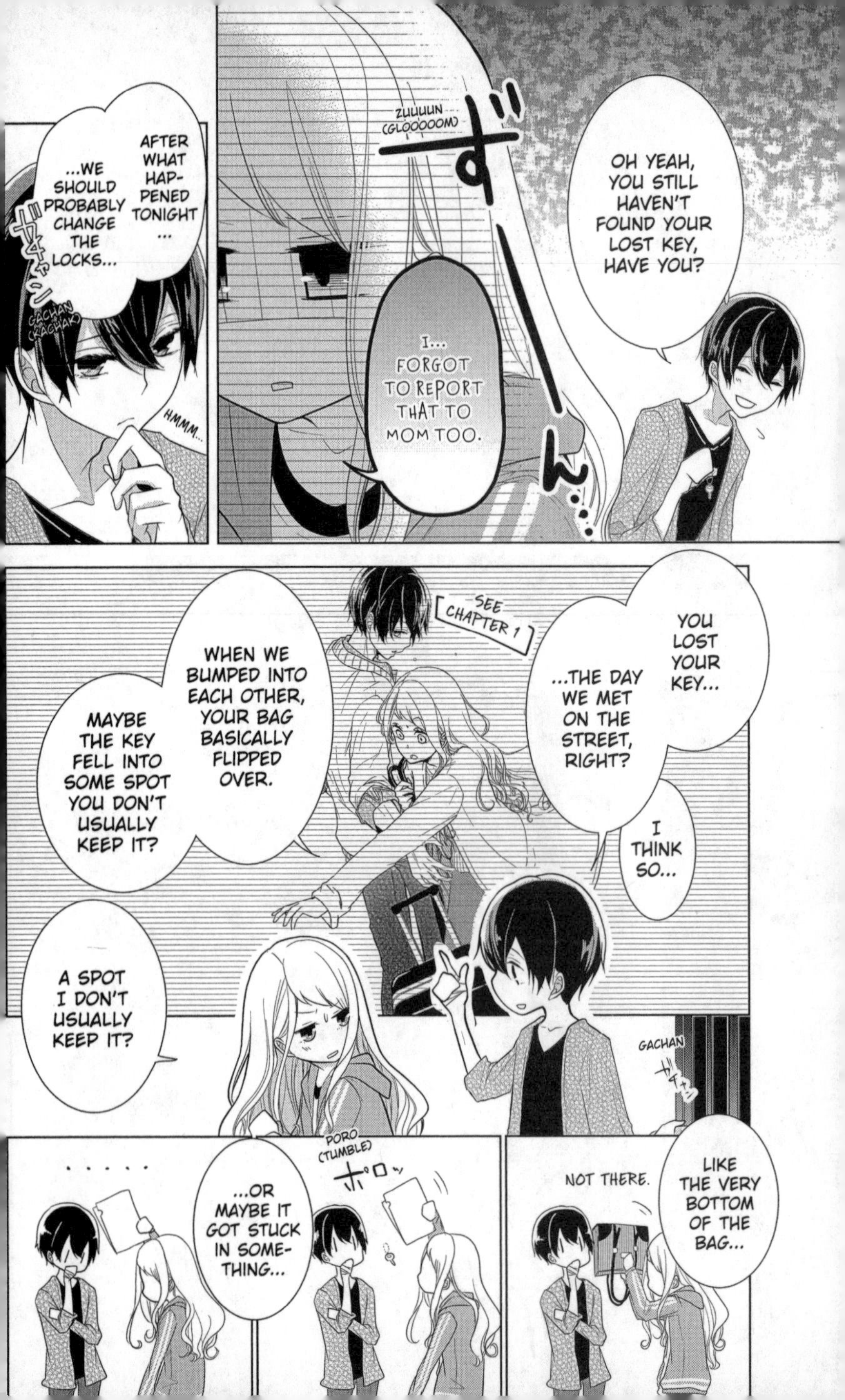
OH YEAH, YOU STILL HAVEN'T FOUND YOUR LOST KEY, HAVE YOU?
ZUUUUN (GLOOOOOM)
I... FORGOT TO REPORT THAT TO MOM TOO.
AFTER WHAT HAP-PENED TONIGHT...
...WE SHOULD PROBABLY CHANGE THE LOCKS...
GACHAN (KACHAK)
HMMM...
YOU LOST YOUR KEY...
...THE DAY WE MET ON THE STREET, RIGHT?
SEE CHAPTER 1
I THINK SO...
WHEN WE BUMPED INTO EACH OTHER, YOUR BAG BASICALLY FLIPPED OVER.
MAYBE THE KEY FELL INTO SOME SPOT YOU DON'T USUALLY KEEP IT?
GACHAN
A SPOT I DON'T USUALLY KEEP IT?
LIKE THE VERY BOTTOM OF THE BAG...
NOT THERE.
PORO (TUMBLE)
...OR MAYBE IT GOT STUCK IN SOME-THING...
. . . . .

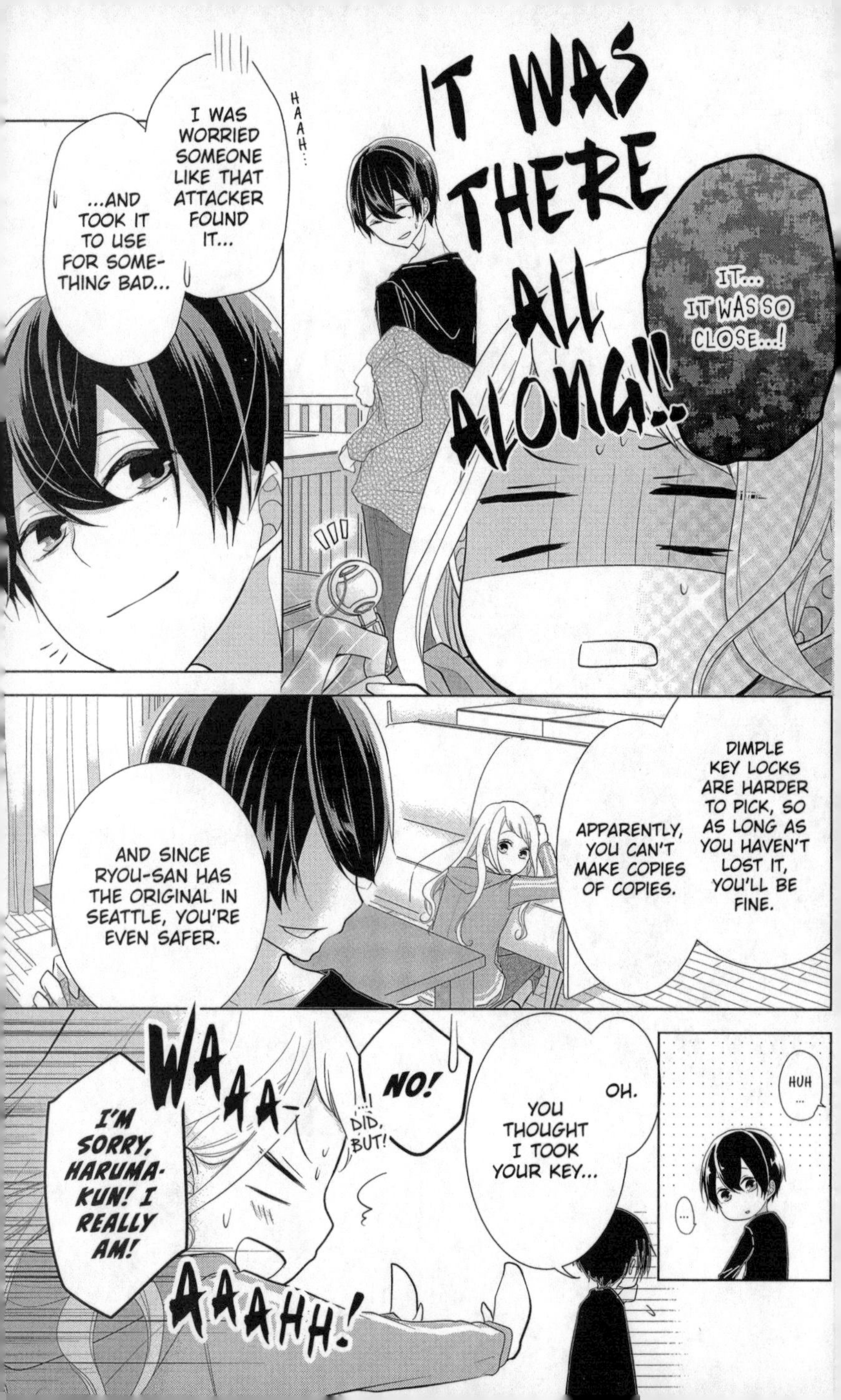
IT... IT WAS SO CLOSE...!
IT WAS THERE ALL ALONG!!
HAAAH...
I WAS WORRIED SOMEONE LIKE THAT ATTACKER FOUND IT...
...AND TOOK IT TO USE FOR SOMETHING BAD...
DIMPLE KEY LOCKS ARE HARDER TO PICK, SO AS LONG AS YOU HAVEN'T LOST IT, YOU'LL BE FINE.
APPARENTLY, YOU CAN'T MAKE COPIES OF COPIES.
AND SINCE RYOU-SAN HAS THE ORIGINAL IN SEATTLE, YOU'RE EVEN SAFER.
HUH...
...
OH.
YOU THOUGHT I TOOK YOUR KEY...
NO!
...I DID, BUT!
WAAAA-AAAHH!
I'M SORRY, HARUMA-KUN! I REALLY AM!

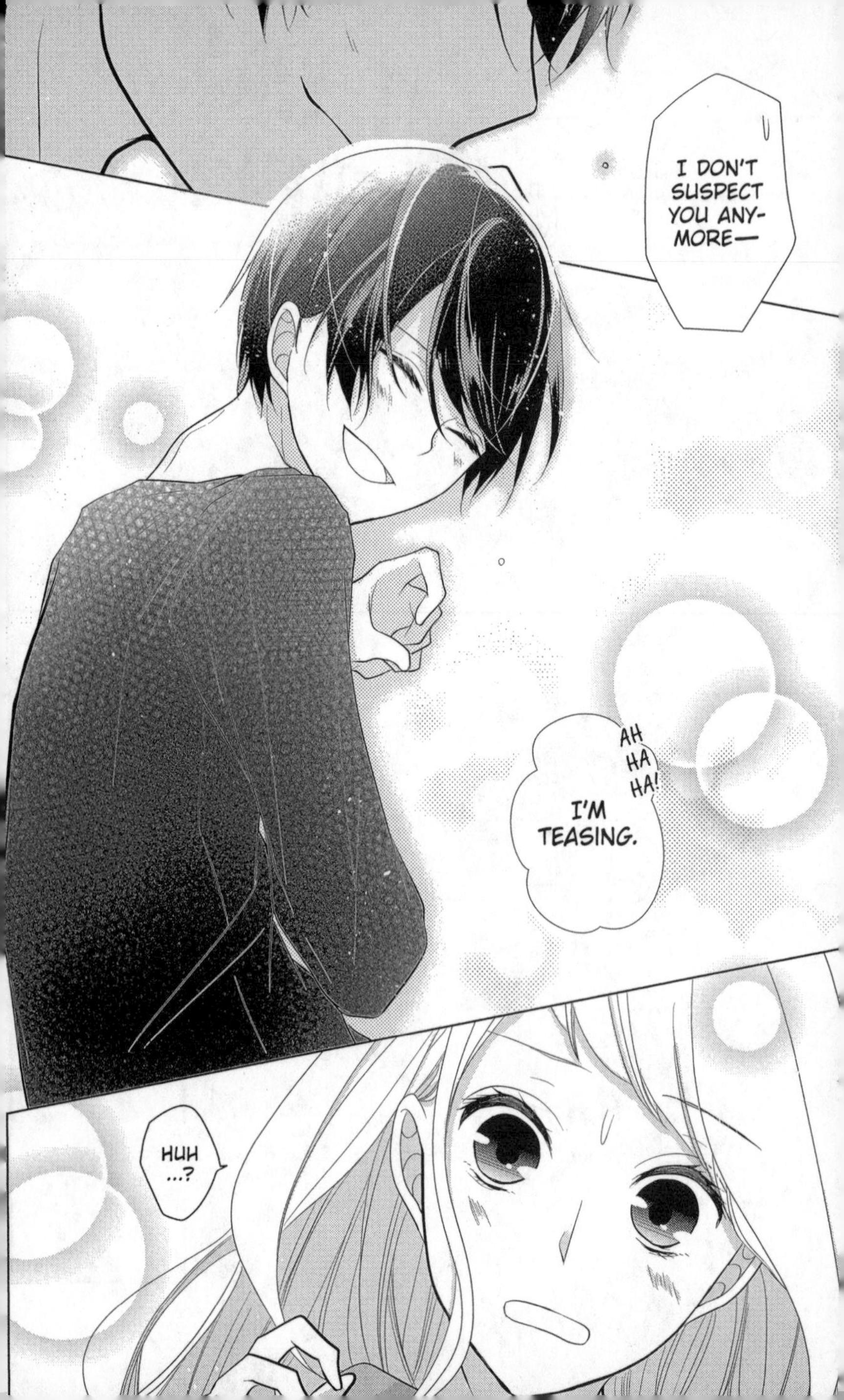
I DON'T SUSPECT YOU ANY-MORE—
AH HA HA!
I'M TEASING.
HUH ...?

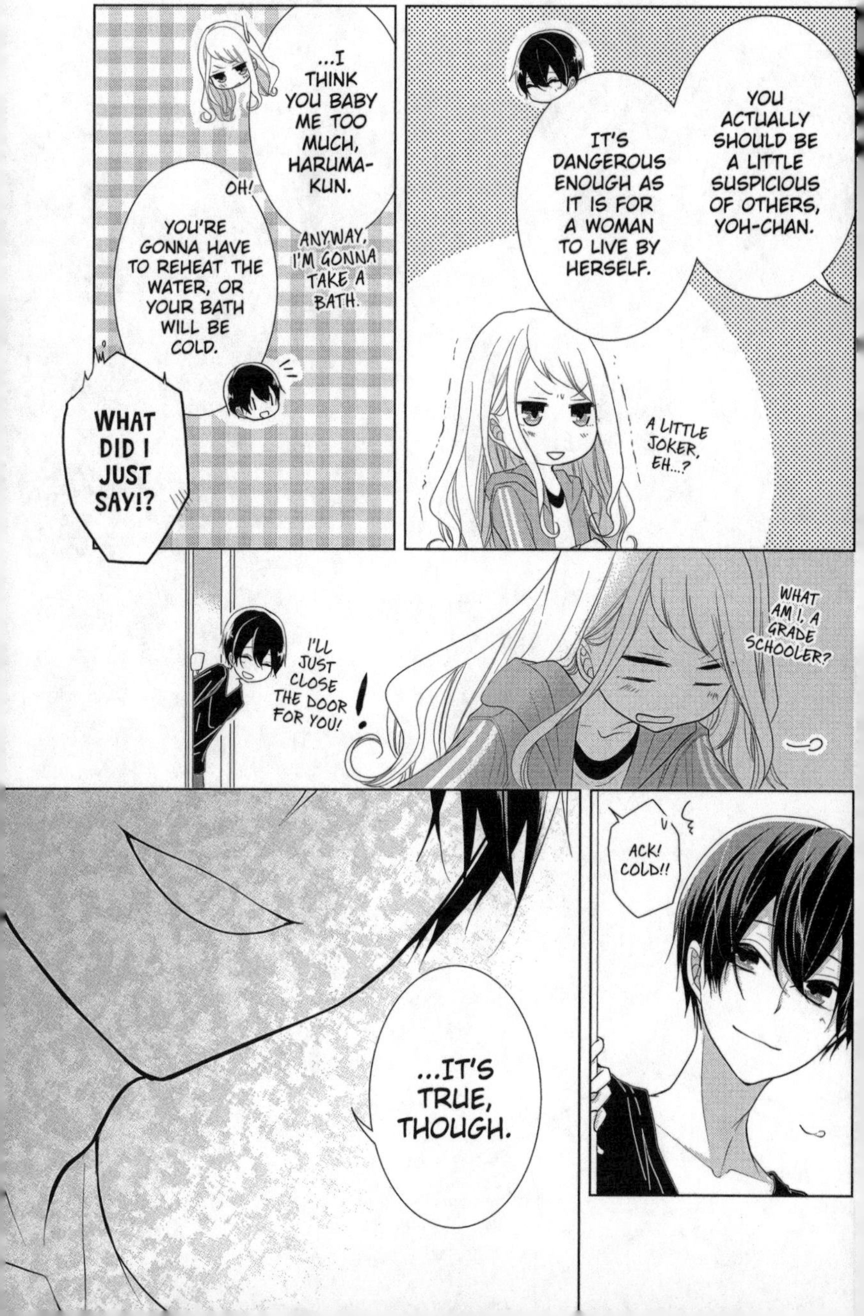
YOU ACTUALLY SHOULD BE A LITTLE SUSPICIOUS OF OTHERS, YOH-CHAN.
IT'S DANGEROUS ENOUGH AS IT IS FOR A WOMAN TO LIVE BY HERSELF.
A LITTLE JOKER, EH...?
...I THINK YOU BABY ME TOO MUCH, HARUMA-KUN.
ANYWAY, I'M GONNA TAKE A BATH.
OH!
YOU'RE GONNA HAVE TO REHEAT THE WATER, OR YOUR BATH WILL BE COLD.
WHAT DID I JUST SAY!?
WHAT AM I, A GRADE SCHOOLER?
I'LL JUST CLOSE THE DOOR FOR YOU!
ACK! COLD!!
...IT'S TRUE, THOUGH.

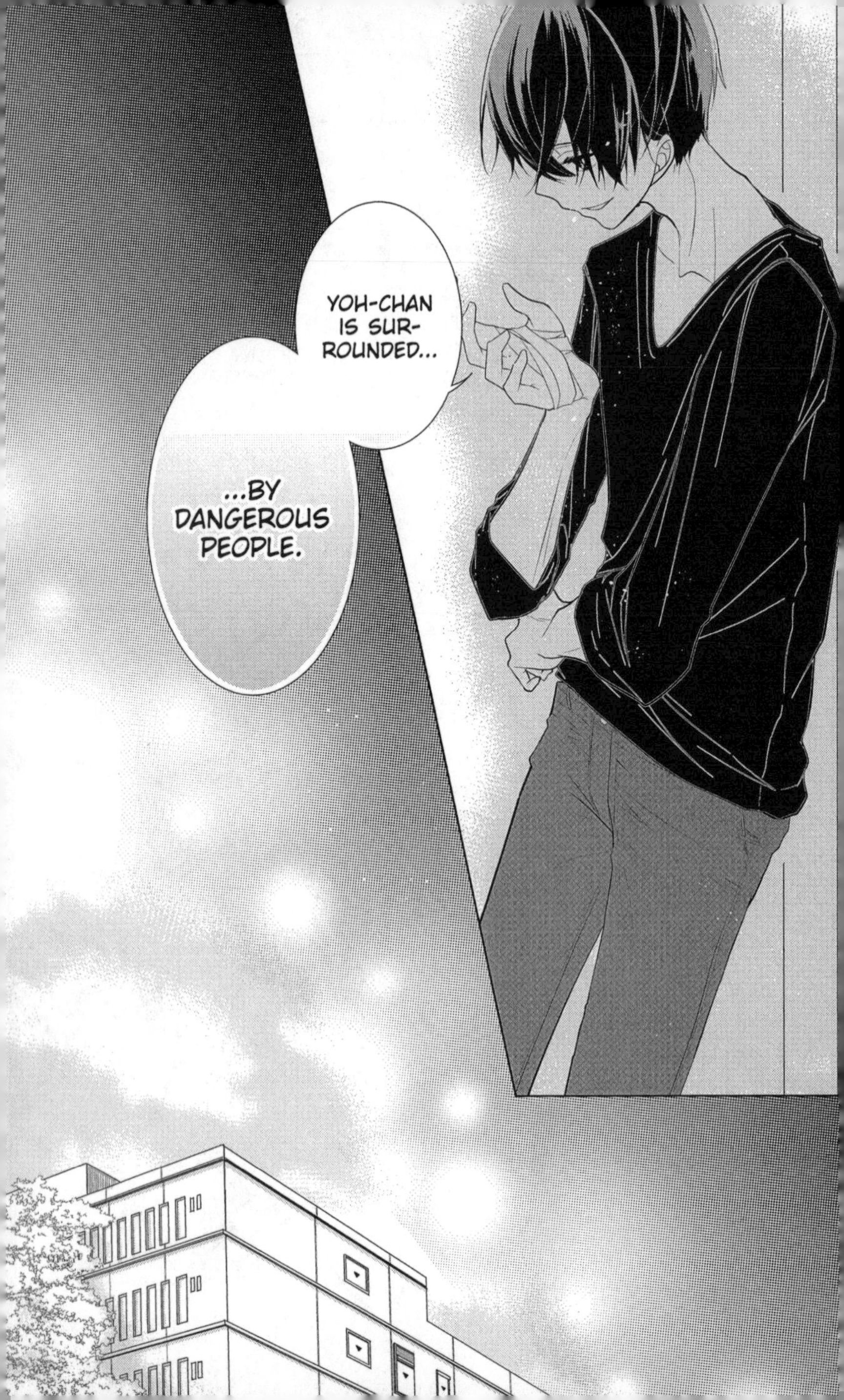
YOH-CHAN IS SUR-ROUNDED...
...BY DANGEROUS PEOPLE.

# #13

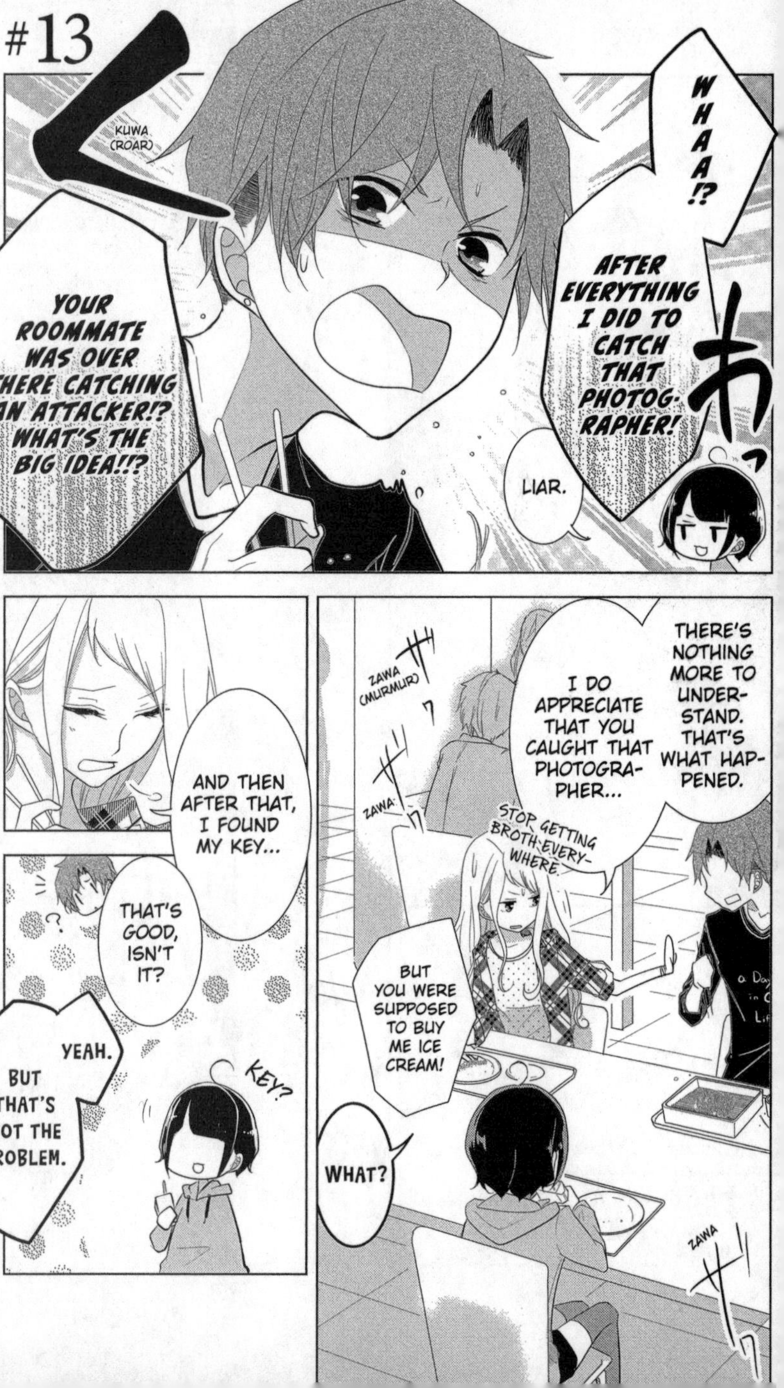
WHAAA!?
AFTER EVERYTHING I DID TO CATCH THAT PHOTOGRAPHER!
わっ
LIAR.
KUWA (ROAR)
YOUR ROOMMATE WAS OVER THERE CATCHING AN ATTACKER!? WHAT'S THE BIG IDEA!!?
THERE'S NOTHING MORE TO UNDERSTAND. THAT'S WHAT HAPPENED.
I DO APPRECIATE THAT YOU CAUGHT THAT PHOTOGRAPHER...
ZAWA (MURMUR)
ZAWA
STOP GETTING BROTH EVERYWHERE.
BUT YOU WERE SUPPOSED TO BUY ME ICE CREAM!
WHAT?
ZAWA
AND THEN AFTER THAT, I FOUND MY KEY...
THAT'S GOOD, ISN'T IT?
KEY?
YEAH. BUT THAT'S NOT THE PROBLEM.

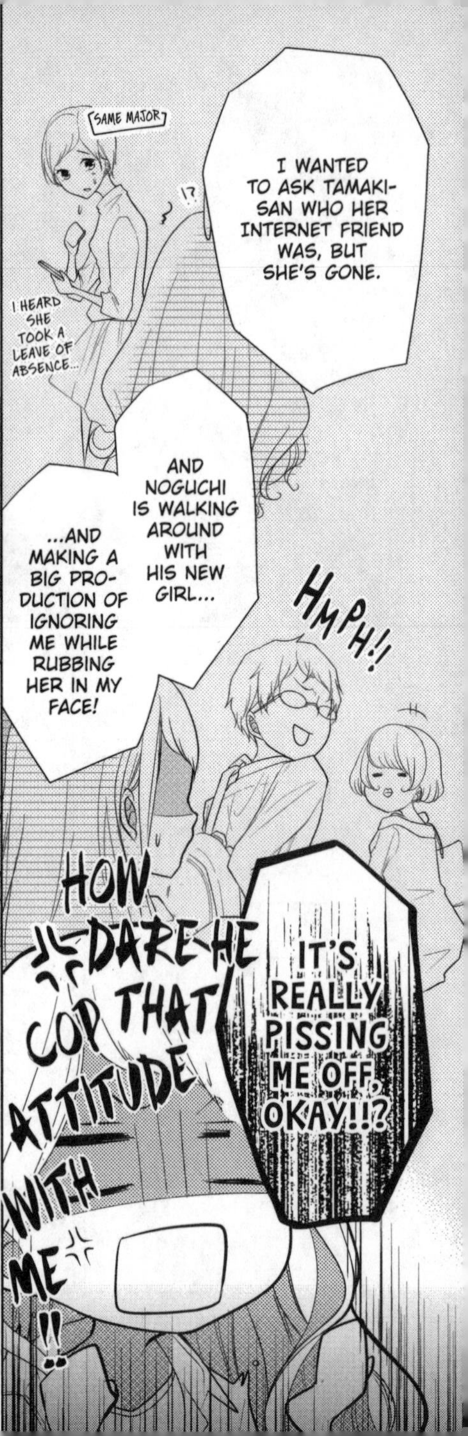
SAME MAJOR
I WANTED TO ASK TAMAKI-SAN WHO HER INTERNET FRIEND WAS, BUT SHE'S GONE.
!?
I HEARD SHE TOOK A LEAVE OF ABSENCE...
AND NOGUCHI IS WALKING AROUND WITH HIS NEW GIRL...
...AND MAKING A BIG PRODUCTION OF IGNORING ME WHILE RUBBING HER IN MY FACE!
HMPH!!
IT'S REALLY PISSING ME OFF, OKAY!!?
HOW DARE HE COP THAT ATTITUDE WITH ME!!

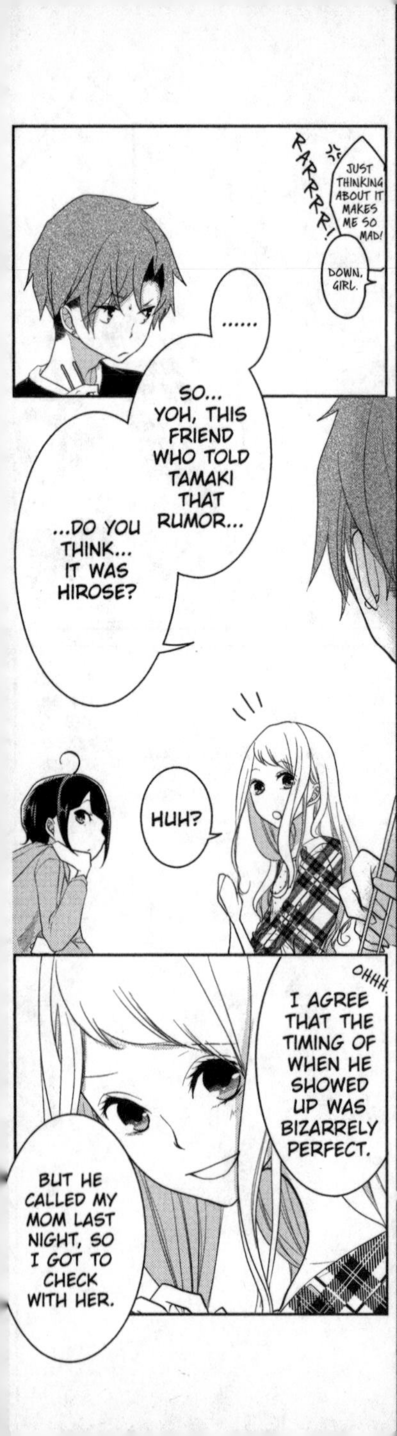
JUST THINKING ABOUT IT MAKES ME SO MAD!
RARRRR!
DOWN, GIRL.
......
SO... YOH, THIS FRIEND WHO TOLD TAMAKI THAT RUMOR...
...DO YOU THINK... IT WAS HIROSE?
HUH?
OHHH
I AGREE THAT THE TIMING OF WHEN HE SHOWED UP WAS BIZARRELY PERFECT.
BUT HE CALLED MY MOM LAST NIGHT, SO I GOT TO CHECK WITH HER.

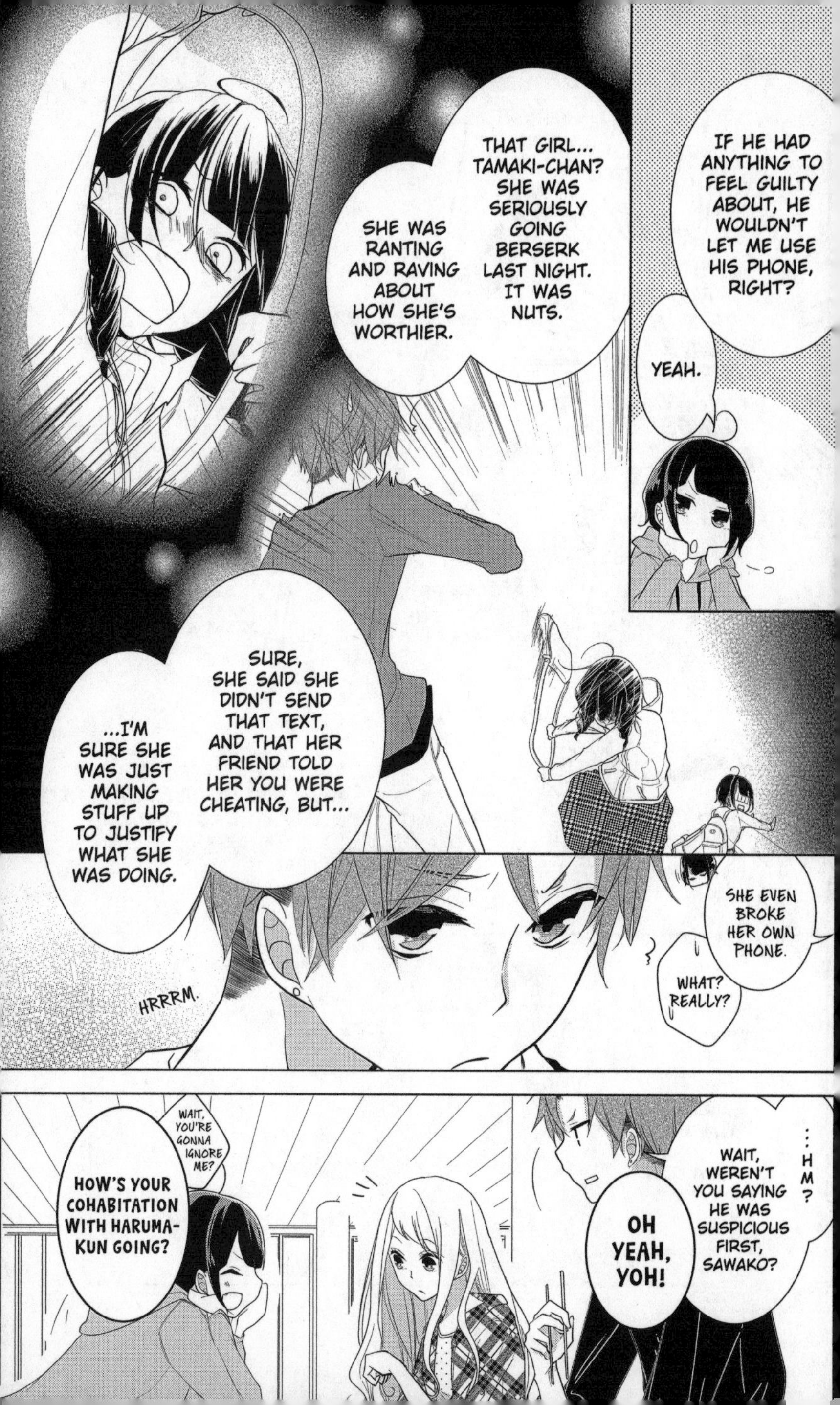
IF HE HAD ANYTHING TO FEEL GUILTY ABOUT, HE WOULDN'T LET ME USE HIS PHONE, RIGHT?
YEAH.
THAT GIRL... TAMAKI-CHAN? SHE WAS SERIOUSLY GOING BERSERK LAST NIGHT. IT WAS NUTS.
SHE WAS RANTING AND RAVING ABOUT HOW SHE'S WORTHIER.
SURE, SHE SAID SHE DIDN'T SEND THAT TEXT, AND THAT HER FRIEND TOLD HER YOU WERE CHEATING, BUT...
...I'M SURE SHE WAS JUST MAKING STUFF UP TO JUSTIFY WHAT SHE WAS DOING.
SHE EVEN BROKE HER OWN PHONE.
WHAT? REALLY?
HRRRM.
...HM?
WAIT, WEREN'T YOU SAYING HE WAS SUSPICIOUS FIRST, SAWAKO?
OH YEAH, YOH!
WAIT, YOU'RE GONNA IGNORE ME?
HOW'S YOUR COHABITATION WITH HARUMA-KUN GOING?

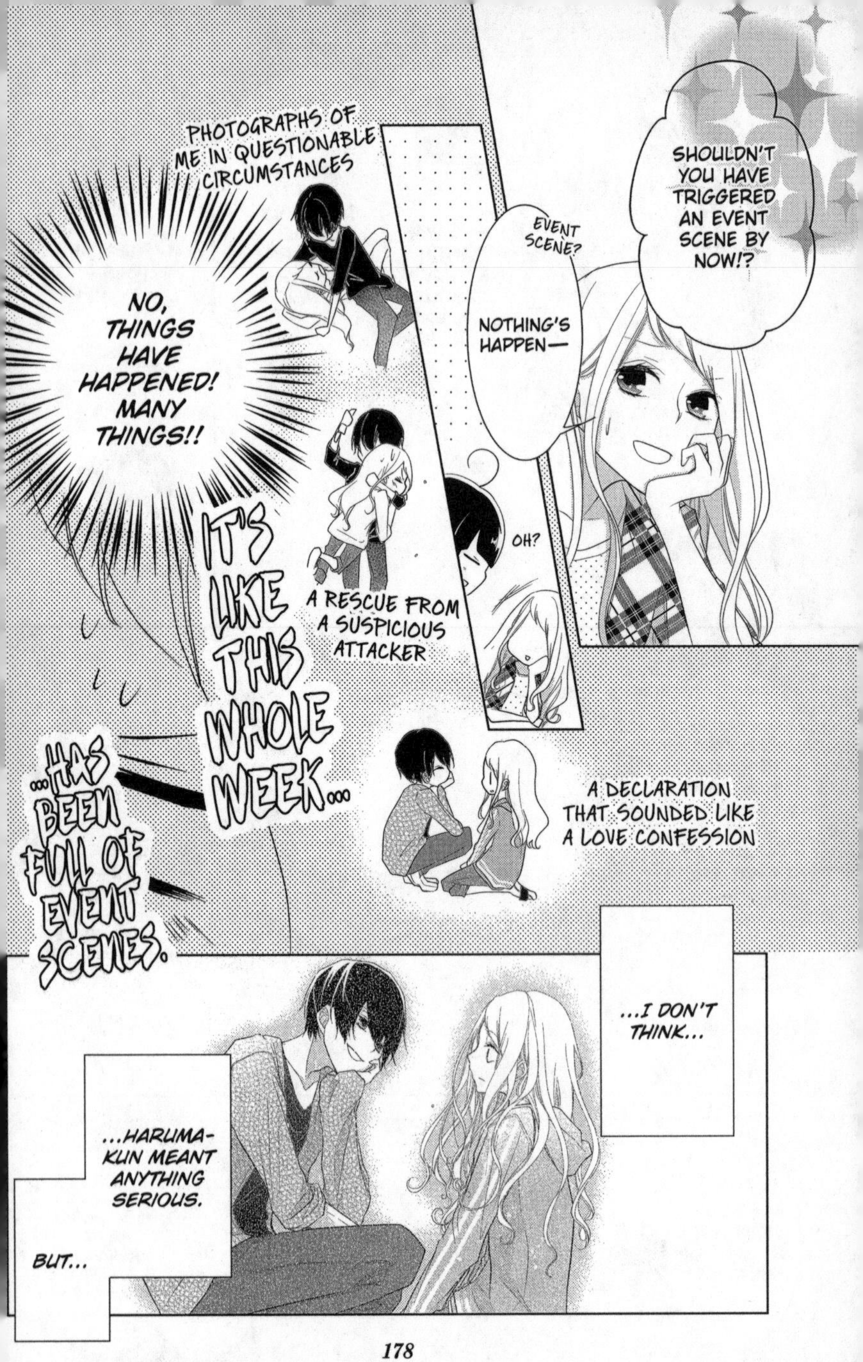
SHOULDN'T YOU HAVE TRIGGERED AN EVENT SCENE BY NOW!?
EVENT SCENE?
NOTHING'S HAPPEN—
OH?
PHOTOGRAPHS OF ME IN QUESTIONABLE CIRCUMSTANCES
NO, THINGS HAVE HAPPENED! MANY THINGS!!
A RESCUE FROM A SUSPICIOUS ATTACKER
A DECLARATION THAT SOUNDED LIKE A LOVE CONFESSION
IT'S LIKE THIS WHOLE WEEK...
...HAS BEEN FULL OF EVENT SCENES.
...I DON'T THINK...
...HARUMA-KUN MEANT ANYTHING SERIOUS.
BUT...

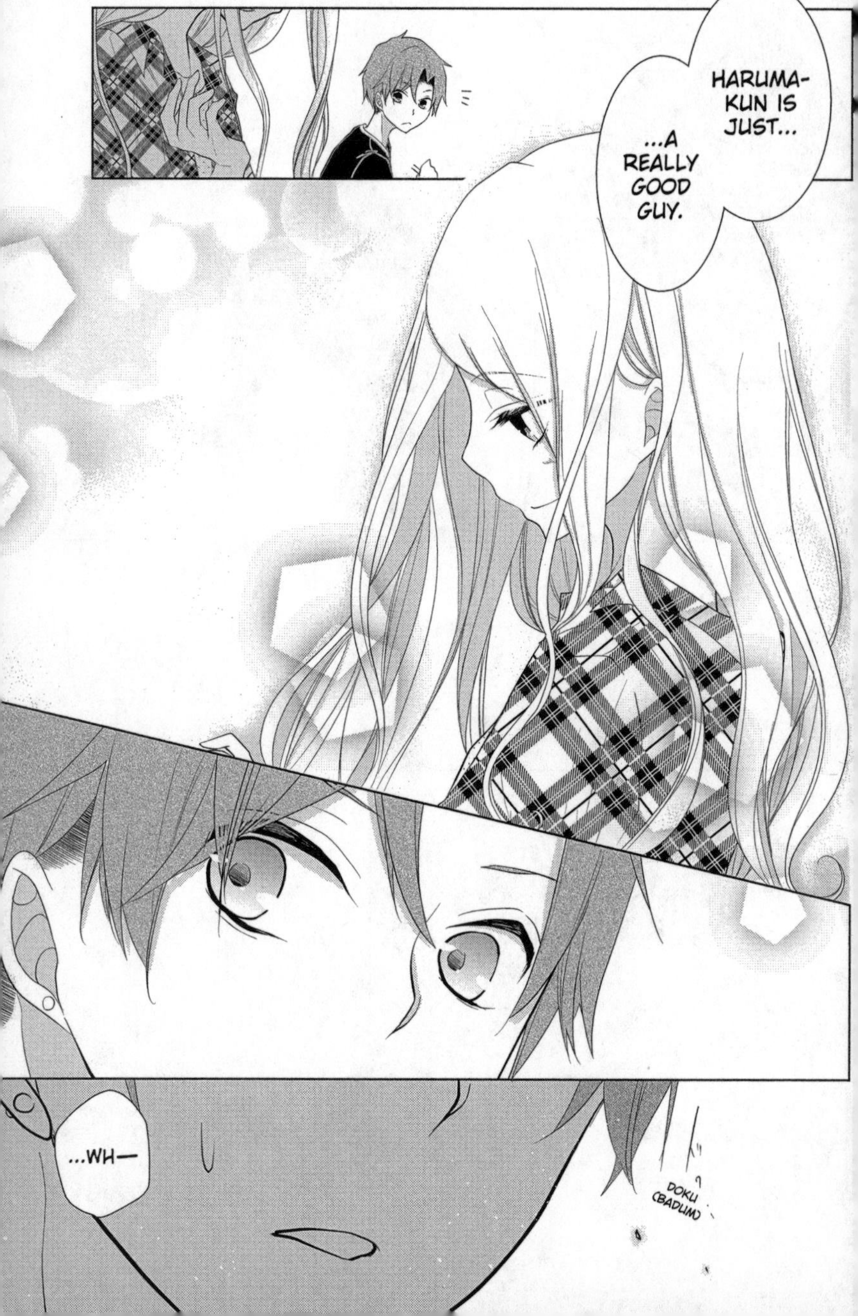
HARUMA-KUN IS JUST...
...A REALLY GOOD GUY.
...WH—
DOKU (BADUM)

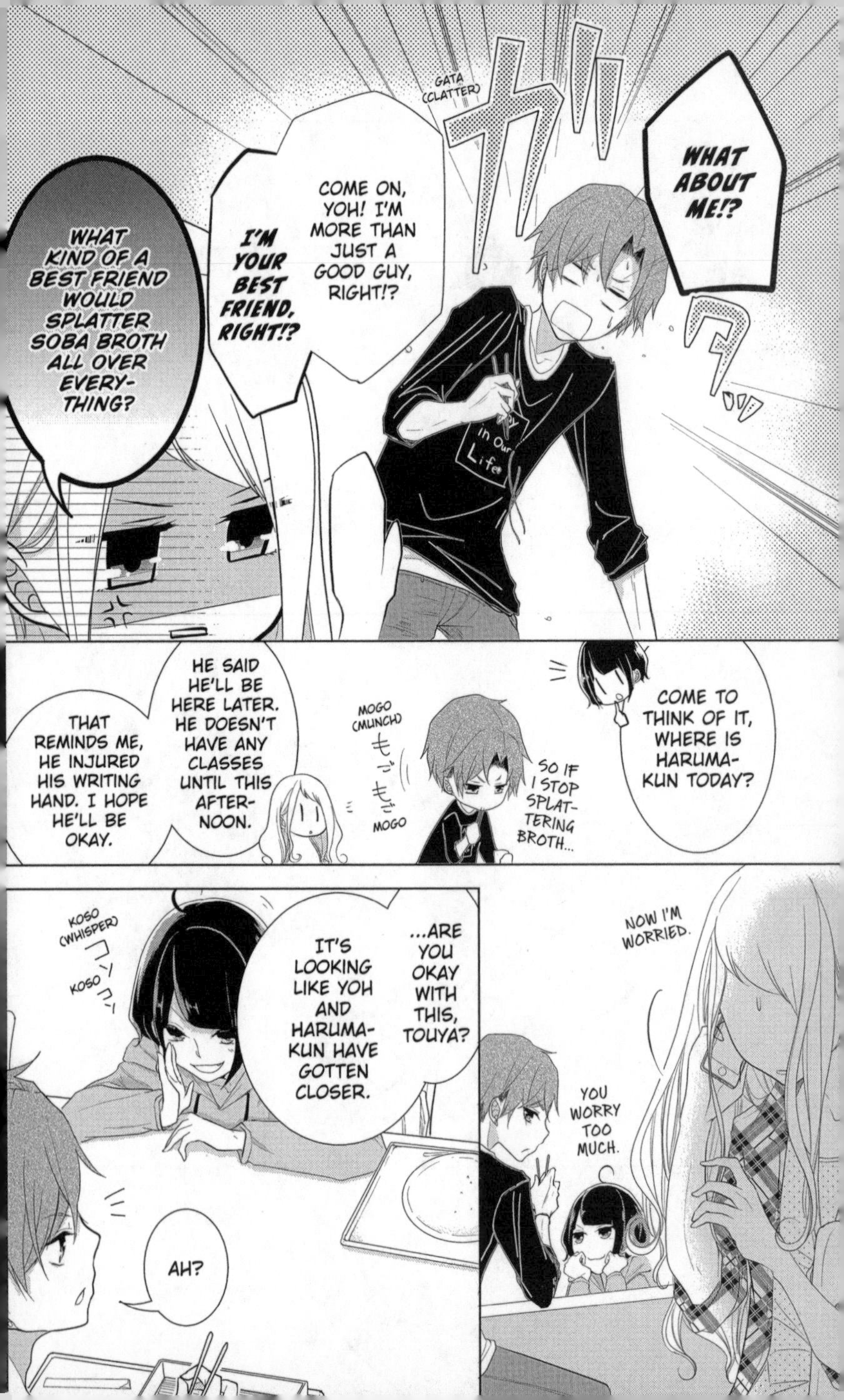
GATA (CLATTER)
WHAT ABOUT ME!?
COME ON, YOH! I'M MORE THAN JUST A GOOD GUY, RIGHT!?
I'M YOUR BEST FRIEND, RIGHT!?
WHAT KIND OF A BEST FRIEND WOULD SPLATTER SOBA BROTH ALL OVER EVERY-THING?
COME TO THINK OF IT, WHERE IS HARUMA-KUN TODAY?
SO IF I STOP SPLAT-TERING BROTH...
MOGO (MUNCH) MOGO
HE SAID HE'LL BE HERE LATER. HE DOESN'T HAVE ANY CLASSES UNTIL THIS AFTER-NOON.
THAT REMINDS ME, HE INJURED HIS WRITING HAND. I HOPE HE'LL BE OKAY.
NOW I'M WORRIED.
YOU WORRY TOO MUCH.
...ARE YOU OKAY WITH THIS, TOUYA?
IT'S LOOKING LIKE YOH AND HARUMA-KUN HAVE GOTTEN CLOSER.
KOSO (WHISPER) KOSO
AH?

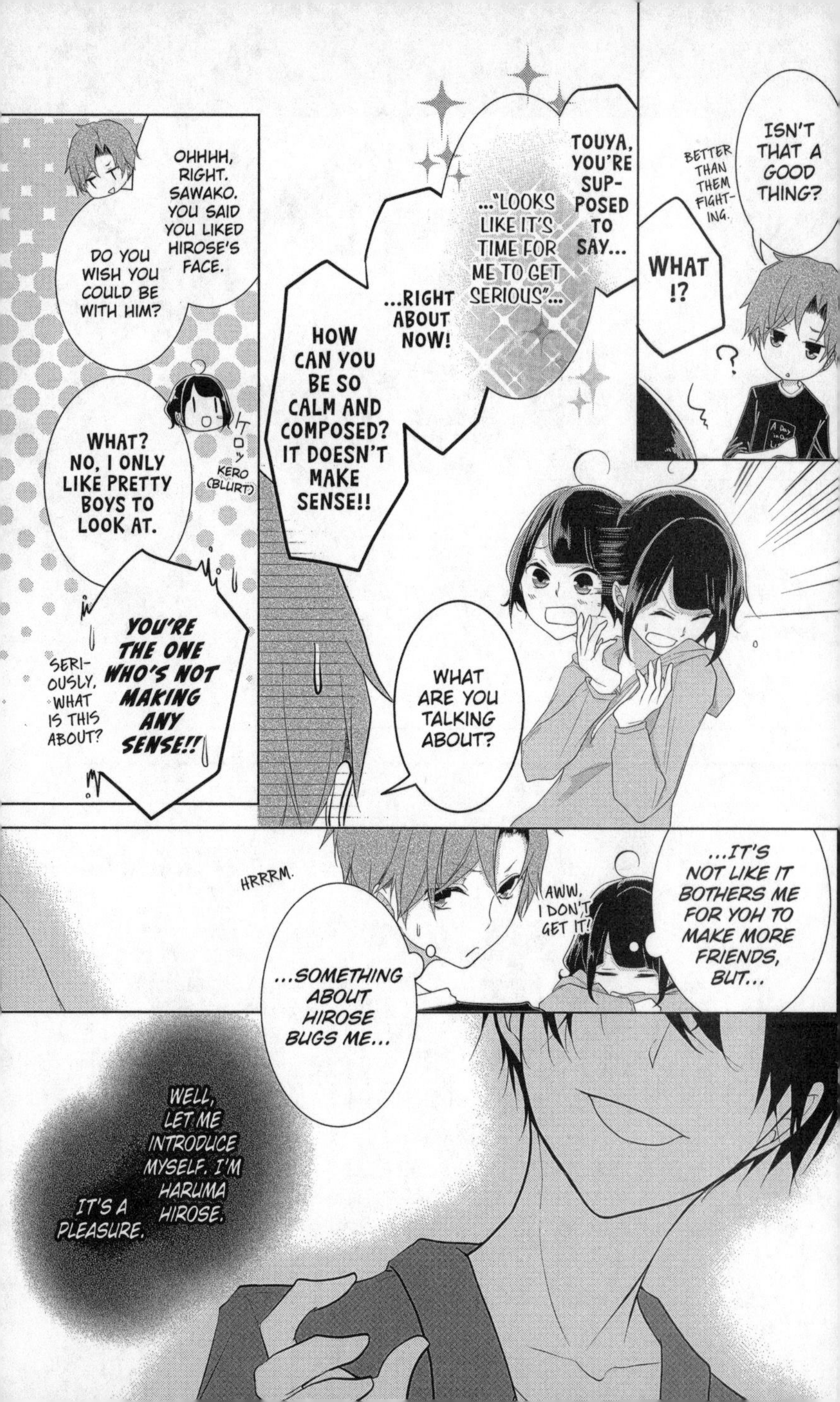
ISN'T THAT A GOOD THING?
BETTER THAN THEM FIGHTING.
WHAT!?
TOUYA, YOU'RE SUP-POSED TO SAY...
..."LOOKS LIKE IT'S TIME FOR ME TO GET SERIOUS"...
...RIGHT ABOUT NOW!
HOW CAN YOU BE SO CALM AND COMPOSED? IT DOESN'T MAKE SENSE!!
WHAT ARE YOU TALKING ABOUT?
OHHHH, RIGHT. SAWAKO. YOU SAID YOU LIKED HIROSE'S FACE.
DO YOU WISH YOU COULD BE WITH HIM?
WHAT? NO, I ONLY LIKE PRETTY BOYS TO LOOK AT.
KERO (BLURT)
YOU'RE THE ONE WHO'S NOT MAKING ANY SENSE!!
SERI-OUSLY, WHAT IS THIS ABOUT?
...IT'S NOT LIKE IT BOTHERS ME FOR YOH TO MAKE MORE FRIENDS, BUT...
AWW, I DON'T GET IT!
...SOMETHING ABOUT HIROSE BUGS ME...
HRRRM.
WELL, LET ME INTRODUCE MYSELF. I'M HARUMA HIROSE.
IT'S A PLEASURE.

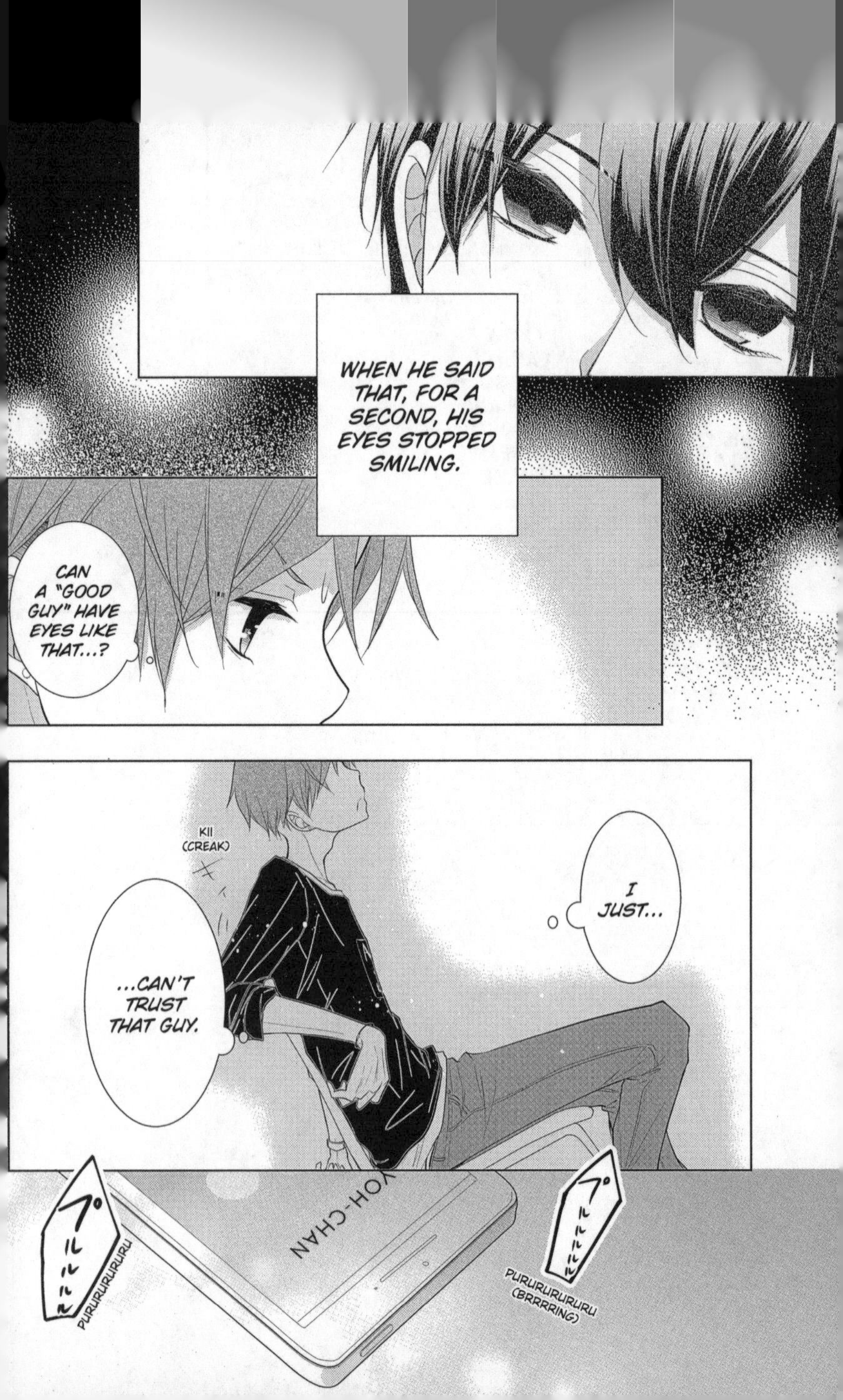
WHEN HE SAID THAT, FOR A SECOND, HIS EYES STOPPED SMILING.
CAN A "GOOD GUY" HAVE EYES LIKE THAT...?
I JUST...
KII (CREAK)
...CAN'T TRUST THAT GUY.
プルルルル
PURURURURU (BRRRRING)
YOH-CHAN
プルルルル
PURURURURU

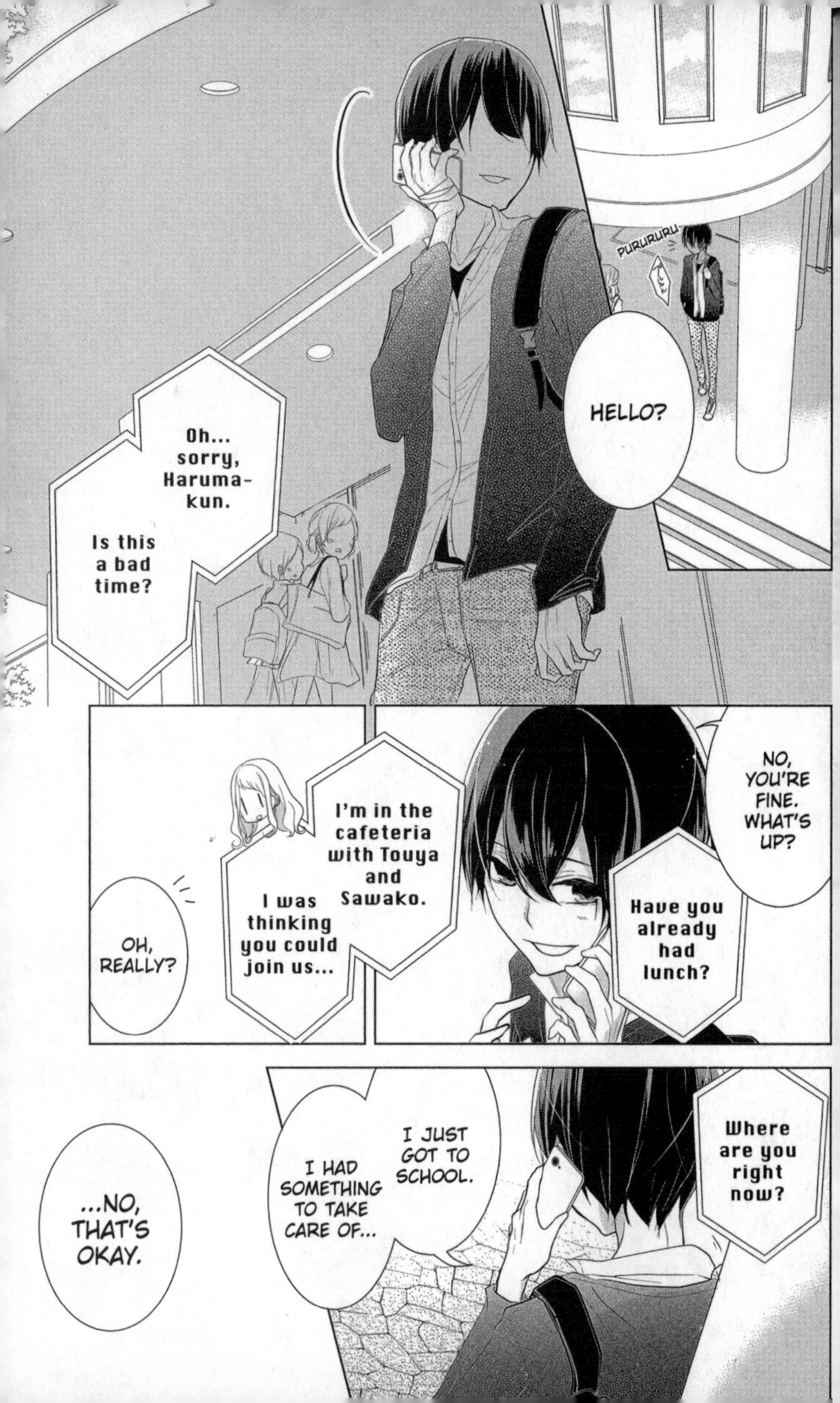
PURURURU
HELLO?
Oh... sorry, Haruma-kun.
Is this a bad time?
NO, YOU'RE FINE. WHAT'S UP?
Have you already had lunch?
I'm in the cafeteria with Touya and Sawako.
I was thinking you could join us...
OH, REALLY?
Where are you right now?
I JUST GOT TO SCHOOL.
I HAD SOMETHING TO TAKE CARE OF...
...NO, THAT'S OKAY.

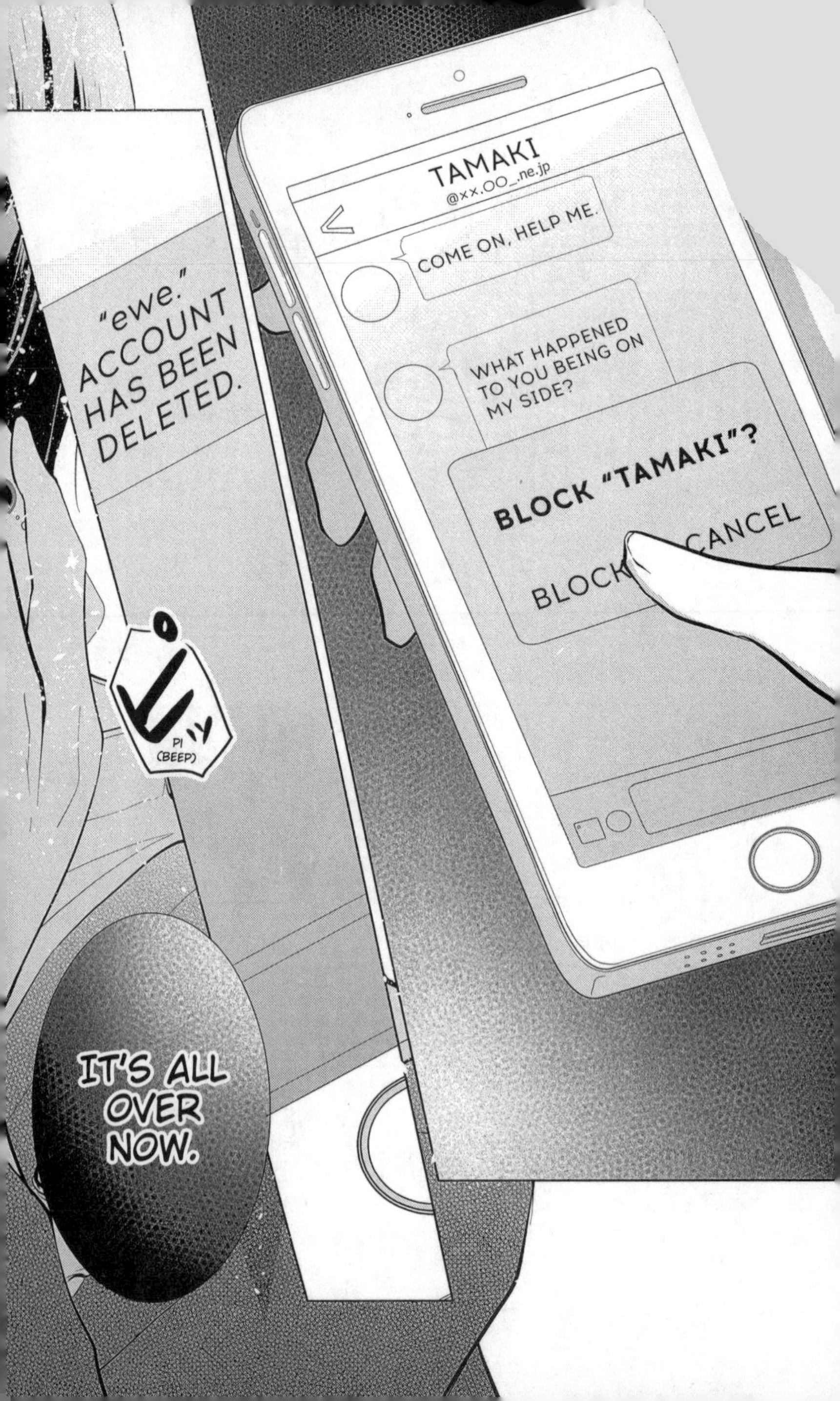
TAMAKI
@xx.OO_.ne.jp
COME ON, HELP ME.
WHAT HAPPENED TO YOU BEING ON MY SIDE?
BLOCK "TAMAKI"?
BLOCK
CANCEL
"ewe." ACCOUNT HAS BEEN DELETED.
PI (BEEP)
IT'S ALL OVER NOW.

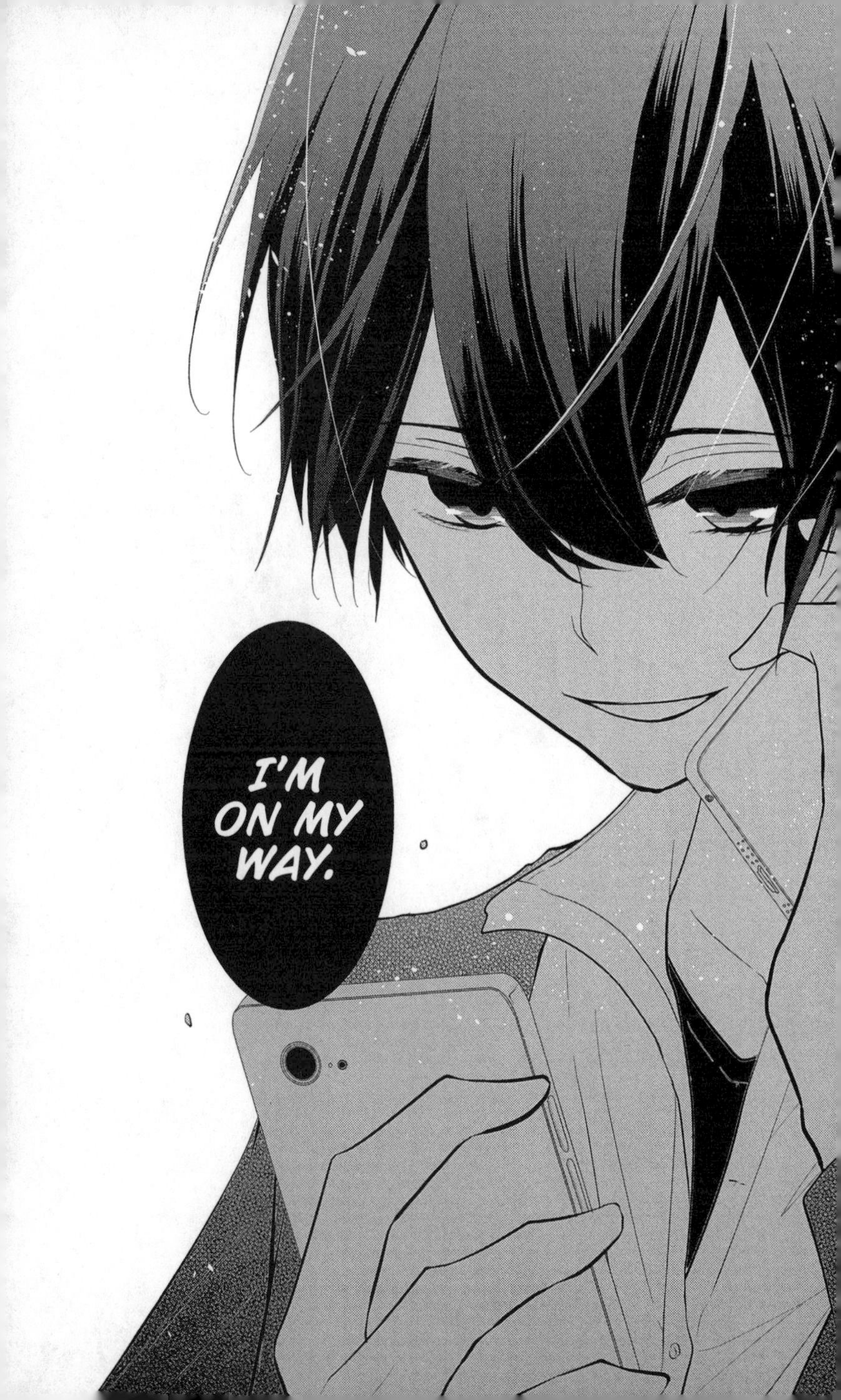
I'M ON MY WAY.

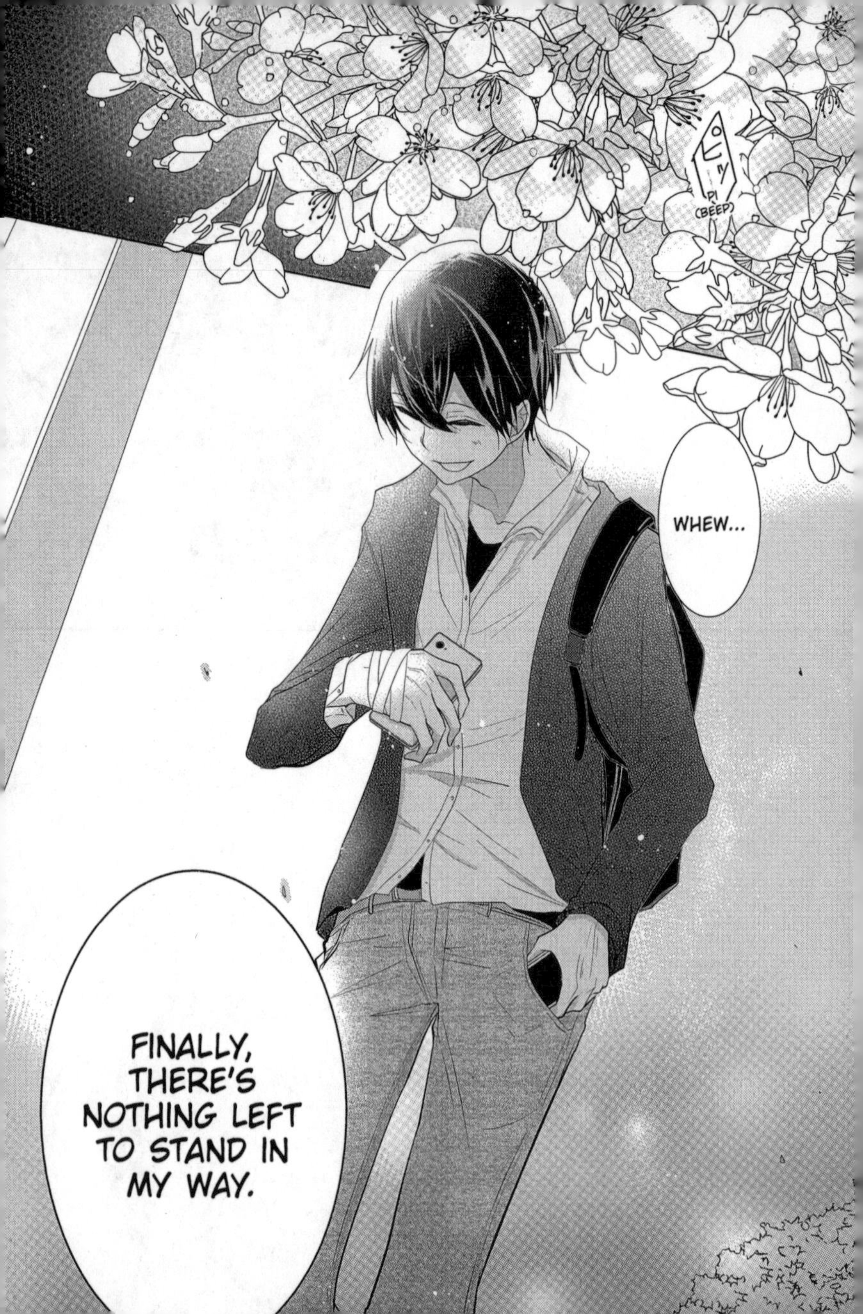
ピッ
PI
(BEEP)
WHEW...
FINALLY, THERE'S NOTHING LEFT TO STAND IN MY WAY.

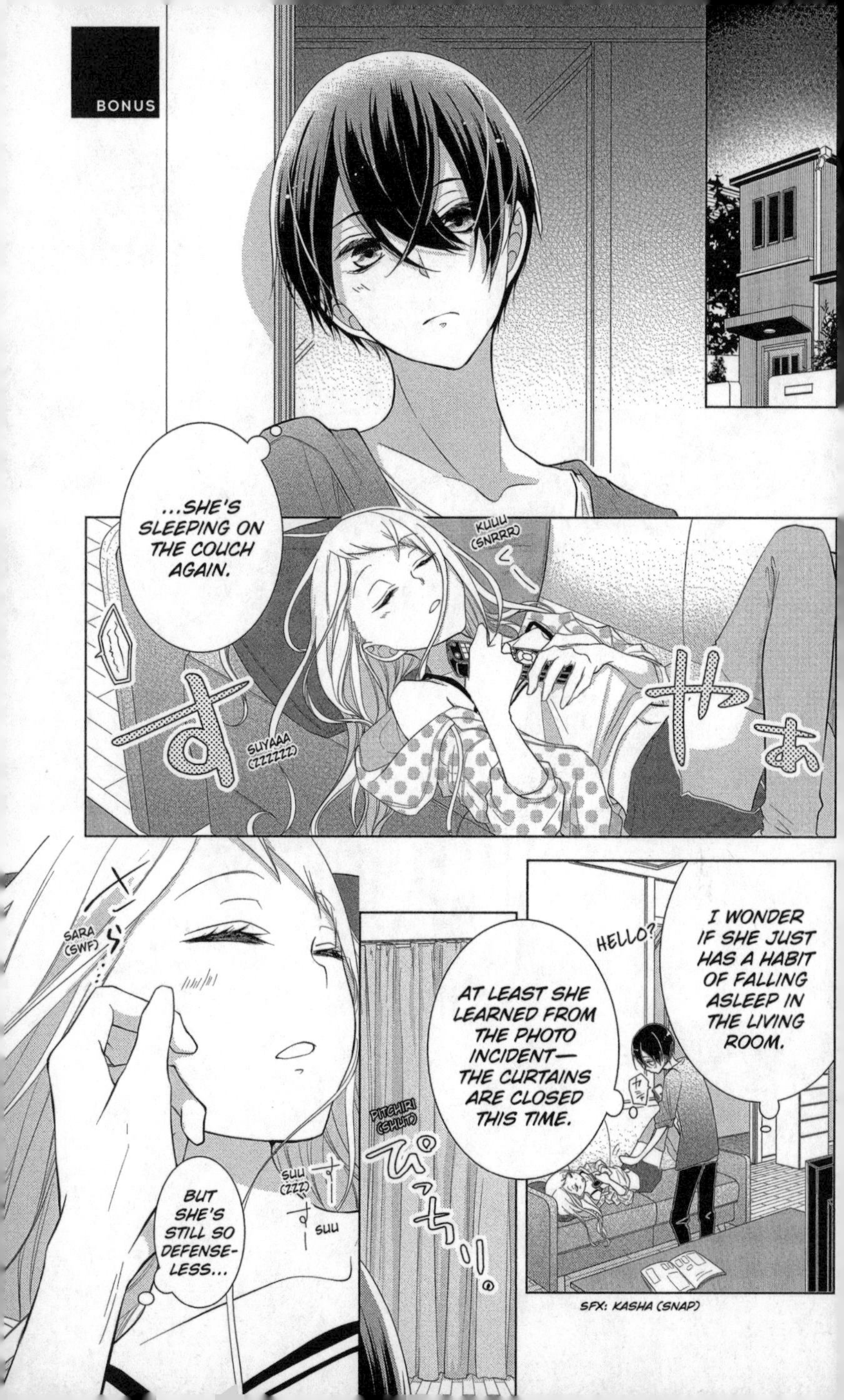

BONUS
...SHE'S SLEEPING ON THE COUCH AGAIN.
KUUU (SNRRR)
SUYAAA (ZZZZZZ)
I WONDER IF SHE JUST HAS A HABIT OF FALLING ASLEEP IN THE LIVING ROOM.
HELLO?
AT LEAST SHE LEARNED FROM THE PHOTO INCIDENT—THE CURTAINS ARE CLOSED THIS TIME.
SFX: KASHA (SNAP)
PITCHIRI (SHUT)
SARA (SWF)
SUU (ZZZ)
SUU
BUT SHE'S STILL SO DEFENSE-LESS...

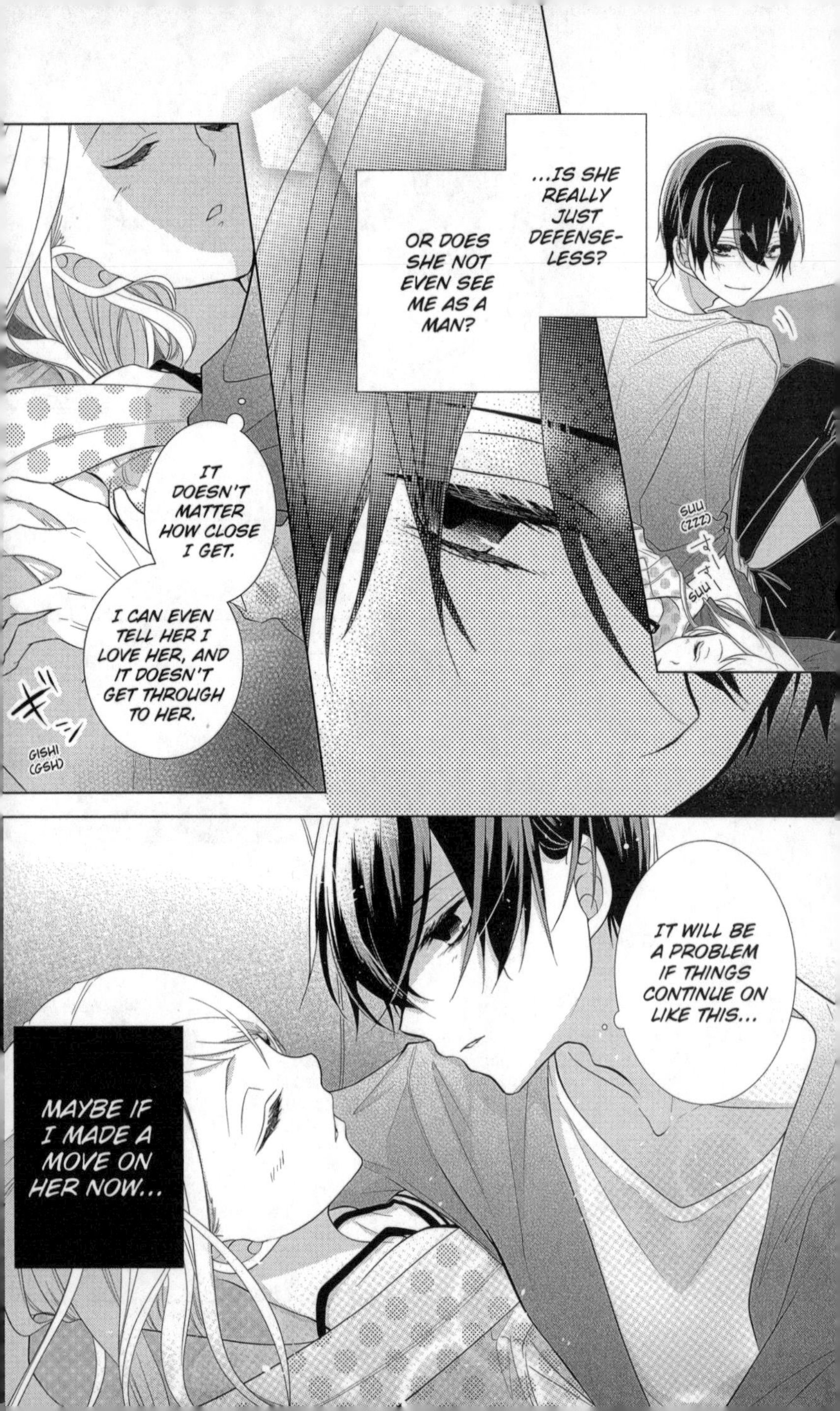
SUU (ZZZ)
SUU
...IS SHE REALLY JUST DEFENSE-LESS?
OR DOES SHE NOT EVEN SEE ME AS A MAN?
IT DOESN'T MATTER HOW CLOSE I GET.
I CAN EVEN TELL HER I LOVE HER, AND IT DOESN'T GET THROUGH TO HER.
GISHI (GSH)
IT WILL BE A PROBLEM IF THINGS CONTINUE ON LIKE THIS...
MAYBE IF I MADE A MOVE ON HER NOW...

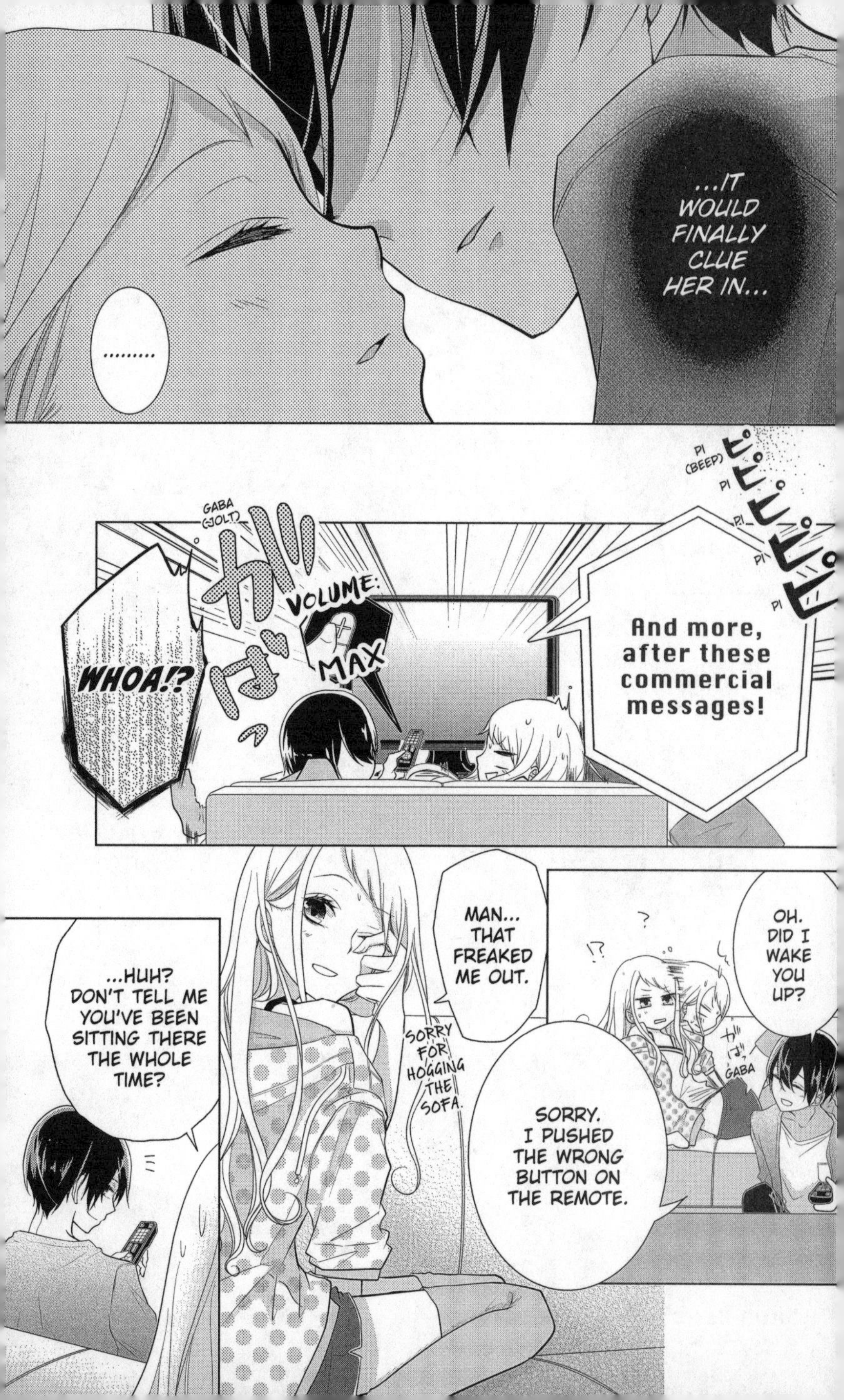
...IT WOULD FINALLY CLUE HER IN...
.........
PI (BEEP) PI PI PI PI
ピピピピピ
And more, after these commercial messages!
VOLUME: MAX
GABA (JOLT)
WHOA!?
OH. DID I WAKE YOU UP?
?
!?
GABA
MAN... THAT FREAKED ME OUT.
SORRY FOR HOGGING THE SOFA.
SORRY. I PUSHED THE WRONG BUTTON ON THE REMOTE.
...HUH? DON'T TELL ME YOU'VE BEEN SITTING THERE THE WHOLE TIME?

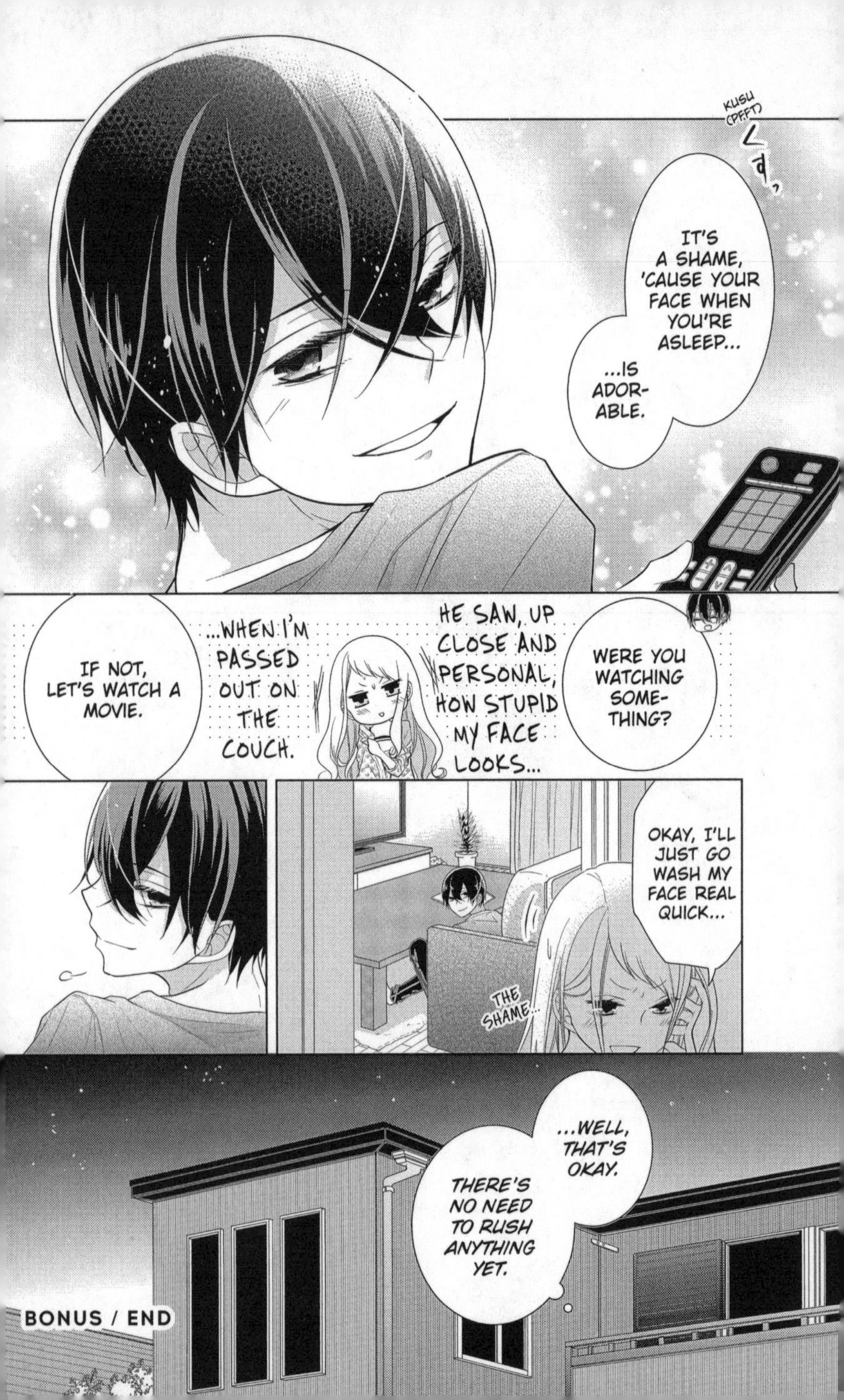
KUSU (PFFT)
くすっ
IT'S A SHAME, 'CAUSE YOUR FACE WHEN YOU'RE ASLEEP...
...IS ADORABLE.
WERE YOU WATCHING SOMETHING?
HE SAW, UP CLOSE AND PERSONAL, HOW STUPID MY FACE LOOKS...
...WHEN I'M PASSED OUT ON THE COUCH.
IF NOT, LET'S WATCH A MOVIE.
OKAY, I'LL JUST GO WASH MY FACE REAL QUICK...
THE SHAME...
...WELL, THAT'S OKAY.
THERE'S NO NEED TO RUSH ANYTHING YET.
BONUS / END

# TRANSLATION NOTES

**Common Honorifics**

no honorific: Indicates familiarity or closeness; if used without permission or reason, addressing someone in this manner would constitute an insult.

**-san**: The Japanese equivalent of Mr./Mrs./Miss. If a situation calls for politeness, this is the fail-safe honorific.

**-sama**: Conveys great respect; may also indicate that the social status of the speaker is lower than that of the addressee.

**-kun**: Used most often when referring to boys, this indicates affection or familiarity. Occasionally used by older men among their peers, but it may also be used by anyone referring to a person of lower standing.

**-chan**: An affectionate honorific indicating familiarity used mostly in reference to girls; also used in reference to cute persons or animals of either gender.

## Page 5

**Kneel**: *Seiza* in Japanese, meaning "proper sitting," refers to a position in which the sitter kneels on the floor with the feet under the buttocks, as demonstrated by Noguchi. This position is often used in formal settings, as well as when one is being reprimanded for misbehavior.

## Page 28

**Dating games** are visual novels about romancing a character of your choice. Touya specifically refers to the subgenre of *otome* games, which are targeted toward women, generally featuring a variety of pretty boys who romance the protagonist.

## Page 31

Spring is the unluckiest season: More specifically, Yoh calls spring the *kimon*, meaning "demon's gate." This concept comes from traditions that hold that certain directions are unlucky, as they are the ones from which demons and other bad things approach.

## Page 33

**EIKEN Grade Pre-1**: EIKEN, short for *Jitsuyo Eigo Gino Kentei* (Test in Practical English Proficiency), is a widely recognized English test, certifying certain levels of proficiency in the language. The most advanced level of the test is Grade 1, and Grade Pre-1 is just before that.

## Page 44

*Izakaya* are a type of Japanese bar that focus on serving small servings of side dishes designed to go with alcohol.

*Ichiban Shibori*, meaning "first press," is a method of brewing beer where the mashed hops are squeezed only a single time, instead of the more common technique of wringing out all available sugars from the mash. This results in a full-bodied beer with fewer bitter flavors.

## Page 48

*Goboten* is tempura made with the root vegetable *gobou* (a type of burdock), often served with udon noodles.

## Page 68

As a privacy measure, under Japanese law all phones are required to play a shutter sound when taking pictures to prevent hidden cameras, and this sound cannot be turned off by the user.

## Page 178

In visual novel games, an **event scene** is any spot in the story where a special image is presented to highlight a notable development.

# LOVE and HEART 1

...TOSE KAIO

Translation: **ALETHEA AND ATHENA NIBLEY**

Lettering: **KIMBERLY PHAM**

KOI TO SHINZO by Chitose Kaido
© Chitose Kaido 2018
All rights reserved.
First published in Japan in 2018 by HAKUSENSHA, INC., Tokyo.
English translation rights in U.S.A., Canada and U.K. arranged with HAKUSENSHA, INC., Tokyo through TUTTLE-MORI AGENCY, INC., Tokyo.

English translation © 2021 by Yen Press, LLC

Yen Press
150 West 30th Street, 19th Floor
New York, NY 10001

Visit us at yenpress.com
facebook.com/yenpress † twitter.com/yenpress
yenpress.tumblr.com † instagram.com/yenpress

First Yen Press Edition: February 2021

Yen Press is an imprint of Yen Press, LLC.
The Yen Press name and logo are trademarks of Yen Press, LLC.

The publisher is not responsible for websites (or their content) that are not owned by the publisher.

Library of Congress Control Number: 2020950226

ISBNs: 978-1-9753-2042-3 (paperback)
978-1-9753-2043-0 (ebook)

10 9 8 7 6 5 4 3 2 1

BVG

Printed in the United States of America